Opera's First Master

Unlocking the Masters Series, No. 8

Series Editor: Robert Levine

Opera's First Master

The Musical Dramas
of Claudio Monteverdi

Mark Ringer

𝄞

AMADEUS
PRESS

Published in 2006 by Amadeus Press, LLC
512 Newark Pompton Turnpike, Pompton Plains, New Jersey 07444, USA
Website: www.amadeuspress.com

Book design by Snow Creative Services

Printed in Canada

ISBN 1-57467-110-3

Library of Congress Cataloging-in-Publication Data is available upon request

For Barbara,
Furty, Clara, and Otto, too

*Monteverdi was born into the world to rule over
people's emotions since no one is so unfeeling that
he could not move them with his talent,
fashioning the music to the words and the passions
so that the singers are compelled to laugh or cry,
become angry, or compassionate, and do everything else
that they command, with the listener led in the same way,
by the variety and strength of the same emotions.*

Remarks by the anonymous librettist of Monteverdi's lost
Venetian opera *Le nozze d'Enea con Lavinia* (1641)

Contents

Introduction

Living with Monteverdi's Operas

Claudio Monteverdi's birthplace, the Italian city of Cremona, is justifiably proud of its great musical figures. A statue of the nineteenth-century composer Amilcare Ponchielli stands in the center of town, commemorating the creator of *La Gioconda* for his stint as the town's music director. The legacies of the instrument makers Amati, Stradivari, and Guarneri are omnipresent on plaques, exhibits, and the living heritage of the numerous luthier workshops in operation. Monteverdi's only statue in his homeland, however, is a meager and disappointing affair, a testament to the tardiness of the early-music revival's establishment in Italy. Erected for the composer's tricentennial in 1967, the smallish modernist sculpture stands in a slightly dilapidated piazza in his native city, removed from the welcoming bustle of the town's center. When I visited the site in late 2001, letters had been effaced from the base, and the surrounding lawn was strewn with debris. Small honor for one of Italy's greatest musical geniuses.

Claudio Monteverdi (1567–1643) was the first great opera composer. His three surviving operas, *L'Orfeo* (Orpheus, 1607), *Il ritorno d'Ulisse in patria* (The Return of Ulysses to his Homeland, 1640), and *L'incoronazione di Poppea* (The Coronation of Poppea, 1643) enjoy an unassailable position of historical importance. During the past century this universal respect has ensured their periodic revival in many of the world's opera houses. Over the years performers and critics have likened Monteverdi's operatic genius to that of Mozart, Wagner, and Verdi, the supreme masters of the genre. Nevertheless, the respect Monteverdi's operas enjoy is far removed from the near-universal love those later masters receive. In the opera houses of the United States and even Europe, Monteverdi remains a chilly icon more than a beloved familiar. One noted critic has stated that "Monteverdi has still, nearly a century after his first modern performances, to establish his centrality for those calling themselves opera goers. . . . By no stretch of the imagination can one speak of Monteverdi as a 'popular' composer even in the late 1990's" (Lindenberger, *Opera in History*, 43). The present book attempts to help rectify this situation by viewing these great works neither as musicological relics nor as the comfortable background sounds of classical "easy listening," but as the vital theatrical experiences that they are.

The Monteverdi operas are perhaps the most innately theatrical in the world repertoire, and they can be best understood and loved when their true nature, as musical drama to be enacted in the theater, is kept firmly in mind. Monteverdi's music speaks to us with unparalleled directness. He found the means for the first comprehensive portrayal of the human subject in music. He taught humanity what we look and sound like on the operatic stage. His music touches the heart and comforts the soul as does that of few other composers. He is one of those artists whose work reconciles us to life. Monteverdi believed that in vocal music the words are "the mistress of the harmony and not the servant" (Fabbri, *Monteverdi,* 50). Although Monteverdi was one of the most memorable and gifted melodists in the Western tradition and a master of counterpoint and harmony, he asserted with almost evangelical fervor throughout his long life that music must serve the text to achieve the most precious of musical and artistic goals: to move the souls of the audience. He believed musical art existed to give a tangible image in sound of the human condition. Music, according to Monteverdi, bears an ethical responsibility to reflect and portray the sensibilities of human beings. The zeal with which Monteverdi pursued this artistic goal would alter the course of Western music. Born in the late Renaissance, Monteverdi would master its musical techniques but would go on to forge a new style utilizing a baroque aesthetic. This new style affected the way virtually all Western music since his time has been composed and experienced.

Opera in Italy may be said to have had two beginnings. First there were the experiments of the early 1600s in Florence and Mantua, where learned societies combined drama and music for the delectation of late Renaissance princes. This phase was superseded by the creation of a fully professional opera in Venice during the 1630s and 1640s. Monteverdi would have a decisive hand in both these births. Monteverdi's operas, historically remote from us yet containing all the passionate contradictions of our own time, are ripe for a popular reevaluation. Monteverdi's operatic legacy awaits a new audience for productions in an intimate performance space with dramatically committed singer-actors. His text- and drama-driven works are the model to which every reformer from Gluck to Wagner has returned to remind audiences of opera's full aesthetic potential.

The intensity of Monteverdi's music encourages listeners to feel bound to his works with an unusual degree of personal identification. The great modernist Igor Stravinsky sensed this when he confessed:

> I feel very close to [Monteverdi.] But isn't he the first musician to whom we *can* feel very close? The scope of his music both as emotion and as architecture . . . is a new dimension compared to which the grandest conceptions and the most profound ardours and dolours of his predecessors shrink to the status of miniatures. The man himself . . . in his own letters, with their moodiness, anxieties about shortage of time, complaints of migraines, sounds not only strikingly contemporary to me, but even, if I may say so, rather *like* me. (Stravinsky 119)

My own approach to Monteverdi derives from experience as a music-loving theater historian and practitioner. I first encountered Monteverdi in recordings I heard as a teenager. The emotional impact of Nadia Boulanger's 1937 recording of the tenor duet "Zefiro torna," sung by Hugues Cuenod and Paul Derenne, was unforgettable. Equally memorable were the opening tracks of Nikolaus Harnoncourt's 1969 recording of *L'Orfeo,* with its striking, astringent period winds yielding to the delicious string ritornello and Rotraud Hansmann's beautiful singing of La Musica. Another revelatory experience came in the television broadcasts in the early 1980s of the world's first cycle of the three operas in productions conducted by Harnoncourt and directed by Jean Pierre Ponnelle at the Zurich Opera. In the years since, I have grown to admire Monteverdi's operas not only for their musical grace, but for their extraordinary sense of theater. These works encompass the entire range of human experience, from ecstatic joy to piercing grief, from bitter loss to miraculous restoration, from spiritual consolation to the most biting cynicism. And nearly everything from Monteverdi's hand—including the nondramatic works such as the religious pieces and the extraordinary books of madrigals—is marked by his uncanny sensitivity to language and human feeling, as well as by a melodic beauty that has never been surpassed.

For the present book I have made abundant use of the wonderful research by musicologists whose work forms the necessary background for anyone's thinking about Monteverdi. I have drawn particular inspiration from Ellen Rosand, Silke Leopold, and Tim Carter, among others who have made and continue to make such a profound impact on Monteverdi scholarship and on our understanding of his music. However, my line of research contains a fresh view of these masterpieces, a view I hope will open the works to wider appreciation among the many opera lovers who have so far shied away from them. I have avoided technical musical terminology wherever possible in order to keep the discussion accessible to the widest audience of music and theater lovers. At the same time, I trust that specialists will find the book of interest. My experience in both theoretical and practical theater has allowed me to find new channels of inquiry into how Monteverdi's operas work in the theater.

In this book I endeavor to place Monteverdi's operatic works within the musical and theatrical framework of his era. The first chapter gives a brief sketch of the composer's early years as well as a description of the complex forces that led to the emergence of opera in late-sixteenth-century Florence. Reference will be made to some of the nondramatic compositions in order to help illustrate Monteverdi's development as a theatrical musician. The second chapter relates the artistic and political machinations that brought the new art form to Mantua in 1607. The third chapter offers a performative reading of *L'Orfeo*. As in later chapters, the focus is placed on the work as a creation intended for performance before an audience in the theater. Chapter 4 examines later Mantuan theatrical works, including *Il ballo della ingrate* (The Dance of the Ungrateful Ladies) and the fragment from *L'Arianna*. *L'Arianna* is the first of some fifteen of Monteverdi's theatrical pieces, spread throughout his career, that have been lost. At least eleven of these works are known to have been performed. Tim Carter offers the best up-to-date survey of the lost works (*Monteverdi's Musical Theater*, 198 and esp. 298–305). Chapter 5 gives an overview of the many years separating the Mantuan from the Venetian operas. Particular focus is given to the "chamber opera" *Il combattimento di Tancredi e Clorinda* (The Combat of Tancredi and Clorinda). Chapters 6 and 7 are devoted to performative readings of the final two surviving Monteverdi operas, *Ulisse* and *Poppea*. Following the main text are a selected discography and videography of the operas.

I am indebted to several translators of Monteverdi's libretti whose work is found in many of the major recordings of these works. I have endeavored to make all the libretto translations my own, but I owe much insight to these earlier translations, a debt recorded in the book's bibliography.

I wish to thank my editor, Robert Levine, of Amadeus Press, for his belief in this book and his shrewd eye. Barbara Norton's careful work has led to numerous improvements to my text. While working on an article for the *New York Times* covering the Brooklyn Academy of Music's 2002 Monteverdi opera cycle, I had the good fortune to interview William Christie, the founder and artistic director of Les Arts Florissants; Pierre Audi, the artistic director of the Dutch National Opera; and Jane Glover, the conductor and baroque opera specialist. I also had the pleasure of meeting and chatting with one of the world's experts on Monteverdi and Venetian opera, Ellen Rosand. I wish to thank them all again for their time and for their wonderful insights into these works. Colleagues and friends at Marymount Manhattan College have helped to make this book possible. I owe the college itself an enormous debt of gratitude for allowing me a leave of absence to devote myself to this project. I am grateful for the generosity of Margaret Sokol, who provided much-needed funds and assistance. Mary Fleischer, Richard Niles, and Bill Bordeau have offered invaluable help and encouragement. I have enjoyed discussing opera and things Italian with John Costello. I also wish to acknowledge my thanks to the late Dean Ashim Basu whose support of this project allowed me the opportunity to begin my work in earnest.

Colleagues and friends from other institutions have been a wonderful resource, especially Jonathan Kalb of Hunter College, City University of New York, and Inga Walther, of Duke University. Simon Williams of the University of California, Santa Barbara, afforded me my first opportunity as a graduate student for researching Monteverdi. Sharon Perkins has offered invaluable help with her discerning comments on earlier drafts of this book. Brian Hurley provided invaluable musical assistance. My music-loving friends Donna Ellis, Steven Mack, Jeffrey Joneikis, Timothy Mangan, John Lowell, Charles Richards, Dennis Green, and David Mermelstein have been wonderful conversation partners. Jon Mullich remains a delightful breath of sanity. Lillian Bosch and Deborah Bosch have, as always, offered indispensable moral and technological support. Nancy Doyle was another technological lifesaver. My greatest inspiration and support comes from my brilliant, talented wife, the director Barbara Bosch, to whom this book is dedicated.

On a sad note, I want to acknowledge friends and family who are now gone with whom I shared my love of Monteverdi. Jeremy Gerber was a gentleman and a scholar. I doubt if anyone derived more pleasure than he from repeated viewings of Janet Baker's Penelope in her performance at Glyndebourne. I know this because I was standing there with him years ago at the Tower Records where we ostensibly worked while finding creative ways to avoid customers in order to watch films of great performers on the store monitor. My friend Desmond Taylor died suddenly just as the idea for this book was formulating. I hope he would have enjoyed the finished product. My mother, Virginia Hartt Ringer, was a philosophy professor who introduced me to history, Italian opera, and theater and helped to convince me that I should carry on her work as a teacher. And finally, my father, Gordon Ringer, a jurist and a poet, passed away as I was beginning my research. In what turned out to be one of our last conversations, he offered me a characteristically inclusive impromptu bibliography, which I have used. He shared my opinion of Monteverdi's position as a musical dramatist. I recall him marveling at the fact that so often the people who begin an art form wind up its greatest practitioners: in drama, the Greek playwrights; in cinema, Charlie Chaplin and Sergei Eisenstein; and in opera, Monteverdi.

Opera's First Master

Monteverdi and the Path to L'Orfeo

Polyphony, Madrigal, and Monteverdi's Early Years

Two events make 1567 a watershed year in the history of music's relationship to words. In Rome, Palestrina (c. 1525–1594), the greatest master of Italian Renaissance polyphony, published his most famous composition, the *Missa Papae Marcelli* (Pope Marcellus Mass); and in provincial Cremona, Claudio Monteverdi was born. One style of music reached its apogee just as the leader of the next phase's development was born. The dominant idiom for "serious" music during the late Middle Ages through the Renaissance (roughly 1400 to 1600) was vocal polyphony. The term "polyphony" derives from the Greek for "in many voices." Polyphony is essentially the same as "counterpoint," a term derived from the Latin *punctum contra punctum,* "note against note." Both counterpoint and polyphony are the musical art of combining different, simultaneous musical lines in a composition. Composers such as Josquin Desprez, Orlando de Lassus, Tomás Luis de Victoria, and Palestrina concentrated on religious compositions, particularly settings of the Mass for a cappella choir. These works set the Latin text in intricate, mellifluous counterpoint. Renaissance contrapuntal vocal music embodies the Renaissance ideals of balance and harmony such as could be encountered in the architecture and sculpture of the Greco-Roman past. After all, "Renaissance" referred to the "rebirth" of the humanistic attitudes of the classical Greek and Roman world, which placed human beings at the center of rationalist inquiry.

Just as Renaissance artists and draftsmen discovered and utilized perspective to vivify the pictorial plane and create a realistic space in which to place figures on a mural or canvas, Renaissance composers utilized the feeling of perspective created by the layering of a choir's voices—sopranos, altos, tenors, and basses—to create a similarly pleasing sense of sonic depth in their compositions. The dominant religious and ethical concepts of the Renaissance postulated a vision of the cosmos and mankind's place in it as an intricate, immaculately balanced, and hierarchical construction. The all-important earth, the home of mankind, was the stable center of creation, orbited by the sun and other stars in a harmonious cosmic dance. This sense of balance, proportion, and harmony, this intuition of an essential order to the universe, can be perceived in Renaissance polyphonic music. Dissonances are present, but they are not allowed to jar the listener for long before they are resolved within the harmony of the whole. The multiple vocal parts are equal in importance, weaving a sonic web of reassuring, idealizing form.

According to a legend, later dramatized in Hans Pfitzner's still underappreciated opera *Palestrina* (1917), sixteenth-century criticism of High Renaissance polyphonic style led to an artistic crisis shortly before the birth of Monteverdi. The Protestant Reformation had split Europe into two hostile camps, which, during Monteverdi's lifetime, would lead to unprecedented religious violence. The central tenet of Protestantism was the dissolution of the barrier between the common people and their faith. Luther insisted that the Bible and religious services be available in the vernacular languages of Europe, thus weakening the elitist authority of a Latin-literate Catholic clergy. Parishioners should understand the words spoken—or, for that matter, sung—to them in church. The Counter-Reformation of the 1540s–60s was Catholicism's response to the challenges posed by Protestantism. The issue of music's role in church services was a powerfully divisive one. Renaissance polyphony in Catholic services can invite a sense of sublime calm, but many Catholics felt that it blurred the verbal sense, even to those listeners who understood Latin. According to legend, Palestrina's *Missa Papae Marcelli* was composed to prove a point: that Renaissance polyphony and verbal intelligibility need not be mutually exclusive. The work was probably composed in 1556 and was dedicated to the memory of Pope Marcellus II, who had reigned for a mere three weeks before his untimely death the year before. Palestrina has been credited, a bit melodramatically, as the man who "saved music." What Palestrina saved was Catholic polyphonic church music from the charge of verbal unintelligibility and inaccessibility. The Latin-versus-vernacular barrier was still there, but if the myth has any truth, even Palestrina, the greatest polyphonist of the sixteenth century, conceded that the problem of intelligibility was indeed real and resolvable only by the most masterly of compositional techniques.

Monteverdi's place of birth was as providential as the year in which he was born. Throughout the next century Cremona would establish itself as the center for the making of violins and other stringed instruments. Monteverdi's first position at the Mantuan court was as a string player. The violoncello, the viola da gamba (which Monteverdi would master), and the relatively new violin were notable for their expressive abilities and for their striking similarity to the human voice. The violin's greater projective power and capacity for brilliant rhythmic articulation would cause its popularity to soar during the seventeenth and eighteenth centuries. Monteverdi was to make significant, at times highly innovative use of stringed instruments in his compositions.

Claudio's father, Baldassare Monteverdi (1542–1617), was a barber-sugeon and apothecary, as his father and grandfather had been before him. Medicine of one kind or another ran in the family: Claudio's youngest son, Massimiliano, became a doctor. The medical heritage of Monteverdi's family taught the musician to observe humanity with compassion allied to unflinching specificity, a point of view reflected in the composer's startling ability to portray psychological states musically in his mature works. This scientific or at least quasi-scientific background may also be detected in the theorizing impulse in Monteverdi's prefaces to some of his scores and in his letters. The pseudoscientific heritage of the barber-surgeon may also resonate in the composer's notable non-musical hobby, alchemy, which occupied his few idle hours.

Baldassare married his first wife, Claudio's mother, in 1566. Maddalena (née Zignani), the daughter of a goldsmith, gave Baldassare two daughters and four sons. Claudio, the eldest child, was baptized in Santi Nazaro e Celso on May 15, 1567. Their second son, Giulio Cesare, who would also become a musician and an important advocate for his more famous brother, was born in 1573. During Claudio's childhood, Baldassare made modest moves up the social and economic ladder. Tragedy repeatedly struck the family, however. Maddalena died when Claudio was eight or nine years old. Baldassare quickly remarried in 1576 or 1577 (as was customary at that time for widowers with young children) and fathered three more children by his second wife, Giovanna Gadio. Giovanna, too, died young, and by 1584 seventeen-year-old Claudio was adjusting to a second stepmother, Francesca Como. Baldassare's marriage to Francesca was childless. Claudio appears to have been emotionally close to his father throughout the older man's life. The acute pain of losing a spouse would come to Claudio himself in due time. His father's repeated tragic losses and the inevitable feelings of sorrow and abandonment seem to have made a profound impression on the future composer of *L'Orfeo, L'Arianna,* and *Il ritorno d'Ulisse in patria.*

At some point in his boyhood—it is not known exactly when—Claudio became a student of the composer Marc'Antonio Ingegneri, the music director of Cremona Cathedral and a composer with an international reputation. Ingegneri solidly grounded his pupil in the techniques of Renaissance polyphonic writing, as well as singing and mastery of the violin and the viol family. The young Monteverdi was a precocious student. The first opus from the fifteen-year-old boy from Cremona, a collection of three-part works, was published under the title *Sacrae cantiunculae* by a Venetian house in 1582. A year later a second volume, entitled *Madrigali spirituali,* made it to press with a publisher in Brescia. At seventeen he published his third volume and first secular work, a collection entitled *Canzonette,* again from a Venetian press. These teenaged efforts reveal palpable ambition matched with a convincing mastery of contemporary style. Like Beethoven's juvenilia, they are remarkable for displaying their creator's competence at an early age rather than for the blazing originality of a young Mozart, Schubert, or Mendelssohn. The year 1587 saw the appearance of his *First Book of Madrigals,* in five voices. This publication by the twenty-year-old composer inaugurated a series of compositions that would stretch throughout the composer's life and alter the course of Western music.

Besides opera, the madrigal was to be Monteverdi's most personal and characteristic musical idiom. The eight books of madrigals published during his lifetime shed light on all aspects of his creative development and in many ways led the way to his achievements in opera. Any examination of Monteverdi's operas needs to include at least a passing glance at some of the madrigals. Monteverdi began composing them just as this popular Renaissance genre was reaching its zenith. The madrigal in Italy was the major genre of secular vocal music. Love poetry supplied most of the texts for these ensemble songs, which typically utilized two to five voices woven into a contrapuntal setting. Madrigals epitomize the largely amateur nature of much Renaissance musical performance. They were written largely to be sung for pleasure by groups of musically literate people who took delight in both listening and performing. The Renaissance madrigal at its height in the mid-six-teenth century was a communal art form that spoke to shared notions of harmony and balance. Like the church music of the era, it was a vehicle for contrapuntal craftsmanship. It also afforded the composer opportunity to suggest musical pictures to illustrate the sung text. The French composer Clément Janequin (c. 1485–1558) offers an extreme and entertaining illustration of this pictorial tendency in his chansons (the French version of the madrigal), with their charming evocations of birds and nature. Throughout his career Monteverdi used this genre as a vehicle for ever bolder experimentation. Like Beethoven's piano sonatas, Monteverdi's madrigals are an extraordinarily rich musical articulation of a great artist's changing techniques and changing per-ception of the world.

At twenty, Monteverdi was looking for a position and a patron in a court. He dedicated his *First Book of Madrigals* to Marco Verità, a count in Verona, Ingegneri's hometown. These works reveal Monteverdi's compositional voice gaining in assurance, but they still lack the clear marks of distinctive genius. Monteverdi's *Second Book of Madrigals* (1590) was dedicated to a potential patron in Milan, Giacomo Ricardi. Here the composer has found his personal voice. The Second Book is distinguished by a strong impulse to dramatize the poetry being set. More than before, the five voices seem to imitate the passions or objects being described. The use of silence and repetition not only makes musi-cally pleasing shapes but serves to create a vivid sense of living action and emotional reaction. One madrigal in particular from the Second Book, "Ecco mormorar l'onde" (Now the waves murmur), indicates

Monteverdi's growing melodic and picture-making powers in creating a musical portrayal of sun, wind, sky, and water. Silke Leopold writes: "The inner balance and the lively composure of this madrigal represent the culmination of the Renaissance spirit, the outcome of an emotional attitude towards life which derives its strength from the consciousness of having a fixed place in the universe, and which manifests itself in harmonious equilibrium and measured serenity" (39). Sometime between 1589 and 1590 Monteverdi left Cremona to serve as a string player among the musicians of Vincenzo I Gonzaga, the Duke of Mantua. The Mantuan court loved spectacle and music and was an ideal site for the young composer to observe and participate in courtly theatrical activity, especially the conventions of the *intermedi*.

Intermedi, Monody, and Operatic Experimentation

The late 1400s saw the advent of the *intermezzo* in Italian court performances. *Intermezzi* or *intermedi,* as they were referred to in the sixteenth and seventeenth centuries, were the Italian equivalent of the masque tradition in England. Elaborately staged vignettes on allegorical or mythological themes, usually containing fulsome praise of the sponsoring nobility, the *intermedi* grew to enormous popularity during the 1500s and were a regular staple of courtly theater. Neoclassical rules of playwrighting stipulated the five-act structure for Italian Renaissance comedies and tragedies. Italian Renaissance spoken drama also labored under the dictates of the neoclassical unities of time, place, and action. The concept of the unities derived from Italian literary critics and their often faulty and heavily proscriptive reading of Aristotle's *Poetics*. The unities dictated that no play should portray more action than could take place within a day, that no more than one scene setting could be portrayed, and that the play should contain no subplot. Always more adept in making rules than in following them, the Italians enjoyed the *intermedi* as an escape from the suffocating dictates of neoclassicism. The five-act play proper, standing as a testament to the patron's educated taste, could languish under the burden of the unities while the *intermedi* afforded the artists and audiences the stimulating variety their natural temperaments craved. *Intermedi* would be performed between the acts of nonmusical dramas, offering the audience singing, dancing, and sometimes dialogue performed by elaborately costumed actors along with perspective scenery. Perspective scenery, another Renaissance innovation, utilized flats and backdrops painted and positioned to create the illusion of spatial depth onstage. The *intermedi* were important forerunners of opera, though for many decades into the seventeenth century they would continue to be produced alongside early operatic performances (see Fenlon, "Origins" 3). *Intermedi* soon became more popular than the spoken dramas they ostensibly complemented. One sixteenth-century playwright lamented, "Once *intermedi* were made to serve the comedy, but now comedies are made to serve the *intermedi*" (Antonfrancesco Grazzini, qtd. in Arnold 97). The staging exigencies of rapid set changes between the five acts of a spoken play and anywhere from four to six *intermedi* on a given evening encouraged Italian designers to develop increasingly sophisticated staging technologies for shifting flats, which were adopted by the early producers of opera during the seventeenth century. The results of the *intermedi*'s influence on opera may be found in the unity-violating change of scene from the pastoral world to the Inferno during the course of Monteverdi's *L'Orfeo* (see also Fabbri, *Monteverdi* 68). The *intermedi* stimulated a longing for greater visual spectacle. Their extravagance and self-conscious artificiality signaled the beginnings of a baroque consciousness.

The most famous of *intermedi* performances of the late Renaissance took place in Florence in a grand hall in the Uffizi Palace in 1589. There, in the city that would host the first opera performances a few years later, an elaborate spectacle of lavish allegorical vignettes utilizing dazzling song, dance, and special effects was staged in honor of the marriage of the grand duke, Ferdinando de' Medici, and the French princess, Christine of Lorraine. Ferdinando was widely suspected of having had his brother, Francesco, and sister-in-law poisoned two years earlier in order to gain his title. The 1589 *intermedi* successfully burnished Ferdinando's dubious public image. They were so successful that the grand duke ordered repeat performances, and it is possible that Monteverdi witnessed one of these. Whether or not the first master of opera was physically present, he would doubtless have become familiar with the published musical score and lavish descriptions the grand duke had published to capitalize on his artistic and political coup.

In this performance, Girolamo Bargagli's comedy *La pellegrina* was framed by a magnificent succession of six *intermedi* celebrating the power of music and the taste and discernment of the grand duke. A whole team of poets, composers, designers, and performers created the vignettes. Several of these artists would in only a couple of years be making history with the earliest experiments in Florentine opera. Significantly, these *intermedi* thematically represented "a cycle of abstract theorizing and Platonic longings for the music of antiquity, which survived more in fable than reality" (Pirrotta 222). Most of the texts for the *intermedi* were provided by the poet Ottavio Rinuccini (1562–1621), who would soon become the world's first opera librettist and a future collaborator with Monteverdi in Mantua. The young, multitalented Alessandro Striggio (c. 1573–1630), the future librettist of Monteverdi's *L'Orfeo,* performed in the instrumental ensemble. Jacopo Peri (1561–1633), a great singer and important composer, and Giulio Caccini (c. 1545–1618), another noted musician, both contributed music for the *intermedi.* Another composer, Emilio de' Cavalieri (c. 1550–1602), who was also an admired dancer, helped to coordinate the complex multimedia production. Cavalieri contributed the music for the grand finale of the last *intermezzo,* "Il dono di Giove ai mortali di ritmo e armonia" (Jove's Gift to Mortals of Rhythm and Harmony). Cavalieri's rousing finale would sweep Europe as "Il ballo dell' Granduco" (The Grand Duke's Dance). Modern audiences are familiar with it as a number in Ottorino Respighi's early-music pastiche *Ancient Airs and Dances.*

Several features of early opera are already apparent in the score. In the first *intermezzo,* "L'armonia delle sfere" (The Harmony of the Spheres), Armonia descends from the heavens singing music marked by virtuosic, florid decorations. Such "stratospheric" vocal ornamentation will figure as a musical device to indicate the divine status of singing characters throughout Monteverdi's career (see also Carter, *Monteverdi's Musical Theater* 22). Mozart's Queen of the Night in *The Magic Flute* stands as a striking later example of this tradition of musical divinity.

Most of the specifically prescribed stage action occurs during the frequent sinfonias or brief instrumental passages that pepper the score.
In the *intermedi,* as in early opera, sinfonias provide musical variety to
solo song while serving to emphasize physical action and mask stage
noise. The music of the *intermedi* is often lovely. The *intermedi* of *La
pellegrina* display brilliant showmanship, the talented poets, composers, designers and performers creating a memorable fusion of the arts.
Nevertheless, they are far from opera. The separate vignettes stand as
self-contained units with minimal dramatic action. The effect is similar to the still frames of a movie flickering past our eyes, too slowly
to create the illusion of animation. (For more detailed information on
these *intermedi,* see Saslow.)

The goal of all Italian art in the wake of the Counter-Reformation
was to create an immediate emotional impact on the audience. The polyphonic technique Palestrina had so eloquently defended was increasingly
perceived as an antiquated, exhausted style, a music that appealed more
to the intellect than to the emotions. Some critics actually accused
polyphony of being a "decadent" style, believing that counterpoint prevented a sung text from being intelligible to its listeners. In the 1580s
and 1590s a flock of young composers and performers, such as Peri,
Caccini, and Cavalieri, emerged who gave serious attention to monody,
or solo song, the oldest form of musical expression. What was different about the late-sixteenth-century monodists was their conviction
that the translation of poetry into vocal music was in need of radical
reinvention, privileging the text over the rules of polyphony.

Monody could not have arisen without the simultaneous development of one of the principle features of baroque music: the basso
continuo. Basso continuo, throughbass, or just plain continuo, as it is
more often called, served as a harmonic foundation for solo vocalists or
other instrumentalists. Basso continuo ("continuous bass") is an instrumental bass line running throughout a score that indicates chords so
players may improvise or "realize" their accompaniment. Continuo was
designed for chordal instruments such as harpsichords, organs, lutes,
theorbos (bass lutes), harps, and stringed instruments such as cellos or
viole da gamba. Continuo technique, as it began to emerge in the late
sixteenth century, had a vital purpose. Like the rhythm section of a

jazz ensemble, basso continuo serves to underpin and organize a larger ensemble. It provides a self-effacing harmonic support for solo voices, liberating the human voice from the necessity of filling in the harmony and allowing the listener to focus on the foregrounded soloists, be they vocalists or other instrumentalists. Continuo practice, with its important improvisatory element, has been successfully recreated by modern performing musicians, and audiences have come to appreciate the beautiful and surprisingly varied sonorities skilled continuo players give to music. As Joseph Kerman observes, "Rhythm, line, and dissonance were actually freed [by the continuo] for the most expressive contortions" ("Orpheus: The Neoclassic Vision" 130). The move from Renaissance homogeneity and balance toward a baroque appreciation of individualism is one of the cultural forces that led to the development of the basso continuo convention. With more freedom being given to the soloist, music was now capable of exploring a greater sense of rhythmic and expressive contrast. The soloistic foregrounding of a voice or an instrument allowed the individual performer to explore virtually limitless performative choices, using all levels of tempo and dynamics to create the most delicate nuances of expression. In the realm of vocal monody in particular, the basso continuo liberated the composer to reflect every detail of a text's changing meaning and emotion. The most important collection of monodist compositions was Caccini's *Le nuove musiche* (The New Music), published in 1602, a work that reveals an important minor master. Caccini helped pave the way for serious composers to concentrate on setting vernacular poetry for the solo voice. Italian medieval and Renaissance literature had provided a rich repertory of settable lyrics, usually on the time-honored themes of love, lust, and loss, that allowed a composer ample opportunity to express strong personal emotion without touching on politically explosive issues in the atmosphere of increasing intolerance fostered by the Counter-Reformation. In Mantua, Monteverdi paid keen attention to the emergence of monodic and basso continuo writing, adapting these techniques to his own developing style.

Although monody like Caccini's was clearly a product of the growing baroque need for individual self-expression, it was also deeply connected with late Renaissance neoclassical aspirations. The Italian-speaking world, politically divided as it was into separate, often small principalities, was home to dozens of Cameratas ("learned societies" or salons). Usually attached to princely courts, these Cameratas were made up of intellectuals of various backgrounds and interests. As the sixteenth century progressed and more and more of these separate principalities shifted from republican to autocratic rule, "the artistic and intellectual pursuits of the late-sixteenth- and early-seventeenth-century academies took on added importance. Cultural achievement became a safe outlet for talented individuals who might otherwise have been attracted to political activities. At the same time, the princes grasped the propagandistic potential of the products of these academies" (Bokina 15). Being good citizens of the late Renaissance, these Camerata men were dedicated to the exploration of the Greco-Roman classical heritage. The Camerata enterprise attested to a profound nostalgia for the golden age of Greek culture and a passionate desire, as the Renaissance came to its close, to rekindle the lost ancient unity of word and musical tone hinted at in ancient texts. The Greeks viewed poetry and music as interwoven arts that found their most notable expression in the tragedies performed in fifth-century Athens at the Theater of Dionysus. Classical theater was enjoying a resurgence of interest. Some of the first texts to be printed in the Italian Renaissance had been the surviving heritage of Greek and Latin drama. Scholars had been poring over these texts, and in Italy attempts were made to restage them. The year 1585 saw the opening of the Teatro Olimpico under the auspices of the Olympic Academy, a Camerata in Vicenza. Built by Andrea Palladio and Vincenzo Scamozzi under the inspiration of Renaissance interpretations of Vitruvius, the Teatro Olimpico was an imitation of a Roman-style amphitheater built into a preexisting structure. The oldest surviving indoor theater in the world, the Teatro Olimpico was inaugurated by a production of Sophocles' *Oedipus Tyrannus* in an Italian translation with incidental music by the Venetian composer Andrea Gabrieli. Just as *Oedipus* gains in impact when it can be staged in a supposedly authentic space such as the Teatro Olimpico, members of the Cameratas in Florence believed that the musical style of declamation, which had been such an important feature of performance in the ancient theater, had to be resurrected.

Italian classical scholarship mistakenly imagined that Greek tragedy had been entirely sung throughout. In actuality, the tragic dialogue in iambic verse was probably spoken in a declamatory or incantatory way. These spoken passages contrasted with the self-contained solo song passages that give lyrical expression to emotional moments in the plays, as well to as the rhythmically complex choruses that were sung and danced in the orchestra. (For up-to-date studies of Greek performance style see Walton and Rehm. John Herington's *Poetry into Drama* is an evocative interpretation of the Greek idea of poetry and music merging into a unique "song culture.") The Camerata dei Bardi in Florence, made up of scholars and musicians, were dedicated, like their Vicenzian counterparts, to the rebirth of ancient Greek–style theater. They met in the house of Count Giovanni Bardi between 1576 and 1582. Bardi, in his capacity as the official in charge of court spectacles, would serve as the driving force behind the 1589 *intermedi.* The group's members included Caccini, a personal friend of both Bardi and Vincenzo Galilei, the father of the astronomer. Galilei published a treatise in 1581, *Dialogo sulla musica antica e moderna,* advocating a rejection of polyphony and a return to the musical style of ancient Greece. Greek music had been a highly developed art, but only a few small scraps of it had survived to the age of printing. The Camerata dei Bardi realized that without music the great plays of Aeschylus, Sophocles, and Euripides were missing an important element, one that had helped to captivate their first audiences.

The new popularity of monody and basso continuo was seen by the Camerata dei Bardi and a slightly later Florentine group, the Accademia degli Alterati, as a possible means to recreate the conditions of Greek drama as they were then understood. Accademia degli Alterati, which was under the direction of the musician Jacopo Corsi, included Peri and Rinuccini. A third Camerata may also have existed that included Cavalieri. These learned societies represented intellectual and artistic rivals whose experimentation and theories would lead to the birth of opera. As may be seen from this brief overview, there was no one "Florentine Camerata" that "invented opera." Later history has tended to simplify a much more complex process of gestation. The term "Florentine Camerata" is useful only as a loose rubric to describe different organizations comprising different people all working at roughly the same time in Florence during the closing years of the sixteenth century. (See also Pirrotta 218.)

The idea of a play sung from beginning to end created devilish problems for the early experimenters. Musical form usually depends on repetition for comprehensibility. In other words, melodic material has to be repeated for an audience to recognize the motifs, and the repetition can create pleasure for listeners. Drama, on the other hand, requires a sequence of ongoing events moving toward a crisis and resolution. How could a drama, which is inherently forward moving and evolving, be continuously linked with music, which demands some form of repetition to generate comprehensibility as well as pleasure? One of the musicians working with the Florentine societies, either Peri, Caccini, or Cavalieri—historians have never been certain which one—broke the creative crisis with the invention of recitative. It is characteristic of the intensely collaborative and intensely competitive nature of the Cameratas' work that a single composer cannot be confidently singled out as the definite inventor of recitative. All three claimed credit for it at various points in their lives. *Stile recitativo* or the recitative style is the compositional innovation that made opera possible. Realizing that a forward-moving drama cannot be created with closed musical forms (i.e., a succession of songs that of necessity repeat tunes), the Florentine creator(s) of recitative developed an open-ended style of solo vocal declamation. Peri himself described the thinking that led him and his colleagues to this all-important innovation: "I decided that the ancient Greeks and Romans (who according to the opinion of many, sang their tragedies throughout on the stage) used a harmony which, going beyond that of ordinary speech, fell so short of the melody of song that it assumed an intermediate form . . . [taking] an intermediate path between the suspended and slow movements of song and the fluent, rapid ones of speech" (Peri's preface to *Euridice,* qtd. in Carter, *Monteverdi's Musical Theater* 25). Recitative was not created out of a vacuum. Pirrotta notes that recitative style "corresponds to a kind of expression that was already coming to maturity in the field of the madrigal" (232).

Recitative is vocal music that imitates the spoken word. The pace and tempo are dictated by the pulse of the words the singer sings.

For the most part, recitative avoids clearly defined melody, moving in a realm of continuous musical progression. A fluid and dynamic solution to a musical and dramaturgical problem, recitative is very flexible; at one moment allowing the plot to hurry forward, at another slowing to permit the composer to lavish ornamental or other expressive devices on any word or phrase that inspires his or her illustrative skills. It seemed that the equivalent of the ancient Greek speech-song was at last within reach. For variety and to accent heightened dramatic situations, closed forms such as songs, choruses, or instrumental interludes could be added to the score as needed. At the conclusion of such passages recitative would be restored to carry the action forward. Recitative may feature ariosos, brief lyrical passages that give variety to the declamation without becoming full-fledged arias.

The last years of the sixteenth century saw a rapid flurry of experimental performances that heralded the beginnings of the operatic medium. In late 1597 Rinuccini composed the world's first opera libretto, *Dafne,* a verse drama based on Greek mythology. Corsi, the leader of the Accademia degli Alterati, began setting the libretto to music, a task completed by Peri. Unfortunately the music for this earliest opera is now mostly lost. Sponsored by Florentine noblemen and performed in Corsi's home during the Carnival season of 1598, *Dafne* represents the first attempt at the genre we know as opera. In 1600 Cavalieri, who had been a part of the Florentine experiments and created musical plays (now lost) in Florence in the 1590s, went to Rome to present his sacred musical drama, *Rappresentatione di anima et di corpo* (The Play of the Soul and the Body), on a text by Agostino Manni. The new Florentine recitative style was now being presented to a Roman audience during Carnival season, uniting the supposedly pagan idea of musical drama with a Christian morality play. Cavalieri's score was published, and it was revived occasionally in the later twentieth century.

Cavalieri's opera is composed with bold strokes containing strong hints at the nascent art of musical characterization. The raucous chorus of "Pleasure with His Companions" tempts "Body" (an earthy bass) and "Soul" (an appropriately airy soprano) in a scene that shows genuine musical-dramatic instinct. Cavalieri favored arioso declamation over the comparatively dry recitative that characterized Peri's operatic writing. Peri was a more delicate craftsman, Cavalieri a more immediately engaging personality. *Rappresentatione* began the tradition of Roman opera, which would prove to be a strong influence on the Venetian version of the genre when it began in the late 1630s. We may regret all the more sharply Cavalieri's death in 1602 and the loss of his contributions to theater music in the following years.

Later in 1600 Rinuccini, the *Dafne* librettist, collaborated with Peri once again on another Greek-based "drama in music," *Euridice*. As with *Dafne,* the new project was instigated by Corsi. *Euridice*'s premiere at the Pitti Palace on October 6, 1600, was part of the wedding celebrations for Henry IV of France and Maria de' Medici. The new opera appears to have caused an even greater stir than *Dafne*. Peri, a much-admired singer (and nicknamed "Il Zazzerino" for his shock of reddish blond hair), made a great impression as Orpheus. Euridice was portrayed by Vittoria Archilei, a famous singer and lutenist (see O'Grady 11). [Peri's second opera received the honor of publication, ensuring that the new style of musical drama could be easily disseminated throughout Italy. *Euridice,* like *Dafne,* is a fascinating signpost in the early history of opera. Although both works lack the dramatic tension or musical interest needed to sustain them on their own artistic and not historical merits, they served as inspiration for those who would follow.] The ferment of early experimentation in opera may be seen as an act of blatant artistic one-upmanship: Caccini was to come out with his own operatic treatment of *Euridice* the same year Peri's version was produced. Caccini's work was not as successful as his rival's, however, and Caccini's disappointed jealousy eventually led him to denounce the recitative style for good.

Euridice, with its five-act structure—each act punctuated by a closing chorus—asserts the courtly opera's neoclassical ambitions. Monteverdi and Striggio were to emulate this pattern in *L'Orfeo*. (For the influence of *Euridice* on *Orfeo,* see Pirrotta 236–45.) Peri's music reveals an appreciation of the meaning of Rinuccini's text, suggesting many of the musical devices Monteverdi was to adapt later for his own recitative. But the differences between Peri's recitative and Monteverdi's are greater than their similarities. Monteverdi's recitative

seems less an "imitation of speech" than a *genuine* speech, a speech flowing with all the unpredictable variety of living thought and spontaneous
expression. Peri seldom utilizes the method of verbal repetition that
Monteverdi later used in his settings to animate and interpret text and
dramatic character. As in the later *L'Orfeo,* the musical and dramatic
high point of *Euridice* comes when Orpheus pleads to the powers of the
underworld for the restoration of Euridice. This long plea, "Fueneste
piagge" (Funereal shores), demonstrates Peri's compositional skill.
Orpheus's impassioned declamation is broken by pregnant pauses as
the performer-composer confronts the void of sound and silence, life
and death. But for all of *Euridice*'s accomplishments, the work pales
beside Monteverdi's first opera owing to the latter's greater sense of
dramatic tension, created by Striggio's even more skillful libretto and
by the sharper contrasts in Monteverdi's music and its infinitely greater
emotional power. Had Monteverdi's operas never come to Mantua, the
new Florentine operatic medium might not have been able to hold its
own against the allure of the *intermedi.* One contemporary listener to
Euridice groused that its recitative was like the "chanting of the Passion"
(cited in Fenton, "Origins" 33). An audience member of Caccini's
Il rapimento di Cefalo, performed later in 1600, complained that "the
style of singing easily led to boredom" (cited in Fenlon, "Origins" 33).
Among the many visitors to Florence during 1600 who saw the premiere of Peri's *Euridice* was Vincenzo Gonzaga. He must have recognized the novelty of this Florentine invention and something of the
genre's potential for attracting attention to its aristocratic sponsors.
His servant Monteverdi probably accompanied him to the performance
(O'Grady 14; see also Fabbri, *Monteverdi* 64).

Monteverdi's Mantuan Career Begins

By late 1606, when Monteverdi undertook *L'Orfeo,* his Mantuan years
had already molded his life and work in indelible ways. Serving the
duke of Mantua was an honor and an onus. The frequent lateness and
unpredictability of the ducal treasury's allocation of his salary was a
continuing frustration. Despite his loyalty and increasing fame as a

published composer, in 1596, when the position of court music director (*maestro della musica*) opened up with the death of Giaches de Wert, Monteverdi was passed over. He was finally to assume that position in 1601. The extra salary was helpful, for the composer had married a court singer, Claudia Cattaneo (daughter of a string instrumentalist at court, Giacomo Cattaneo) on May 20, 1599, and had a growing family. The young couple's first child, Francesco Baldassare, was born in 1601 and would follow in his parents' footsteps as a musician. A daughter, Leonora Camilla, died soon after her birth in 1603. Their third and last child, Massimiliano Giacomo, a future doctor, was born in 1604. In 1602 Monteverdi was granted Mantuan citizenship and moved the family from lodgings on the outskirts of Mantua to a dwelling close to the palace. All these changes marked the composer's rising status at court, despite the often disdainful treatment he received. These years were filled with personal frustrations and modest triumphs. The madrigals composed and published during this period reflect an exciting stylistic and emotional evolution.

Monteverdi's *Third Book of Madrigals* (1592) shows the composer experimenting with more solo passagework, which imparts greater intelligibility to the words. One critic observes Monteverdi's use of "motifs that have a monotonous declamation of considerable length on one tone only," lending the music "poignant" and "passionate" force (Schrade 183). The five-voice settings, of Torquato Tasso's epic poem *Gerusalemme liberata,* reveal a newfound grandness of utterance. The *Fourth Book of Madrigals* (1603) represents another landmark in Monteverdi's creative development. Although there is much contrapuntal writing for the five voices, the music suggests that the composer is already leaning toward the use of basso continuo, though not accompanimental instruments. Schrade detects "a new counterpoint . . . [in which] an upper part . . . functions as the vehicle of the melody and the lower part . . . affords harmonic support" (192). One of the most memorable pieces in this collection is "Sì, ch'io vorrei morire" (Yes, I would like to die), perhaps the most erotic of all Monteverdi's compositions before *L'incoronazione di Poppea*. Here the languishing chromatic lines and the pulse-quickening shifts of tempo create one of the frankest and most beautiful expressions in music of sexual passion.

The *Fifth Book of Madrigals* (1605), for five voices, graphically depicts the fault line of the Renaissance style's shift into the baroque. Six madrigals out of the nineteen contained in this collection require genuine basso continuo support. The title page suggests basso continuo may also be added "ad libitum" to the rest of the collection. The contrast between styles is still shocking even to modern ears when the cycle is presented as a whole. This shift within a single publication must have seemed even more freakish in the early seventeenth century. One of these basso continuo madrigals, "'T'amo, mia vita,' la mia cara vita," may stand as a convenient marker for gauging the significance of the composer's development since the First Book of 1587.

The whole poem needs to be examined before listening to Monteverdi's musical interpretation.

> "T'amo, mia vita," la mia cara vita
> dolcemente mi dice, e'n questa sola
> sì soave parola
> par che trasformi lietamente il core,
> per farmene signore.
> O voce di dolcezza e di diletto!
> Prendila tosto, Amore;
> stampala nel mio petto.
> Spiri solo per lei l'anima mia;
> "T'amo, mia vita," la mia vita sia.

> ["I love you, my life," my beloved
> says sweetly to me, and, with this one
> most lovely phrase,
> she seems serenely to change her heart,
> to make me master of it.
> O sweet and delightful words!
> Make haste, Love,
> to imprint them on my heart!
> Let my soul breathe through them alone:
> let "I love you, my life" be my whole life.]

Guarini, trans. Philip Weller

The basso continuo supports the composition's harmony and maintains its musical coherence, freeing the voices not only for solo passages but to assume "roles" within the composition. A solo soprano voice sings the "beloved," who utters a languishing, sighing phrase, "T'amo, mia vita" (I love you, my life). The male voices, which form a trio representing the lover, perform the majority of the poem while the soprano reiterates her opening phrase. The use of repetition makes the role assignment all the clearer: the solo soprano represents each man's lover. The final line of verse allows for a suggestive blurring of identity as the soprano joins her male colleges and a second soprano is at last added to the overlapping musical lines. Monteverdi has created a musical drama with an exposition, development, and denouement, which Guarini's lovely words hardly suggest by themselves. Monteverdi has absorbed the dramatic implications of monody into the madrigal. We can see from our vantage point that such music is very close to opera. Music like this represented a disturbingly personal vision that seemed to threaten the long-standing compositional tenets of the past several centuries. Indeed, in the first few years of the seventeenth century, Monteverdi and his methods sparked an important controversy.

The "Artusi" Quarrel

In 1600 a dispute began that articulated Monteverdi's role in the emergence of a post-Renaissance musical aesthetic. A priest from Bologna, Giovanni Maria Artusi, had heard performed at a gathering some of the madrigals that would eventually be published in the Fourth and Fifth Books. A keen musical amateur trained in the polyphonic style, Artusi was mystified, offended, and disturbed by this new music. He went to the length of publishing a polemic devoted solely to attacking Monteverdi's works as a wanton violation of musical grammar and syntax. With great aplomb, he called his treatise *Artusi, or the Imperfections of Modern Music (L'Artusi, Overo della Imperfettione della moderna musica).* Artusi delineated all the violations of the rules of traditional polyphony that he detected in Monteverdi's madrigals: grating dissonances, faulty intervals, accidental alterations, modal ambiguity, and recitativelike declamation. (For a lucid outline of the quarrel, see Fabbri, *Monteverdi* 34–52.) The priest was particularly offended by

Monteverdi's frequent use of dissonance, which Artusi found "rough, crude, harsh, and insupportable to the ear." An arch-traditionalist, he proclaimed that "music made by the ancients without these jokes produced marvelous effects, and this music produces tomfooleries" (qtd. in Fabbri, *Monteverdi* 46–47). Artusi's attack focused on the musical notes in Monteverdi's scores while neglecting the verbal texts being set. By ignoring the texts, Artusi was ignoring the purpose of the composer's work as Monteverdi saw it—to move the passions of his listeners by vivifying the emotional meaning of the words being sung. Although Artusi would eventually be won over to the "new music," the controversy forced the composer to construct a more theoretical basis for his compositional aims. Monteverdi's letters and other writings, as well as the writings of his loyal brother, Giulio Cesare, clearly delineate the composer's views of his aesthetic process and his mission. In an appendix to his *Fifth Book of Madrigals,* Monteverdi defended himself against Artusi: "I do not compose my works haphazardly. . . . With regard to the consonances and dissonances, there is still another way of considering them, different from the established way, which, with satisfaction to the reason and to the senses, defends the modern method of composing. . . . The modern composer builds upon the foundation of truth" (qtd. in Fabbri, *Monteverdi* 48).

Throughout his career Monteverdi would cultivate two distinct styles of composition: the new basso continuo technique of the baroque and the heritage of Renaissance polyphony. For all his radical innovation, Monteverdi never disdained or discarded polyphony. In his writings he referred to the old, balanced polyphonic style of the Renaissance as "the first practice" (*la prima pratica*) and the new basso continuo method, which privileges a more direct communication with the audience "the second practice" (*la seconda pratica*). Giulio Cesare Monteverdi, himself a member of the Gonzaga court's musical retinue, published a statement appended to his brother's *Scherzi musicali* of 1607 giving a clear description of his brother's use of both traditional and innovative genres:

> By First Practice [my brother] understands the [compositional style] that turns on the perfection of the harmony, that is, the one

that considers the harmony not commanded but commanding, not the servant, but the mistress of [the poetic text], and this was founded by those first men who composed . . . music for more than one voice. . . . By Second Practice, . . . he understands the [style] that turns on the perfection of the *melodia,* that is, the one that considers harmony not commanding, but commanded, and makes the oration the mistress of the harmony.

In a subsequently famous phrase, Giulio Cesare stated that Claudio's controversial music had "made the poetry the mistress of the music and not the servant" (qtd. in Fabbri, *Monteverdi* 50).

This theory of two practices is behind all Monteverdi's works from the start of the century until his death. There is an element of stylistic self-consciousness here that should find resonance in the postmodern world's sensibility for differing styles coexisting and gaining nourishment from each other within the same work. Silke Leopold summarizes the major issues at stake in the Artusi-Monteverdi schism.

Up until then scholars were in agreement that the intellect (*intel-letto*) and not the feelings (*senso*) were the last resort when judging a work of art. Monteverdi, however, perceived the goal of music as being an appeal to the emotions of the audience, not to their understanding. In order to attain this goal, music was justified in using any means, even that of infringing on the rules. For Artusi "art" meant skill, a craft at the highest level, constrained by a theory which established its rules and this made it teachable and learnable, debatable and comfortable. "Art" for Artusi was on the same plane as science. . . . For Monteverdi "art" was a private artistic expression, wherein rational criteria such as "right" and "wrong" lost ground in relation to emotional ones such as "moving" or "stirring." A perfect approach to a work for Artusi lay in being able to understand it, if one were only at the same intellectual level as the composer; for Monteverdi, on the other hand, a work of art distinguished itself by the very fact that it could not be completely understood, that it possessed something disconcerting, mysterious, not entirely explicable. . . . Within the idea of the *secunda pratica* are found the origins of the later aesthetic theory of genius in which genius breaks the shackles of tradition and creates its own rules. (48–49)

By the early seventeenth century, the "knowableness" of the world Renaissance scholars and intellectuals postulated had begun to shatter, owing to the forces of inquiry unleashed by science and philosophy. The new baroque sensibility in the arts reflected the needs of a new world: one full of restless searching and an equally restless sense of instability as new discoveries led to seemingly infinite questions. Human beings learned in this era that they were no longer at the center of a cosmic order. Just as the telescope would prove the size of the universe to be beyond measure, so too the microscope would suggest the possibility of a tiny world, equally elusive for human comprehension. Christianity, which for centuries had provided stability to its followers, was now torn between Catholic and Protestant factions. It is not surprising that artists of the early seventeenth century, such as Monteverdi, would both cling to the older, seemingly stable forms (*prima pratica*) and at the same time find eloquent means for expressing their individual sense of instability and mutation (*seconda pratica*). The double-sidedness of the seventeenth-century sensibility has often been remarked upon: its schizophrenic division between the sacred and the secular, the longing for purity and stability and the awareness of omnipresent change and decay. One sees this in Vermeer's genre scenes immortalizing paradoxically transient moments in an eternal prismatic perfection. Much of Rembrandt's work is a loving meditation on change and decay experienced in flesh and other materials. This duality finds expression at the dawn of the century in a speech of Hamlet: "What a piece of work is a man! How noble in reason, how infinite in faculties, in form and moving how express and admirable, in action how like an angel, in apprehension how like a god—the beauty of the world, the paragon of animals! And yet to me what is this quintessence of dust? Man delights not me" (act 2, scene 2, lines 293–98).

The awareness of a duality at the heart of things lies behind the "two practices" articulated by Monteverdi and imparts disquieting animation to much of his music. Monteverdi did not want or attempt to replace one discredited worldview with another. Instead he sought to depict and communicate the only subject a person can claim to know in an unstable universe—the human soul. The results of his experiments continue to work in the laboratory of performance. They still speak to audiences after four centuries because Monteverdi, like Shakespeare, discovered a cartography of the human heart that is ever relevant because it is true.

The Style of Early-Seventeenth-Century Opera

Late Renaissance artists and theorists—Monteverdi included—were profoundly influenced by aesthetic precepts in Plato and Aristotle. Of especial interest were the Greek philosophers' theories on imitation or mimesis. Aristotle's *Poetics* represents the most important exposition of classical literary and artistic theory. According to Aristotle, all art, including music and drama, is a form of mimesis (imitation). Although Plato's idealism mistrusted mimesis, Aristotle boldly asserts that mimesis is an innate part of human nature and that its efficacy rests in its educational value. (Thomas Gould's *The Ancient Quarrel between Poetry and Philosophy* is an excellent analysis of Plato's and Artistotle's conflicting views.) Humans learn by studying mimesis. In the *Politics,* Aristotle writes:

> When men hear imitations [in music], even apart from the rhythms and tunes themselves, their feelings move in sympathy. . . . Rhythm and melody supply imitations of anger and gentleness, and also of courage and temperance, and of all the qualities contrary to these, and of the other qualities of character, which hardly fall short of the actual affections, as we know from our own experience, for in listening to such strains our souls undergo a change. The habit of feeling pleasure or pain at mere representations is not far removed from the same feeling about realities; for example, if any one delights in the sight of a statue for its beauty only, it necessarily follows that the sight of the original will be pleasant to him. (Aristotle, *Politics* 8.1340a.11–29)

In other words, Aristotle suggests that music can both replicate an emotional state and by some mysterious alchemy instill something of that emotional state in its listeners. Music consequently inhabits a potentially dangerous region between representation and essence (see also Aercke 69; Kivey 34–35).

There are three distinct modes of solo vocal music in early-seventeenth-century opera:

1. Recitative (from the Italian *recitatare,* "to recite"): a speechlike musical declamation, which, though it may call for verbal ornamentation and other forms of musical emphasis or illustration, is fundamentally a nonmelodic, flowing, open-ended form.
2. Aria (from the Latin *aer,* "air," "atmosphere"): a song of a certain length which is musically intelligible in and of itself.
3. Arioso (from the Italian, "melodious" or "like an aria"): ostensibly recitative passages that under the emotional and dramatic pressures of the moment are allowed to blossom into brief melodic writing.

Recitative, aria, and arioso are the fundamental building blocks of early opera. Ellen Rosand writes: "The shift between these different modes challenges the audience to define and understand their experience. Are the characters speaking or singing? What is the difference? The multiple layers of musical/dramatic illusion amplify those in the text" (Rosand, *Opera* 118). Rosand detects the listener's appreciation of "the distinction between speech [recitative] and song [aria or arioso]" as "the basic premise of the genre" (*Opera* 333). F. W. Sternfeld has discerned a dramaturgical pattern in the employment of the three operatic musical modes. Arias tend to occur once an emotional "stage (or 'station') of the action has been reached, and during the aria the music does not deviate from the '*affetto*' [emotional state]. . . . It is the shifting from one '*affetto*' to another, the fluidity of transition, that makes recitative (and arioso) such an indispensable carrier of dramatic action" (Sternfeld, "Aspects of Aria" 117). Aria and arioso would occur more frequently once opera became commercialized in Venice during the 1630s and 1640s. Early opera's shifts between recitative, aria, and arioso are beautifully described by Nino Pirrotta. Although Pirrotta, like Rosand, is specifically addressing the style of early Venetian opera, his words easily apply to court operas such as *L'Orfeo:*

> To be sure, [early opera is] not lacking in melody—sometimes very beautiful melody—but it always arises without a break from recitative, as, in an eloquent speech, there surges up at a given

moment a rounder and more sonorous voice which falls again and dies off. For music is still ruled by the word, is adjusted to it, and tries to reinterpret, stress, and embellish it, without exceeding the function of an obedient and faithful servant. (357)

It would only be in much later baroque opera, such as Handel's, that music would assert itself in opera above and beyond consideration for the text and dramatic situation. In this latter style of baroque opera, the aria will rule, while recitative will be banished to the role of mere "connective tissue" (Pirrotta 357). Monteverdi's operas contain an embarrassment of melodic riches, but they can never be listened to as mere background music, as one might a recorded collection of Rossini, Verdi, or Handel arias. His music demands that the listeners prepare themselves by reading the text beforehand and that they concentrate on every verbal inflection to comprehend better the way the music vivifies the dramatic situation. Such preparation is customary for audiences encountering works such Wagner's *Ring* or Berg's *Wozzeck*. The mistaken attitude that baroque music is "easy listening" has prevented many listeners from bringing the appropriate "Wagnerian" attitude toward fully engaging in Monteverdi's textual and dramatic situations. Monteverdi's actual sound is of course hardly Wagnerian, with its delicate, comparatively bare textures. But the attention both these masters paid to verbal and psychological detail reveals that opera was for them above all a site of drama with music, not a costumed concert with negligible dramatic action.

Another important feature of seventeenth-century opera is the tradition of allegorical prologues, which feature in all three surviving Monteverdi operas and are found in the later works of Francesco Cavalli, Jean-Baptiste Lully, and Marc-Antoine Charpentier, among others. These prologues feature mythical or allegorical figures who introduce the opera and enunciate the thematics of the musical play to follow. Monteverdi's prologues are more intimately linked to his operas than are those of many early operatic composers. Verbal and musical echoes of the prologues may even be woven throughout an opera. In *Poppea,* one allegorical figure from the prologue is actually inserted physically into the main action of the opera.

It is an interesting paradox that the late Renaissance, an era that set great store by verisimilitude (the attempt to create lifelike representations of the world) also created opera, that most outlandishly nonrealistic of art forms. Artists and theorists of early opera were keenly aware of the violations of verisimilitude presented by singing characters, and this conflict between the demands of verisimilitude and the attempted re-creation of ancient dramatic form finds a reflection in the subject matter as well as the style of the earliest operas. Greek subject matter was an obvious choice for an art form that was intended to emulate Greek theater. It is no accident that both Peri and Monteverdi choose the Orpheus myth for their separate treatments. They could argue that their operas did not violate verisimilitude, since Orpheus was a notable *singer.* What could be more lifelike than a lead character who is famous as a singer, doing onstage what he does best? Orpheus was also a demigod, and divine figures might easily be imagined singing to express their elevated status. After all, did not the heavens themselves resonate the "music of the spheres"? This interest in verisimilitude in operatic aesthetics can be found in the depiction of divine or semidivine characters who feature in *Dafne, Euridice,* and *L'Orfeo,* particularly in some of the celebratory songs and dances in *L'Orfeo*'s first two acts. Rosand notes, "The development and persistence well beyond the middle [of the seventeenth century] of conventional situations in which singing was either natural or purposely unnatural—songs within the drama, for instance, or scenes of madness and sleep—bear witness to the irresolvable contradiction posed by the mixing of music and drama" (Rosand, *Opera* 45). Indeed, opera loves "'singing about singing," whether it is Nerone and Lucano's grotesque singing match in *Poppea,* *Carmen*'s "Habanera," or the "Brindisi" of *La traviata.* Recitative, aria, and arioso contribute to the subtle "levels of musical illusion" (Rosand's phrase) that have helped audiences from the seventeenth to the twenty-first century fall under opera's spell.

Renaissance theorists could also look to spoken language itself as a latently musical phenomenon. Gary Tomlinson observes: "The effectiveness of correspondence between word and tone in late Renaissance song was conceived as arising from an innate harmony within words that was muted in normal speech. It was not a question of music assimilating itself to signifying words but of *words disclosing* in song, the hidden harmony that *underpinned their significance*" (Tomlinson, *Metaphysical Song* 14). Tomlinson writes that the human being in the late Renaissance imagination "inhabits the borderline between material and immaterial worlds. Unlike all higher things, it has a coarse, congealed material body; unlike all lower things, it has an immaterial soul. In merging material and immaterial worlds it repeats the structure of the cosmos in miniature; it is microcosm to the macrocosm of the cosmos" (*Metaphysical Song* 10).

Early opera, whether of the courtly (*L'Orfeo*) or commercial kind (*Ulisse* and *Poppea*), privileges the text over the music, just as it privileges the singers over their instrumental accompaniment. Even in such a lavish performance as the Mantuan premiere of *L'Orfeo,* the orchestral accompaniment was no larger than a small chamber orchestra. The weaker projective force of early instruments and the relatively small performance venues further ensured that the singers' voices would dominate the proceedings. Early opera contains numerous sinfonias (short instrumental pieces, often in several sections) and ritornelli (from the Italian for "little returns": short instrumental passages repeated either as preludes or postludes). Sometimes ritornelli appear as interludes occurring throughout a strophic aria. (Strophic arias or songs employ the same musical material for setting each stanza of a lyric.) These instrumental passages punctuate and enrich the action, but there is never any question as to the focus of the audience's attention. The singer-actor is the most important element in performance and dictates the pace of virtually the entire musical performance (see also Aercke 73). Monteverdi opera requires intelligent, sensitive singers who, more than merely producing attractive sounds, can project words and convey their characters' changing psychological states. The instrumentalists who accompany these singers must work in close relationship with them and with the dramatic situation. Frequently an element of improvisatory freedom is required from the instrumentalists based on seventeenth-century performance practice. This wonderful element of improvisation ensures that each performance of a Monteverdi opera, more than works from the traditional operatic canon, is a unique experience, a true "happening," to borrow a favorite phrase from the dramatic theorist Antonin Artaud. Whenever we encounter the earliest operas in performance, we are keenly aware of the genre's newness. Words, drama, and music are coming together before our senses for the first time. In the words of the conductor Jane Glover, "We must forget about Handel and Mozart, Wagner and Puccini. This combination of drama and music has never happened before. We are experiencing something new" (personal interview, December 2001, New York City).

"Lend Me a Castrato"
Opera Comes to Mantua

I have decided to have a play in music [una favola in Musica] performed at Carnival this year, but as we have very few sopranos here, and those few not good, I should be grateful if Your Excellency would be kind enough to tell me if those castrati I heard when I was in Tuscany are still there. I mean the ones in the Grand Duke's service, whom I so much enjoyed hearing during my visit. My intention is to borrow one of them (whichever Your Excellency thinks the best), as long as you agree that the Grand Duke will not refuse to lend him, if you yourself do the asking, for a fortnight at most.

Letter from Francesco Gonzaga in Mantua to
Ferdinando Gonzaga in Pisa, January 5, 1607

The letter excerpted in the epigraph marks the first reference to Monteverdi's *L'Orfeo* in the historical record. Francesco was the twenty-one-year-old son and heir of the reigning Duke Vincenzo. He wanted to emulate his father's reputation as a patron of the arts and was perhaps more than a little envious of his brother Ferdinando's reputation as a music connoisseur. Ferdinando, just a year younger than Francesco, was a passionate musical and literary amateur who had close ties with such musicians as Peri, Caccini, and Marco da Gagliano (1582–1643) through his sponsorship of the Florentine Accademia degli Elevati. Gagliano dedicated his *Fourth Book of Madrigals* to Ferdinando and may have even given him composition lessons. Ferdinando composed at least two works—now lost—for the Carnival seasons of 1605 and 1606 for the Medici court, which traditionally passed that season in Pisa. One of these works was a comedy for which Ferdinando wrote both poetry and music. Francesco lost little time in attempting to rival his younger brother. Francesco shared none of Ferdinando's practical artistic aptitude, but that would not hinder him from attempting to outdo him as a patron of ambitious artistic endeavor. Francesco determined that for the 1607 Carnival in Mantua he would sponsor a musical play to rival anything the Florentine court or his younger brother could come up with. Francesco displays marvelous courtly aplomb in his letter to Ferdinando. The "play in music" is announced as a fait accompli. His request for supplementary singers is also subtly designed to let the Tuscan grand duke know that the recent Florentine innovations in musical drama are being seriously challenged by the rival court of Mantua. If Florence can produce Peri and Rinuccini's *Euridice,* in the newly discovered "representative style" (*stile rappresentativo*) of drama with music, Mantua can present its own version of the myth with *L'Orfeo.*

The Mantuan court was one of the most dazzling centers for the arts in Renaissance Italy. There one of the greatest painters of the era, Andrea Mantegna, in 1474 executed his greatest masterpiece, the frescoes of the palace's Camera degli Sposi. In 1480 the Gonzagas hosted a performance of Angelo Poliziano's *La favola di Orfeo* (The Play of Orpheus), the first vernacular Italian play based on a classical subject. At least half of Poliziano's play was designed to be sung. Poliziano's music is lost, but his telling of the Orpheus story is an important harbinger of the later sixteenth-century Florentine experiments, as well as embodying a still lively cultural memory in early-seventeenth-century Mantua. Poliziano's memory was also immortalized by Mantegna as one of the courtly personages in the Gonzaga frescoes, the poet-musician-Orphean portrayed standing amid the ancestors of the reigning duke (see also Schrade 225). Mantegna also portrayed Orpheus on Parnassus for a fresco for the studio of Isabella d'Este. Other local Orphean traditions include the atrium frescoes at the Palazzo del Giardino in nearby Sabbioneta (see Fabbri, *Monteverdi* 69). Sabbioneta also featured an indoor neoclassical theater inspired by Vicenza's Teatro Olimpico.

In more recent years, Duke Vincenzo had hosted the great poet Torquato Tasso, as well as producing, in 1598, a staging of another watershed theatrical work, Giovanni Battista Guarini's *Il pastor fido*. Written in the 1580s, *Il pastor fido* was a conglomeration of the ancient tradition of pastoral poetry (idealized visions of shepherds and shepherdesses complaining of the sorrows of love in elegant, courtly poetry) and tragicomedy. Guarini's play incorporated so much singing, dancing, and instrumental accompaniment that Monteverdi and the entire musical staff at the palace had to have been involved. Guarini's idealized country folk were to be the inspiration for the Italian craze for pastoral drama (Shakespeare's *As You Like It* is the nearest English equivalent of this style) as well as the direct precedent of the shepherds and nymphs in Monteverdi's *L'Orfeo*.

Along with the more distant influence of Guarini and Poliziano, the strongest literary precedents for *L'Orfeo* would be the telling of the Orpheus myth in Ovid's *Metamorphoses,* books 10 and 11, and Virgil's *Georgics,* book 4, as well as Rinuccini's *Euridice* libretto of 1600. The opera's Apollonian ending, which appears in the published score of 1609 and in the reprint of 1615 (but not in the published libretto of 1607) is based on a version of the myth by an obscure author of late antiquity, Hyginus, in his *Astronomia* (2.7).

Even ostensibly nondramatic music making at the Gonzaga court contained a strong theatrical element. A Roman visitor around 1628 recounted the style of madrigal performance at both the Mantuan and Farranese courts in terms that no doubt described the performance style current when Francesco first contemplated his friendly rivalry with his brother.

> [The court singers] moderated or increased their voices, loud or soft, heavy or light, according to the demands of the piece they were singing; now slow, breaking off sometimes with a gentle sigh, now singing long passages legato or detached, now groups, now leaps, now with long trills, now with short, or again with sweet running passages sung softly, to which one sometimes heard an echo answer unexpectedly. They accompanied the music and the sentiment with appropriate facial expressions, glances and gestures, with no awkward movements of the mouth or hands or

> body which might not express the feeling of the song. They made
> the words clear in such a way that one could hear even the last syl-
> lable of every word, which was never interrupted or suppressed by
> passages [*passaggi*] and other embellishments. (Letter of Vincenzo
> Giustiniani, qtd. in Whenham, *Orfeo* 5)

Francesco's musical play was produced under the auspices of the court's own learned society, the Accademia degli Invaghiti (Charmed Ones' Academy). Open to aristocrats and clergy, the society was for men only. The princely Gonzaga brothers were members, as was Alessandro Striggio, the *L'Orfeo* librettist, but Monteverdi was not. The son of a prominent composer, also named Alessandro, Striggio the younger was a diplomat and served as the court secretary. In addition to his regular courtly duties, Striggio the younger was himself a musician. As a teenager he had participated as a viol player in the epoch-making Florentine *intermedi* of 1589 and must have been deeply impressed at the power implicit in the successful union of even limited stage action with music. Striggio was to prove Monteverdi's closest ally at Mantua and to remain a dear friend until the librettist's death in 1630. Most of Monteverdi's surviving letters are addressed to him. Monteverdi, the *maestro et de la camera et de la chiesa sopra la musica* (master of chamber and church music) was already a firmly established composer with a reputation spreading far beyond Mantua. Francesco knew he would be perfectly adept at rivaling the Florentine masters at their own invention. But not even he could have known that the ephemeral courtly rivalry he was engaged in would lead to the creation of the first permanent work of the operatic repertoire and ensure that his name would be remembered forever for this Carnival entertainment, which would be seen by only a couple of hundred spectators during Francesco's lifetime.

Along with Monteverdi and Striggio, a large company of singers, instrumentalists, designers, and stage technicians could be counted on to lend their talents to Francesco. Nevertheless the enterprise—an entirely sung play—was novel and taxing. At this earliest stage of the genre's development, there were no professional opera singers: the singers in the early court operas made their livelihoods as solo or madrigal singers, choristers in ducal chapels, and instrumentalists. Some were courtiers with good voices and, it is to be hoped, histrionic talent.

We may recall Peri's fame not only as a composer but as a singer in the early Florentine performances. As we shall see in chapter 4, actors from the spoken theater could easily be drafted for the operatic stage. The focus of all the action in *L'Orfeo* is unambiguously placed on the singer playing the title role. The tenor Francesco Rasi (1574–after 1620) is believed to have created the role of Orfeo for the 1607 premiere. An impoverished nobleman originating from the town of Arezzo, Rasi had studied with Caccini and had been close to the Florentine Camerata before moving to Mantua in 1598. In 1600 he briefly returned to Florence to sing a role in Peri's *Euridice*. Iain Fenlon notes: "As a member of the first generation of monodists, and one with practical experience of early opera, Rasi may well have been of some importance to Monteverdi's assimilation and adaptation of the monodic style in *Orfeo*" ("Mantuan Stage Works" 265). *L'Orfeo* is filled with striking supporting characters who enrich the opera immeasurably, but no other role places demands on a singer like that of the title character (see also Fabbri, *Monteverdi* 64). In Rasi, Monteverdi had a performer steeped in the tradition of monody who could presumably identify with the mythic poet and musician. As an impoverished nobleman, Rasi must have attempted to cut a distinguished figure in the palace. He was allowed to eat his meals with the duke's chamberlains rather than the lowlier musicians and reportedly bragged that the duke had once loaned him a horse from his private stables (Rosselli, *Singers* 9). Rasi's keen sense of his status in adversity must have lent him authority as he strode the Mantuan stage in the role of the demigod Orfeo.

Orfeo is the first of Monteverdi's great tenor roles. It is important to note that tenor roles in the early seventeenth century were often written for a lower tessitura, or general range, than those of the eighteenth or nineteenth century. Orfeo, like Ulisse over thirty years later, is such a "baritone-tenor" (Celletti 7). The lower notes required of Orfeo have led to the role's being sung in several modern revivals by high baritones.

The role of Orfeo may have been specifically tailored to Rasi's vocal and dramatic gifts. Such an important role might easily have gone to a higher voice, such as an alto or a soprano, given the age's preoccupations. In the baroque mentality, higher sounds were considered generally superior. As Rosselli notes, "'Soprano' means 'higher,' a notion not to be taken lightly by a society that was at once hierarchical minded and used to displaying hierarchical order in forms perceived by the senses" (*Singers* 34). But Orfeo was designed for a tenor, satisfying, if only by accident on this occasion, the twenty-first century's taste for operatic realism. Realistic, too, was the dramatically evocative use of bass voices for the roles of Caronte and Plutone. Basses, however dramatically appropriate their use, seemed, like tenors and baritones, less then optimal singing voices to baroque ears. Their natural male sounds were regarded as vulgar or common when set beside the higher ranges. The most prized voices were sopranos, female or male.

Prince Francesco needed to supplement the cast with at least one extra soprano. Since *L'Orfeo* was a product of the all-male Accademia, the cast was likewise to be all male. Necessarily, female roles would be sung by castrati in drag. We come here to the most exotic—and, for many, the most repellent—aspect of early opera and music: the existence of the castrato. The castrati, male singers castrated before puberty to maintain their soprano, mezzo-soprano, or contralto voices, were the most popular kinds of singers in the late Renaissance and the entire baroque period. Although technically illegal, the creation of castrati was a thriving clandestine practice fueled by the hopes of poor families that their children might have a chance to prosper as musical virtuosi. The church's complicity stemmed from the need for mature singers in the soprano and mezzo range for church music, coupled with the ancient proscription against women choristers issued by St. Peter. Although male falsettists were frequently employed in seventeenth- and eighteenth-century music, the countertenor's weaker, reedy sound was no match for that of his surgically altered rivals. Many great composers up until Rossini, early in the nineteenth century, would compose important roles for the castrato voice. The practice died out completely only in the mid-nineteenth century. (For more on this vocal type, see two engaging studies, Patrick Barbier's *The World of the Castrati* and Angus Heriot's *The Castrati in Opera*. The 1994 Belgian film *Farinelli* is a highly evocative, if largely fictional, depiction of the life of the eighteenth century's greatest castrato singer.) Castrati sang with the vocal range of a woman and the lung capacity of a man. At its best, this vocal type produced an unearthly blending of male and female sound. The female parts in *L'Orfeo* lose nothing of their dramatic effectiveness when sung, as they always are nowadays, by female singers. In the later *L'incoronazione di Poppea,* the composer was to utilize the unique potential of castrati more fully in the roles of Nerone and Ottone.

And so we return to Francesco Gonzaga's urgent request to borrow one of the Tuscan grand duke's castrati. Ferdinando came to the rescue, not with one of the singers Francesco had heard but with one who nevertheless "has performed with great success in musical plays on two or three occasions. He is a pupil of [Caccini]" (Ferdinando's letter of January 14, qtd. in Whenham, *Orfeo* 168). The singer in question, Giovan Gualberto Magli, was sent the words and music for the important role of La Musica, the allegorical figure of Music herself, who sings the opera's prologue. He was also assigned the small part of Proserpina, as well as one other unidentified role, which caused him a great deal of difficulty because "it contains too many notes" (the most likely rendering of the ambiguous locution "troppo voci"; Whenham, *Orfeo* 170). The especially difficult part was probably that of Silvia, the Messaggiera (messenger), whose recitative declamation is one of the highlights of seventeenth-century opera. Magli applied himself with great diligence, however, and learned all his parts in time for the premiere. Later correspondence indicates that Euridice was sung by a castrato referred to as "that little priest" (Fabbri, *Monteverdi* 64). In all likelihood this is a reference to Padre Girolamo Bacchini, a castrato in the Duke's musical retinue and the only other singer from the premiere of whose name we can be fairly certain.

On February 23, 1607, Carlo Magno, an attendee of the Mantuan Carnival celebrations, wrote to his brother in Rome: "Tomorrow evening the Most Serene Lord the Prince is to sponsor a [play] in a room in the apartments which the Most Serene Lady of Ferrara had the use of. It should be most unusual, as all the actors are to sing their parts; it is said on all sides that it will be a great success. No doubt I shall be driven to attend out of sheer curiosity, unless I am prevented from getting in by the lack of space" (qtd. in Whenham, *Orfeo* 170). That same day Francesco Gonzaga wrote his brother Ferdinando in Pisa: "The musical play [*favola cantata*] is to be performed in our Academy tomorrow, since Giovan Gualberto has done very well in the short time he has been here. Not only has he thoroughly learnt the whole of his part by heart, but he delivers it with much grace and to great effect; I am delighted with him. . . . The play has been printed so that everyone in the audience can have a copy to follow while it is sung" (qtd. in Fabbri, *Monteverdi* 63). The site of *L'Orfeo*'s premiere was a room in the apartments of Margherita Gonzaga, widow of the duke of Ferrara. Although the exact room is impossible to prove, most scholars believe it to have been the one now known as the Galleria dei Fiumi. One hundred feet long and thirty feet wide, this probable site of the makeshift theater is a moderate-sized hall on the second story of the ducal palace. It is just big enough for the mounting of the kind of chamber opera that *L'Orfeo* was. Carlo Magno's concern about "the lack of space" for the audience was justified. Both Monteverdi and Striggio may well have been envisioning a larger venue for the performance of their ambitious project. The court theater, however, was apparently out of the question: it was being used for a lavishly staged spoken comedy that was to be presented under the duke's patronage just two days before the opera. The 1609 preface to the published score refers to the opera's first performance space as a less-than-ideal narrow stage (*angusta scena*). As we shall see, this space was so small and the opera so successful that a second performance was commanded.

At one end of the hall a makeshift platform was erected, with a curtain to be drawn to reveal the stage action at the start of the prologue. For reasons of visibility, the platform would probably have been raked. Acts 1, 2, and 5 have the identical pastoral setting, and acts 3 and 4 are both set in the Inferno. The Mantuan premiere probably utilized background paintings on flats similar to the ones that had been used seven years earlier for *Euridice* at the Pitti Palace in Florence and described by Buonarroti:

> Behind the curtains, and within a great arch . . . appeared the most beautiful woods, both painted and in relief . . . and, through the clever placing of the lights, seemingly full of daylight. But when it became necessary to see the Inferno, everything changed, and we saw frightful and horrible rocks . . . leafless tree stumps and scorched grass. And beyond, through a fissure in a rock, we could

see the city of Dis burning, tongues of flame licking between its
towers, the air around blazing, copper colored. (Qtd. in Pickett,
"Behind the Mask")

Scene changes were effected before the audience's eyes by sliding the
different background flats along grooves in the floor of the temporary
stage (see Pirrotta 261). The score makes it clear that all five acts were
performed continuously, without intermission. Modern revivals show
that with a tautly paced performance, no intermission is necessary or
even desirable. Ritornelli cover the two necessary scene shifts.

The costuming of all the operatic characters would have been lavish.
Even shepherds and nymphs, products of the deliberately artificial
pastoral tradition, would have worn gorgeous, expensive headgear
and clothing nonetheless carefully designed to prevent their outshin-
ing the principal characters. A seventeenth-century Italian manual for
stage production insists that even ostensibly humble characters must be
dressed richly: "The fur pieces or skins which they are to wear must be
properly lined and decorated with gold and silk flowers. They must have
jeweled collars and shoulders, the tunic underneath should be of a very
fine golden fabric, and the caps must be in some sort of interesting style
with a jeweled or feathered trim, above all the hat must be beautiful.
All this will help the interpretation of the role for the actor" (from *Il
corago,* qtd. in Pascucci 229–32). In courtly productions given in honor
of a particular family, care might be given to integrate the colors from
that family's coat of arms into the color scheme (Pascucci 241). Another
contemporary source suggests a possible inspirational image for Orfeo
himself. The surviving costume design for Jacopo Peri as Orfeo in his
1600 *Euridice* in Florence reveals a delicate, gentlemanly outfit with
smock and breeches. His headdress is a small violinlike instrument
serving as a rather fantastical hat. With rich colors and ornaments, such
an Orfeo could easily fit into and dominate a lavishly dressed ensemble
of shepherds and nymphs. Gods and other supernatural beings, such as
Apollon, Plutone, Proserpina, and Caronte, would also be splendidly
attired, "but with certain symbols of their divinity so that they could be
easily recognized." Above all, the costuming aimed at stirring the emotions of the audience (see Pascucci 232–34, 220, 216). As consumed as

Monteverdi was with the musical aspects of his first opera's premiere, it is easy to imagine his keen fascination with all the other elements of the performance as it developed in rehearsal. Gagliano went so far as to include in the printed score for his opera *Dafne* (which would be staged in Mantua in 1608) staging suggestions for future performers of his work. He commented, with a fine sense of theatrical know-how, that "in such matters the music is not everything; there are many other necessary requisites, without the which even the finest harmonies would be worth little" (qtd. in Guccini, 130). The keen sense of theatricality Monteverdi displayed in all his operas suggests that he would have agreed.

The instrument list Monteverdi specifies in the published score is a small chamber ensemble of richly varied late-Renaissance timbres. It comprises two harpsichords, two violones (double-bass viols), ten members of the violin family, one double harp, two piccolo violins or *pochettes* (French dancing-masters' fiddles), three chitarroni (theorbos or bass lutes), two small pipe organs, two bass viols, five sackbuts (early trombonelike instruments), one regal (a small reed organ), two cornetti (woodwind instruments played with a trumpetlike mouthpiece), two soprano recorders, and four trumpets. The *L'Orfeo* score uses these instruments in often symbolic ways suggested by the *intermedi* tradition. Jane Glover delineates "two completely separate instrumental colors" in the opera's scoring. Strings, recorders, organs, and plucked continuo instruments create the dominant sonority for *L'Orfeo*'s Arcadian scenes of acts 1, 2, and 5, while cornetti, sackbuts, and regal characterize the infernal ones of acts 3 and 4 (Glover, in Whenham, *Orfeo* 142–43). This is a sizable instrumental ensemble to be sure, even if several players played more than one instrument, as was almost certainly the case. The continuo instruments—keyboards and chitarroni—were probably placed in two groups at opposite sides of the stage, as the composer specifies at the start of act 5. Such a "stereophonic" placement was typical of seventeenth-century interest in antiphonal effects and would have enhanced the already vast range of timbral possibilities. Monteverdi had planned for some of the instrumentalists accompanying the performance ideally to be placed in the wings, or even in closely adjacent rooms, acoustics permitting, out of the audience's direct line of sight. These positions would create antiphonal effects associating a particular character with a particular instrumental color, to contrast with the main body of the orchestra, which would presumably be in full view of the audience. We cannot tell if such ingenuity was possible on the "narrow stage" of *L'Orfeo*'s premiere. Pirrotta imagines that the cramped *angusta scena* may have led to the first placement of the orchestra in its modern, familiar position, directly in front of the stage and performers (214). Whatever the configuration, the chitarrone and keyboard players would have to have been close enough to the singers that the instrumentalists could watch their faces and movements.

The first audience enjoyed the advantage of following the opera with a libretto in hand. This practice of issuing libretti to the audience would continue throughout the baroque period. The *L'Orfeo* libretto published for the 1607 premiere poses a problem, however. The conclusion of the fifth act in these texts differs from the ending preserved in the two published scores of 1609 and 1615. It is likely that the first audience saw a conclusion whose music has since been lost, one that depicts Orfeo quickly leaving the stage after making his misogynistic declaration at the end of his act 5 monologue. According to the 1607 libretto, the stage is then filled with a chorus of Bacchantes. Both Virgil and Ovid relate that the Bacchantes avenged themselves on Orfeo for his misogyny by tearing him limb from limb. Striggio's text in the 1607 libretto makes a rather muted reference to this bloody act: A Bacchante declares, "[Orfeo] will not escape, for heavenly anger is wont to be all the more severe the later it descends on his guilty head." Two other Bacchantes chime in, "Let us sing, meanwhile, of Bacchus," which is exactly what they do for the remainder of the act, creating a disappointing anticlimax for anyone who has not recently read Ovid or Virgil and is unable to fill in the gaps about the fate of the character who has absorbed their attention for the past two hours.

Fortunately, the Apollonian ending that appears in the two scores published under the composer's auspices is dramaturgically superior to the 1607 ending. The revised ending ties together the themes of light, music, and immortality that have been woven throughout the text. The music for this ending is beautiful and always convincing in performance. As we shall see, the Apollonian closure, a decidedly muted happy ending, creates its own fair share of interpretive questions. Scholars have come to no consensus about the meaning of these two divergent endings, one with music, the other without. It is hard to imagine that the 1607 premiere was performed without the Bacchantic ending, since that was the version of the text in the printed libretti the audience would have had at hand. But the composer used the Apollonian ending *twice* in publishing his score. There can be little question that, whatever the genesis of these different endings, Monteverdi believed the Apollonian apotheosis was the correct one for his opera. Without the score for the 1607 ending, we have no alternative but to submit to the composer's will. Pirrotta persuasively reasons that "the *deus ex machina* and the apotheosis of Orpheus were part of the original plan, later modified because the place available for the performance did not allow the use of theater machinery. . . . The Apollo finale was restored by Monteverdi when, with the printing of the score, his opera was no longer presented 'on a narrow stage' but [to use Monteverdi's words] in the great theater of the world" (259). The opera's last act has had detractors in the secondary literature. One repeated reservation is its perceived brevity compared to the acts that preceded it. In fact, the fifth act is approximately the same length as the first—yet another indication of the opera's exquisite feeling of balance and proportion (see also Solomon 47, n. 53).

A letter from Francesco Gonzaga to Ferdinando of March 1, 1607, reports: "The play was performed to the great satisfaction of all who heard it. The Lord Duke, not content to have been present at this performance, or to have heard it many times in rehearsal, has ordered it to be given again; and so it will be, today, in the presence of all the ladies resident in the city. For this reason Giovanni Gualberto is to remain here at present; he has done very well, and given immense pleasure to all who have heard him sing, especially to My Lady" (qtd. in Whenham, *Orfeo* 171). So a second performance was given especially to accommodate ladies, who were excluded from the first staging under the Academy's auspices. There was talk of a third performance a few weeks later to grace a state visit, but that one seems to have been canceled along with the diplomatic visit it was intended to enliven. Some evidence exists of a possible performance "in the grand theater with most noble scenery," but it is far from proven (E. Cagnini, quoted in Solomon 29, n. 7). On August 22, 1607, Francesco returned Giovan Gualberto back to the Tuscan grand duke's service and to the obscurity from which he came, but only after the young castrato had helped make history. "He now returns to Your Highness's service," Francesco writes to the grand duke, "having given me nothing but satisfaction; I am infinitely obliged to you and thank you as is right and proper" (Whenham, *Orfeo* 172).

3

"So That Memory of His Glory May Live"

L'Orfeo

Along with Henry Purcell's *Dido and Aeneas, L'Orfeo* is probably the most frequently performed and recorded of seventeenth-century operas. The opera deserves the attention it receives. Before *L'Orfeo* appeared, "drama in music," as opera was then known, was still a primitive curiosity. The premiere of *L'Orfeo* revealed an art form that had come to a state of genuine maturity, a medium capable of addressing the most serious concerns of human life with the emotional depth and intellectual complexity found only in the greatest art. It should be noted from the outset that *L'Orfeo* is blessed with a superb libretto. Alessandro Striggio, probably with much help from Monteverdi, molded a text with uncanny instinct for effective music and stagecraft. The libretto's succinct exposition and its masterly alternation of rising and falling dramatic tension show a theatrical instinct missing from earlier Florentine experiments. Striggio's text is art that conceals art.

In *L'Orfeo,* the elements of music, words, and drama are brought into a perfect synthesis. One critic dubs the opera "a musical cosmos which peers, Januslike, into the past of the [*intermedi* tradition] as well as into the future" of Gluck and Wagner (Redlich 97). What lifts *L'Orfeo* beyond even this historic achievement, however, is not only Monteverdi and Striggio's success in articulating the binary nature of the new medium (music and words), but also the ways in which that binary nature opens up our perception of ourselves and the world. *L'Orfeo* abounds in dichotomy and dualism. The opera's characters frequently call attention to oppositions—male and female, divine and human. As the son of the god Apollo and the Muse Calliope, the title character is a *semideo* (demigod), the very embodiment of duality. Along with the human/divine divide, the boundaries of life and death are explored, as is the primal opposition of light (Apollon in heaven) and dark (Plutone in the Inferno). Classical Greek paganism finds itself in an uneasy alliance with Italian Renaissance Christianity. The metaphysical go-between binding all these opposites is art. Art in *L'Orfeo* is represented by the demigod's song, which unites words with music and the sound of the voice with that of instruments in a harmony resonant with the music of the spheres. This harmony of Orfeo the artist serves as his passport into the underworld and very nearly allows him to transcend the laws of nature. Art reflects the human being, its creator, with the human's characteristic mixture of reason and passion, discipline and abandon. Art is produced by mortals, yet, paradoxically, partakes of the immortal. The deepest paradoxes of the opera involve the artistic triumph and defeat of Orfeo. The psychological oppositions that inspire his art, an art which seems ready to transcend time and death and partake in the superhuman, are the very elements that defeat his mighty enterprise. His weak human passion causes him to break his vow and lose his wife forever. Ironically, it was this very passion and Orfeo's ability to express it in poetry and song that led to Plutone's extraordinary act of clemency. *L'Orfeo* serves to interrogate music itself and its paradoxical strength and powerlessness (see also van der Kooij and Riehn; Chafe 12).

At the end of the opera the demigod is definitively confronted by the painful lot of humankind. Like many creative people, Orfeo attempts to reject the very notion of moderation, ordinary humanity's means of coping with the tragedy of existence. Lurking behind Orfeo's triumph and defeat lies the Neoplatonic trope of earthly versus heavenly love articulated in Plato's *Symposium* and disseminated in the commentaries of Ficino and other Renaissance scholars working to synthesize pagan and Christian philosophies. The ultimate goal for the human soul is to aspire upward toward the light of God and reason, away from worldly entrapments. Orfeo's passion has destroyed his quest for Euridice and jeopardized his own soul. The crisis finds its uneasy resolution when Orfeo's father, Apollon, leads the singer to a bittersweet apotheosis. Orfeo's mortal existence will be changed to an immortal one; his longing for Euridice may find sublimation when he contemplates her likeness in the sun and stars. Orfeo moves to the heavens and eternity with only a terrestrial metaphor to comfort his loneliness. This is surely cold comfort for the hot-blooded artist. Orfeo's defeat represents the tragic position of mankind as the Greeks would have recognized it—a lonely mixture of passion and reason, confronting the harsh boundaries of existence with the unquenchable desire for transcendence. Although Orfeo's aspiration for a physical triumph over death and time is lost, *L'Orfeo,* the opera, gently suggests another kind of victory. Art, which briefly suspends the laws of time and space, exists outside of us. In spite of all our weakness, human endeavor and art are never in vain—as the chorus notes at the close of act 3. Art, particularly the kind that unites word with music, hints at the divine within us, allowing us to communicate with each other as well as with those of the past and future. Like many of the ancient Greek heroes, Orfeo wants to have it all: eternal life in the flesh *and* eternal art. *L'Orfeo* presents the balance in between: its poetry and music afford glimpses of transcendence, giving assurance that something of our aspirations will survive—if only in the metaphor of words and notes.

Prologue and Act I

After an instrumental toccata is performed, La Musica, the spirit of Music, appears in the allegorical prologue to bid the princely audience be attentive to the story of the Thracian poet and singer Orfeo. La Musica relates that Orfeo "drew wild animals to his singing and made the Inferno submit to his entreaties." The first act is set in Arcadia, the region of Greece most closely associated with the pastoral poetic tradition. Shepherds and nymphs happily celebrate the marriage of their friends, Orfeo and Euridice. Solemn and joyful choruses fit for the occasion are sung, and the new couple proclaim their love for each other. All the characters resolve to go to the temple to offer thanks to the gods.

The dichotomy of transience and permanence is memorably embodied in the first moments of *L'Orfeo,* an opening that immortalizes that first performance in the Gonzaga Palace in 1607. No other opera of permanent interest so emphatically asserts the time and place of its creation as does *L'Orfeo*. *L'Orfeo* opens with a toccata (meaning here "prelude") for wind instruments in five parts "to be played three times, with all the instruments, before the curtain is raised." Muted trumpets strut their fanfare above a droning bass. Evidence exists that such martial-sounding flourishes were the expected signal for the start of performances at the Mantuan court. A contemporary description of the performance of a spoken play at the court in 1608 describes its opening moments with clear parallels to *L'Orfeo*. "The torches being lit in the theater, the usual sign of the sound of the trumpets was given within the stage; and as the trumpets began to sound a third time the great curtain which masked the stage disappeared so quickly, as it were in the batting of an eyelid, that even though it rose high above, there were few who noticed how it disappeared" (Follino, qtd. in Whenham, *Orfeo* 190). The same fanfare motto of the *L'Orfeo* toccata is the basis for the opening chorus of Monteverdi's 1610 Vespers, another composition for the duke of Mantua; this fanfare was in all likelihood the duke's personal ceremonial entry music. *L'Orfeo* and the Vespers preserve this most ephemeral of occasional music from their original Mantuan environment. Kelly envisions "the court trumpeter Giovanni Srofenaur [leading] a threefold playing of [the] trumpet fanfare before the curtain went up. The first called the audience to attention; the second announced the arrival of the duke; and the third signaled the beginning of the play" (38). The toccata, especially when performed by rasping period winds, may still startle an audience; Redlich describes its sound as "shattering" (97). No better example could be imagined for the bracingly "new" feel of "old" music.

One of the most distinctive features of Monteverdi's musical dramaturgy is the use of startling shifts and transformations from one musicodramatic section to the next. This is already apparent in the opening moments of *L'Orfeo,* as the bracing, "masculine"-sounding wind toccata yields to the gentler, more "feminine" string ritornello, ushering in La Musica's prologue. The first Florentine operas had revealed their overriding literary concerns in their allegorical prologues. The Roman poet Ovid set his seal of approval by introducing Peri's *Dafne,* and the Muse

Tragedia herself had opened Peri's *Euridice*. Striggio and Monteverdi give the introductory honors to music as an affirmation of their own artistic orientation (see also de' Paoli 174). Music's bittersweet power is elegantly conveyed by this ritornello, a mellifluous, melting tune in D minor which alters the dramatic temperature from the pompous, martial expectancy of the toccata. This tune, the first appearance of the strings by themselves, will haunt *L'Orfeo* until its reappearance in the fifth act. It serves as a kind of proto-leitmotif associated with the idea of music itself, the medium of Orfeo's art. The ritornello that punctuates La Musica's five-stanza aria can be played jauntily to suggest a feeling of joy or slowly to create a sad or wistful mood. It is the very embodiment of music's ambivalent power: at once happy and sad, music is a medium pliant enough to take the impression of all human feelings.

La Musica is a soprano role. The opera was composed for the Mantuan Accademia, so all the singers in the original performance would have been male—just as the opera had been premiered for an all-male audience. Giovan Gualbert Magli, the soprano castrato who sang La Musica, would have been the perfect embodiment of this allegorical character: a castrato was, in essence, a "singing machine" who had sacrificed his sexual potency and its promise of family life to the Muse. The art of music is literally such a singer's entire life. The assignment of a castrato to the role of La Musica is but the first example of Monteverdi's talent for dramatically and musically apt vocal casting in his operas. La Musica's text is set as a strophic song. (A strophic song or aria is one in which the same melody is used to set each strophe of the text.) La Musica's prologue, like the preceding toccata, links us to the first audience. In the first stanza La Musica flatters the "noble blood of kings" who have summoned her from Permessus (in classical mythology, a retreat for the Muses). The numinous world of Greek antiquity is ready to oblige Renaissance princes. In the next stanza she identifies herself as Music, able to inspire such desperate emotions as "noble anger" or "love."

> I am Music, who through sweet accents
> knows how to calm every troubled heart
> now with noble anger, now with love,
> and can enflame even the coldest hearts.

> [Io la Musica son, ch'ai dolci accenti
> So far tranquillo ogni turbato core,
> Et or di nobil ira, et or d'amore
> Poss'infiammar le più gelate menti.]

The drawn-out elaboration on "poss[o]" (can) hints at Musica's reveling in her power. The phrase "le più gelate menti" (the coldest hearts) provokes "an icy dissonance" (Whenham, *Orfeo* 49). In the third stanza she links "the golden lyre" we will be hearing in this performance with "the sonorous harmony of heaven's lyre" (i.e., the music of the spheres), which she will "invoke" in her listener's hearts.

> I sing with my golden lyre
> giving delight to mortal ears,
> and in this guise, I invoke in the soul
> the sonorous harmony of heaven's lyre.

> [Io su cetera d'or cantando soglio
> Mortal orecchio lusingar tal hora,
> E in questa guisa a l'armonia sonora
> De la lira del ciel più l'alme invoglio.]

The melodic lift on the word "alme" (soul), the goal of Musica's (and the composer's) aspirations, is a sublime touch. Notable also are the remarks about Musica's "solo singing," reminding the audience that *L'Orfeo* is a highly self-conscious work. As mentioned before, early opera was particularly concerned, out of a regard for verisimilitude, with justifying singing characters. In the next stanza Musica introduces the subject of the opera to follow.

> Now my desire spurs me to speak of Orfeo,
> of Orfeo who drew to his song the beasts
> and the servants of hell to his pleadings,
> winning immortal glory of Pindus and Helicon.

She concludes her aria by urging the audience to be silent and attentive.

> Now, as my songs alternate between happy and sad,
> may the birds not move on the trees
> nor the waves sound upon the shore of this bank,
> and may every breeze stop in its path.

Musica's final lines are a mimetic tour de force. The sweet and bitter harmonies on "now happily, now sadly" (hor lieti, hor mesti) are delectably suggestive. The numerous rests that punctuate the concluding verses are more complex in effect: "May they not move [*rest*] the birds [*rest*] on the trees [*rest*] nor the waves [*rest*] sound upon the shore of this bank [*rest*] and every breeze [*rest*] in its path stop [*rest*]." One critic has detected a touch of "gentle humor." "The sudden silence ought . . . to be interpreted in theatrical terms as a trick to catch out any members of the audience who might be talking and to remind them that they, too, should be attentive" (Whenham, *Orfeo* 50). At the same time these rests, though they possess delicate comic potential, also demonstrate the power of music to literally take our breath away by suddenly arresting its established pulse. La Musica's aria ends with the last iteration of the full ritornello, setting the seal on the prologue and helping to ensure that this bittersweet D minor melody lingers in the audience's imagination until its significant restatements later in the opera. It also serves the purely functional purpose of covering the exit of La Musica and the entry of the characters who begin the first act proper.

Act 1 gives a succinct, orderly exposition of the story, introducing Orfeo and Euridice and their friends in the pastoral world, and suggesting the sorrows that prepared the way for the present joy. The First Shepherd, a tenor, launches the act with an expository text set as a supple da capo aria. The da capo (literally, "from the top") aria, with its ABA form, was to become the major building block of later baroque vocal music and opera. It would be wrong to intuit any special prescience on Monteverdi's part in launching the first act of his first opera with a form that would develop such importance in operatic structure only later (see Carter, *Monteverdi's Musical Theater* 119, 129.) Nevertheless, the first da capo aria in the first opera of the permanent repertoire exhibits great subtlety and a measure of ambiguity. The words—"On this happy and fortunate day which has put an end to love's suffering for our demigod Orfeo"—inform us that Orfeo is marrying his Euridice after a protracted courtship. Rather than sounding joyous, however, the shepherd sings a sad tune that shares the prologue ritornello's somber key of D minor. Although the D minor tonality links this aria to the ritornello, it is not easy to reconcile the joyful text with the dolorous music. The sad melody recalls Orfeo's previous suffering; the shepherd is describing a situation that has only recently turned happy. The mood lightens slightly for the B section: "Today has pity stirred the soul of the beautiful Euridice, which had been disdainful." The shepherd uses rests for mimetic effect as he describes Euridice, "for whose sake in these woods [*rest*] Orfeo sighed and wept." But the sad mood is firmly reasserted by the repetition of the initial text and its music, neatly justified by the substitution of the word "dunque" (therefore) for "in questo": "Therefore on such a happy morning . . . ." This surprisingly somber tone suggests an awareness of opera's ironic potential. The shepherd sings a "sad" tune describing the happy result of an initially unpropitious courtship. The audience, however, appreciates the ironic aptitude of the sad music for describing events soon to become much more painful than any that had gone before. From the opera's opening moments, Monteverdi reveals a profound understanding of the seemingly limitless potential of this new musical and dramatic idiom. Pirrotta observes: "Even in the opening scenes joy is, as it were, veined with melancholy, happy innocence is knowingly caressed as an unreal vision, a nostalgic aspiration, an impossible evasion of the sorrows of humanity" (245).

The shepherd's injunction for his comrades to join him in song, "Cantiam," justifies the first chorus, a formal hymn to Hymen: "Vieni, Imeneo, deh, vieni" (Come, Hymen, oh, come). "All the instruments are to play together in this song," the score notes. The G major tonality of this stately chorus brightens the dour tonal palette of the shepherd's aria and marks the score's gradual move toward jubilant celebration. The nymphs and shepherds invoke the sun's light, reminding us of Orfeo's father, the sun god, Apollon, who will resolve the action in the last act. (The sun was also a symbol for the duke of Mantua.) They ask the sun to "dispel far away the grief and suffering of horror and shadow."

The score has so far used instrumental music for winds and strings, strophic song, da capo aria, and a formal unison chorus. The next musical section utilizes the first instance of pure recitative for the Nymph's invocation of the Muses of Parnassus. The Nymph bids her friends to "let your sonorous lyres rip away all the mists of gloomy veils" in lively song and dance. Her eleven-bar section of music with simply notated chordal accompaniment reveals Monteverdi's prowess in recitative. As in the early Florentine experiments, the recitative here serves as a declamatory passage moving the plot forward. But unlike the Florentines, Monteverdi has created a declamation that seems to flirt continuously with the contours of arialike melody. This melodic potential from a master melodist creates the tension that makes Monteverdi's recitative writing more satisfying than that of many another composer before or since. It is a musical language tied intimately to the words it sets, illustrating images and emotions with exactitude and speed. The fluttering motion on "squarcino d'ogni nub'il fosco velo" (rip away all the mists and veils) lends the words and music an onomatopoeic immediacy. This subtle touch of musical and verbal animation serves to usher in the next chorus, "Lasciate i monti, lasciate i fonti" (Leave the mountains, leave the fountains). This is a joyfully explosive, highly danceable sequence featuring contrapuntal and unison singing and instrumental ritornelli. This chorus is accompanied by bowed and plucked strings and a descant (soprano) recorder. "The bowed strings represent the Muses' *liras* [in answer to the Nymph's request], while the plucked strings represent their *cetras,*" Pickett notes. The soprano recorder recalls "the tabor pipe so frequently associated with ...wild dances in the 16th century" ("Armonia" 147–48). The stage is set for the introduction of the protagonist.

The Second Shepherd, sung by either a high tenor or a male alto, introduces Orfeo in recitative, bidding him sing "with [his] famous lyre songs of love." Orfeo's role as a "great singer" is immediately established with his first vocal "performance" in the opera as he greets his offstage father, Apollon, and then turns to Euridice. His words to his father are a hymnal arioso.

> Rose of heaven, life of the world and worthy
> offspring of him who leads the universe,
> Sun, who surrounds everything and sees everything,
> from your circle between the stars,
> tell me, did you ever see
> a happier or more fortunate lover?

Fabbri reminds us that "the meaning of this declaration to the sun is made clear only with reference to the device of the Accademia degli Invaghiti, an eagle with its eyes fixed on the sun, accompanied by the motto 'Nihil pulcherius'('Nothing more beautiful')" (*Monteverdi* 69). Orfeo's first words, directed to the heavens, fit in with medieval and Renaissance ideas of the character as a proto-Christlike figure, whose earthly sufferings were emblematic of the sorrows of mankind. Orfeo's first reference to the sun marks the beginning of his spiritual journey, which will end with the sun god's descent onto the stage and Orfeo's own transference to heaven. The light of the sun also serves as a Neoplatonic symbol of the divine enlightenment toward which the philosophical acolyte moves during his life (see Solomon 27–47). The music's solemn key of G minor and its slow, expansive phrases reawaken something of the tone of the act's opening. Orfeo's role is sung by a tenor with a strong baritonal quality (see chapter 2). Although Orfeo is emphatically human in his emotions, the august dignity with which Monteverdi imbues his melodic phrases reminds us at the outset of the singer's status as a demigod. The porous musical texture of Monteverdi's operas is apparent in Orfeo's first speech as he seamlessly moves from the melodic arioso passage that sets the first half of his speech to the recitative style he uses to describe his successful courtship of Euridice.

> Blessed was the day,
> my beloved, when I first saw you,
> and happier still the hour
> when I sighed for you,
> since for my sighs you sighed.
>
> [Fu ben felice il giorno,
> Mio ben, che pria ti vidi,
> E più felice l'ora
> Che per te sospirai,
> Poich'al mio sospirar tu sospirasti.]

The shift to recitative suggests Orfeo's musical virtuosity. Within less than two pages of music Orfeo (like Monteverdi) has demonstrated an absolute supremacy in the art of uniting words and music in perfect dramatic harmony. Schrade notes:

> When Orfeo sings his first song of joy, posing the challenging question whether there is anyone as happy as himself, the melody is an organic mixture of recitation and arioso, with no clear separation of one from the other. . . . Striking intervals, accidentals, or modulations may alter the course of the recitation and give it a melodious character, though they are not introduced for the sake of melody, but in order to do justice to the text. (230–31)

Euridice, a soprano, responds in a lovely recitative, pledging her complete devotion to her love. It is interesting to note how tiny the role of Euridice is in the opera relative to her importance in the story. Monteverdi wrote the part of Orfeo's love interest with a castrato soprano in mind, the "little priest" Girolamo Bacchini. As with figures such as Caronte, Plutone, and Proserpina, the character is created with great musical concision.

The introduction of the two lovers signals a repetition of both the "Lasciate i monti" and "Vieni, Imeneo" choral and instrumental sequences. This recapitulation of such attractive music allows for more dancing and pastoral spectacle, so popular in Italian court entertainment. It also suggests the composer's quest to impose a musical architecture upon the work. The tenor First Shepherd summons all to go to the temple to solemnize Orfeo's marriage in a brief recitative. Dramatically speaking, because the opera was performed continuously, with no break between acts, the First Shepherd is motivating Euridice's exit so that her death may be reported in the next act (see Whenham, *Orfeo* 52).

The next musical section is a three-part variation sequence adorned with a ritornello in G minor for a five-part string consort, music that seems to waft down a divine benediction on the marriage of the happy lovers. The shepherd's reference to the temple has suggested appropriately churchlike music to the composer. This solemn ritornello serves to punctuate three stanzas assigned respectively to a duet, a trio, and a second duet of shepherds and nymphs. The vocal music, for all its variety in each of the verses, is bound together by a similar pattern in the basso continuo. The first duet is for two tenor shepherds. "No one shall fall prey to despair nor be given to sorrow, though it assail [*assaglia*] us so powerfully that it endangers [*inforsa*] our life." The tenors sing in unison and take turns in overlapping soloistic passages, creating expressive emphasis with their divisions (ornamentation) on "assaglia" and "inforsa." The trio for soprano, high tenor or countertenor, and bass reminds the audience that "after the dark [*nembo*] clouds laden with tempests which have frightened [*inorridito*] the world are dispelled, the sun's rays [*rai*] shine all the more brightly." The melody is elaborated with added ornamentation and rhythmic variety, which allows for more words to be decorated. The last strophic variation is a duet for high tenor and tenor: "And after the bitter cold of bare winter, the spring [*primavera*] clothes [*veste*] the fields with flowers." The virtuosic decorations of "veste" and "primavera" bring this long processional passage to a conclusion. This is the most static passage in the entire opera and seems to have been designed to cover some kind of staging necessity. This sequence allows for a number of characters—Orfeo, Euridice, and some of the shepherds and nymphs—to exit the stage. The first act ends with a vigorous five-part chorus, "Ecco Orfeo" (Here is Orfeo), the text didactically underlining the theme of Orfeo's cyclical move from sorrow to joy. The "Ecco Orfeo" chorus with its skipping rhythm reanimates the musical pulse, paving the way for Orfeo's reentry and the continuous flow of action into the start of act 2.

Act 2

The scene is still Arcadia. Orfeo and his pastoral friends continue their celebrations, which build in excitement until the nymph Silvia, the Messaggiera (messenger), enters to reveal the tragic news that Euridice has just died as the result of a snakebite. The grief-stricken Orfeo vows to retrieve Euridice from the "king of Shadows," leaving his friends to mourn in funereal music.

After establishing the characters and dramatic situation, Monteverdi and Striggio now build a seamless arc of excitement and happiness for the newly wed Orfeo, who is celebrating with his shepherd friends. This will make the messenger's news, when it comes, all the more tragic and wrenching. The sinfonia linking acts 1 and 2 springs from a melody and rhythm similar to those heard in the "Ecco Orfeo" chorus. It serves to introduce Orfeo's upcoming aria, "Ecco pur ch'a voi ritorno" (Here I return to you, dear woods and beloved hills, made blessed by that sun through which alone my nights have turned to day). One ancient tradition credited Orpheus as the inventor of the violin. As Nigel Rogers observes, "In the sixteenth century the legendary lyre was considered to be a bowed rather than a plucked instrument, and Monteverdi frequently employs string ritornelli to evoke the sound of Orpheus's lyre" (185). Both acts 1 and 2 begin with brief minor-key arias. The music's tone and rhythm at the opening of act 2 however, are more vigorous and optimistic than that which we encountered at the start of the first act.

Orfeo and the orchestra have barely established his new, attractive tune before the music and the instrumental timbre shift—the score specifies the harpsichord, two chitarroni, and two violini piccoli. These "little violins" are the *pochettes* mentioned in the last chapter's instrument list. The sound of the *pochette,* an octave above that of the standard violin, suggests birdsong, an effect inspired by Orfeo's reference to the "sun through which alone my nights have turned to day." The rising bass line beneath the "birds" suggests the rising sun itself (Pickett, "Armonia" 149). This new ritornello, with an even more pronounced dancelike character, will punctuate a two-verse aria for the First Shepherd, "See how the shadow of these beeches entices" (Mira ch'a sé n'alletta). This shepherd's aria has charming music and text that quicken the pulse. The shepherd's second verse implores: "On these grassy banks let us rest and let each join his voice to the murmuring stream." These words seamlessly trigger yet another ritornello—different music with different instrumental timbres, now for two full-size violins, bass viol, and two chitarroni. The violins imitate the murmuring stream. Again the contrasting rhythm heightens the sense of exultant tension. This new ritornello serves to introduce and punctuate a strophic duet for two tenor shepherds, "In questo prato adorno" (In this beloved meadow). After two verses in Monteverdi's most delicious pastoral style, the ritornello suddenly shifts its instrumental sonority to two chitarroni, harpsichord, and two recorders playing a beautiful ornamented version of the tune, which is then picked up by the two shepherds. The shift in instrumental color here was suggested by the reference to "Pan, the shepherd's god, who has sometimes been heard lamenting here, sweetly recalling his unhappy loves." A repetition of the ornamental ritornello ushers in another surprise—the tenor's tune is now sung by the entire chorus of shepherds in "Dunque fà degni, Orfeo" (Then, Orfeo). The chorus implores Orfeo to, "with the sound of your golden lyre, make worthy these fields over which the aura of oriental odors wafts." This wonderful contrast of vocal sonorities, tenor solo, tenor duet, and now full chorus works to propel the spirits to their highest pitch. The score reinforces this impression of a nearly reckless acceleration of ecstatic feelings by launching yet another danceable ritornello tune, scored for five viole da braccio (recalling again the hero's role in creating the violin), a contrabass, two harpsichords, and three chitarroni. This music of unforgettable rhythmic vigor is the basis for Orfeo's great strophic aria of rejoicing, "Vi ricorda, o boschi ombrosi" (Do you recall, O shady woods, my long bitter laments when the stones to my plaints made piteous response?). This aria has been the musical and dramatic goal since the act began.

As in his first arioso, "Rosa del ciel," Orfeo is "singing" both in the context of the operatic performance and within the fictive world of *L'Orfeo*. On one level this new aria projects a vigorous, healthy sense of Dionysian rapture. Ostensibly a simple strophic aria expressing Orfeo's newfound marital happiness after "years of sorrows," the music shares something of the emotional ambiguities of several of Schubert's ostensibly "happy" songs, such as "Das Fischermädchen" or "Fischerweise." Like Orfeo's aria, these songs have a vigorous, outdoorsy feel created by melodies of such purity that they could be folksongs. When well performed, this aria and these songs leave a sense of intangible sadness—a feeling that the underlying tragedies of existence are ever present, lying just beneath the present moment of bliss. And that is exactly the dramatic point of "Vi ricorda, o boschi ombrosi." Indeed, the tide of joy is about to turn. Orfeo's iterations about his "torments," "laments," "woe," and "sad and mournful" existence seem at odds with such a joyous melody. Chafe discerns the delicate irony of the aria: its words, its music, and its dramatic placement within the opera.

> "Vi ricorda" is music for its own sake, giving no attention whatever
> to the expression of the textual contrast but allowing one idea—
> carefree joy—to dominate to the exclusion of all else. From the
> standpoint of the text setting, Orpheus's past suffering has no
> reality. Only the present matters. . . . Orpheus refers to his past
> sufferings in every one of the four strophes, without suspecting
> that the possibility of a reversal exists. He is sympathetic because
> he enjoys his happiness to the full. Nevertheless, the final stanza
> of his solo hints at the dangerous viewpoint that the only meaning
> of sorrow is as a foil to joy. (Chafe 139–40)

The aria ends touchingly on a repetition of the name of Euridice—
the sole cause of Orfeo's present joy, the center of his life—reminding
the listener of the fragility of all human happiness at the very moment
before Orfeo's joy turns to desolation. This aria and its melody must
have lodged stubbornly in the composer's mind. In his last opera he
would recall it for a similar poignant effect in the middle section of the
"Non morir, Seneca" chorus in *Poppea.*

Now Monteverdi embarks on one of the most dramatic passages in
all opera: the Messaggiera's revelation of Euridice's death. This scene is
set in a long sequence exhibiting an emotional depth and resonance that
is rare not just by Monteverdi's standards but in the whole of Western
vocal music. The sequence begins innocuously enough, with one of the
shepherds bidding Orfeo to continue with yet another song in order to
"sweeten the air on such a beautiful day." The tenor shepherd sings this
request in an innocent C major arioso, "Mira, deh, mira, Orfeo" (Look,
ah, look, Orfeo). His delicate ornamentation on "ride" mimetically
indicates the "laughing meadows," and the delightful melisma (melodic
ornament) on "beato" emphasizes the day's "blessedness," all miraculous
responses on nature's part to the demigod's song. The time seems ripe
to usher in more songs of rejoicing. But the rhythm and accompanimental texture are gentler than before. Perhaps now Orfeo will sing more
temperately of happiness. Instead, the scene of bucolic joy is rent by
entrance of the Messaggiera, Silvia, and the introduction of recitative
that brings the bright harmony into a wrenching minor-tonality world.

For all its individuality and beauty, the first act and the first portion
of the second act breathe the artistic air of the *intermedi* and pastoral

play. With the Messaggiera's entrance a newer and still uncharted world of musical and dramatic expression has strode onto the stage. The Messaggiera's scene "rivals the *Lamento d'Arianna* as the most famous passage of lamentation in early Italian opera" (Chafe 140). As mentioned at the beginning of our exploration of *L'Orfeo*, sudden, almost violent contrast is one of the hallmarks of Monteverdi's dramatic style. These works, like Shakespeare's plays or van Eyck's panels, aspire to contain the widest breadth of human experience. Each of Monteverdi operas contains worlds.

"Ahi, caso acerbo!" (Ah, bitter event! Ah, impious and cruel fate!), sings the Messaggiera, in a grating minor-key recitative line that will reappear later in the scene as a "strongly marked leitmotiv" that will "dominate" the scene with great effect (Redlich 98). Incredulous, the tenor shepherd keeps to his major key; the musical line of his dialogue still resembles his last aria when he asks, "What sounds of mourning perturb this happy day?" But the setting of the last word, "perturba," creates a brief dissonance, suggesting the upward inflection of the voice at the end of a question and a sense of foreboding. The Messaggiera sings, "Alas, then must I, while Orfeo consoles the heavens with his music, pierce him through the heart with my words?" Orfeo's lyric "music" is to be arrested by Silvia's recitative, her "musical speech." Her recitative brings back the minor key and touches on mournful chromaticism. An alto shepherd identifies the Messaggiera as "gentle Silvia, sweetest companion of the beautiful Euridice." His ethereal high notes and the suave melodious tendency of his recitative are stifled by Silvia's next response: "Shepherd, leave off singing [*lasciate il canto*], for all our joy has turned to sorrow." There is nothing to sing songs about any more. This provokes Orfeo's first musical reaction to Silvia.

He enters into recitative with urgent questions: "Where did you come from? Where are you going? Nymph, what are you bringing?" Silvia's reply, in recitative, creates drama of the utmost vividness. She sings, "I come to you, Orfeo, unhappy messenger [*delicate dissonance here*] of the most unhappy and fatal occurrence [*dissonances again*]. Your beautiful Euridice——." On these last words ("la tua bella Euridice") Silvia's vocal line displays a bittersweet lyricism akin to the shepherd's aria "Mira, deh, mira, Orfeo," subliminally referring to the joy of only a few moments before. The phrase is broken off by a notated rest; she cannot finish the sentence. Stung with apprehension, Orfeo interjects, "Ah, me, what do I hear?" (Ohimè, che odo?), to a line tinged with dissonance. Silvia seems to draw a new breath, then sings another version of her last lyrical phrase. "Your delightful spouse" (La tua diletta sposa)—followed by another notated rest, the opera's action and Orfeo's life hanging in the balance—"is dead" (è morta). Her vocal line sinks to a desolate pair of E's on "morta." Again a rest indicates the rupture in the pastoral world. "Ohimè," sings Orfeo, to two sinking notes. This is an exchange made almost unbearably poignant by the composer's use of sound and silence to suggest quickly fluctuating psychological states. Schrade observes: "In this scene Monteverdi attains an unmatched greatness. . . . He revived something of the Greek tragic sense, according to which extreme joy and serene happiness, to which only the immortals seem to have a right, are a challenge to Fate. This is accompanied by that utter unawareness of catastrophe which, in Greek tragedy, always has a terrifying effect" (232). Another marked pause prefaces the beginning of the Messaggiera's story.

Silvia sets the offstage scene of Euridice's death:

> In a flowering meadow with her companions she was gathering flowers to make a garland for her hair, when an insidious serpent [quand'angue insidioso] that was hidden in the grass bit [punse] her on the foot with its venomous teeth. And behold, immediately her beautiful face lost color and from her eyes vanished that radiance for which the sun envied them [Ed ecco immantinente scolorirsi il bel viso e nei suoi lumi sparir que' lampi, ond'ella al Sol fea scorno].

The musical settings of "ange" and "punse" are piercing. Pauses emphasize "ed ecco" (and behold), leading into a deeply expressive passage setting the words "her beautiful face lost color and from her eyes vanished that radiance for which the sun envied them." Monteverdi creates moments of horrified musical stasis by reiterating the same note on "immantinente" and "e nei suoi lumi sparir," making the dissonance on "scolorirsi" (lost color) and the pathetic drooping notes on "bel viso" and "lampi" all the more vivid. The setting of "for which the sun envied them" is especially remarkable. "Ond'ella al Sol" is set to four ascending notes—as if the Messaggiera's memory of Euridice is brightening the musical line. But a notated pause indicates the intrusion of bitter reality, and "fea scorno" sends Silvia's voice back down from where it had ascended, like a descent into numbing grief.

Silvia describes Euridice's last moments: "She briefly opened her languishing eyes" (ch'ella i languidi lumi [*rest*] alquanto aprendo). Silvia's vocal line begins to move upward, as if representing the dying woman's struggle for life. Another suggestive silence follows, then she sings, "And she called to you, Orfeo" (E te chiamando Orfeo [*rest*], Orfeo). The vocal line ascends to the highest note in her narration. The rest prefacing the last utterance of Orfeo's name makes the passage all the more poignant. Another rest follows, which marks the moment when life yields to death: "After a deep sigh she expired in these arms [*spirò frà queste braccia*]." The vocal line sinks dejectedly. Although these lower notes are certainly grave enough to suggest Euridice's death, they seem to slip past Silvia before she notices them. The import of what has just happened can only be realized during the two notated pauses, which indicate the stunned silence of both the speaker and her audience. The realization of Euridice's death permeates Silvia's concluding lines: "And I remained, my heart full of pity and fear." "And I remained" (ed io rimasi) dwells in the same vocal depths as her last phrase describing Euridice's death, only now her voice stays on five iterated D's for the whole phrase, projecting an image of shell-shocked immobility as the enormity of what has just occurred sinks in. The realization is expressed in her closing words: "My heart is full of pity and fear [*spavento*]." "Spavento" is treated to a climactic dissonance. Striggio's studied neoclassicism is apparent in this clear reference to Aristotle's theory in the *Poetics* that tragedy serves to stimulate "pity and fear" in its audience. Monteverdi's setting of the text ensures that Aristotle's tragic formula is made vividly real for the audience.

The first reaction to Silvia's report comes from the tenor shepherd, who sings the same words and virtually the same musical line with which the Messaggiera had entered the opera, "Ahi, caso acerbo." This passage of repeated text and music imparts an obvious musical and verbal symmetry to the scene, yet it makes psychological sense as well. Now the shepherds and Orfeo experience the grief Silvia felt when she interrupted their celebrations. The baritone shepherd now declaims in dissonant and angular music, "Ah [*Ahi*], one would have the heart of a tiger or a bear who didn't feel pity for your sorrow." The two high notes to which "ahi" is set suggest a jagged cry of anguish—a device that will reoccur with great effect in this act.

A full bar of vocal silence prefaces Orfeo's next speech as the basso continuo sounds grief-stricken chords. The score requires Orfeo's continuo accompaniment to shift from the "clavicembalo, chitarrone e viola da braccio" that had been the backup for his joyful music to the "organo di legno [pipe organ] e un chitarrone," the same instruments specified to accompany the Messaggiera. One critic observes that Orfeo's "shift to the messenger's continuo sonority... indicates his greater acceptance of fate" (Chafe 144). We have waited some time for a response from the protagonist to the Messaggiera's news. Schrade notes: "This holding Orfeo back from any spontaneous reaction to the story makes the sudden shock convincing; he was totally unaware and now he is stunned. It is as though he had not even heard what the Messaggiera recited at great length" (Schrade 233). "You [*rest*] are dead, [*rest*] you are dead, my life [*rest*]," sings Orfeo, in recitative expressive of the most anguished recognition. The rests throughout this passage act like catches in the voice, a voice on the edge of tears. His halting declamation continues. "And am I breathing [*rest*]? You have departed from me [*rest*], you have departed from me, never [*rest*], never to return." Orfeo's journey from shock and despair to fierce determination can be followed in his defiantly ascending vocal line, especially as he rejects his fate on the ascending notes of the repeated "mai più" (never) and the reiterated "no"s. In an instant Orfeo's plan is clear: "If my verses have any power, I shall fearlessly go down to the deepest abysses [*profondi abissi*]," his voice dropping mimetically from E to C. "And, moving to pity the heart of the king of shadows, lead you back to look again upon the stars [*meco trarrotti a riveder le stelle*]"—a clear reference to the last line of Dante's *Inferno*. This Dante reference seamlessly links the world of Hellenic myth with Christian epic, a quintessentially Renaissance mixture. The rising stepwise motion of the voice on "meco trarrotti" (lead you back) is vividly suggestive, as are the high notes on "le stelle" (the stars). His resolution to reclaim his bride or "remain with [her] in the company of death [*rest*]" (in compagnia [*rest*] di morte [*rest*]) utilizes rests and a descending vocal line to convey his steady determination. His last line in the act is beautiful poetry, simply set: "Goodbye, earth, goodbye, heavens and sun, goodbye" (A Dio terra, a Dio cielo, e sole, a Dio). This elegant line, punctuated with written pauses, creates for the protagonist a gloriously effective exit line. The lines here recall those of Sophocles' Oedipus as he bids farewell to light and physical sight before his self-blinding (*Oedipus the King*, lines 1182–85).

The horrible news affects all the opera's characters differently. Orfeo, the most deeply wounded, has just left on a superhuman quest that embodies the denial of grief. The chorus sings a passage that emulates so many in Greek tragedy, "Ah, bitter event!" (Ahi, caso acerbo!). The words and music recall the Messaggiera's first words, which have already been repeated soloistically by one of the shepherds. The dramatic shift in texture from an act that has been almost entirely soloistic to a five-part harmonization for the chorus is breathtaking. Their reiterated cries of "ahi," sometimes in unison, sometimes in counterpoint, cut through the musical texture like vivid stabs of pain. The chorus warns the audience, "Mortal man, don't trust the perishable and frail good that soon flees [*che tosto fugge*]." This last phrase is given a mimetically appropriate fluttering five-note figure—the very picture of impermanent, fleeting happiness. Silvia, the Messaggiera, is next granted an exit speech. Calling herself a "night bird of ill omen" (nottola infausta) in music of dreary dissonance, she resolves to find "a solitary hole and lead a life that conforms to my grief." Her voice climbs a steep chromatic line above a dragging bass, an image of masochistic suffering (see also Whenham, *Orfeo* 64–65).

Now a solemn sinfonia plays, marking the Messaggiera's exit and inaugurating a final expression of grief from the shepherds, set in an elaborate madrigal of mourning. The shepherd soloists express individual, personalized grief for Euridice and Orfeo, while the full chorus expresses a more generalized tragic lesson about the cruelty of fate and heaven. In this way "Monteverdi imparts a dramatic significance to the [musical] style of . . . soli and contrasting tutti" (Schrade 233). The insistently held first note, played by the orchestra in the sinfonia, recalls the jarring "ahi"s of the chorus. The sinfonia introduces a funereal duet between the two tenor shepherds, sung above grave harmonies in the basso continuo: "Who will console us?" (Chi ne consola?). The physical sensation of their flowing tears is suggested by the three-note ornamentation they share on the word "un" in the phrase "un vivo fonte da poter lagrimar" (a living fountain of tears). The tears' bitterness is manifested in the chromatic phrases on "da poter lagrimar," which they sing soloistically. The way the vocal lines color the words and the emotive impact of the contrasting sonorities of soloists, chorus, and instrumental accompaniment, all create an intensity of feeling that will hardly be encountered in baroque music until Bach's *St. Matthew Passion*. Another interesting passage where the shepherds sing distinct soloistic material comes when they individually describe the two stricken lovers, Orfeo and Euridice. The First Shepherd has the line "the one bitten by a snake" (l'una punta da l'angue) all to himself just before the second tenor sings "the other stricken by grief" (l'altro dal duol trafitto). They close their first duet with a unison exclamation, "Ah, consumed by grief" (Ahi, lassi ha spenti).

The chorus interjects a truncated version of their "Ahi, caso acerbo" refrain, contrasting the more individually expressed grief of the preceding duet with that of a group ("a final stroke of genius"; Arnold, *Monteverdi* 103). The tenor-shepherd duet resumes with different music as they propose to go and claim Euridice's body—a smoothly neoclassical dramaturgical device to empty the stage in preparation for the third act. They sing "Come, shepherds [*Andiam, pastori*], come, full of pity" to a slightly more animated phrase to begin the process of clearing the stage. Their duet closes with passages of poignant chromaticism. The last vocal "word" goes to the full chorus with a final (truncated) version of "Ahi, caso acerbo."

As the stage empties a remarkable thing happens. The strings play once more the D minor ritornello associated with Musica in the prologue. Here the later Wagnerian idea of leitmotif is clearly anticipated. Monteverdi is repeating this music, which has been heard six times during the prologue, firmly setting its association with "Music," the patron spirit of the entertainment before us. The Musica ritornello strikes us as something obviously familiar, yet oddly new, for we have already experienced much joy and sorrow since it was first heard. This musical recollection serves as a promise of Orfeo's power. The prologue told us this great musician will almost triumph over death and win "the immortal fame of Pindos and Helicon." Orfeo is about to test the powers of music, and this reprise of Musica's ritornello reminds us of Musica's omnipresence in the opera's unfolding action. This repeated ritornello stimulates the audience to make inferences and associations about the drama they are witnessing. Wagner's use of this kind of musical tag will, of course, be far subtler. But one can only marvel at Monteverdi's prescience in suggesting this idea at the very inception of the operatic medium.

Act 3

The scene is the Inferno, on the banks of the river Styx. Led by Speranza (Hope) to the entryway to Hades, Orfeo pleads with Caronte, the boatman of the Styx, to be allowed to enter the underworld. Caronte is moved by Orfeo's extraordinary solo—the opera's centerpiece, "Possente spirto"—but refuses to help. Orfeo's instrumental music does put Caronte to sleep, however, and Orfeo jumps into the boat and enters Hades. A chorus of spirits sings in praise of human endeavor.

Although the confrontation between Orfeo and Caronte has precedents in passages of Ovid and Virgil, Striggio and Monteverdi will use their audience's familiarity with Dante's vision of the Inferno to animate act 3, creating a perfect fusion of pagan and Christian elements typical of Renaissance art. As Whenham notes, "Doubtless it did not escape Striggio that Dante (a Florentine poet) developed his description [of hell] from that of Virgil (a Mantuan poet)" (*Orfeo* 67). The darkened instrumental palette of sackbuts, cornetti, and regal was suggested to Monteverdi by the *intermedi* tradition for presenting underworld scenes. A sublime eight-part sinfonia heralds the opening of the act. Scored for trombone, cornetti, and the rasping sounds of the regal, this sinfonia represents the august and terrifying boundary to the underworld. During the act's climax it will sound again and create new and startling resonance for the dramatic action that it punctuates. Led by Speranza

(Hope), Orfeo, a living man, approaches the gates of hell. Speranza is an allegorical figure who, as Arnold observes, "seems to have been brought in from an *intermedio*" (*Monteverdi* 98). Orfeo addresses Speranza, "the only blessing of afflicted mortals," in a mellifluous, somber arioso. The reiterated F's sinking to E-flats on "tenebrosi regni" (shadowy kingdom) are subtly mimetic. Orfeo bids Speranza to "support my weak and trembling steps, wherefore I hope today to see again those blessed lights which alone bring the day to my eyes." Speranza, an alto, responds with her own recitative, describing the place to which they have come. A brief dissonance colors "pianto" (lamentation) as Speranza gestures to "those fields of lamentation [*pianto*] and sorrow." A "bitter law forbids" Speranza from leading Orfeo any farther. This law "is inscribed with iron on the hard stone . . . 'Abandon Hope, you who enter here.'" "Lasciate ogni speranza, voi ch'entrate," the famous proclamation carved before Dante's Inferno (*Inferno,* canto 3, 9), is stated twice by Speranza in an arioso passage that highlights the imprecation by transposing the phrase up a tone upon its repetition. Dante's poem, as noted earlier, had been recalled moments before when Orfeo, at the end of act 2, vowed to lead Euridice "back to see the stars again" (a riveder le stelle)—the last line of the *Inferno* (canto 34, 139). These references to Dante make Orfeo's "pagan" dilemma all the more compelling to an Italian Catholic audience. Speranza sings, "Therefore, if your heart is really steadfast and you feel able to enter the city of sorrow [*dolente*], I will flee from you and return to my normal abode." Another delicate dissonance adorns "dolente," and Speranza leaves Orfeo before the grim boatman. "Where, ah, where are you going, sole comfort of my heart?" Orfeo's vocal line climbs to a higher, more plangent range, suggesting his apprehension. "What good remains for me if you fly, sweetest Hope?" The rest that punctuates the verse before "sweetest Hope" (dolcissima Speranza) is wrenching in its expression of Orfeo's vulnerability.

Caronte's first words astonish Orfeo (and the audience) with their threatening vehemence. Monteverdi specifies the supernatural-sounding regal as the grim ferryman's personal accompanimental instrument. His part is assigned with consummate musical and dramatic logic to a deep-voiced bass—the lowest voice yet heard in the opera.

O you, who before death dares
come to these shores—halt your steps!
Crossing these waves is not allowed to mortal man,
neither can he who dwells with the dead be living.
Who are you?

The cavernous-sounding voice and its snarling, sepulchral accompaniment are given a slithering arioso melody that will serve during all Caronte's speeches as his theme. The characterization is one of the most masterly in early opera. When well performed, his brief, menacing appearance creates one of the most memorable impressions in *L'Orfeo*. Striggio and Monteverdi economically use the character to stand for virtually all of Orfeo's superhuman opposition in reaching Euridice in the underworld. Facing Caronte, Orfeo braces himself for his task. As he does, a mysterious sinfonia sounds a somber, slow theme on the strings and organ, an instrumental benediction before Orfeo's prayer to the underworld. This sinfonia is frequently interpreted as representing the sounds of Orfeo's divinely inspired instrumental prelude on his lyre. Pickett makes a plausible argument that it is actually "a musical representation of Apollon's benign magic, sent down without Orfeo's knowledge by a watchful father to calm him and inspire him for the task ahead" ("Armonia" 151). The instrumental passage will recur just before Caronte falls asleep after the great aria. It makes a third appearance in the final act before Apollon descends from the heavens. Of course there is no reason why this passage may not carry multiple meanings. The grave tune prefaces the opera's centerpiece and one of the greatest tours de force in Western music. Monteverdi dares to write a lament displaying the musical power and invention worthy of a demigod. It is music capable of opening the portals of the underworld, worthy to represent the power of music and of art itself in its most important function: as the means by which mortal endeavor achieves immortality, the only way human beings can be said to conquer death. Orfeo's plea is the first important set piece in operatic history (see also Fenlon, "Mantuan Stage Works" 274–75).

Orfeo's solo, "Possente spirto," is a sequence of four strophic variations followed by two contrasting recitative or arioso passages. The slow instrumental bass line remains the same while Orfeo sings his four strophes with increasingly virtuosic ornamentation. The verses of his plea are punctuated by elaborate instrumental interludes. The published score gives two versions of Orfeo's aria printed side by side, with directions that "Orfeo sings only one" of these. One version is simple, without ornament. The other, which is the one usually heard in performances and recordings, is extremely florid. It seems obvious that the ornamental version is the one best suited for performance. The simple reduction is presented, didactically, to help orient future performers to the textual and melodic foundations for their own ornamentation (see also Carter on the two versions, *Monteverdi's Musical Theater* 130–31). Celletti observes that "the 'plain' version, . . . apart from being far less noteworthy, largely defeats the purpose of the orchestral interventions, which were clearly devised with virtuoso vocalism in mind" (28). Variations in instrumental color are provided by virtuosic duets of violins and cornetti and a solo for the double harp. These instruments will perform exquisite obbligatos during each verse and in ritornelli between verses. Orfeo's voice is accompanied by a chitarrone, which probably represents his lyre, along with one of the wood pipe organs. The obbligato instruments represent "the three main classes of late Renaissance instruments—bowed string instruments, wind/brass instruments, and plucked string instruments . . . [suggesting] that Orpheus conquered all the available forces of music to aid his pleas to Charon" (Whenham, *Orfeo* 68). As will be seen, these three instrumental groups also serve to represent the three spheres through which Orfeo will pass during the opera: the earth, the underworld, and heaven. "Possente spirto" is a consummate realization of operatic theater wherein the needs of the drama and the needs of musical expression are identical. It is a wildly virtuosic display piece, perfectly integrated into the opera, its virtuosity being an integral part of its expressive and spiritual content and purpose. In this sense its analog in the baroque repertory is the Chaconne from Bach's D Minor Violin Partita, a piece that recent scholarship has suggested is also a musical lament for a lost wife—a real one, in Bach's case. The technical difficulty of "Possente spirto" must be surmounted by the virtuosic singer, yet the audience must still sense its difficulty; its technical difficulty is part of its expressive content.

In the first verse Orfeo sings, "Mighty spirit and formidable divinity [*Possente spirto e formidabil nume*], without whom the souls free of their bodies hope in vain to reach the other bank." Orfeo's voice rises above his basso continuo accompaniment of chitarrone and wood pipe organ with vocal decoration magically illustrating the things he sings about. The words "spirto" and "formidabil nume" are treated to florid divisions (rapid coloratura), aided by the fluttering "stereophonic" conversation of two obligato violins. One recalls Orfeo's close association with these instruments and their use in the pastoral world in the preceding act. The florid ornamentations of this aria clearly suggest the state of the art for early-seventeenth-century professional singers. As always with Monteverdi, the words highlighted for ornamentation are meaningful and usually convey mimetic force. The ornamentation of "altra" in the phrase "altra riva" (the other bank) suggests the desired journey across Styx. In "Without you, souls presume in vain to enter the underworld," the rapid divisions on "alma da corpo sciolta in van presume" (the souls presume in vain) offer Caronte a very musical form of flattery. As a close to the aria's first stanza, the two obbligato violins play in unison a ritornello whose rapid figurations complement Orfeo's with their own instrumental virtuosity.

The texture shifts back to voice and basso continuo for the start of Orfeo's second strophe: "I am not alive, no, after my dear wife was deprived of life, my heart is no longer with me, and without a heart, how can I be alive?" Here contrast is achieved from the first strophe by a striking simplicity of ornamentation in the vocal line and the continuo. The words "Vivo, mia cara sposa" and "è più meco" receive brief, pointed accentuation, and a simple dissonance colors the reference to "vita" (life), of which Euridice has been deprived. The idea "without a heart, how [*può*] can I be alive" stimulates a slightly longer division on "può" suggestive of Orfeo's disdain for life without his wife. The other striking difference in the second strophe is that the duetting obbligato instruments are now two cornetti, which in the *intermedi* tradition had associations with the underworld. The cornetti join together to play the ritornello tag ending the second strophe, as the violins had done for the first strophe.

Florid tendencies reemerge with a vengeance for the third strophe. "To her have I turned my way through the dark air, not toward the Inferno, for everywhere is paradise that has such beauty"—the thought of nearing his goal inspires Orfeo to the most spectacular divisions yet heard as the ornamentation on "a lei" (to her), "tanta [bellezza]" (such [beauty]), and "paradiso" seem to stretch into an infinity of sound and longing. This direct response to Euridice's beauty is aptly complimented by the obbligato double harp, whose mellifluous rejoinders punctuate the rests in the vocal line. At the strophe's end the harp plays an extended variation on the ritornello tag that seems to squeeze out the ritornello melody's last expressive potential. The effect, Pickett writes, is "as if time stands still for Orfeo when he thinks of Euridice" ("Armonia" 152). The harp sonorities—fingers on strings—suggest an even more intimate dimension to the strophe, and this new, deeper sense of intimacy triggers the fourth stanza, which brings the strophic vocal variation sequence to a climax. The harp, an instrument long symbolic of heaven, was suggested by Orfeo's references to "paradiso" and contrasts its "celestial" harmonies with the infernal gloom on stage.

"I am Orfeo, who follow the steps of Euridice through these dark arenas, to which no mortal can go." The singer's divisions on "Orfeo son io" are even more florid and virtuosic than all that have gone before. As the great singer introduces himself he is joined by three solo instruments, the two violins from the first strophe coupled with a cello, creating a string trio whose sonorities complement the voice's musical phrases. This newly enriched obbligato texture is joined to the even greater instrumental quality of the vocal writing for Orfeo: in the last strophe, particularly in its fluttering pattern on the climactic lines "ove già mai per huom mortal non vassi" (through which no mortal can go), the vocal writing seems more appropriate for a string instrument than a human voice. Yet Orfeo demonstrates that his voice, the quintessential human voice, is the prototype of all musical instruments.

At this moment, just as Orfeo's vocal style is at its most instrumental, the texture of Orfeo's solo shifts to a simpler setting. As Schrade observes, "The more intense Orfeo becomes, the more direct his approach" (Schrade 235). The words "O serene lights of my eyes, if only a glance from you can return life to me! Ah, who can deny me comfort in my pain?" are set to arioso, with the last phrase, "Ah, who can deny me comfort in my pain?," repeated as a refrain. The arioso melody to which "O serene lights of my eyes" (O de le luci mie luci serene) is set will be poignantly recalled in act 5 as Orfeo grieves for Euridice for the last time (at "Tu bella fusti"). This simple passage of arioso declamation makes for a perfect contrast and shift of tone from the building emotion of the four variations that preceded it. The simpler texture, just voice and continuo without obbligato commentary and with only modest touches of ornamentation, offers a momentary lessening of the musical and dramatic tension. The final sequence of four lines brings the solo to conclusion by uniting this new simplicity of vocal decoration with another suggestion of the depth of sonority available from the orchestra: "Only you, noble god, can help me; don't be afraid, for the only weapon for my fingers is the sweet strings of the golden lyre against the rigid souls to whom it is in vain to plead." Kerman describes this final stanza as set "in a style [that is] vaguely ecclesiastical, part music to which Orfeo kneels with the viols, exposing most purely the quiet bass pattern which had united the earlier stanzas" ("Orpheus" 133–34). This whole concluding arioso passage affords only one word for florid decoration, "invan" (in vain), which, appropriately enough, given the immediate situation, serves as the climactic musical gesture of the whole aria.

There may be implicit humor in the effect of Orfeo's long, complex aria being followed by Caronte's blunt arioso. Caronte sternly warns Orfeo that "pity is far from this breast." But this warning comes after he admits to being "rather flattered, delighted at heart . . . by your pleas and your song." Caronte's music is stubbornly the same, but his words hint that for all his bluster even he is not completely immune to music's charm. Caronte's initial rejection spurs Orfeo to a passionate recitative. His voice moves from agitated repeated E's on "Ahi, sventurato amante!" (Ah, unhappy lover!) to the grim, despairing descent on "e pregando, e piangendo io mi consumi" (and begging and pleading myself). This declamatory passage climaxes in a thrice-repeated phrase, "Rendetemi il mio ben, Tartarei Numi" (Give me back my beloved, gods of Tartarus)—a musical line that, in Whenham's phrase, "unleashes the full emotional power of the new recitative style" (*Orfeo* 69). At its first appearance we had heard the sinfonia as a kind of instrumental prelude to "Possente spirto." It now sounds as a gentle postlude, to be "played softly by viola da braccio, a wooden piped organ and contrabasso de Viola da gamba" as the score directs. This repeated sinfonia gives a pleasing sense of musical architecture to this central section of the score, and now, in its repetition, it gains in dramatic significance. Orfeo's vocal music has lulled the boatman to sleep. As noted earlier, this interlude may represent Apollon's unseen intercession for his son.

Orfeo seizes his opportunity: "He sleeps, and even if my lyre awakens no pity in the hardened heart, at least his eyes cannot escape sleep at my songs." Orfeo sings this gentle recitative with barely any harmonic motion, to the accompaniment of the wooden pipe organ. Any loud noises might awaken Caronte. I believe the gentle laughter this scene often receives in performance was intended by the opera's creators. The sleeping Caronte is the first in opera's long line of comic philistines, one that includes Beckmesser in Wagner's *Die Meistersinger von Nürnberg* and the unseen nobleman in Richard Strauss's *Ariadne auf Naxos*. Orfeo's "operatic" stylings are not for everyone; Caronte proves this. But even Caronte is vulnerable enough to the charms of melody to at least fall asleep!

As Orfeo moves into action, his recitative style rises in pitch: "So then, why do I delay? It is a good time to land on that other shore, if no one is there to prevent it." The wooden pipe organ is directed to play while Orfeo enters the bark. At the moment of departure for the realm of Hades he brings the act to its climax by repeating "Rendetemi il mio ben, Tartarei Numi," the emotion-laden tag he had sung earlier. His departure into the inner reaches of the Inferno is signaled by another meaningful musical repetition, the majestic sinfonia that began act 3. When first heard at the start of the act, the stately music seemed to herald a new and appropriately impressive sound palette for portraying the gate to Plutone's kingdom. Now, played at the moment when Orfeo has penetrated hell itself, it serves as a fanfare exalting not the infernal powers of the underworld but the extraordinary achievement of the man and artist.

Orfeo makes his exit in the boat, and the chorus of spirits, made up of tenors and basses, begin their act-concluding song in reaction to Orfeo's performance. Virgil provides a description of the effect of the singer's pleas that seems to resonate in Striggio and Monteverdi's work.

> Startled by the strain, there came from the lowest realms of Erebus the bodiless shadows and the phantoms of those bereft of light, in multitude like the thousands of birds that hide amid the leaves when the evening star or a wintery shower drives them from the hills—mothers and men, and bodies of high-souled heroes, their life now done, boys and unwed girls, and sons placed on the pyre before their father's eyes. But round them are the black ooze and unsightly reeds of Cocytus, the unlovely river enchaining them with its sluggish water, and Styx holding them fast within her nine circles. Indeed, the very halls of Hell were spell-bound, and inmost Tartarus, and the Furies with livid snakes entwined in their locks. Cerebus held agape his triple mouths, and Ixion's wheel was stayed by the still wind. (*Georgics,* book 4, modified from Fairclough trans., 229–31)

The chorus in acts 3 and 4 of *L'Orfeo* consists of spirits, like Virgil's audience. After hearing Orfeo's song and witnessing his triumph over Caronte, they intone a paean to the human spirit.

> No enterprise by man is taken in vain,
> nether can Nature arm herself against him.
> From the unstable plane
> he has plowed the wave like fields and sown seeds
> of his labors, so that he receives a golden harvest.
> So that memory
> of his glory may live,
> Fame has loosened its tongue to speak of him,
> for he's placed a bridle on the sea of fragile wood,
> for he's disdained the anger of the east and north winds.

Here Striggio's debt to Sophocles becomes apparent. The chorus is largely inspired by the famous "Ode to Man" from Sophocles' *Antigone* (lines 332–75). Striggio's original text contains two extra stanzas, which give the chorus a carefully layered ironic ambiguity, recalling the ambivalent triumphs of Jason, Daedalus, and Phaeton. Monteverdi has cut these extra stanzas from the score. Consequently, *L'Orfeo* at this moment avoids a haunting sense of man's paradoxical mix of beneficent and malevolent potential. Monteverdi sculpted his librettist's text to create his own "Ode to Man," or, to be more precise, "Ode to Man the Artist" (Carter reads these deleted lines into his interpretation of the opera, despite their exclusion by the composer; *Monteverdi's Musical Theater* 113–14). The chorus's dramatic placement at the end of act 3 makes it deeply significant for all that has already occurred in the opera and all that will follow. Not all the pious references to Orfeo's "tragic flaw" of passion at the close of the next act can erase this decidedly pagan humanistic idea from *L'Orfeo*. The chorus sings its glorious five-voice madrigal in praise of man to the accompaniment of both the regal and wooden pipe organ, five sackbuts, two bass viols, and a violone, creating one of the richest textures in the opera. Their lines are contrapuntal, but, notably, all voices are in unison as they sing, "Ch'ei pose freno al mar con fragil legno" (For he's placed a bridle on the sea of fragile wood)—which Orfeo has, in effect, just done before their eyes. As Kerman observes, "The solemn Venetian madrigal polyphony, stiffly controlled as though sculptured, answers and deepens the [work's] impassioned voice" ("Orpheus" 133). Their sonorous anthem closes, and the sinfonia sounds for a third and final time, providing music for the entry of Plutone and Proserpina at the top of the next act and setting the seal on another musical and dramatic sequence, which has seldom if ever been surpassed in the long history of opera.

Act 4

The scene is still the Inferno. Moved by Orfeo's musical pleadings, Proserpina persuades her husband, Plutone, the god of the underworld, to show mercy and return Euridice to her husband. Plutone's one condition is that Orfeo may not look at his wife as they journey back to the world of the living. In the midst of a celebratory aria, "Qual honor di te," Orfeo, seized by sudden anxiety, turns to face his wife, who is then once again consigned to eternal darkness. The chorus of spirits philosophizes about humankind's need to conquer its unstable passions if it is ever to attain true virtue.

Proserpina informs us that she and Plutone have witnessed Orfeo's musical skills. Some commentators have perceived here a mysterious gap in the opera's dramatic strategy. The audience has just witnessed Orfeo's pleading to Caronte in act 3. Did Proserpina and Plutone hear the same performance we experienced in act 3 or another one? Are composer and librettist cannily avoiding the challenge of depicting Orfeo's performance before Plutone and Proserpina, since no mortal artist would dare to represent so sublime an act of song? (See Abbate 19–27 for a summary of this view.) These arguments are intriguing but unnecessarily convoluted. It seems doubtful that a theater audience in either the seventeenth or the twenty-first century would attach importance to this perceived incongruity. With a fine sense of dramaturgical economy, Striggio's text indicates that Proserpina and Plutone have indeed overheard Orfeo's lament to the boatman, music that has soothed Caronte while moving Proserpina to pity. Plutone tells her that Orfeo's song has moved him to thoughts of love. These three reactions are a beautiful microcosm of song's potential to affect its audience. Proserpina, like the demigod Orfeo, is a character caught betwixt and between. As the earth goddess Demeter's daughter, she does not belong fully to the environs of her husband's underworld kingdom. Perhaps this duality in her nature makes the living Orfeo's plight all the more affecting to her.

Proserpina opens act 4 with one of the loveliest recitatives in the opera: "Deh, se da queste luci amorosa dolcezza unqua traesti, se ti piacque il seren di questa fronte che tu chiami tuo cielo" (Ah, if from these eyes you have derived love's sweetness, if you have taken delight from this serene brow). It is music of liminal melodiousness, so characteristic of Monteverdi. The melodic purity and ardor of the passage cuts to Plutone's (and the audience's) heart. Orfeo's eloquence has inspired Proserpina to combine word, sense, and tone with the utmost economy and sensitivity. This is one of the countless passages in the Monteverdi operas in which music that is ostensibly recitative is graced with a greater melodic felicity than is encountered in many later composers' best arias. "I beg you" (pregoti) she repeats emphatically, the reiteration rising musically, "to let Euridice return to delight in those days which she spent living in festival and song" (fa ch'Euridice torni a goder di quei giorni). This thought inspires a new lovely arioso melody, which is over as soon as its immediate dramatic purpose is fulfilled. Her pleading has its desired effect. Plutone cannot refuse "such beauty conjoined with such entreaties." He orders Euridice's release, contrary to the "severe and immutable Fate" that normally contravenes such requests. The god offers his famous caveat that "a single glance" at Euridice on their journey back to life will mandate Orfeo's "eternal loss." Like Caronte, Plutone is cast as a deep and imposing bass. Plutone's speech, as befits his character, is straightforward recitative probably accompanied by the wind instruments, signifying his supernatural power.

Two spirits, one tenor and one baritone, appear from the ranks of the chorus to indicate in brief recitatives that Plutone's command will be enacted and to underline for the audience the important test Orfeo faces. "From these terrible caverns will Orfeo lead his wife, if, using his intelligence, he is not vanquished by his youthful desire, nor forgets your stern decree." Proserpina registers her gratitude to her husband with more ravishing recitative and arioso. Particularly affecting is the melody adorning "Sia benedetto il dì che pria ti piacqui, benedetta la preda e 'l dolce inganno" (Blessed be the day on which I first pleased you, blessed the abduction and the sweet deception). Though their presence is brief in quantity of text and music, Proserpina and Plutone's scene serves as an important divine parallel to the opera's central couple, Orfeo and Euridice. Both couples represent myths of life's conflict with death, the separation of light and darkness and an achieved or attempted act of metaphysical compromise. Proserpina's words accent this parallel: "Blessed the abduction and the sweet deception, since to my good fortune in losing the sun I gained you." After a recitative by Plutone, the chorus of spirits sings a five-voice madrigal covering Plutone and Proserpina's exit. The chorus declares, "Today pity and love have triumphed in the Inferno." It is a short passage: six bars of choral singing with only a bass-line accompaniment. At its close, a tenor spirit from the chorus's ranks announces in recitative, "Here is the gentle singer who conducts his wife to the light of heaven."

Orfeo, leading Euridice behind him, enters to the strains of a gloriously triumphant strophic aria, "Qual honor": "What honor is due
to you, my omnipotent lyre, since in the realms of Tartarus you have
subdued every hardened mind?" This happy aria is enhanced with a
jaunty violin duet ritornello, recalling Orfeo's special bond with these
instruments and anticipating his return to the living world. The vocal
and instrumental writing express the utmost joy, and the walking bass
illustrates Orfeo's confident strides toward the light. The second verse
allows Orfeo to indulge in exciting and pointed ornamentation: "You
[the lyre] shall have a place among the most beautiful images of heaven,
where to your sound the stars will dance in orbit [*giri*], now slow, now
fast [*presti*]." Both "giri" and "presti" are decorated with mimetically
appropriate ornamentation. Ironically, Orfeo and his lyre will indeed
find a place "among the stars" by the opera's end. The third and last
verse of the aria reserves all its ornamentation to a single word that is
both suggestive of Orfeo's character and dramatically apt. In "Because
of you I am finally happy, I will see her beautiful face and on the pure
breast of my wife I shall [*sarò*] recline," "sarò" is the only word elaborated with a vocal decoration. This gesture points to Orfeo's overeager
anticipation, which is about to lead to disaster.

The anticipatory joy embodied in the ornamentation on "sarò" effectively halts Orfeo's aria in its tracks, and he now expresses himself in
anxious recitative. The frequent notated rests in the vocal line indicate
the direction of Orfeo's thoughts: "But as I sing [*rest*], ah me [*rest*], who
will assure me that she is following [*rest*]? Ah me [*rest*], who hides from
me the sweet light of her beloved eyes?" Another rest marks a transition into a rapid-fire recitative passage that suggests Orfeo's sudden
paranoiac doubts, fueled by a touch of egotism. "Perhaps the envy of
the Avernian deity, so that my joy is not complete [*rest*], takes away my
sight of your beautiful and blessed eyes, that can with one sole glance
[*rest*] bless others?" Another fateful rest. The die is cast. "What do you
fear, my heart [*rest*]? What Plutone forbids, Love commands [*rest*]! I
must obey a more powerful divinity, who conquers men and gods."
Now voice and instruments are directed to go silent as a threatening
noise (*strepido*) is heard from backstage. This noise, the embodiment

of unmusical, unpoetic, uncontrolled sound, marks the decisive rupture in the fabric of the opera and Orfeo's near-triumph over death
through art. It marks the moment Orfeo, in the self-defining moment
of "spiritual blindness," turns to look at his wife (see also van der Kooij
and Riehn 99). The inspiration for this passage of tragic reversal comes
from Virgil's handling of the story.

> And now as he retraced his steps he had escaped every mischance,
> and the regained Euridice was nearing the upper world, follow-
> ing behind . . . when a sudden frenzy seized Orpheus, unwary in
> his love, frenzy worthy of pardon, did Hell know how to pardon!
> He stopped, and on the very verge of light, unmindful, alas! and
> vanquished in purpose, on Euridice, now his own, looked back! In
> that moment all his toil was spent, the ruthless tyrant's pact was
> broken, and thrice a crash was heard amid the pools of Avernus.
> (*Georgics* 4, modified from Fairclough trans., 231)

The recitative resumes. The score specifies that Orfeo is accompanied by harpsichord, viola da braccio, and chittarone as he hesitantly
sings, "But [*rest*] what do I hear [*rest*], ah me! Wretch that I am [*rest*]!
Could it be that [*rest*] with such fierce arms the enamored Furies attack
me to rob me of my beloved [*Orfeo halts now for the most poignant and
pointed rest of all*]—and that I consent?" The ultimate dramatic recognition and catastrophe having been reached, the accompanimental
sonority shifts to the sound of chords to be played softly on the wooden
pipe organ as Orfeo looks at Euridice for the last time. "O sweetest
eyes, I can indeed see you [*rest*], I can [*rest*]." Again the accompanimental sonorities change: the harpsichord, viola da braccio, and chittarone
replace the organ. "But what eclipse, ah me! obscures you?" A third
spirit, a dark bass like Plutone and Caronte, blocks their contact.
"You've broken the law and are unworthy of grace!" he declares.

Euridice now sings her second and final passage in the entire opera.
Her arioso is a passage of exceptional poignancy, every turn of phrase
and choice of word delicately reflected in the vocal line. The exclamation "ahi" is sung to a doleful yet jabbing D. The setting of "dolce"
already suggests she is singing about something bittersweet, as the next
phrase "and too bitter [*amara*]," confirms.

Ah, sight too sweet and too bitter;
is it for too much love then that you lose me?
And I, miserable one, lose
the chance of happiness
and light and life and lose also
you, the dearest one, O my husband.

Her realization of Orfeo's folly never hints at recrimination. Her love for her husband is too strong for her to blame him for his all-too-human weakness. That love is embodied in the piercing tenderness expressed in her voice as she calls him "the dearest one" (più caro), moving from G to a ringing, affirmative C. A tenor spirit directs her back to the Inferno forever in a recitative that paraphrases Dante yet again: "never hope again to see the stars" (né più sperar di riveder le stelle). As Ovid writes, "Euridice, dying now a second time, uttered no complaint against her husband. What was there to complain of, but that she had been loved? With a last farewell which scarcely reached his ears, she fell back again into the same place from which she had come" (*Metamorphoses* 10, Innes trans., 226). Orfeo tries to rejoin Euridice but is stopped by invisible forces: "Where are you going [*rest*], my life [*rest*]? Here, I follow you [*rest*], but who stops me, ah me! Do I dream or rave?" This final recitative is appropriately wrenching and dissonant as Orfeo, utterly defeated on the verge of triumph, is ignominiously expelled from the Inferno he had nearly conquered.

David Freeman offers an intriguing view of Orfeo's "sin" as exposed in this most harrowing of scenes.

> One interpretation of Orfeo's turning around to see Euridice in Hades is that it represents a . . . dramatic version of the idea that he must not let the past that she represents come between himself and the future. If he succeeds in getting out of Hades, he must love a new Euridice, not the old one who is dead, just as in any relationship the person one knew yesterday is in a sense dead, and one can only effectively relate to the person one now sees. It is not the act of turning around, not a childish condition imposed by a spiteful Pluto, which leads to Orfeo's downfall; and Orfeo's weakness is not just a question of curiosity or lack of steadfastness,

as with Elsa in *Lohengrin*. It is a question of man's place in time. ("Telling the Story" 162)

A new sinfonia plays as Orfeo exits, its music pompous and ceremonial, like the sinfonia that began and ended act 3. But this new sinfonia is darker still, as if it were the Inferno's imperious rebuke to Orfeo's frailty. This instrumental passage introduces the act-closing five-part madrigal by the chorus of spirits. Pickett is surely correct in detecting another resonance of Dante in Monteverdi's depiction of the underworld. The low-lying, dense textures, the repetitions of rhythmic figures, "and the constant use in all the parts of a rising/falling motif" recalls passages from the *Inferno* "where the many souls are described as being packed closely together, endlessly repeating their actions, and crying out in their anguish" ("Armonia" 151). Here, with the accompaniment of sackbuts, viols, violone, and both organs, the spirits sing of an ideal man, steady and true, who is "not frightened, rather magnified to greater splendor" by the "ravages of Time." The hapless Orfeo is not such a man, since he "conquered the Inferno yet was defeated by his own passion." The tone of their words is conventional, as is the predictable ornamentation on such words as "apprezza" (prize), "maggiore" (magnifies), and "splendore." Orfeo's failure is described with (gratuitously cruel) ornaments on "vinto poi" (defeated at last). Lest the lesson's moral be lost, the five voices soloistically banter the phrase "fia sol colui": he alone deserves glory "who has triumphed over himself." But the powers of expression that led to Orfeo's near-triumph are the same forces of sensitivity and artistic ego that led to his failure.

Humankind is like the character of Orfeo, and not like the abstract "huom" eulogized by the spirits. This rift in perception serves to isolate Orfeo from the frame of the operatic world that surrounds him and makes the "happy ending" required by neoclassical standards all the more disturbing and unsatisfying. As the chorus exits, the solemn sinfonia sounds again, like a stern injunction punctuating this chorus and preparing for the shift into the fifth act. The positive humanism of the last act now seems a chimera. For all mankind's potential and achievement, as expressed in the final chorus to act 3, the chorus that closes act 4 perceives a tragically limited creature. Monteverdi has deliberately heightened this contrast by cutting the stanzas of Striggio's text for the act 3 chorus, which specifically problematize the heroic human subject. Like *Hamlet*'s, *L'Orfeo*'s view of humanity is dualistic: torn between intoxicating hope in man's limitless potential yet darkened by a more medieval awareness of the transience of this world. Man in Monteverdi and Shakespeare is both godlike and pitifully bestial. Neither artist attempts to reconcile or remove this paradox. Humanity longs for transcendence, which art seems almost capable of achieving. But art is created from a fusion of godly discipline and human passion. Without this very passion the spirit chorus denounces, Orfeo would never have caught the ear of the underworld. The victory and defeat of art is the victory and defeat of mankind. But perhaps humanity's longing for the permanent and transcendent may be realized through art after all. Shakespeare's sonnets often make this assertion, and Musica's prologue intimated that Orfeo has already attained a kind of permanence. The final act as it is represented by the published score will make good on the prologue's promise of achieved immortality.

Act 5

We return to the Arcadian setting. Orfeo, alone except for an offstage Echo, sings a final despairing threnody for his lost wife and grows increasingly bitter. Apollon, the god of harmony and Orfeo's father, descends from heaven and persuades his son to renounce sorrow on earth for transcendence in the heavens, as a reward for his sufferings. As the god and demigod ascend to heaven, the chorus of nymphs and shepherds sings that "he who sows in sorrow reaps the fruits of grace."

Orfeo reenters the Arcadian setting of the first two acts accompanied by the final repetition of Musica's ritornello. This melodic recapitulation is the simplest musical device imaginable for imparting structural cohesion to the opera. Just as the stage setting has brought *L'Orfeo* back to where the story started, the orchestra musically recapitulates the melody most often heard in the opening of the work. We are musically and scenically back where we started. But why is this recapitulation so breathtaking? Again Monteverdi anticipates something of Wagner's leitmotif effect: a melody with specific dramatic associations is repeated in a different context to shed light on the developing dramatic situation. Later composers of the classical era, from Haydn to Schubert and the romantics, would exploit in the recapitulations of sonata structure the psychological implications of revisiting melodic material in light of far-reaching musical development that has expanded the consciousness of the listener. Rehearing the Musica ritornello as the dejected Orfeo enters reminds us of his past happiness and his bitter loss. It is a masterstroke of musical and dramatic irony that stings while wrenching the heart with its associations with Orfeo's lost Eden.

The self-conscious symmetry imparted by this repetition also hints at a shift in meaning. Music and art are a way of imposing order on the apparent chaos of life. Musica's ritornello is painfully ironic in its final appearance, while at the same time giving a strange sense of consolation in the familiar. All music, all art, we can hope, remains to be encountered again at the different stages of our own lives, just as in Orfeo's. Music and art change their resonance for us as we change and begin to derive different things from them. Claudio Arrau, the great pianist, once remarked that "music rebukes us" in that there is always more to be derived from it than we are able to mine. Perhaps Musica's ritornello rebukes Orfeo in something like the way Arrau meant. We thought we had its full implications, but there is more to be learned. Its reappearance reminds us of its inscrutable depths. A man-made thing, it seems to have a life of its own, the embodiment of an eternal quest in performance and perception whose failure to be fully realized is part of its power and, paradoxically, its consolation for the human soul. Its final recapitulation has something of the effect of hearing a song with happy associations during a time of inconsolable grief. The music reminds us of irrecoverable loss while perhaps hinting at a dimension of experience that our instincts tell us relates to the eternal. Monteverdi's final use of Musica's ritornello is a statement about the meaning of music and art, its fragility, its apparent futility, and its paradoxical indestructibility. "Musica" literally heralded Orfeo's entrance to the Inferno and now heralds, however sadly, his return from it.

Virgil describes Orpheus's reaction on losing Euridice again and his sad return to the land of the living.

> What could he do? Whither turn himself, twice robbed of his wife? With what tears move Hell, with what prayers its powers? She, alas! even now death cold, was afloat in the Stygian bark. Month in, month out, seven whole months, men say beneath a high cliff by lonely Strymon's wave, he wept, and deep in icy caverns, unfolded his tale, charming the tigers, and making the oaks attend his strain; even as the nightingale, mourning beneath the poplar's shade, bewails the loss of her brood. . . . No love, no wedding song could bend his soul. Alone he would roam the northern ice, the snowy Tanais, and the fields ever wedded to Rhipaean frosts, wailing Eurydice lost, and the gift of Dis annulled. (*Georgics* 4, modified from Fairclough trans., 233)

Ovid, in his handling of the story, describes "shady trees moving" to the singer's side, enchanted by his mournful music (*Metamorphoses* 10, Innes trans., 227). This part of the story is encapsulated in the opening sequence of *L'Orfeo*'s fifth act, where the idea of inanimate nature responding to Orfeo's music will find articulation in Monteverdi's echo scene.

Alone in the pastoral setting he had once shared with the frolicking shepherds and nymphs, Orfeo begins a last solo, a grand recitative with arioso passages and an echo sequence. The score here gives interesting indications for the continuo accompaniment and the placement of the instruments: "Two organi di legno and two chittaroni concertize in this song, the one [group] sounding from the left and the other from the right side of the stage." One set of these particular instruments has given color to Orfeo's words twice before: when he mourned Euridice for the first time in the second act and when he lost her for the second time in the underworld. This antiphonal deployment may suggest the broken, bifurcated state of Orfeo's soul when he returns to the living world as essentially a dead man, unable to go on (see also Chafe 156). On the other hand, it may also be intended to serve as dueling continuo groups for Orfeo's onstage singing and the ghostly offstage Echo. Another possibility is that the doubling and physical opposition of continuo instruments may serve primarily to create a more sonorous effect. A parallel may be found in a very different artistic form, Bunraku (traditional Japanese puppet theater). There, in the final scene of a tragic play the audience may experience a dramatic increase in the number of singer-reciters and their accompanying musicians. This intensified sound helps to build dramatic tension for the stage action it is supporting.

Orfeo's first three verses form a moving passage of arioso. Again the use of rests enhances the dramatic effect of the declamation: "These [rest] are the fields of Thrace [rest], and this the place [rest] where my heart was pierced [rest] with grief at the bitter news." The arioso writing is suggestive of shell shock, the pauses and the initially static iteration of D's vividly projecting a soul racked by inconsolable grief. As he recollects first hearing of Euridice's death, his voice rises from its nearly somnolent monotone to a brief stabbing figure on the phrase "passomm'il core" (pierced my heart). The musical setting of these lines is of the highest personal intensity, anticipating such works as "Ardo, e scoprir" and "Or che 'l ciel et la terra" from Monteverdi's much later *Eighth Book of Madrigals*. This tone of personal intensity, the sense of one individual human soul communicating intimately with its fellows in the audience, represents what is new in Monteverdi's musical achievement. In his music Monteverdi strives to represent the mind of a great figure on the verge of collapse. His music colors and punctuates the words in ways analogous to Shakespeare's use of blank verse in his great soliloquies. (For a virtuosic comparison of Orfeo's solo with Antony's similarly suicidal speech in *Antony and Cleopatra,* act 4, scene 12, see Osthoff 161–62.)

After this arresting opening arioso, Orfeo shifts to recitative: "What can I do but turn to you, gentle woods, once upon a time the comfort of my torments, when it pleased heaven out of pity for me to move you to languish at my languishing [*languire al mio languire*]." Orfeo's voice rises unexpectedly on "al mio," heightening the personal intensity of the declamation. It creates a kind of out-of-body musical experience, the setting of "al mio" seeming to come from another musical world distinct from that of the other notes surrounding it. This passage anticipates the echo scene that is about to begin. Orfeo now recalls how the mountains and stones grieved and wept with him when he began his courtship.

Now he shall weep with them forever: "And never more shall I sleep, ah, grief, ah, tears!" (e mai sempre dorommi, ahi, doglia, ahi, pianto). As if in answer to Orfeo's prayers to an anthropomorphic nature, an offstage tenor voice echoes back his music and slightly altered words, "Hai, pianto" (Yes, tears).

At first Echo seems an answer to Orfeo's loneliness, an embodiment of the pathetic fallacy to which he resorted in the time before Euridice died. He continues his recitative. "Courteous, lovely Echo, who though unhappy yourself would console me in my grief . . . I still have not wept enough [*basti*]." Another echo of "basti" resonates in the woods surrounding the singer. It is as if nature itself is telling the singer that he has indeed mourned "enough." Chafe observes, "The very voice of indifferent, obdurate nature contains more comfort than Orpheus will allow himself" (Chafe 155). But rather than being consoled by Echo, the mysterious voice drives Orfeo to new extremes: "If I had as many eyes as Argus and all were to pour a sea of tears it would not conform enough to such grief [*guai*]." Instead of "guai," Echo responds with a sigh: "Ahi." Echo's inability to reflect Orfeo's words and feelings fully heightens his sense of alienation. "Why do you respond only with final accents?" Orfeo demands. "Render all laments to me completely." A notated silence marks Echo's nonresponse, and Orfeo is more alone than ever. The echo scene was a conventional borrowing from spoken pastoral drama, but in *L'Orfeo* Monteverdi puts his own distinctive touch on this trope: it is used and then dismissed. Orfeo's rejection of the device after its dysfunction suggests a growing alienation between the trappings of courtly performance and the modern human drama being forged before our eyes and ears. Orfeo's character and situation have been rendered in too human, or, dare one say, too realistic a manner to countenance the external device of the echo scene to suggest a reestablished concord between man and nature.

Orfeo endeavors one last display of his art, a "last praise" of Euridice with which he will "sanctify my lyre and song." His music shifts from recitative to a short-breathed but mellifluous arioso that serves as a final requiem for Euridice.

You were beautiful and wise. In you reposed
all the graces of courteous heaven
while giving to all others too little.

Every praise from every tongue becomes you,
who housed in a beautiful body a soul more beautiful,
the more worthy of honor, being without haughtiness.

The plangent melody, broken by rests, is the last trace of lyricism Orfeo can produce. It is simple and poignant, recalling an arioso melody heard near the end of "Possente spirto" as Orfeo pleaded with Caronte, "O de le luci mie luci serene." This haunting melodic fragment expresses complete exhaustion. The concluding lines of his monologue reveal that Orfeo's grief has pushed him past the breaking point. The music now shifts back to recitative and to G major as Orfeo begins a neurotic attack against womankind.

Striggio's words subtly hint at Orpheus's shift to homosexuality as recorded in Ovid and Virgil. More important in the context of the opera's theme is the tone of startlingly violent aggression. These misogynistic lyrics, with their coarse rhythms and blunt declamation, represent Orfeo's ultimate rejection of life and the life affirmation of the sexual drive itself. As is Euridice in fact, he is now metaphorically wedded to death. His words having degenerated into irrational rant, he resorts once more to his lyre for a final attempt at musical sublimation. The ancient mythographer Hyginus supplies the inspiration for the opera's conclusion. After mentioning Orpheus's violent death at the hands of angry Bacchantes—a fate hinted at in the 1607 libretto— Hyginus laconically reports that "the Muses gathered the scattered limbs and gave them burial, and as the greatest favor they could confer, they put as a memorial his lyre, pictured with stars, among the constellations. Apollo and Jove consented, for Orpheus had praised Apollo highly and Jupiter granted this favor to his daughter [Orpheus's mother, the Muse Calliope]" (Hyginus, *Poetica Astronomica,* 2.7, in *The Myths of Hyginus,* trans. Mary Grant, 191; see chap. 2 for a discussion of the controversy over the Bacchantic ending of the published libretto of 1607 vs. the Apollonian closure of the published score of 1609). This prosaic text belies the lyrical and theatrical power of *L'Orfeo*'s climactic sequence.

The "lyre" sinfonia heard twice in act 3 before and after "Possente spirto" is intoned by the stringed instruments. Perhaps Orfeo's last resort, now that hope and poetry have seemingly failed him, is instrumental music. After Orfeo's unlyrical tirade, the sinfonia works as a balm upon the audience's senses and signals the arrival of Orfeo's father, Apollon. Dionysus's more temperate brother, Apollo was the god of intellect, light, and music, one of the consolations of human sorrow. The sinfonia also serves the practical purpose of helping to mask the noise of Apollon's descent from the space over the stage singing "in a cloud" ("Apollo descende in una nuvola cantando," notes the score). This simple, economic linkage of necessary mechanical stage business with profound poetic suggestiveness reveals Monteverdi as a born musical dramatist. It is the same effortless fusion of spiritual meaning and hard-headed practical acumen that is evident to anyone who stages a Shakespeare play in the theater.

Like father, like son: Apollon is a tenor. As in the Renaissance *intermedi* tradition, this Olympian would probably have represented the Mantuan duke sponsoring the performance. In simple, graceful recitative Apollon lovingly chastises his son. "It's not the counsel of a great heart to be the servant of one's own passion." Orfeo needs to heed Apollon's warning to avoid looming disaster and win "fame and life." The composer chose to color only four operative words in this nine-verse speech: "figlio" (son), sung to a lovely cadence of C–B-flat; "aita" (help), "ascolta" (listen), and "lode" (fame) are similarly accented. Orfeo is suitably rebuked by his father's appearance and offers to obey his father's "command" (imponi), the one word whose delicate elaboration gives the cadenced end to the recitative. In response, Apollon delivers a reiteration of the self-conscious neoclassical moral Striggio's text had asserted at the end of act 4. "Too much you rejoiced at your happy fortune, now you weep too much at your bitter fate." Apollon invites his son to join him in heaven, singing "come with me to heaven" (vientene meco al ciel) to a stepwise ascending line of recitative that will inaugurate Orfeo's final journey, not to the Inferno but to the heavens. "Shall I never see again the sweet eyes of my beloved?" Orfeo asks.

Apollon's response offers only cold comfort: "In the sun and the stars you will see her beautiful semblance." The sentiment expressed by the god is the purest Neoplatonism. Solomon observes of the libretto:

> The conclusion . . . is cosmically, philosophically perfect. A chosen man who has experienced the sweetness and bitterness of a single lifetime yearns for spiritual happiness by overcoming death. Because he has been earnest and virtuous in his quest, he is escorted by his divine father in an ascent to the permanent celestial bliss of joy and peace. . . . Beauty is a required aspect of the ascent to God because it is the visual attraction that allures us to desire and pursue it. The higher the ascent, the greater the beauty, until the soul reaches the Idea of Beauty which God/the Good emits. . . . By gazing at the beauty of Euridice, Orfeo's soul will be able to contemplate God/the Good. Whereas he once before was restricted completely from looking backwards towards "bella Euridice" just to revive her and restore her to mere earthly existence, he can now look upwards in the heavens to make his soul immortal. Euridice is, symbolically speaking, the "celeste bellezza" referred to at the end of act 4. (37–39)

Orfeo consents to follow his father to heaven. The two tenors—one the god of music, the other, his son, the greatest of all singers—ascend together in a duet that joins their voices together in florid, virtuosic divisions. In the *intermedi* tradition florid singing had stood as the most important musical signpost for representing divine characters. Orfeo's voice is now fused with that of his father in coloratura (rapid ornamentation) that sets the seal on his apotheosis. The score directs that they "ascend to heaven singing." Their elaborate ornamentations on "saliam" (let us ascend) cue the slow ascent of Apollon's cloud back to the heavens.

> Let us ascend, singing, to heaven
> where true victory has
> its worthy prize, delight and peace.

The two take turns delivering soloistic divisions to "saliam" (let us ascend) and "cantando" (singing), suggesting their equal abilities as singers. Apollon initiates the duet just as he renders the first coloratura to "saliam" and "cantando." The duet ends as both father and son make their exit into the heavens singing florid decorations to the word "diletto" (delight) in the phrase "delight and peace." Orfeo and his father leave the opera in this somber G minor duet, Orfeo's final act of musical sublimation and self-abnegation. The music is less personal than any he has yet sung. It is formal, like its verbal sentiments, and has more the feel of religious music than a passage from an opera. *L'Orfeo*'s premiere was as part of courtly Carnival celebrations. The Carnival season was "traditionally a period of pre-Lent celebration and contemplation," as Carter notes (*Monteverdi's Musical Theater* 115). The emotional rhythm of the opera, charting a course from death to ascension, is easy to associate with Christian traditions, despite its pagan veneer. But there is an equally compelling pagan resonance in this happy ending as the suffering hero ascends from the bitterest grief to divine status. The influence of Sophoclean tragedy could be felt earlier in the libretto, and now the reader may recall the hero's final transcendence in *Oedipus at Colonus.*

The G major ritornello and chorus of nymphs and shepherds makes a sharp, almost jolting contrast to Orfeo and Apollon's august exit. The jaunty ritornello tune that introduces the chorus's song is similar to the pastoral festivities of the first two acts and is scored for the instruments associated there with the pastoral world. Its insistent syncopation, coupled with the wishful moralizing of the chorus that Orfeo is "now completely happy," resembles the "Ecco Orfeo" chorus at the close of act 1. This reminiscence of the earlier act's tone and spirit is an obvious attempt to give a formal closure to the act, binding it with the beginning of the opera. It is also a masterstroke of musical and dramatic irony. Striggio's words may suggest the transfigured sorrow of the closing moments of *Oedipus at Colonus,* but Monteverdi's music does not attempt to sculpt a similar catharsis (see also Davies 40). The consolation of the neoclassic *lieto fino* (happy end) that brings the opera to its close satisfies the dictates of seventeenth-century Italian aesthetic form but does not satisfactorily resolve the tragic emotions *L'Orfeo* has produced. The Neoplatonic "poetic justice" of a transfigured Orfeo gazing at the "semblance" of Euridice points with surprising sophistication to the unbridgeable gulf between life and death, to art's need to embrace and impose form on the terrors of existence, and, like Orfeo's underworld endeavor, to the paradoxical triumph in failure of the whole human and artistic endeavor.

The chorus's second stanza proclaims, "So he receives grace from heaven who tasted the Inferno down here, and he who sows in sorrow will gather the fruit of every grace." The opera's need for an acceptable formal close—which convention dictated must be happy—clashes with the tragic emotions Monteverdi has created with such unprecedented skill. *L'Orfeo*'s final moments are dominated by jubilant dance music, just as the first two acts were. The courtly tradition prescribed a closing dance for a final *intermezzo,* often a moresca (see Fenlon, "Origins" 23; Arnold, *Monteverdi* 104). The moresca that closes *L'Orfeo* requires frenetic dancing from the nymphs and shepherds, whose comparatively generic responses to the dramatic situation clash pointedly with the profoundly personal music that had been given to Orfeo. This concluding sequence represents a rupture between the Renaissance's humanistic certainties and the growing perception of the individual soul's experience of pain and isolation. The closing dance recalls the jigs danced at the close of Shakespeare's tragedies in the contemporary English theater—a kind of "satyrs' dance" full of wild and grotesque movement, which imparts a Dionysian joy (and violence) to the conclusion of Monteverdi's great tragedy, with its seemingly happy end. The comparatively impersonal moresca asserts by its microcosmic choreography an image of the macrocosmos of creation. The moresca eases the Mantuan audience—and all their successors over the centuries—back into the everyday world, just as the toccata had led them into another realm some two hours before. The toccata and the moresca unite courtly reality with operatic illusion.

The First Lost Opera and Other Works for Mantua

L'Arianna

The February 24, 1607, premiere of *L'Orfeo* was an enormous success, but the composer had little time to savor it. His wife, Claudia, was becoming seriously ill. Monteverdi took her with him to his hometown of Cremona in July so she could recuperate while the couple visited with his father. However, Claudia died in Cremona on September 10, 1607. Unlike his father, the composer would never remarry. Within two weeks the grieving husband was ordered back to Mantua to create another opera as well as a *ballo* and a prologue for a set of *intermedi* for Guarini's play *L'idropica,* all music to celebrate the marriage of Francesco Gonzaga, heir to the throne, and Margherita of Savoy. The widowed father with two small sons now was being called upon to provide festive music for someone else's wedding only days after burying his own wife. The planned wedding festivity performances sought to expand upon the success of *L'Orfeo* at the same time it served as an overt advertisement for Mantuan power and prestige. The marriage between the Gonzaga heir and a member of the house of Savoy represented a great political coup: it was an alliance that would neutralize any military threat to Mantua's possessions from the Savoyard princes (Leopold 184). In the best of times Monteverdi was unhappy in his Mantuan position. He had complained justifiably that he was underpaid, overworked, and severely underappreciated. A reassuring letter dated September 24, 1607, from his friend Federico Follino, the court chronicler, may well have steeled the composer's heart for renewed efforts for the Gonzaga family:

> I do not know how to dissemble nor am I a flatterer, so please
> believe me that I have seen in the eyes of the prince and I have
> heard from his voice such things in praise of your genius that I
> have good, even excellent hopes for you; I believe that in the past
> you have known me to be affectionate, even most affectionate to
> my friends, and in particular to you yourself in such matters; so
> accept my advice, which is to forget now all these troubles, to
> return here and quickly, since this is the time to acquire the great-
> est fame which a man may have on earth and all the gratitude of
> the Most Serene Prince. (Qtd. in Arnold, *Monteverdi* 17)

Although Follino's prediction of princely gratitude never fully
panned out in the years to come, his prophecy of coming fame proved
to be on target. Monteverdi's execution of the wedding projects would
make him the most famous composer in Italy. Soon Monteverdi was
back in Mantua, busily working on his second opera, *L'Arianna,* with
a libretto by Rinuccini. The Mantuan court was tapping even deeper
into the Florentine heritage of operatic experiment. In February 1608,
as Monteverdi was completing his second opera, Gagliano presented
his new opera, *Dafne,* at the Mantuan court. Gagliano had made his
own setting of Rinuccini's revised text, which in its original form had
served Peri at the beginning of operatic history only ten years before.
Gagliano's nymphs and shepherds recall Monteverdi's opera of the preceding year with their tuneful bounce. There is also an interesting echo
scene between the shepherds and an offstage Apollo. Gagliano's compact
work is attractive and entertaining but utterly lacks *L'Orfeo*'s humanity.

The royal wedding was scheduled for May 1608. Monteverdi no
doubt channeled his grief into his necessarily rapid work. He must also
have proudly anticipated the success Caterina Martinelli would enjoy
as Arianna. Still in her late teens, Martinelli had lived and trained in
the Monteverdi household as a vocal protégé. She was a brilliantly talented young woman with whom the duke was much taken and to whom
the composer must have had a deep emotional bond. Since the new
opera was not connected to the all-male academy that had sponsored
L'Orfeo, wedding guests would be allowed to see men *and* women in
Monteverdi's new opera, and the composer took this opportunity to
develop opera's first great heroine for Martinelli to sing. But tragedy

struck again when she died of smallpox on March 9, a great personal and professional blow to the composer. Martinelli's replacement came from within the assembled troupes of performers. Virginia Ramponi Andreini was an actress in a theater company called the Fedeli that was rehearsing the Guarini play. Ramponi Andreini went by the stage name "La Florinda" following her success in a tragedy of that name written by her husband, the company manager, Giovan Battista Andreini. La Florinda rescued the opera, learning the large title role in only six days.

May 28, 1608, saw the premiere of Monteverdi's second opera, *L'Arianna*. *L'Arianna* was presented in a temporary theater built for the purpose on one side of the Prato di Castello, with a capacity for some five thousand spectators. The stage machines required "more than three hundred men" to operate them (contemporary, qtd. in Pirrotta 256). This was a far cry from the chamber-opera staging of *L'Orfeo* the year before. Contemporary accounts praise the lavish costuming and staging and the effectiveness of placing the musical instruments "disposed behind the scene" (see Fabbri, *Monteverdi* 86). One witness wrote: "All of the beautifully dressed singers did their job very well, best of all though, Arianna, the commedia dell'arte actress; . . . and in her *lamento in musica,* which was accompanied by viols and violins, she brought many people to tears with her misfortune. A singer by the name of Rasi also appeared, who sang divinely; but compared to the part of Arianna, the castrati and the others appeared to be nothing." It is interesting to note the reappearance of Francesco Rasi, presumably singing the role of Teseo, after his success as Orfeo the previous year. The poet Giovan Battista Marino joined other contemporary witnesses in praising La Florinda's operatic debut: "In such a way you heard Florinda, O [Mantua], / There in the theaters of your royal roofs / Unfold the harsh torments of Arianna / And draw from a thousand hearts a thousand sighs" (qtd. in Leopold 12; Fabbri, *Monteverdi* 83). After the drag casting of castrati necessary at *L'Orfeo*'s premiere, Monteverdi must have relished creating a female role for a real female performer to sing. The musical and dramatic honesty must have meant much to the composer—as it did to the audience member quoted above. Rinuccini's libretto was published for the 1608 premiere, but all that remains of Monteverdi's music is the famous "Lamento d'Arianna," published as a bleeding chunk in 1623. The libretto and the account of the performance by Follino, the court chronicler, give us some tantalizing glimpses of the lost whole.

L'Arianna portrays the love of Arianna (Ariadne) for Teseo (Theseus), the notorious womanizing adventurer of Greek myth. Teseo abandons Arianna on the island of Naxos, leaving her to vent her grief, fear, and sense of betrayal in her powerful lament. The opera ends happily when the god Bacchus arrives to whisk Arianna off to immortality as his bride. The story line alone suggests that *L'Arianna* was very much a companion work to *L'Orfeo* in its tale of love lost and a divine intervention bringing transformation and immortality to the afflicted lover. Gagliano remarked that "Signor Monteverdi, the most famous musician, . . . composed the arias in so exquisite a manner that we can affirm in all truth that the power of ancient music has been restored [*che si rinovasse il pregio dell'antica musica*] because they visibly moved the whole audience to tears." Such praise from a Florentine competitor indicates the growth of Monteverdi's reputation in the operatic medium and represents "the first time that an outsider had compared Monteverdi's music to the music of Ancient Greece" (qtd. in Schrade 236).

Follino published descriptions of the performances for the political purpose of disseminating something of the court spectacle to the thousands who had no hope of witnessing such dynastic splendor. His words convey the excitement of the opera's premiere.

> There was present at this performance princes, princesses, ambassadors, . . . ladies . . . and that greatest number of foreign gentlemen that the theater could seat, which, although it has a capacity of six thousand and more persons . . . was not able to contain all those foreigners who sought to enter. . . . [*L'Arianna*] was very beautiful in itself, and for the characters who took part, dressed in clothes no less appropriate than splendid, and for the scenery, which represented a wild rocky place in the midst of the waves, which in the furthest part of the prospect could be seen always in motion, giving a charming effect. But . . . to this was joined the force of the music by Signor Claudio Monteverdi . . . who in this work proved to excel himself, combining with the union of voices

the harmony of the instruments, disposed behind the scene, which
always accompanied the voices, and as the mood of the music
changed, so was the sound of the instruments varied . . . [and] in
the lament which Arianna sings on the rock when she has been
abandoned by Theseus, which was acted with so much emotion
and in so piteous a way that no one hearing it was left unmoved,
there was not one lady who did not shed some little tear at her
beautiful plaint. (Qtd. in Fabbri, *Monteverdi* 85–86)

L'Orfeo had been courtly chamber opera. *L'Arianna* exposed
Monteverdi to opera as an entertainment for a large audience, perhaps
the largest that had ever attended the new art form (Leopold 130).
Like *L'Orfeo, L'Arianna* would have been performed without an interval. The disappearance of the score of *L'Arianna* was the first of the
losses that would befall the majority of Monteverdi's operatic projects,
one made all the more tragic because the work was one of immense
importance to the composer. He revived and revised the opera for the
Venetian public opera in 1639 as a way of easing himself into activity
in the newly emerging commercial operatic theater. The lament, shorn
of the choral interjections that punctuated it in the complete opera,
was published in 1623. A contemporary observed that *Arianna* "was so
appreciated that there has been no house which, having harpsichords
or theorbos therein, did not have its lament" (Bonini, qtd. in Fabbri,
Monteverdi 98). Monteverdi's *Sixth Book of Madrigals* (1614) would
include a five-voice madrigal version of the lament. In his old age he
would adapt the solo version to a religious context as "Pianto della
Madonna sopra al Lamento del'Arianna" (Lament of the Madonna Based
on the Lament of Arianna): with a Latin text, Arianna becomes the
Virgin lamenting her dead Son. Monteverdi made this unlikely revision
the pièce de résistance of his last publication during his lifetime, the
Selva morale e spirituale (1641), a compendium of his religious works
for St. Mark's basilica. At least we have these versions of the lament,
which Monteverdi called "the most essential part of the work" (letter
from the composer, March 20 or 21, 1620). In a letter dated October
22, 1633, Monteverdi attaches even more importance to the lament,
viewing it as one of, if not the single most important milestone in his
stylistic development.

I found out in practice that when I was about to compose "the Lament of Arianna"—finding no book that could show me the natural way of imitation, not even one that would explain what an imitator ought to be (other than in Plato, in one of his shafts of wisdom, but so hidden that I could hardly discern from afar with my feeble sight what little he showed me)—I found out (let me tell you) what hard work I had to do in order to achieve the little I did do in the way of imitation. (Stevens, *Letters* 410) 1633

At the time of Monteverdi's death in 1643, the "Lamento d'Arianna" would figure as the only work mentioned by name in *Fiori poetici,* a published funerary tribute: "Who has the strength to hold back tears when he hears the just lament of the unfortunate Arianna?" (qtd. in Leopold 128). Shorn of its original operatic context, the lament is featured in modern concerts and recordings, proving its ability to move audiences. The "Arianna" lament relates to Monteverdi's life's work in a way analogous to the *Tristan und Isolde* "Prelude and Liebestod" in Wagner's corpus some 250 years later. Both passages by Monteverdi and Wagner, performed apart from their surrounding operatic contexts, became emblematic of their creators' discovery of new expressive frontiers for the musical articulation of emotion, especially erotic longing.

The lament depicts Arianna's tortured reaction when she discovers she has been abandoned on Naxos by her feckless lover, Teseo. In the original opera her great monologue was broken up by the sympathetic comments of a chorus of fishermen. The lament embodies a moment of powerful recognition on the heroine's part. Its range and depth of expression is easily comparable to that of some of Shakespeare's most searching soliloquies. It was set "just before dawn, that characteristic period of introspection where things untenable and inexpressible in the harsh light of day may be given voice" (Carter, *Monteverdi's Musical Theater* 209). The first phrase sung by Arianna, "Lasciatemi morire" (Let me die), will form a refrain heard twice in the first section of the piece, an arioso built out of an unforgettable chromatic stab of pain. "Let me die!" Arianna sings. "How can I be consoled in so harsh a fate, in so grievous a torment?" These questions are sung to recitative that breaks the speech into breathy bursts of language and tone. Again she sings the "Lasciatemi morire" arioso, signaling the climax of her initial shocked realization that she has been abandoned. This anguished phrase is immediately contrasted by a new, even briefer arioso, "O Teseo, o Teseo mio," heard four times throughout the lament, suggesting her still-tender feelings for her betrayer. These two refrains stand for Arianna's violently contrasting emotions. Arnold remarks that "Monteverdi has no compunction about repeating words (the repetitions are already present in Rinuccini's verse), and right from the start he uses this to create balanced phrases and a natural development of the melody as melody not just declamation" (Arnold, *Monteverdi* 104–5).

Arianna begins to plead in recitative, "Turn back, Teseo—O God!—Turn back and look again at her who left her homeland and kingdom for you, and who upon these shores will leave her bones as prey to desperate and cruel beasts!" The "O Teseo, o Teseo mio" arioso sounds again. The next recitative passage highlights Arianna's words with great poignancy. Music's ability to contrast joyful and sorrowful ideas through pulse and turn of melodic phrase is utilized to the full as Arianna contrasts Teseo's happy voyage and welcome back to Athens and his parents' arms with her own weeping, physical danger, and desolation. She contrasts Teseo's happy state with her misery in three balanced pairs of verbal comparisons. "With serene breezes you are happily on your way [*rest*] and I am weeping [*rest*]. For you Athens prepares joyful, splendid celebrations [*rest*], while I remain, food for animals on a solitary shore [*rest*]. You will happily embrace both of your two old parents [*rest*], and I will never see—oh, Mother, oh, Father mine!" The music illustrating Teseo's situation forms an upwardly moving, lyrical melodic sigh. The words describing her misery droop painfully in their musical setting. The reference to her parents brings this act of comparison to a climax, the iterations of "oh" set to emotionally piercing ascending notes.

From these stark contrasts Arianna's voice rises in mounting indignation as she wonders, "Are these the diadems you placed upon my brow [*rest*]? Are these the sceptters [*rest*], the jewels, and golden ornaments? To leave me, abandoned to animals who will devour me?" The emotional pendulum swings back for a brief return of the "O Teseo, o Teseo mio" arioso. But this return of tender feeling brings her again to despair, and from despair to a building rage. "Will you leave me to die, weeping in vain [*rest*], in vain crying for help [*rest*], the miserable

Arianna [*rest*] who put her trust in you [*rest*] and gave you fame [*rest*] and life?" The now swiftly moving recitative gives violent coloration to "O thunderclouds, whirlwinds, and gales, thrust him beneath those waves. Rush, sea monsters and whales, and fill the chasms of the deep with his corrupt limbs!" Leopold writes: "Arianna's dammed-up feelings overflow with a torrent of the shortest declamatory note values, forced out in a tempo that can hardly be understood. This is the place in the lament which comes closest to the aesthetics of *Sprechgesang*" (132–33). *Sprechgesang* (a German term meaning, literally, "speech-song") emerged at the turn of the twentieth century to denote vocal declamation that was halfway between speech and song. Schoenberg notably used this device in such works as *Pierrot lunaire.* Another critic writes: "Arianna's anger is musically irrational in every possible way; her word rhythm is unpredictable; her phrasing loses all sense of poetic lines; the falling minor third motive on which she has called Teseo's name becomes the motive by which she calls storms and tempests to drown him; nonsensically her melody peaks at the image '*voragini pro-fonde*' ('deep caverns'), contradicting the conventions of word painting" (Cusick 32). But Arianna's rage is over as soon as it has been expressed. Pauses indicate a return of her loving, trusting nature, making her torment all the more poignant. "What am I saying?" she asks in more temperate recitative; "Ah, what is this raving? Miserable me, what am I asking for?" This leads to a final iteration of "O Teseo, o Teseo mio," followed by "wretched woman, I still harbor hope betrayed, and still the fire of love burns unquenched by contempt." The lament ends in recitative in which Arianna calls on the listening chorus, and by association the audience itself—"faithful friends" (fidi amici) all—to behold her as a paradigm of betrayed love: "See [*rest*] what grief has been given to me as an inheritance by my love [*rest*], my faith [*rest*], and the one who betrayed me! That is the way it stands for one who loved and trusted too much." This final sentence, "Così va chi troppo ama e troppo crede," is set to a sinking line that brings the lament to a fitting close.

The grandeur of Monteverdi's Arianna, the first great operatic heroine, rests in the composer's ability to reflect the wildly shifting, contradictory feelings within the character's psyche. It is no wonder the passage so moved its first audiences, nor that it loomed so large in the composer's own esteem. Nothing in *L'Orfeo* equals the emotional range of Rinuccini's text and the varied, expressive audacity of Monteverdi's setting. More than in any other early opera, the music "revealed what could only be felt between the lines" (Leopold 130–31). Perhaps only Penelope's lament at the start of *Ulisse* and Ottavia's "A Dio, Roma" in *Poppea* will create anything comparable in effect.

Without the surrounding operatic context, the lament can still give only a glimpse of what excited audiences in 1608. The work paradoxically assumes more of its full theatrical stature, however, when it is heard in the five-voice version of the *Sixth Book of Madrigals*. Although the idea of such a personal utterance being given to a small vocal ensemble seems ludicrous in theory, Monteverdi's setting, with its richer texture and contrapuntal overlapping, asserts the work's highly charged emotionalism. Monteverdi allows the five singers to "become" Arianna, the voice of suffering humanity itself. A monodic theatrical work is made into contrapuntal concert music and consequently enjoys the best of both worlds. The dramatic tension created by the interaction of the five voices articulates a personal expression that digs deeper into the heart of human suffering than even the best of *L'Orfeo*'s music. After *L'Arianna,* most early Italian opera would include a lament, sometimes several.

Il ballo delle ingrate

Monteverdi's triumph with *L'Arianna* is all the more remarkable when one realizes that the opera was only the largest of his contributions to the court wedding celebrations. Monteverdi and Rinuccini were also responsible for the prologue to Guarini's comedy *L'idropica* (the music is now lost) and, more important, *Il ballo delle ingrate,* performed on June 4, 1608, only a week after the opera. *Il ballo delle ingrate* (The Dance of the Ungrateful Ladies), like *L'Arianna,* was to enjoy fame far outside of Mantua and found a place of honor in the exceptionally heterogeneous *Eighth Book of Madrigals* (1638). This published score shows evidence of textual and musical revision during the 1620s or 1630s for an intended or realized revival in Vienna. Rinuccini's original textual references to the Mantuan court have been changed to Viennese and Habsburg corollaries. Monteverdi was then cultivating Habsburg patronage, owing to the marriage of Eleonora Gonzaga to the Austrian emperor Ferdinand II in 1622. Their court in Vienna became a haven for Italian musicians and performers, including the Fedeli company, which had performed in the 1608 Mantuan festivities and probably restaged *Il ballo,* in slightly altered form, for the imperial court. Although *Il ballo* is not an opera like *L'Arianna* or *L'Orfeo,* its obvious theatrical elements warrant an overview here. *Il ballo* affords an example of a comparatively weak though decorous text inspiring music of almost inappropriately tragic depth.

Balli were courtly performances that, like the *intermedi,* required singing, dancing, and spectacle, performed to flatter the noble person who sponsored them. Originating in the court of France, the *balli* were freestanding works with a relatively strong narrative (see Fenlon, "Origins" 16). Rinuccini had been in France several times between 1600 and 1604 as a courtier attending Maria de' Medici and had absorbed something of this performative tradition. The *balli* usually included passages where the courtly patrons themselves were encouraged to dance, penetrating the boundary between the stage illusion and the spectators. The theme and practice of dancing in courtly entertainment held powerful political resonance between earthly authority and order and the cosmic dance of the spheres (see Fenlon, "Origins" 16). The noble audience of a *ballo* or masque expected direct flattery, sumptuous costuming, and stage effects that impressed the eye and suggested the wealth and taste of the patron. (See Aercke for a wide-ranging exploration of these kinds of seventeenth-century courtly performances.) Monteverdi probably wrote many *balli* during his career, but *Il ballo delle ingrate* is the only major example to survive, along with the brief *Tirsi e Clori.* (The *Eighth Book of Madrigals* includes a minor work in this genre, "Volgendo il ciel per l'immortal sentiero," an "introduction to a *ballo.*")

Il ballo's plot focuses on the plight of ladies' souls who have been condemned to hell for "ungratefully" failing to consummate their relationships with their lovers. The theme of *ingrate* or "ungrateful lovers" was a familiar one often encountered in the madrigal texts of

Monteverdi and his contemporaries. Gordon notes: "While the fate of the ingrates, coupled with the moralizing commentary of the gods, shows what can befall those who do not love enough, Arianna's story [in the opera performed the previous week] demonstrates the perils of loving too much" (6). Venus (Venere), accompanied by her little son Cupid (Amore), pleads with Pluto (Plutone) before the gates of the Inferno to allow the souls of the ungrateful women to appear on earth as an object lesson for the theater audience. One critic writes that Venere's words, "addressed to the emerging *ingrate,* [describing] the splendor of the . . . court, which they are about to enter, . . . bridge the gap between their world and that of the court" (Chafe 160). Plutone orders them back to the underworld, and in *Il ballo*'s concluding sequence "one of the ungrateful souls" (una dell'ingrate) sings a solo lament, affording her the opportunity to stand in for all her "ungrateful" sisters. The moral of *Il ballo* is reminding court ladies, including the newlywed princess, to gratify their lovers. This work, with its none-too-subtle encouragement of promiscuity, would have been particularly attractive to the males of the Gonzaga family, a line noted for its womanizing. As so often in *ballo* or masque performances, the entire court is implicitly flattered for sponsoring a performance of self-conscious delicacy and learned classical allusions.

The work premiered in the permanent theater where *L'idropica* had been presented; it had been turned into a ballroom in front of the stage to allow for the expected social dancing after the performance. (See also Gordon. There is doubt that dancing preceded the performance; Carter, *Monteverdi's Musical Theater* 165.) The court chronicler, Follino, gives a vivid impression of the work's spectacular visual effect.

> The duke had decided to perform . . . a *balletto* of very beauti-
> ful invention, . . . in which the duke and the prince-groom par-
> ticipated, with six other knights and with eight ladies from the
> principal ones of the city in terms as much of nobility as of beauty
> and of grace in dancing, so that in all they reached the number
> sixteen. . . . Now when all were comfortably seated, the sign
> having been given with a frightening banging of discordant drums
> under the stage, the curtain was raised with . . . wondrous speed
> . . . and in the middle of the stage one saw the large mouth of a

wide and deep cavern, which, stretching beyond the confines of
the scene, seemed that it went so far beyond it that the human eye
could not reach to discern its end. That cavern was surrounded
within and around by burning fire, and in its darkest depths, in a
part very deep and distant from its mouth, one saw a great abyss
behind which there rotated balls of flames burning most brightly
and within which there were countless monsters of the inferno
so horrible and frightening that many did not have the courage
to look upon it. . . . In front of that fiery mouth . . ., where some
small misty and gloomy light shone, beautiful Venus . . . held her
beautiful son Amor by the hand, who, to the sound of sweetest instruments which were behind the stage, sang with a very
suave voice. . . . [Later, Follino reports,] Venus, turning to the
spectators and looking at the ladies who were before her, sang in
this manner: "Udite donne, udite!" (Listen, Ladies, listen!) (All
Follino's descriptions of *Il ballo* are taken from Fabbri, *Monteverdi*
89–92.)

Supple recitative declamation sets the initial dialogue between the
sopranos Amore and Venere before the gates of the Inferno. When
Amore pleads with his mother to "back up" (seconda) his pleas to the
king of the underworld, the word "seconda" is treated to a six-note
arabesque underscoring Amore's objective. Venere's motherly concern
is evident in her reassurance to her son that her voice "will not cease
its sweet flatteries and prayers until the wild spirit [*l'alma feroce*] of the
dread king yields to your desires." Venere indulges in delicate mimesis
as her voice colors "l'alma feroce" with notes from its lower range.
The audience may now hear the connection between the ominous,
fearful setting and the heavenly figures who stand expectantly before
it. Amore, protective of his mother, enters the infernal gates, while
Venere is left to address the audience in an arioso punctuated with
a solemn ritornello, which is a disguised prologue recalling Musica's
address in *L'Orfeo*. "Listen, ladies, listen! [*Udite, Donne, udite!*] These
wise words of heavenly speech keep in your heart [*nell cor serbate*]. She
who is an enemy of love will cruelly strengthen her heart in the flower
of her youth [*il cor nella fiorita*]." "Il cor nella fiorita" is treated to pictorial decoration. After the repeat of the ritornello, Venere continues:

"She will suffer burning [*arda*] and pain when she has lost her grace and beauty, and in vain will resort to tardy repentance and the false assistance of unguents [*acque*] and perfume." "Arda" receives an appropriately fiery, virtuosic decoration spanning nearly two measures, but the less dramatic "acque" balances the musical rhetoric with a six-note ornament that hints at a kind of musical tongue-in-cheek. These contrasting decorations of "arda" and "acque" reveal Monteverdi's awareness of the lightly satiric intent behind Rinuccini's words and dramatic situation, a lightness that the music will later subvert.

Plutone emerges from the Inferno accompanied by Amore. As in *L'Orfeo,* Plutone is cast as a bass. He indulges in mimetically appropriate and perhaps lightly comic explorations of his upper and lower vocal registers to project his sepulchral character when he refers to the "serene and pure" (sereno e puro) regions from which Venere has descended and "this dark abyss" (quest'abisso oscuro) where she now finds herself. Venere explains that she is accompanying her son on a mission to restore the potency of Amore's arrows. Plutone voices surprise and professional concern that so powerful a god's instruments are losing their effect. Venere explains that "there, in the German Empire [the Mantuan court, in Rinuccini's original text], the ladies are armed against Cupid's golden arrows" and treat his weapons "as a joke" (scherzo e gioco), words adorned with appropriately mocking decoration. Worthy lovers, from poets to warriors, are receiving mockery for their amorous pleas. Venere's music utilizes the soon-to-be-ubiquitous *stile concitato* (agitated style) when describing "the gentle warrior who in vain moves gracefully and proudly into the field of honor" (invan gentil guerriero move in campo d'honor, leggiadro e fiero). This passage almost certainly represents a revision by the composer either for the 1638 publication of the score or for a Viennese revival (Fenlon, "Origins" 18). The *concitato* style is found in the "warlike," agitated rhythm, considered by Monteverdi and his contemporaries to signify violent emotion in music. It will be discussed more fully in the following chapter.

Amore reveals his plan to Plutone. He asks that the "impious and cruel ladies" being punished in hell for their sins against courtship be brought briefly into the light once more. That way, "let every proud soul [at court] see the martyrdom destined for cruel beauty." Plutone is predictably affronted by such a breach of infernal etiquette but is won over at last by Venere's pleas. A new expressive depth begins to emerge in the music as Venere recalls her intervention in helping Plutone to meet Proserpina. "So you do not remember how I led the lovely Proserpina to gather flowers upon the mountain of eternal passion? For the sake of those noble joys, for the sake of those sweet loves, let the grieving shades appear on earth." Venere, like Orfeo in the opera from the preceding year, is using all her skills to win Plutone to her will. As in Orfeo's "Possente spirto," Venere's expressive music, here supplely molded arioso, supports her words, charming Plutone yet again to yield up souls under his dominion. The reference to Proserpina also naturally recalls the tender relationship between Plutone and his wife from the earlier opera. Venere's wish that "every soul . . . see displayed the punishment cruel beauty can expect" is gratified. Plutone sings, "Too, too powerfully, beautiful mother of Love, do the arrows [*strali*] of your prayers reach my heart!" Plutone's acquiescence is signaled in his elaborate melisma on "strali," an indication that with his help, Amore's arrows will soon be sharp again. Plutone orders the infernal shades to do his bidding and allow the *ingrate* to revisit the earth. Venere apostrophizes the *ingrate* as they are about to make their much-anticipated entrance with words linking the fictive world of *Il ballo* with the world of the audience: "It is not without delight that you will walk beneath the roof of these glorious kings!" She directs the still-offstage spirits to be sure to admire the "incredible works and marble sculptures of peerless artists." Venere is particularly proud of the theater's "superb [*superbe*] walls, resplendent with purple and gold." "Superbe" is treated to a wonderfully pompous ornamentation spanning several bars. Here the text of *Il ballo* flatters the patrons in the audience, who are told that they are sitting in "crowded theaters and stages that put to shame the Tiber and learned Athens!"

As the ungrateful women emerge from hell's mouth, Amore and Venere sing a duet tinged with a sorrowful chromatic character, "Here comes the sorrowful troupe" (Ecco ver noi l'addolorate squadre). This duet marks another musical heightening of *Il ballo*'s emotional temperature. Mother and son paint the moral of the *ingrate* to the noble audience: "You would have been happy if fate had let you be less cruel and harsh or less fair and beautiful!" Plutone bids Venere and Amore to "return to [their] blue heavens" as he orders the spirits of the *ingrate* to dance with him. An extended passage of instrumental music follows. The music for the ladies' entrance and dance, the *entrata* and the ensuing *ballo,* is a set of instrumental variations based on an unforgettably solemn tune, notable for its noble and mysteriously affecting sense of loss and nostalgia. This is some of Monteverdi's most affecting purely instrumental writing, creating an atmosphere of melancholy and otherworldliness. (The melody was borrowed and adapted by William Walton to create a passage of Renaissance pastiche in his film score for Laurence Olivier's *Richard III.*) The somber strings play as "with sorrowful gestures the ingrates begin to dance . . . solemnly, two by two, while Plutone remains in the center, moving with a natural, solemn walk." Such a stage image coupled with such music must have riveted and moved the courtly audience. The performance of the eight ungrateful women and their eight male escorts would have galvanized the attention of the entire audience, since the duke himself and his son played two of the escorts. Such princely participation deliberately blurred "the demarcation between fantasy and reality" (Leopold 187). The performance mixed courtly amateurs with professional musicians and singers in a way typical of both the *ballo* and masque traditions. Follino described the appearance of the *ingrate.*

> These condemned souls were dressed with garments in a very extravagant and beautiful style, which draped to the ground, made up of a rich cloth that was woven precisely for this effect. It was gray in color, mixed with most subtle threads of silver and gold with such artifice that to look upon it it seemed to be ashes mixed with flashing sparks; and thus one saw the dresses, and likewise the cloaks (which hung from their shoulders in a very bizarre manner), embroidered with many flames made of silk and gold, so well arranged that everyone judged that they were burning; and between the said flames, there could be seen scattered in most beautiful order garnets, rubies, and other jewels which resembled glowing coals. Their hair was also seen to be woven

with these jewels, which part cut short and part spread around
with wondrous art, seemed destroyed and burned; and although
it was all covered with ashes, nonetheless it showed between the
ash and the smoke a certain splendor, from which one could well
recognize that at another time they were blondest of blondes like
gold thread; and their faces, showing signs of a former beauty,
were changed and palled in such a way that they brought terror
and compassion together on looking upon them. They moved (but
with great grief indicated by gestures) two by two in a pleasing
descent from the stage, accompanying their steps with the sound
of a great number of instruments which played a melancholic and
plaintive dance tune; and having reached the floor of the theater,
they did a *balletto* so beautiful and delightful, with steps, movements, and actions now of grief and now of desperation, and now
with gestures of pity and now of scorn, sometimes embracing
each other as if they had tears of tenderness in their eyes, now
striking each other with rage and fury. They were seen from
time to time to abhor each other's sight and to flee each other in
frightened manners, and then to follow each other with threatening looks, coming to blows with each other, asking pardon and
a thousand other movements, represented with such affect and
with such naturalness that the hearts of the onlookers were left
so impressed that there was no one in that theater who did not
feel his heart move and be disturbed in a thousand ways at the
changing of their passions.

Although it fulfilled his obligations to create a picturesque masque,
Monteverdi's commitment to portraying the human condition led him
beyond the hollow courtly dalliance of Rinuccini's text. The plight of
the *ingrate* has become personalized. These ladies have become the
emblem not merely of a lover's frustrated sexual goals, but of the tragic
condition of humanity itself. *Il ballo* fascinates not so much as a relic
of a long-forgotten courtly tradition, but as a moving quasi-operatic
sketch suggesting the transience of human happiness, an anthem for
all lost human potential. This most decorative of courtly performative
traditions has now become, according to Follino, a site of Aristotelian
"terror and compassion." Follino again:

> After these *ingrate* had danced so much, that weaving among
> themselves in various ways they found themselves occupying the
> whole space of the floor, they stood still at a sign from Plutone
> (who was standing before the stage) in a group along it, eight on
> each side, and he, moving among them toward the princesses
> with great gravity, who were in view facing the stage, once he had
> approached them, full of horrid majesty he began to sing, accom-
> panied by instruments, in a very courteous manner the following
> verses: "Dal tenebroso orror del mio gran Regno. . . ."

"Don't be afraid, Ladies. I have not come from the dark horror of my
kingdom, burning with a new passion in order to steal a lady or a girl."
Plutone's remarks are frequently interrupted by a lively instrumental
ritornello. His address to the princess contains notable ornamentation
on words such as "lieto" (the "happy" face of the princess) and "monar-
chi e regi" (monarchs and kings), serving as a form of musical flattery.
His tone of deference to the earthly royalty before him allows him some
playful license with his decorations on "rapir." "I have not come here
to steal [*rapir*] a lady or girl" (à la Proserpina!). His ornaments also
reinforce the moral of the stage spectacle when he decorates the word
"sagge" (wise), remarking that "the unhappy ones" before us "grieve in
vain that they were not wise [*sagge*]." Plutone orders the *ingrate* back
to the Inferno—their dance on earth is at an end. The score directs,
"They return to the same music as their first entrance, with the same
movements and steps as before." Follino reports:

> Those Ingrates began another *balletto* with gestures full of greater
> desperation and of greater grief, and with a thousand interweav-
> ings and a thousand changes of effect they came, approaching the
> stage little by little, and mounting it in the same order in which
> they descended. When they were all on it, Plutone, with a voice
> of horror and of fear, said, singing: "Tornate al negro chiostro"
> [Return to the black cloister]. . . . Scarcely had Plutone spoken
> than one of the *ingrate,* who had stayed on the stage when the
> others descended to dance, burst forth in such tear-filled accents,
> accompanied by sighs and sobs, that there was no woman's heart in
> that theater that did not loose from their eyes some pitying tear.

The solo *ingrata,* first performed by Virginia Andreini, La Florinda, fresh from her triumph as Arianna, addresses the audience in "Ahi troppo, ahi troppo è duro": "Ah, it is too hard, too hard the cruel sentence, and more pain to come! To return to weep in the gloomy cavern! Clear, pure air, farewell for ever, farewell, O sky, O sun, farewell shimmering stars! Learn pity, matrons and maids." Sung to an arioso of wrenching pathos, this passage shocks the listener with its personal expression of anguish and loss. Arnold notes that the "dissonant broken arioso is given added point as [Monteverdi] contrasts it with the consonance and smoothness and simplicity of the 'serene and pure air' [*Aer sereno e puro, addio*] which now the *ingrate* must leave behind forever" (*Monteverdi* 106). The single *ingrata* is thus suddenly foregrounded like a Caravaggio saint in extremis. Her reiterated "Addio"s are set to a descending vocal line. "Learn pity, matrons and maids" (Apprendete pietà, donne e donzelle) becomes a refrain sung first by the solo *ingrata,* then echoed back by a chorus of four *ingrate* placed behind her. Just as the composer creates contrast between dissonance and consonance in the soloist's arioso, the dramatic shift in sonority between her solo voice with continuo accompaniment and the four-part chorus singing a capella startles the ear and deepens the expressive intensity. After this choral injunction, the soloist returns to compare the "smoke, groans, sighs, and eternal torments" of the Inferno with the *ingrate*'s lost "splendor" and troops of "lovers." Again the dissonant arioso shifts to exquisite consonance as she repeats, "Aer sereno e puro, addio." Again the refrain "Apprendete pietà, donne e donzelle" is shared by soloist and then a capella chorus, closing the work with the unmediated human voice. Chafe writes: "As in *Orfeo,* but far more directly, these final moments of the *Ballo delle ingrate* break the barrier between the drama and the courtly reality, a device that underscores the merging of dramatic action and moral that characterize the piece" (Chafe 160). Follino describes the final moments of the performance: "At the end of so beautiful a plaint they again entered the cave, but in such a manner that they seemed pushed by a lively force; no sooner were they swallowed up by it than, closing its great mouth, the scene remained with a beautiful and delightful view." The audience is left not with a tone of winking provocation, but instead with an unexpectedly stark expression of the fleeting nature of human life and opportunity and a surprisingly somber admonition to seize the day before we the audience find ourselves participating in Plutone's ballet. As so often in Monteverdi's work, his commitment to expressive truth has opened vistas that before him could scarcely have been imagined. Just as his style was rupturing the boundaries of conventional madrigal composition, in *Il ballo* this same expressive need has added unforeseen dimension to the courtly masque. Both genres, madrigal and *ballo,* seem ready to implode under the force of what we can now see as Monteverdi's fast-developing operatic style.

The hurried creation of *L'Arianna, Il ballo delle ingrate,* and the (lost) prologue for the Guarini play, coupled with the grief for his wife, took a serious toll on the composer. After the triumph of the wedding performances Monteverdi retreated once more to his father's home in Cremona, in a state of even more desperate exhaustion than before. Years later Monteverdi referred to himself as being at death's door during this period, and he was not exaggerating. In addition to suffering from exhaustion, Monteverdi was also angry and frustrated that the Gonzaga family had given him no extra money for his labors. Without his wife's income, the composer had been forced to take money from his father to support his Mantuan household. Monteverdi attempted to leave the duke's services but was cajoled back one last time by the promise of a significant raise and a pension. It was characteristic of Monteverdi's experience with the Gonzaga court that for the rest of his life he would have to wrangle for the money and pension promised him. In 1613 Monteverdi assumed his position as *maestro di capella* at St. Mark's basilica in Venice, free from the caprices of the Gonzaga family. The following chapter will examine some of his Venetian activities during the last phase of his career. As a Mantuan citizen, however, he continued to contribute music to his former patrons, especially operatic or semioperatic compositions. His new responsibilities in Venice necessitated correspondence with Mantuan courtiers, which has, thankfully, survived. These letters, often involving works that have been lost or were never completed, offer invaluable insight into Monteverdi's methods as a musical dramatist.

Tirsi e Clori and a Lost Comic Opera

Tirsi e Clori, a *ballo* on pastoral themes with text possibly written by
Striggio, is a brief but significant semioperatic work. It was written
for Mantuan performance in 1616, several years after Monteverdi had
moved to Venice. This new *ballo* was probably conceived as part of
the festivities marking the coronation of Duke Ferdinand. *Tirsi e Clori*
appears as the final work in the *Seventh Book of Madrigals* (1619). Barely
a third the length of *Il ballo delle ingrate, Tirsi e Clori* delights the ear
and eye with its opportunity for spirited dances. Indeed, the work is a
concise and exuberant ode to dance itself and the cosmic (and princely)
order it symbolizes. Tirsi and Clori are pastoral lovers, refugees, as it
were, from the first two acts of *L'Orfeo.* The "plot" of the *ballo* is simple:
Tirsi bids Clori to dance, and she acquiesces. On paper it is difficult to
disagree with Carter, who remarks that "the piece gives the impression
of just going through the motions" (*Monteverdi's Musical Theater* 160).
In a good performance, however, *Tirsi e Clori* emerges as a masterpiece
of concision, a true "apotheosis of the dance," to steal Wagner's famous
description of Beethoven's Seventh Symphony. The work's first section
comprises a meltingly lyrical dialogue between the two pastoral lovers.
They describe the dancing of their fellow shepherds and shepherdess
in gorgeous aria writing worthy of the pastoral sections of *L'Orfeo.*
"Only we are standing alone here," Clori observes. Tirsi picks up the
hint and with his "outstretched hand," surely an internal stage direction
for the *ballo* performers, invites her to to join them. The lovers sing
in duet, "Let us dance, and by our skill and our song extol the praises
of dancing." These words serve as the motto for this *ballo.* The chorus
now joins the lovers with the reiterated imperative "Balliamo" (Let us
dance), a bold, thrilling musical motto, foreshadowing the iterations
of "Cantiam" in the Bacchanalian scene between Nerone and Lucano
in *L'incoronazione di Poppea.* The remainder of the work is the *ballo*
proper, the singing and dancing of the pastoral characters. Their lyrics
take account of the whole Neoplatonic universe, from their flocks,
the winds, and the flowers on earth to the heavenly bodies above that
move "to the sound of the spheres." All things are engaged in a cosmic
dance, reflected in the catchy choral lyrics and lively accompaniment

that generates the dancing of the performers on stage. A letter dated
November 21, 1615, from the composer to a Mantuan courtier reveals
Monteverdi's keen interest in the staging of the new *ballo*.

> I would think it proper to perform [the *ballo*] in a half-moon, at
> whose corners should be placed a theorbo and a harpsichord, one
> [on] each side, one playing the bass for Clori and the other for
> Tirsi, each of them holding a theorbo, and playing and singing
> themselves to their own instruments and to the aforementioned.
> If there could be a harp instead of a theorbo for Clori that would
> be even better. Then having reached the ballet movement after
> they have sung a dialogue, there could be added to the ballet six
> more voices in order to make eight voices in all, eight viole da
> braccio, a contrabass, a spinetta arpata, and if there were also two
> small lutes, that would be fine. And directed with a beat suitable
> to the character of the melodies, avoiding over-excitement among
> the singers and players, and with the understanding of the ballet
> master, I hope that—sung in this way—it will not displease His
> Highness. Also, if you could let the singers and players see it for an
> hour before His Highness hears it, it would be a very good thing
> indeed. (Stevens, *Letters* 107–8)

Presumably the dancing took place either within the semicircle or
before it; it is unclear whether the performers he mentions took part
in the ballet itself. These directions reveal a concern not just with
dynamic variations in sonority, but also with the visual effect of what
might be called today a "semistaged" performance. It also indicates that
Monteverdi could imagine more voices and instruments being employed
than his score might indicate. As Whenham observes, "Music that may
appear quite thin on paper may in fact have been rich and colorful in
performance" ("Later Madrigals" 224). Such considerations must necessarily influence contemporary musicians as they prepare Monteverdi's
music for performance.

The year 1627 found the composer at work on the opera *La finta
pazza Licori* (The Phony Madwoman Licori), with a libretto by Giulio
Strozzi, commissioned by the Mantuan court. This opera is especially notable because it represents the first attempt at comic opera.
Unfortunately, the death of the duke necessitated the cancellation of the

opera, and the music—like so much of Monteverdi's operatic work—
has been lost. Many letters from the composer survive, however, that
give valuable insight into his thinking on this project. Most revealing
is the composer's discussion of the challenge he faces in creating the
music for the feigned madwoman, Licori. Monteverdi's concern with
the acting abilities of his projected performers is especially apparent.

> The part of Licori, because of the variety of moods, must not fall
> into the hands of a woman who cannot play first a man and then
> a woman, with lively gestures and different emotions. Therefore
> the imitation of this feigned madness deserving consideration
> (provided it is in the present, not in the past or future), it must
> consequently derive its support from the word, not from the sense
> of the phrase. So when she speaks of war she will have to imitate
> war; when of peace, peace; when of death, death, and so forth.
> And since the transformations take place in the shortest possible
> time, and the imitations as well—then whoever has to play this
> leading role, which moves us to laughter and to compassion, must
> be a woman capable of leaving aside all other imitations except
> the immediate one, which the word she utters will suggest to her.
> (Letter of May 7, 1627, in Stevens, *Letters* 315)

These comments shed light on Monteverdi's later setting of Iro's
final solo in *Il ritorno d'Ulisse* of 1640. The pointillistic, fragmented
style of word painting described here may be found in the monologue
in which that comic character descends into madness.

"Singing Speech" and the Demands of Opera

In 1616 Monteverdi was requested to compose dramatic music for a text
called *Le nozze di Tetide,* a "maritime fable" by Scipione Agnelli, for a
performance at the wedding of Duke Ferdinando Gonzaga and Caterina
de' Medici. This proposed project and Monteverdi's difficulties with
the material occasioned a famous letter from the composer in Venice
to his old friend and *L'Orfeo* collaborator Alessandro Striggio back in
Mantua. This letter, dated December 9, 1616, gives much insight into
Monteverdi's thoughts about composing for the theater and constitutes

one of the most revealing letters by any major composer about the process of operatic composition. The letter also suggests Monteverdi's sense of humor as well as his often surprising candor.

> If His Highness approves of this fable it ought therefore to be very beautiful and much to my taste. But if you add that I may speak my mind, I am bound to obey Your Lordship's instructions with all respect and promptness. . . . I have noticed that the interlocutors are winds, Cupids, little Zephyrs and Sirens; consequently many sopranos will be needed, and it can also be stated that the winds have to sing—that is, the Zephyrs and the Boreals. How, dear Sir, can I imitate the speech of the winds, if they do not speak? And how can I, by such means, move the passions? Arianna moved us because she was a woman, and similarly Orpheus because he was a man, not a wind. Music can suggest, without any words, the noise of winds and the bleating of sheep, the neighing of horses and so on and so forth; but it cannot imitate the speech of winds because no such thing exists. . . . And as to the story as a whole—as far as my no little ignorance is concerned—I do not feel that it moves me at all (moreover I find it hard to understand). . . . *Arianna* led me to a just lament, and *Orfeo* to a righteous prayer, but this fable leads me I don't know to what end. So what does Your Lordship want the music to be able to do?

If the duke does order the text set to music, Monteverdi suggests that each of the various prospective performers could compose his or her own music for it.

> Because if this were something that led to a single climax, like *Arianna* and *Orfeo,* you would certainly require a single [compositional] hand—that is, if it led to singing speech, and not (as this does) to spoken song. . . . Forgive me, dear Sir, if I have said too much; it was not to disparage anything, but through a desire to obey your orders. (Stevens, *Letters* 115–18)

Behind the deferential posturing suitable to his position as the servant of his former employers, Monteverdi reveals the deeply humanistic sensibility that governs his artistic choices and his courage to potentially curry disfavor with his honesty and commitment to his artistic convictions. Operatic art must move us by the humanity of its characters. The focus of musical drama, as Monteverdi sees it and as he demonstrated in *L'Orfeo* and *L'Arianna,* is the honest portrayal of the human condition. Empty gesture and excessive artifice (e.g., singing winds) are forbidden in Monteverdi's serious musical drama—unless, of course, the duke insists.... Monteverdi's distinction between "singing speech" (e.g., *Arianna* and *Orfeo*) and "spoken song" (which the text of *Le nozze di Tetide* requires) articulates the distinction between the highly demanding, largely unadorned recitative style that serves the human characters and a more elaborate compositional style suitable for deities—and for concealing a weak text. This 1616 letter ranks with those of Mozart, Verdi, and Richard Strauss in which these later masters reached a similarly clear-headed sense of theatrical truth in the operatic theater.

Monteverdi's problems with *Le nozze di Tetide* were resolved when he learned that the text was intended merely as a decorative *intermezzo,* not a full-fledged opera. Monteverdi happily went to work, but the performance was canceled, and the music, which had stimulated one of the most interesting documents in operatic history, has been lost.

5

"Contraries to Move the Mind"

Il combattimento di Tancredi e Clorinda and the Journey toward the Venetian Operas

The long period from *L'Arianna* to the final surviving operas contains the majority of the lost works. Nevertheless Monteverdi's madrigal compositions and letters, as well as the unclassifiable *Il combattimento di Tancredi e Clorinda,* offer a surprisingly vivid image of his developing style as a musical dramatist. In 1612 the dissolute Duke Vincenzo died, leaving a financially shaky state to his heir, Francesco. Francesco, in his brief reign, attempted to repair some of his predecessor's financial extravagance by dismissing many in Vincenzo's retinue. Monteverdi seems to have quarreled with the new duke and was dismissed from service. But Duke Francesco, the erstwhile proponent of *L'Orfeo,* quickly regretted firing Mantua's most illustrious musician and attempted to win Monteverdi back. Any chance of rapprochement was destroyed by Francesco's sudden death in an epidemic later that year. Monteverdi must have been concerned about his and his sons' future, yet it is difficult not to imagine that he saw his dismissal as at least a partial blessing, liberating him from the morass of drudgery, overwork, and broken promises that attended so much of his time serving the Gonzagas.

Monteverdi's long sojourn of personal hardship and artistic triumph came to a happy end when he was appointed *maestro di cappella* at Saint Mark's basilica in Venice on August 19, 1613. But his years of grief and frustration since his wife's death and the increasing aggravations in Mantua were marked by one last danger and indignity: as he was traveling to Venice in early October to assume his new post, he was attacked by highwaymen and robbed.

Upon reaching his new home, Monteverdi quickly settled into one of the most desirable and powerful musical posts in Italy. His compensation included lodging and a better and punctually paid salary. Also, there was opportunity for freelance work in Venice, and Monteverdi was often allowed to work on projects outside the city. Although he would occasionally consider returning to the life of a court musician, he appears to have been largely satisfied with his Venetian appointment. Like J. S. Bach a century later, Monteverdi was a disciplined choirmaster. The performance standards at the basilica had lapsed in recent years, and Monteverdi strove to restore the choir to its previous glory. Unlike Bach, however, Monteverdi was lucky to enjoy the appreciation of his employers, and his choristers recognized and appreciated his genius. Although the Gonzagas would long campaign to win him back to their court, Monteverdi remained loyal to his Venetian home and the dignity, respect, and rewards it offered for his services.

For all of his necessary concentration on religious music during his thirty years at Saint Mark's, Monteverdi remained dedicated to the madrigal. In 1614, a year into the Venetian appointment, he published his *Sixth Book of Madrigals,* his only madrigal book without a dedication. Tomlinson is surely right that this action must signify "Monteverdi's newfound independence from princely patrons" (Tomlinson, *Monteverdi* 151). In 1617 Monteverdi's father died. He had lived to see his son become the greatest composer of his era and to at last find a position of security and appreciation for his talent. As Claudio Monteverdi grew in fame as a composer and choir director in Venice, his own two sons developed into promising young men. Francesco joined the musical profession, despite his father's longing for him to enter law. Francesco became a singer at Saint Mark's in 1623, where he served until 1677. In addition to dabbling in composition, Francesco also participated in the very first public opera productions in Venice in the late 1630s. Massimiliano studied medicine in Bologna and practiced both in Mantua and in Venice.

Monteverdi's *Seventh Book of Madrigals* (1619) marks a radical break from the previous books. Banished forever is the five-voice madrigal of the Renaissance. The book offers a wide selection of formal and expressive possibilities. Monteverdi signaled this increasingly baroque spirit by christening the volume *Concerto: Settimo libro di madrigali* (here the term *concerto* denotes "ensemble music"). The Seventh Book is rich in accompanied vocal duets, wherein two singers of the same vocal range (sopranos, altos, or tenors) explore the pictorial and expressive possibilities of a body of poetry largely devoted to the more joyful aspects of amorous relationships. The tenor duet "Soave libertate" (Sweet freedom) is a setting of a poem by Chiabrera in which the lover wistfully laments the freedom he will lose in exchange for his new romantic engagement. The tenor "lovers" bid farewell (addio) to "their" former liberty with plaintive repetitions that foreshadow Nerone and Poppea's leave-taking by nearly a quarter of a century. The two so-called love letters in the Seventh Book, "Se i languidi miei sguardi" (If my languishing looks), described as "Lettera amorosa a voce sola in genere rappresentativo" (Love letter for solo voice in the representative [i.e., dramatic] style), and "Se pur destina: Partenza amorosa a voce sola" (If the heavens decree: Amorous parting for solo voice), serve as soloistic etudes in the still-new art of recitative writing. Opera production was still the preserve of the Italian courts, and such demonstrations of the effect of recitative declamation would have been of keen interest to Venetian listeners in the 1610s. Monteverdi returns in the Seventh Book to courting princely favor—and the Mantuan moneys still owed him—by dedicating the opus to Caterina de' Medici, duchess of Mantua.

Il combattimento di Tancredi e Clorinda

Monteverdi gave his Venetian admirers another, far more significant taste of the *stile rappresentativo* in 1624 when his setting of *Il combattimento di Tancredi e Clorinda* (The Combat of Tancredi and Clorinda) was premiered in a semistaged performance in the palace of the Venetian patrician Girolamo Mocenigo, one of the composer's patrons. *Il combattimento* is a setting of passages from the twelfth canto of Tasso's Renaissance epic *Gerusalemme liberata* (The Liberation of Jerusalem). First published in 1581, Tasso's classic inspired many operas during the following two centuries, including, by way of Voltaire's dramatic adaptation, Rossini's first great opera seria, *Tancredi*. The story of *Il combattimento* involves Clorinda and Tancredi, a Saracen woman and Christian soldier who fall in love during the First Crusade (1099). Monteverdi's work opens with Clorinda dressed as a man in full armor, battling for her people, when she is confronted by the armed Tancredi. The lovers do not recognize each other. As night falls they battle savagely. They rest momentarily out of sheer exhaustion, but soon their chivalric vaunts compel them back into the most brutal fighting until Clorinda receives a mortal wound. She asks to be baptized before her death. Suddenly full of pity for his fallen "foe," Tancredi removes his opponent's helmet and discovers Clorinda, who dies peacefully by his side.

The singing parts are taken by a soprano and two tenors in the roles of Clorinda, Tancredi, and the Testo (narrator). The scoring is for a small string ensemble of soprano, alto, tenor, and bass viola da braccio with a contrabasso da gamba and harpsichord continuo. A musicologist notes that "the string parts were written out by Monteverdi for the first time in a complete, continuous quartet texture which embodied many original directions for performance [i.e., the first use of string tremolo and pizzicato]. It was the birth of the modern string quartet score and of the violin technique of a new age!" (Redlich 107). The work would be published fourteen years later in the *Eighth Book of Madrigals*. Monteverdi's Venetian friends and admirers were doubtlessly curious to see and hear for themselves what Monteverdi had created in the way of operatic drama for his former Mantuan patrons. Without an operatic theater of their own until the late 1630s, curious Venetians could briefly glimpse something of the new style of musical drama in *Il combattimento*. It is a demonstration piece by baroque music's master realist, displaying a striking range of musical mimetic devices. The tenor narrator has the lion's share of the work's declamation, Tancredi's and Clorinda's parts being quite small. For all its brevity, *Il combattimento* is a remarkably complete musical-dramatic work containing, as Carter notes, "all the elements that a good Aristotelian would call tragic—peripeteia (reversal), catastrophe and purgation—while, as Testo notes, ... Tancredi exhibits the pride that conventionally leads to a tragic fall" (*Monteverdi's Musical Theater* 189).

The published score gives an evocative description of the first performance in 1624. Monteverdi writes:

> It was performed in the palace of the most illustrious and most excellent Signor Girolamo Mocenigo, my particular lord, with all refinement, given that he is a knight of excellent and delicate taste, and in carnival time as an evening pastime in the presence of all the nobility, which remained moved by the emotion of compassion in such a way as almost to let forth tears; and [the audience] applauded it for being a song of a kind never before seen or heard. (Qtd. in Fabbri, *Monteverdi* 188–89)

Monteverdi had first set poetry of Tasso in his *Third Book of Madrigals.* In early-seventeenth-century Italy, Tasso's *Gerusalemme liberata* was viewed as one of the greatest works of literature. The epic articulates powerful oppositions between West and East, between Christianity and Islam, and between men and women—and, especially in the section set in *Il combattimento,* the mysterious connection perceived during the Renaissance between sexuality and death, between lovemaking and warfare. In this work the composer sought to discover new avenues of musical expression. Having already explored the means for portraying more tender emotions, Monteverdi found in Tasso's epic an excellent vehicle to express the most violent of feelings and experiences. In the preface to the *Eighth Book of Madrigals* the composer wrote:

> I have reflected that the different passions or affections of our mind are three, namely, anger, moderation, and humility or supplication; so the best philosophers declare, and the very nature of our voice indicates this in having high, low, and middle registers. The art of music also points clearly to these three in its terms "agitated," "soft," and "moderate" [*concitato, molle, temperato*]. In all the work of [earlier] composers I have indeed found examples of the "soft" and the "moderate," but never of the "agitated," a genus nevertheless described by Plato in the third book of his [*Republic*] in these words: "Take that Harmony that would fittingly imitate the utterances and the accents of a brave man who is engaged in warfare." And since I was aware that it is contraries which greatly move our mind, and that this is the purpose which all good music should have—as Boethius asserts, saying "Musicam nobis esse coniunctam, mores, vel honestare, vel evertere" [Music is related

to us, and either ennobles or corrupts the character]—for this reason I have applied myself with no small diligence and toil to rediscover this genus.

After reflecting that according to all the best philosophers the fast pyrrhic measure was used for lively and warlike dances, and the slow spondaic measure for their opposites, I considered the semibreve, and proposed that a single semibreve could correspond to one spondaic beat; when this was reduced to sixteen semiquavers, struck one after the other, and combined with words expressing anger and disdain, I recognized in this brief sample a resemblance to the passion which I sought. . . . To obtain a better proof, I took the divine Tasso, as a poet who expresses with the greatest propriety and naturalness the qualities which he wishes to describe, and selected his description of the combat of Tancredi and Clorinda as an opportunity of describing in music contrary passions, namely, warfare and entreaty and death. (Qtd. in Fabbri, *Monteverdi* 239–40)

Monteverdi alludes in this passage to his love for musical contrast, which has always figured in his music but will become more and more pronounced in his later works as a formerly Renaissance aesthetic becomes more baroque. Perhaps the nearest contemporary tradition to which this utterly original work conforms is that of the *abbattimenti,* a specific genre of Renaissance *intermedi* that featured "an engagement between armed warriors, often stylized with musical accompaniment" (Pirrotta 289). Monteverdi's still-powerful connection to Renaissance thinking is also evident in his earnest search for guidelines in ancient philosophy. With *Il combattimento* Monteverdi believed he had created "a style indispensable to music and without which music is in truth imperfect, possessing only two styles, the sweet and the tempered" (Pirrotta 289). This *stile concitato* or "agitated style" informs much of *Il combattimento.* The composer believed that he had at last found the musical means to express all of human emotion, even its most violent aspects. *Il combattimento* is consequently one of the most notable and extreme examples of the baroque aesthetic in music. Monteverdi's ruthless mimetic impulse is unsettling in its ability to involve the audience in the heat of battle and the sorrow of Clorinda's death. Chafe reflects: "The *stile concitato* might even be viewed as an emblem of human assertiveness, of a positive viewpoint on anger that seems almost to anticipate the emphases of modern psychology. . . . At its worst it depicts the ungovernable violence of Nero, who, in his confrontation with Seneca in *L'incoronazione di Poppea,* generates several different manifestations of the style" (239–40).

Monteverdi's skill as a showman is evident in his description of the 1624 premiere:

> [*Il combattimento*] is intended to be done in the representative genre [i.e., scenic production. Therefore its performers should] enter unexpectedly, after some madrigals without action have been sung, from the side of the room in which the music is performed, Clorinda fully armed and on foot, followed by Tancredi also armed but on horseback, and the Testo will immediately begin singing. They will perform steps and gestures in the way expressed by the oration, nothing more or less, carefully observing tempo, beat and steps, and the instruments should sound excited or soft, and the Testo delivering the words in measure, in such a way that they create a unified interpretation. Clorinda will speak when appropriate, the Testo silent; and similarly Tancredi. The instruments . . . should be played in imitation of passions of the oration. The voice of the Testo should be clear, firm and with good delivery, somewhat distanced from the instruments, so that the oration may be better understood. (Pirrotta 188)

Fabbri imagines that in this "hybrid" work

> it would seem that at the Palazzo Mocenigo the musicians were placed in a room apart from that which contained the [audience]. . . . With the instrumentalists hidden from the audience, only Tancredi and Clorinda offered themselves to view, plus the Testo, whose voice was kept "somewhat distanced from the instruments, so that the oration may be better understood." And the entrance of these characters "unexpectedly, after some madrigals without action have been sung" must have had a significant effect on the guests, who were certainly not expecting the surprise that "the Testo will then begin the singing." (Fabbri, *Monteverdi* 190)

The magnificent chamber where *Il combattimento* premiered may still be seen today in the Mocenigo Palace. What "unexpectedly" walked into that room on a Carnival evening of 1624 was a new-minted musical audacity that, as Caravaggio's paintings had done in the visual arts some years before, pushed the limits of acceptable musical expression of human action and emotion. Its stark power remains palpable to this day. *Il combattimento* defies classification; it appropriates musical and dramatic devices from the worlds of opera, madrigal, pantomime, and the epic tradition. Leopold calls it "a Janus-headed" work that "in some of its details is among the most innovative of [Monteverdi's] compositions" (196).

Some modern performances of *Il combattimento* incorporate sinfonias from other contemporaneous works to introduce the piece. Monteverdi's score begins abruptly with the Testo's first words, plunging directly into the action, surely the composer's goal at that 1624 premiere. The Testo drives the work, standing "outside the field of dramatic action, like the evangelist in the Baroque Passion" (Redlich 107), and his declamation literally animates Tancredi and Clorinda. His opening words have an incantatory effect, establishing the subject matter for the startled audience: "Tancredi, believing Clorinda to be a man, decides she is worthy to challenge." The string quartet unexpectedly launches a steady, striding motif that, the Testo implies, represents Clorinda's "going round the mountain peak" before the fateful confrontation. This image established, the strings next depict the trot of Tancredi's horse, moving ever more rapidly toward the armored woman. "He follows impetuously," the Testo sings, his recitation interrupted by quickening bursts of "riding" music from the instrumentalists. Music has become sound effect, as the illusion of the clattering of horse and armor in the instrumental ensemble alerts Clorinda to his approach. "She hears the noise of armor sound, of armor sound, of armor sound," sings the Testo, the repetitions compelling the audience to recognize the blatant musical mimesis in operation. The next surprise occurs within seconds as both Clorinda and Tancredi, who have been pantomiming the actions the Testo describes, find their own voices in brief recitative exchanges. After a "slow, warlike passage" (passagio bellicoso grave) that pits blocks of instrumental writing against passages of narration, beautifully suggesting the slow build toward combat between the erstwhile lovers, a lovely sinfonia interrupts the declamation and action. This creates an unexpected moment of retro-spection. From the very heat of battle the music boldly arrests narrative time in its tracks, the musical equivalent of cinema's freeze-frame. This instrumental passage forms a ritornello framing the Testo's retrospec-tive, choric remarks, set in haunting arioso, which remind us that the story we are seeing and hearing is from the distant past, a heroic act fit for epic recitation and remembrance. This moment of unexpected stillness is emblematic of the entire work and its complex mixture of tone and effect. Monteverdi's eclectic setting—part cantata, part opera, part pantomime—allows the actors to be viewed from a number of perspectives: it is both a historical moment being described from a temporal distance and a gripping incident occurring directly before our eyes. A listener is reminded of Bach's similar temporal awareness in his *St. Matthew Passion*. The Testo's role intensifies the action, yet also serves as a distancing device between the audience and the struggling lovers, whose own vocal music takes a back seat to the requirements they must fulfill in pantomiming the action.

The Testo sings some of the most lyrical music in the work to evoke the nocturnal setting of the combat in the section beginning "Night" (Notte): "Night, who has enclosed [*chiudesti*] in your deep, dark breast, a hidden deed so great; since works so memorable are worthy of the light of day, and of a crowded theater, grant that I may illuminate them thus. . . . Long live their fame, and may their glory shine out from your darkness, noble memory [*l'alta memoria*]." The two phrases enclosed here in brackets are granted florid melismas, particularly "l'alta memo-ria." These ornaments help to slow the pulse of the arioso even further, making the resumption of the battle scene all the more effective. Again the Testo's solo expository declamation intermingles with instrumental patterns of increasing excitation as Tancredi and Clorinda enact their struggle before our eyes. The great crashes depicted by the strings and keyboard when the lovers abandon all chivalric decorum as their rage builds and the contorted patter singing of the Testo are still shocking in their vividness. In 1624 these effects must have seemed as violent as those of Stravinsky's *Rite of Spring* when it was new. Monteverdi the showman is evident in the setting of the Testo's words "Odi le spade" (Hear the swords). Carter observes, "Testo directly addresses the audience" with these words, "followed one bar later by representations of clashing weapons in the strings, whereupon Testo pointedly repeats 'Odi, odi le spade'; here Testo seems to speak less as Testo than as the composer himself, doubtless to the audience's delight" (*Monteverdi's Musical Theater* 191–92).

During the height of the battle the instruments are directed to shift volume from *piano* to *forte,* creating innovative contrasts in dynamics that would soon become a familiar element of baroque and classical orchestral technique. Monteverdi directs that when the Testo sings the words "they strike with their pommels and, more cruelly, with their helmets together and their shields," the strings are to be plucked pizzicato—the first Italian use of this device in published music. Leopold pointedly observes that for the composer, "it was a theatrical, a dramatic idea which led to these innovations" (195).

The new musical depiction of violence and rage is but one aspect of *Il combattimento.* Monteverdi's music allows the erotic subtext of the situation to insinuate itself, especially in the suggestive passage "Thrice does the knight grasp the woman in his strong arms, and just as often does she break from his retentive grasp, the embrace of fierce enmity and not of love." The words are set to an arioso that underscores the sexual subtext. Just seconds after the pizzicato passage, the string players are directed, "Qui si ripigna l'arco" (Here resume playing with the bow), creating a warm, supportive texture reminiscent of an amorous madrigal. Another energetic burst of instrumental combat leads to a vivid depiction of the fighters' exhaustion. Limping five-note patterns sound between brief, breathless interjections by the Testo: "[They] are tired . . . and panting." Tancredi preens before his weaker opponent as the two fighters stop to regain their breath. The Testo, in his choric role, declaims against humanity's capacity for self-delusion: "Oh, our folly, that refuses every offering of Fortune! Poor man, what joy is this? . . . Those eyes of yours—if you survive—will pay for her blood with a sea of tears." Tancredi tries to get Clorinda to reveal her name. Instead she lets him know that it was she who helped to "set the great tower ablaze." This incites Tancredi to even more furious attack. The ensuing passage is marked simply "Guerra" (Fighting). Again the instruments play passages of rapid figuration contrasted by *piano* and *forte* markings.

But this time the violence is short-lived, for Tancredi deals Clorinda a fatal wound. References to her "weakness" and "staggering" are sung to a drooping note pattern. The Testo describes her now "failing voice" with successions of static notes, depicting the effects of shock on the wounded woman. In a broken arioso passage she sings, "Friend [*rest*], you have won [*rest*]; I forgive you [*rest*], you forgive me too." These words are accompanied by the strings playing a panting phrase requiring a decrescendo—the first use of such a device for instruments rather than for the voice. The effect is that of a slowing heartbeat. The dying Clorinda asks Tancredi to baptize her.

The Testo depicts Tancredi's moment of recognition after he has removed his fallen opponent's helmet to reveal Clorinda. "The sight, the sight [*rest*] and the recognition [*one measure rest*]! He stands [*rest*], without voice [*rest*], motionless" (La vide e la conobbe e restò senza e voce e moto). The rapid declamation with the horrified repetition of "la vide" slows into a deathly vocal monotone. The decrescendo of Clorinda's string accompaniment has transferred itself into the Testo's vocal line. The music for the dying Clorinda evokes an uncanny sense of calm and religious ecstasy. The work ends with the soprano giving voice to her character's dying thoughts: "The gates of heaven are open; I go in peace" (S'apre il ciel; io vado in pace). The vocal line and its string accompaniment gently expire into a silence all the more profound for the tumult that has preceded it.

Il combattimento reveals Monteverdi's fearless pursuit of expressive truth, which still resonates with the shock of the new. It demonstrates his ever-expanding ambition to dramatize the human condition through music. Tasso's text enabled him to portray the widest range of emotions, from rage, to love, to horror, to religious exaltation, within a compact twenty minutes of performance time. It would be another fifteen years before the Venetians would become fully acquainted with Monteverdi not as a church musician and madrigal composer but as the master of musical drama in the theater. As a performative genre, *Il combattimento* represents a "stylistic dead end. . . . Monteverdi, as so often, used the experience gained to good advantage in another context"—that is, the later operas (Arnold, *Monteverdi* 108). The last word on this unique work should be given to Chafe, who notes that it has always provoked, and perhaps will always provoke, disagreement on the score of its artistic quality, all such viewpoints reducing in the final analysis to the acceptance or lack of acceptance of its highly descriptive nature. . . . For [Monteverdi] an artwork was in some respects more an experience than an object, profoundly the opposite position from the one that has come to dominate modern musicological writings. . . . [*Il combattimento*] holds the aesthetic issue of representational and autonomous forms before our eyes, teaching us to value art that moves and provokes rather than standing as an object of reverence. (245–46)

Monteverdi's Last Decade

The dawn of the 1630s brought the trauma of war and plague to northern Italy. In 1630 Mantua was plundered by Austrian troops in the War of Mantuan Succession. Many unpublished Monteverdi manuscripts were probably lost forever in the ensuing conflagration. The troops brought with them plague, which soon spread to other cities. Among the victims was Alessandro Striggio, the *L'Orfeo* librettist who had remained Monteverdi's closest friend from the Mantua years. The composer's brother Giulio Cesare Monteverdi died of the sickness around 1630. Soon plague would devastate Claudio Monteverdi's current home, lasting over a year and killing nearly fifty thousand people, roughly a third of Venice's population. It is impossible to know how these horrors effected the aging composer or whether they were part of the spiritual journey that led him to take up holy orders in 1631 and become a priest the following year. Like J. S. Bach's, Monteverdi's later years suggest the composer felt a need to consolidate his life's work in the areas of the secular madrigal, religious works, and opera. In 1632 the *Scherzi musicali* was published, a collection of madrigals that included the tenor duet chaconne "Zefiro torna," one of Monteverdi's most beloved compositions. In 1638 he would crown his secular compositional career with the publication of his last and largest collection, the *Eighth Book of Madrigals,* subtitled by the composer *Madrigals of Love and War*

(*Madrigali guerrieri et amorosi*). The Eighth Book was dedicated to the Habsburg emperor Ferdinand III. It contains many of Monteverdi's most sublime creations in the madrigal form, including such masterpieces as "Or che 'l ciel e la terra," "Mentre vaga angioletta," "Vago augelletto," and "Lamento della ninfa." It also preserves *Il combattimento di Tancredi e Clorinda* as well as the 1608 *Ballo delle ingrate*.

Among the madrigals of the Eighth Book, the "Lamento della ninfa," described by the composer as "a little theatrical work," represents an interesting creation from the perspective of Monteverdi's operatic style. It is a setting of a poem by Rinuccini, opera's first librettist and Monteverdi's collaborator for the 1608 festivities. A narrative voice describes a "nymph's" lamenting for a faithless lover, a description that is sandwiched around the woman's direct speech. Monteverdi creates a miniature musical-dramatic masterpiece: three male singers represent a kind of Greek chorus, setting the scene and interjecting their observations, as the solo soprano, unambiguously cast as the nymph, sings of her grief, oblivious to the men's presence. It is interesting to compare Monteverdi's musical dramatization of Rinuccini's poem with his earlier transformation of "T'amo mia vita" in the *Fifth Book of Madrigals.* In the "Lamento della ninfa," the singers' roles are even more explicit without the more conventional depersonalizing passages of contrapuntal madrigalisms found at the close of the earlier work. In this later madrigal the singers seem to occupy imaginary upstage and downstage spaces. Monteverdi creates another archetypal lament to rival that of Arianna, yet the musical effect is quite different. The nymph's actual lament, "Amor, dov'è la fè che il traditor giurò?" (Love, where is the faith the traitor swore?), is an aria sung over a ground bass in the continuo, interrupted frequently by the chorus. The tension between the ostinato ground bass and the high female voice floating its mournful arabesques above, with the discreet comments of the chorus, sometimes in unison, sometimes soloistically, closely shadowing the ground bass, creates a five-minute work that contains more drama than many a full-fledged opera. The contrast of freedom versus inexorable rigidity, expressed in soloistic versus unison singing, serves to build a musical scene of extraordinary tension that foreshadows the emotional power and musical concision (but not the volume) of the "Miserere" sequence in Verdi's *Il trovatore,* a work more than two hundred years in the future. During the seventeenth century the "Lamento della ninfa" would serve as a potent model for many operatic laments set to an ostinato (repeating-pattern) bass (see also Bianconi, *Music in the Seventeenth Century* 213–15).

Yet another ambitious publication, the *Selva morale e spirituale,* a collection of religious works for Saint Mark's, appeared in 1641. The Eighth Book and the *Selva* would seem by themselves to form an appropriate capstone for Monteverdi's career. But 1639–40 was the beginning of an Indian summer for Monteverdi the opera composer. In the years since *L'Orfeo* and *L'Arianna,* opera had made significant inroads into many of the Italian courts. By 1637 opera would establish itself in Monteverdi's Venice.

Il corago

Before its arrival in Venice, opera performance was beginning to acquire many of the features associated with the genre today. An anonymous handwritten treatise has survived from the late 1620s or early 1630s that gives evidence of the increasing sophistication with which courtly operas could be mounted in the years just before its professionalization. *Il corago* is a manual designed to give instruction in the art of stage direction for spoken and sung drama. Modern scholars attribute the work to Pierfrancesco Rinuccini (1592–1657), the son of the Florentine poet and librettist Ottavio Rinuccini. The word *corago* is an adaptation of the Greek word *coragos,* which referred to a wealthy producer of fifth-century Athenian tragedy. The Italian term signifies almost everything from the modern stage director to the impresario. The author of *Il corago* was well aware of the exigencies of operatic acting. It is heartening to discover that so many of opera's familiar elements were already being discussed and debated during its earliest years. The text offers invaluable insight into early-seventeenth-century Italian musical theater in the years immediately preceding Monteverdi's late operas.

The singer must accompany the song with gestures fitting the variety of emotions in the same way as does the simple actor. . . . Since acting in music moves at a slower pace than spoken acting, it is necessary that gesture likewise move more slowly, so that the hand does not stop before the voice. . . . Broad gestures are in order. . . . Singing must stop briefly at every break in the sense, and the player may sometimes stop as well. Sometimes he may linger on the same note, and at others play a particular and distinct music—provided singer and player have rehearsed thoroughly together in advance. . . . Words must be uttered distinctly, the last syllables in particular, because hearing only the voice and the change in vowels, not the distinct articulation of the syllables, much offends the ears of the listeners. . . . From time to time the singing should be broken up by walking, at which point there should be instrumental music, the musician either making a suitable ritornello or playing other notes, or at least gracefully arpeggiating on the same note. . . . To be a good actor-singer, one should above all be a good speaking actor. . . . It is sometimes asked whether one should cast a tolerable musician who is a perfect actor or an excellent musician with little or no talent for acting. . . . Just as some few connoisseurs of music have in the main appreciated excellent singers however cold their acting, so common spectators have found most satisfaction in perfect actors with mediocre voice and musical skill. Meanwhile, the musical director who has to allocate the parts and get the best out of everyone at his disposal will, as far as possible, make sure to cast the excellent but weak and aged singers in roles which are not very active and which are surrounded by stage trappings such as clouds and other airborne machines, where there is little call for movement or the striking of histrionic poses.

Il corago offers fascinating advice for dealing with some of the contraptions and problems peculiar to the early baroque operatic stage.

When it comes to singing on a machine, it is essential that it manifest itself or move only very slowly while the singer is acting, so as not to trouble him. This is especially the case because of the jolts that sometimes occur, but also because it is not proper to hold forth earnestly while being moved through the air. . . . [The *corago*] must take care as far as he can that none of the actors or other stage personnel lean out of the perspectives because—apart from the ugly sight they make—they may hinder the movements of the *periaktoi* and cause many other mishaps. However, this may be a very difficult thing to achieve, since the late Grand Duke Cosimo [? de' Medici, d. 1621] was only able to do it by keeping two dwarfs who would shoot with crossbows at anyone leaning out. (Excerpts from *Il corago* in Fabbri and Pompilio; translated in Savage and Sansone 500–2, 504–5)

Opera Comes to Venice

Ideas like those found in *Il corago* would have been familiar to the singer and composer Francesco Manelli (1595?–1667), the leader of a troupe of itinerant Roman operatic musicians. After successful performances in Padua, Manelli's troupe was invited to Venice to perform opera at Teatro San Cassiano under the sponsorship of the patrician Tron family. The premiere of Manelli's (now lost) *L'Andromeda* took place on March 6, 1637, to enormous acclaim, and his company was encouraged to settle in Venice. Within only a few years Venice could boast of four separate commercial opera houses, all owned by patrician families and offering performances for a wide cross-section of the paying public. Modern commercial opera was born.

Venice, an enlightened oligarchy, perceived itself as the liberal antithesis of the largely repressive regimes controlling much of Italy and Europe. According to legend, the city was founded by the refugees of the crumbling Roman Empire, and Venice linked its model constitution and its political ethos not with the decadent empire but with the Roman Republic. In fact, some seventeenth-century Venetians saw the corrupt Roman Empire as a metaphor for the current Vatican. Unlike the Mantuan or Florentine court, Venice elected its duke, or doge. Venice had its own version of nobility: the ruling patrician families, self-ennobled members of the merchant classes. These families—for example, the Trons and the Grimaldis—sought additional wealth and status by investing in the burgeoning operatic industry. Bokina observes: "Like the absolutist princes who produced court operas, the various noble families regarded their opera houses as expressions of their splendor and power. But unlike the princes, individual Venetian aristocrats could not afford to underwrite the entire expense of staging opera; their financial limitations required that Venetian opera become a commercial venture" (24). The Venetian Carnival was the context for the operatic seasons, a period of approximately six to ten weeks beginning December 26 and extending to Mardi Gras (the day before the beginning of Lent). During Carnival, Venetians would don masks, enjoying the liberating blurring of class and all other forms of workaday social hierarchy. Carnival time marked the height of the tourist season, ensuring that opera could draw on a truly wide cross-section of Venetians and outsiders for its audience base. One of the greatest strengths of the emerging Venetian opera tradition was the inherently democratic nature of its audience. The cheapest admission fee was half a scudo, which almost any Venetian could afford (Worsthorne 6). Simply buying a ticket could put a gondolier on the same plane as a nobleman. Rosand observes: "The significance of this varied audience cannot be overestimated. It was responsible for the breadth of opera in Venice and the range of its appeal" (Rosand, *Opera* 2). Audiences were bound together, whatever their social rank, by their shared experiences within these theaters, theaters that maintained an atmosphere of intimacy between the spectators and the performers.

Since the mid-1500s, indoor theaters had been built in Italy for the phenomenally popular commedia dell'arte, the spoken improvisational comedies involving such stock characters as Arlecchino and Columbina. These commedia theaters were the buildings the Venetian aristocratic patrons adapted to house the new operatic productions. Soon purpose-built opera houses such as the Grimaldi family's Teatro Santi Giovanni e Paolo (1639) were constructed. The patrician theater-owning families delegated responsibility for the actual running of the operatic productions to an impresario, who was contracted seasonally. The impresario was responsible for hiring all the rest of the necessary artists and staff, and he paid the bills and salaries out of the proceeds from ticket sales. During the early years of Venetian opera, the impresarios discovered that large profits could be made from the rental of private boxes to aristocratic families, the possession of which was seen as a status symbol. Rented boxes quickly became homes away from home for hundreds of Venetians and were passed on to the children of operagoers as a form of inherited property. These boxes ("snug [compartments], holding about three persons in front" and sometimes including "a little withdrawing room behind each box") afforded a semiprivate space. They encouraged "casual yet habitual operagoing," which quickly fostered a well-developed taste for the new art form (Worsthorne 11–12). The public opera house became the unrivaled center for entertainment and intrigue in Venetian society. The model of "the Italian opera house," with its boxes, pit, and gallery, would inspire theater architecture for centuries. These structures were successful in accommodating a large audience within a relatively restricted area by placing many spectators within the walls of the theater building.

A report from an English visitor in 1645 suggests something of the texture of Venetian operagoing in these early years, especially the great importance of stage spectacle and the presence of women on the stage.

> This night, having with my Lord Bruce taken our places before, we went to the Opera where comedies and other plays are represented in recitative music by the most excellent musicians vocal and instrumental, with a variety of scenes painted and contrived with no less art of perspective, and machines for flying in the aire, and other wonderful motions; taken together it is one of the most magnificent and expensive diversions the wit of men can invent. The history was Hercules in Lydia, the scenes changed thirteen times. The famous voices, Anna Rencia [Anna Renzi, opera's first prima donna and creator of the role of Ottavia in Monteverdi's *Poppea*], a Roman, and reputed the best treble of women; but there was an eunuch who in my opinion surpassed her; also a Genoeze that sang an incomparable bass. This held us by the eyes and ears till two in the morning. (From the *Memoirs of John Evelyn*, qtd. in Worsthorne 32)

Women's presence on the Venetian operatic stages would greatly enrich the medium. Their onstage partnerships with male singers encouraged the extraordinary eroticism found in both Cavalli's and

Monteverdi's works. The presence of the castrati, as well as the medium's love for a spectrum of cross-dressing—all proscribed, of course, by the church—added a sense of forbidden allure. Males sometimes dressed as females, females as males, suggesting works of exuberantly open sexuality and helping to establish a cult of sexual ambiguity that would dominate opera until the end of the baroque era (see also Rosselli, *Singers of Italian Opera* 58). Acting ability was of enormous importance for Venetian opera. A French traveler in the 1630s noted the particular strength of Italian opera singers. "They do their best to portray the passions and emotions of the soul and the mind—anger, fury, rage, madness, heartache, etc., etc.,—with a vehemence so unusual that they almost appear to be actually experiencing the feelings they depict as they sing" (Marin Mersenne, qtd. in Celletti 22).

Along with hiring the best singers from all over Italy, the Venetian impresarios spared no expense in securing the finest designers in order to thrill the audience with all the magic that baroque theater could create. The Venetian opera house in the early seventeenth century was the site for some of the most ambitious experimentation in the history of scenography. The new public opera houses featured many of the flamboyant devices developed in court theaters and *intermedi* performances, such as flying characters and deities and heroes in "glory," that is, hovering on artificial clouds made of wood. Trap doors assisted singers and actors in their quick, "magical" disappearances and reappearances. Designers such as Giacomo Torelli made the operatic theaters they worked for more and more spectacular. In the 1640s Torelli invented a system for changing whole sets within a matter of seconds. Sets would appear and disappear without visible human intervention. Such innovations created "the illusion of a world in mutation. No longer merely a backdrop or setting, the scenery actively participated in the drama, changing with, and as part of the action" (Rosand, *Opera* 106; see also Ferrero, "Stage and Set" 50). Innovations like those of Torelli and his competitors would influence stagecraft well into the nineteenth century.

The impresarios gave significant attention not only to their singers and designers, but also to their librettists. The librettist, or "l'auttore," as he was referred to in Venice, would often print his libretto to help the audience follow the performance as well as to assert his claim to works of genuine literary merit. This is a considerably different attitude to libretto composition than anything that would be encountered until the time of Wagner. It was the librettists, not the composers, whose names were associated with the operas they helped create. The composer was regarded more as a "service professional" in the rapid-growth industry that was seventeenth-century Venetian opera (see Rosand, *Opera* 209–10). *Dramma per musica* (drama for music) was the term for the libretto, and this implicit privileging of the verbal text must always be borne in mind when experiencing operas of this era. For Monteverdi and his colleagues, opera was primarily a form of theater in which music served to convey and enhance the dramatic thrust of the story being presented. For all of Venice's anti-Roman attitudes, several aspects of Roman operatic dramaturgy entered the Venetian tradition through Manelli's troupe. Like Roman operas of the 1620s and 1630s, Venetian operas would experiment with mixing comedic and serious elements. The tragicomic nature of Italian libretti in the seventeenth century would lead to the genre's eventual designation as *opera* or "work" (Pirrotta 355). The stock characters of commedia dell'arte infiltrated Roman and later Venetian opera. Emulating Spanish Golden Age playwrights such as Lope de Vega, Venetian librettists would blend aristocratic and plebeian elements and the idea of the confidant, as well as male and female comic characters, usually servants. The Italian taste for the happy ending or *lieto fine* found reinforcement in the non-tragic denouements encountered in many of Lope's dramas (see also Celletti 19–20). The new Venetian opera librettists would seek to follow the ancient Roman poet and critic Horace's formula for art uniting "delight" (deletto) with "usefulness" or "edification" (utile). The Roman taste for religious subjects, however, never caught on in Venice. Neither did the Roman tradition of all-male opera companies, necessitated by the papal ban on female performers. Female roles in Roman opera were played by castrati in drag. Although castrati were an important part of Venetian opera, women were vital to its commercial appeal.

With the attention and financial resources lavished on singers and stage machinery, the public opera houses could not afford the relatively large instrumental ensembles which the Mantuan court utilized for

L'Orfeo. In Venetian opera houses the band was extremely small, consisting primarily of a large continuo ensemble—several harpsichords and theorbos—along with at least two violins. Occasionally a few more instruments might be added, but the Venetian theaters of Monteverdi's time never hired an ensemble that could be called a chamber orchestra in any modern sense. The number of accompanimental musicians would probably seldom if ever have risen above ten. These players were usually positioned in front of the stage action. The surviving manuscripts of Venetian opera scores clearly reflect these performance conditions. The manuscripts of *Ulisse* and *Poppea* contain complete vocal music, but the instrumental accompaniment is usually restricted to a mere indication of chords, the basso continuo. The copyists assumed the instrumentalists knew how to accompany singers and generate sensitive improvisation to fill out the bare bones of the score. Both *Ulisse* and *Poppea* feature sinfonias and ritornelli written in three- to five-part textures, without directions for instrumentation. These more elaborate instrumental passages lend dramatic point to the stage action, gaining emphasis by contrast with the more minimalist accompanimental texture. In the Venetian operatic theater the audience's focus is firmly trained on the singer-actors and the stage action. Just as financial constraints limited the number of instrumentalists, Venetian opera seldom calls for much activity by a chorus, so when required it would have been made up of any singers not otherwise engaged in the action at that moment. Another decidedly Venetian feature is more and more melodies and arias spread thoughout the scores. Audiences liked the tunes. By the middle of the seventeenth century, one historian notes, "the rules of music will supersede the literary text in a manner that no subsequent reform has been able to temper" (Pirrotta 357).

Monteverdi, by this time in his early seventies, must have been gratified that the art he had done so much to develop was becoming so wildly popular. Monteverdi's inauguration as an opera composer in Venice reveals that his sense of showmanship was a strong as ever. After publishing the revised *L'Arianna* libretto in 1639, he mounted his revival of that much-celebrated work to mark the conversion of the Teatro San Moisè to opera. *L'Arianna* had the advantage of being famous while still being unknown to Venetian audiences, except for the lament.

The revival created a sensation. Within weeks his new opera, *Il ritorno d'Ulisse in patria*, opened; it then went on to become one of the most successful operas of the century. Monteverdi's next opera, which has tragically disappeared except for its published libretto, was *Le nozze d'Enea con Lavinia* (1641), based on Virgil's epic. *L'incoronazione di Poppea* (1643) premiered only months before the composer's death. *Ulisse* and *Poppea* represent the summit of Monteverdi's achievement and are among the very greatest operas of all time. Seldom in the history of music have such a profound grasp of the human condition and such distinctive melodic richness been combined with such a faultless theatrical instinct. The fact that these two works, which contain so much palpable energy, were created by a septuagenarian rapidly approaching death represents a miracle of human creativity comparable to Sophocles' late plays and Verdi's extraordinary marshaling of his powers for his final two Shakespearean operas.

"Tempests Are Kind, and Salt Waves Fresh in Love"
Il ritorno d'Ulisse in patria

To the Most Illustrious and most Reverend Signor Claudio Monteverdi Great Master of Music: Not in order to compete with those talented men who, in recent years have publicized their compositions in the Venetian theaters, but to stimulate the imagination of Your Lordship to make known to this city that in warming the affections there is a great difference between a real sun and a painted one, I initially dedicated myself to compose the Return of Ulysses. . . . Now, having seen the opera performed ten times, always before the same [large] audience of the city, I can positively and heartily affirm that my Ulysses is more obligated to Your Lordship than the real Ulysses was to the always charming Minerva. . . . We admire with the greatest astonishment those rich ideas of yours, not without some perturbation, because I can no longer recognize this work as mine.

Giacomo Badoaro, preface to a manuscript of the
libretto for *Il ritorno d'Ulisse in patria*, c. 1640

Giacomo Badoaro (1602–1654) was an amateur poet, an aristocrat, and a member of the Accademia degli Incogniti, a society of rationalist intellectuals who exerted enormous influence in the creation of Venetian opera. The passage quoted in the epigraph to this chapter indicates that he wrote the libretto for *Il ritorno d'Ulisse in patria* specifically to tempt Monteverdi into writing for the new Venetian operatic theater and to reveal to Venetians the old priest's supremacy in the art. The "painted sun" of Manelli and Cavalli would be bested by Monteverdi's "real sun." The idea of a young (and, in Badoaro's case, a first-time) librettist working to lure an older composer out of retirement and back into the operatic theater in order to reinvigorate the Italian lyric theater would be repeated some 240 years later when Arrigo Boito convinced Verdi to compose *Otello* and later *Falstaff.* A comparison of the score to Badoaro's libretto, which survives in several manuscript copies, reveals the extent of the composer's editorial changes. Monteverdi boldly reshaped Badoaro's writing into a coherent and supremely effective foundation for a music drama. Badoaro's comments in the prefatory letter reveal an admirable humility: he acknowledges the composer as, in effect, the master dramatist in his bold manipulation of the raw material the younger man had presented him. (Ellen Rosand details specifics of Monteverdi's changes to Badoaro's text in *Opera* 250–53, "Bow" 383–93, and the forthcoming *Monteverdi's Late Operas.*)

Badoaro's original *Ulisse* libretto followed a neoclassical five-act structure, which Monteverdi appears to have remodeled into three acts. Many commentators and performers opt to restore Badoaro's original divisions or to create divisions of their own: more often than not the work is performed in two acts. Nevertheless, three acts was the preferred form for Venetian opera as well as commedia dell'arte and the Spanish drama, which so influenced Italian commercial opera. As will become apparent, the three-act division of the score, though undeniably lopsided, with two one-hour-long opening acts and a thirty-minute last act, serves the complete opera better than Badoaro's original conception or the practices of most modern productions. The modern two-act division can damage the carefully modulated final scenes, creating so-called *longueurs,* which in turn lead producers to make unfortunate cuts in the score's third act. Monteverdi's act shaping may be "imperfect," just as Puccini's own "opera of waiting," *Madama Butterfly,* is lopsided in terms of the duration of its acts. Like Puccini, however, Monteverdi was unconcerned with arbitrary balances created by stopwatches and entirely concerned with creating his own sense of time in music and dramatic action. Leopold is one commentator who suggests that "Monteverdi's governing hand may be behind" the three-act structure.

> In the score, the entire first act, as an exposition, is filled with the introduction of the characters surrounding Ulisse and Penelope. The second act tells the story of the suitors. The third act proves to be a complement to the first: instead of Penelope's lament at the beginning, there is Iro's parody of a lament before he kills himself because of hunger; a scene with the gods with a following chorus is then found in both acts; and, instead of Ulisse's disguise and Penelope's refusal to give audience to the suitors, there is the difficult task, which lasts half of the act, of convincing Penelope that . . . Ulisse was disguised as a beggar. (Leopold 201)

The opera's success led to a tour to Bologna by Manelli's company, presumably the performers of the Venetian premiere. Bolognese contemporaries record the names of two of these performers and their roles: Maddalena Manelli, the wife of the company director, who had starred as Andromeda in the first Venetian opera three years before, sang Minerva, and Giulia Saus Paolelli took the role of Penelope. The demand for the opera was so great that *Ulisse* enjoyed a revival in 1641, the only time in the century that a Venetian opera enjoyed a revival only one season after its premiere. At the Teatro Santi Giovanni e Paolo, the revival of *Ulisse* would share the stage with Monteverdi's next opera, the lost *Le nozze d'Enea con Lavinia*. Whatever reticence, if any, Monteverdi possessed about writing for the commercial theater had vanished; the short time remaining to him would find him engrossed in the operatic theater.

Monteverdi's *Il ritorno d'Ulisse* survives in a single handwritten manuscript discovered in the Vienna Nationalbibliothek by the historian A. W. Ambros in 1881. It contains the vocal lines, basso continuo, sinfonias, and ritornelli in five parts and lacks indications for instrumentation. The score probably stems from a revival performed for the Habsburg court. We may recall how Monteverdi had cultivated his relationship with these rulers after Eleonora Gonzaga had married Ferdinand II in 1622. One scholar surmises that the opera's themes of marital fidelity and other "high ethical claims" would have made the work particularly palatable for the Viennese imperial court audience in the midst of the Thirty Years' War (Pass 175–82). After its first publication in 1922, some scholars doubted the work's authenticity. Nowadays, *Ulisse* is viewed as a score relatively free of the authorship questions that have in recent years besieged passages in *Poppea*. The *Ulisse* score does contain some scholarly cruxes caused by scribal error; one or two passages of Badoaro's libretto that are necessary for the plot or staging are missing, and some supporting roles suffer various confusions and obvious inconsistencies that require editorial attention to make them performable. All told, however, the score is in coherent condition and has little need for editorial "assistance" or amplification, so long as the instrumentalists are experienced with the improvising skills necessary for supporting the singers and stage action.

Ulisse requires only a small instrumental ensemble of approximately five string players and assorted continuo instruments. The reduced ensemble is typical of Venetian opera and heightens the attention on singers and stage action alike. Although the number of instrumentalists has shrunk from the courtly opulence of earlier years, the number of characters onstage has grown from *L'Orfeo*'s smallish ensemble, and they are far more diverse and colorful. They come from virtually all walks of life, both human and divine. Especially notable is the number of fully developed female characters. Although the roles of Ulisse and Penelope are of prime interest, the opera affords several memorable, three-dimensional portraits of both male and female characters— a notable advance on the dramaturgical achievements of *L'Orfeo*. One scholar notes that "like his contemporary Shakespeare, Monteverdi is an artistic 'democrat,' endowing each of his characters, regardless of status, with the most distinctive and expressive examples of his art" (Bokina 29). As in the Shakespearean theater, the convention of role doubling probably would have been utilized, though the singers portraying Penelope, Eumete, Ulisse, and Telemaco would presumably have had their hands full with just the one role. As in *L'Orfeo,* the title character is assigned to a tenor with baritonal capabilities and, like Orfeo, is occasionally sung by a baritone in modern revivals. *Ulisse* is an opera particularly rich with tenor roles, but the hero's range is lower than that of the supporting tenor parts such as Telemaco and Eurimaco. This

lower tessitura indicates Ulisse's maturity, an act of musical characterization that one critic observes is "simply unheard of at the time and
positively pre-Romantic in flavor" (Celletti 36). Penelope is nominally
a soprano part but, as so often in the seventeenth century, her range
avoids the higher reaches and coincides with the modern notion of the
mezzo-soprano. *Ulisse,* like *L'incoronazione di Poppea,* makes good use
of Monteverdi's *stile concitato* whenever violence or emotional agitation
needs to be expressed. In both *Ulisse* and *Poppea,* Monteverdi differ-
entiates the vocal music of human and divine characters, as he did in
L'Orfeo. But now, in these later operas, even the human characters sing
more luxuriantly lyrical music. The "elevated" style of florid vocal ornament is not alone the province of gods but may now discreetly illustrate
human "youth, gallantry, and sensuous love" (Celletti 32). In addition to
some spectacular special effects that exceed the climactic apotheosis of
the courtly *L'Orfeo*—a flying chariot, a moving ship being transformed
into a rock, and so on—the opera requires only three settings; a palace,
a seascape, and a woodland. The allegorical prologue might well have
been played before the main curtain (see Carter, *Monteverdi's Musical
Theater* 103, 81).

Badoaro's text, which so captured the composer's imagination, is a
faithful adaptation of Homer's *Odyssey,* books 13–23. Badoaro's major
innovation was the expansion of the gluttonous beggar Arnaios, nicknamed Iros, from his minor presence in the epic (book 18, lines 1–107,
wherein he is beaten virtually to death by Odysseus and propped against
a wall as a grotesque scarecrow to ward off stray dogs and pigs) to a far
more significant position in the opera. Badoaro probably was inspired
by Giambattista Della Porta's 1591 play *Penelope,* an earlier Italian
dramatization of Homer's epic. Porta develops the illicit love affair
mentioned by Homer (*Odyssey,* book 8) between Melantho, Penelope's
maid, and Eurymachus, one of the leading suitors, into an important
subplot. Badoaro alters this idea so that the operatic Eurimaco appears
to be a servant from the suitors' entourage rather than a direct con-
tender for Penelope's hand. The story of Ulysses' journey from his years
of wandering to his joyful repossession of his kingdom is perhaps the
greatest and most satisfying adventure story of classical antiquity. With
his propensity for disguise and metamorphoses, Ulysses also constituted

a potent symbol of transformation for the baroque sensibility (see also Aercke 157). Although the Venetian opera was a commercial operation endeavoring to appeal to a wide audience, its ultimate sponsors were the Venetian aristocratic families that owned the theaters. It is not difficult to see that Ulisse and Penelope would appeal to these patrons as worthy aristocratic role models of chastity, continence, patience, and courage. The aristocracy of early-seventeenth-century Venice was suffering increasing setbacks through outbreaks of plague as well as military and political troubles. Ulisse, the beleaguered wanderer reestablishing his dominion over Ithaca, would have been a cheering dramatic symbol of aristocratic legitimacy and resurgence (see also Bokina 24–26). Ellen Rosand has drawn a comparison between Ulisse and the aged Monteverdi. Both men are returning to their home. In Monteverdi's case, "home" is the medium of opera, which he had made his own more than thirty years before in Mantua. Monteverdi is driven to prove to his younger colleagues and himself that he still is the master of this art form, still the master of Apollo's bow, still the man who can make the "string" sing like no other. At least one of the composer's contemporaries noted this identification between Monteverdi and Ulisse (see Rosand, "Bow" 393–95).

This comparison between the composer and Ulisse with his bow as weapon/ musical instrument has authentically Homeric resonances, which Monteverdi, with his great respect for the precedents of classical antiquity, would have certainly recalled. The original epic contains several self-referential descriptions of bardic performances. (On this theme see Segal, *Singers.*) Particularly notable is Homer's description of Odysseus as he takes the bow in his hands at the contest.

> ... but Odysseus of many devices,
> as soon as he had lifted the great bow, and examined it thoroughly,
> just as when a man who understands the lyre and singing
> easily stretches a new string around a peg,
> making fast at both ends the taut sheep gut,
> so without effort did Odysseus string the great bow.
> And holding it in his right hand, he tried the string;
> which sang sweetly under his touch, like the voice of a swallow.
>
> (*Odyssey,* 21.404–11)

Monteverdi's skills in musical characterization may be seen operating in ways similar to Homer's bardic references. The musical "art" of the suitors is pitted against that of Penelope as well as her husband during the course of the opera. The hero and heroine, with their honest musical and verbal declamation, vanquish the suitors, with their exaggerated, overornamented styles.

Ulisse is the most tender and moving of Monteverdi's operas, perhaps even of all his works. It lacks the extraordinary irony and bitterness of *Poppea,* with its profound ambivalence, but in a good performance the audience cannot fail to be swept up in its suspense and to engage emotionally with the characters. The great scenes of recognition between father and son and between husband and wife are unrivaled in their poignancy and emotional depth. The closest parallels reside less in opera than in Shakespeare's drama. One thinks of Lear's brief restoration to Cordelia in *King Lear* and the quasi-religious harmony of the recognition scenes in Shakespeare's late romances—*Pericles, Cymbeline, The Winter's Tale,* and *The Tempest. Ulisse* depicts the eventual triumph of love over time and all the other vicissitudes that afflict humankind. It finds music for the deepest longings of humanity for union with lost loved ones and long-delayed justice, longings that, given the tragic condition of life, are usually realized only through religious observance or art. In this regard the effect of *Ulisse* recalls that of Sophocles' final play, the mystical *Oedipus at Colonus,* another late work in which the artist is sublimated into the figure of the protagonist. The depth of Monteverdi's portrayal of the human subject is based on truths that transcend day-to-day reality or probability and allow his audience to partake in the miracle of Ulisse's restoration to his home and family, as well as the long-delayed punishment meted out to the suitors who have been threatening all he holds dear.

Prologue and Act I

In the allegorical prologue, Human Frailty is beset by Time, Fortune, and Love, who promise to show him no mercy. Act 1 introduces Penelope, who laments the absence of her husband, Ulisse (Ulysses), king of Ithaca,

mysteriously lost on his return from the Trojan War ("Di misera regina").
She is comforted by her loyal old nurse, Ericlea. Melanto, Penelope's hand-
maid, is romantically involved with Eurimaco, an attendant of Penelope's
suitors, and is being corrupted to persuade her mistress to yield to them.
Meanwhile, the god of the sea, Nettuno (Neptune), is angry at Ulisse
for blinding Nettuno's son, the Cyclops. Nettuno vows vengeance on the
Phaeacian sailors who are at this moment conveying Ulisse to his homeland.
Giove (Jove), Nettuno's brother, attempts to placate the sea god, allowing
him to destroy the Phaeacians and their ship, after they have safely deposited
the sleeping Ulisse on the Ithacan coast. Upon awaking, Ulisse laments his
fate and the apparent treachery of the Phaeacians ("Dormo ancora o son
desto?"). Minerva, his patron goddess, appears disguised as a shepherd boy
and tells him that he has been brought to Ithaca. Soon she reveals her divine
identity and discloses that Penelope remains chaste but is in danger from the
suitors. She transforms the hero into the shape of an old beggar to facilitate
her plans for Ulisse's securing his kingdom once again. The hero celebrates
his good luck in an aria, "O fortunato Ulisse!" Back in the court, Melanto
tries unsuccessfully to persuade Penelope to give in and fall in love with one
of the suitors ("Ama dunque, ché d'amore"). We are next introduced to the
faithful shepherd Eumete, who longs for his master Ulisse's return while
celebrating his happy existence close to nature ("Colli, campagne e boschi!")
He is rudely accosted by the foolish glutton Iro, a parasite belonging to the
suitors who are, with Iro's help, feeding off the riches of the royal house in
Ulisse's absence. Eumete drives Iro away and meets Ulisse in his disguise
as a beggar. The "beggar" promises Eumete that Ulisse will soon return.
Eumete promises the disguised Ulisse safe refuge.

Prologue

The Prologue not only launches the opera perfectly but must have
seemed an uncomfortably apt reflection on Europe in 1640. The human
condition is presented in the guise of an allegorical figure, Human
Frailty (L'Humana Fragilità), bullied by Time (Tempo), Fortune
(Fortuna), and Love (Amore). Seldom had the Western world felt more
vulnerable than in the early seventeenth century. As religious wars

and plague ripped apart much of Europe, scientific and philosophical innovations were vanquishing what was left of the medieval worldview. Expanding visions of the universe shook traditional epistemologies to their core. The *Ulisse* prologue compels the audience to view the ensuing opera not as a comfortably distant tale from antiquity, but as a living contemporary document. Like Rubens or Rembrandt, Monteverdi and Badoaro are utilizing a story from the classical tradition to reflect upon the human condition in their own time (see also Leopold 32–42 for her discussion of Renaissance and baroque issues). The vocal casting for the prologue calls for a bass to sing Tempo and three mezzos for L'Humana Fragilità, Fortuna, and Amore. Fortuna and Amore would presumably have been sung by women, castrati, or boys. L'Humana Fragilità is intended for a male or female mezzo.

L'Orfeo, as a courtly entertainment, began with a formulaic toccata fanfare heralding the ensuing opera as a product of Gonzaga patronage. Commercial Venetian opera sublimated such extradramatic concerns, and consequently Monteverdi is at liberty to launch *Ulisse* with a brief, dramatically charged D minor sinfonia, plunging his performers and audience into the center of his opera's emotional and thematic concerns. The use and reuse of this sinfonia during the prologue suggests that this instrumental passage is associated with the precarious human condition. L'Humana Fragilità sings an arioso that she will repeat throughout the prologue with telling variations: "I am a mortal being, fashioned human" (Mortal cosa son io, fattura humana). L'Humana Fragilità's words and their stark musical setting introduces a sense of pathos within the opening seconds of the vocal writing. The languishing ornaments on "humana," which stretch over four bars, suggest humanity's painful vulnerability. She complains, "Everything, everything disturbs me" (Tutto, tutto mi turba). The verbal repetitions are the composer's. The ornamental runs on "combatte" when she sings "Time which creates me, also fights against me" serve as a musical flourish introducing the next figure to sing, Tempo (Time).

Tempo inspires Monteverdi to create another bass villain in the Caronte vein. Tempo sings a solo recitative with fleeting suggestions of arioso. Tempo is too unstable—either rushing, lingering, or limping—to sustain a regular aria melody or meter. His recitative encompasses the sadistic, "gnawing" repetitions on "Ei rode, ei gode" ([My tooth] gnaws, it enjoys) and the threatening vocal flourish on "Non fuggite" (Don't run away). Most striking of all are the humorously effective rests breaking up the line "Though I limp" (Ché se ben zoppo). Each setting of "zoppo" (limp) is broken in two by a rest. Time's menacing aggression is then released in vocal runs on the phrase "I have wings" (Ho l'ali). Time's recitative suggests that the opera to follow will contain not only darkness, but a sense of grotesque humor akin to that found in Homer's epic. Tempo's solo is followed by the opening sinfonia, underscoring his centrality to the opera. Time, the ultimate destroyer of mankind, will also prove the ultimate healer. Ulisse-Odysseus will struggle under Time's yoke until Time leads the hero home again.

L'Humana Fragilità then sings a chastened variant of her opening arioso. The only significant vocal flourish appears on the word "fortuna" in the phrase "for frail life is a game of fortune," which serves as the cue for the next "deity" to appear onstage. The mezzo Fortuna sings an arioso, but its music is bright, her rhythm bouncy and dancelike. She even comes equipped with a brief ritornello that punctuates her lyrics: "My life is desire, joy, and labor." She sings with rapid verbal repetitions suggesting her flighty character: "Riches, greatness I dispense according to my mood" (Ricchezze, grandezze dispenso a mio modo). These words are treated with dizzying repetitions and rapid-fire alliterations sung to her jolly, seemingly unstoppable tune, driving home Fortune's cruelty and her kinship with Time.

L'Humana Fragilità's sings her arioso again, closing her refrain with a florid run on "fugace": "To the tyrant Love is sacrificed my flowing green and fleeting [*fugace*] years." This vocal ornament marks the appearance of the third and final of humankind's abstract opponents. Amore enters with an even more elaborately contrived ritornello than Fortuna. It serves as a jaunty rephrasing of L'Humana Fragilità's sinfonia. This musical similarity suggests a spiritual connection between L'Humana Fragilità and Amore. The "deities" have control over L'Humana Fragilità now, just as they have power over the accompanimental instrumentalists to punctuate their solos and not hers. The mischievous boy, Amore, delights in his role as archer ("saettator") and in his nudity ("ignudo"), which elicits playful vocal decoration. Amore's nudity parallels L'Humana Fragilità's defenselessness, whether this is actualized onstage or not. Like Tempo and Fortuna, Amore also takes pleasure in bandying repetitions at "Non val difesa o scudo" ([Against my arrow] there is no defense or shield of any use). This childish mockery and taunting repetition seems all the more appropriate if Amore is sung by a boy treble.

L'Humana Fragilità sings her refrain a final time. Her deepening depression is accented by a word change and its emphatic repetition: "Misera, misera son ben io, fattura umana: credere a ciechi e zoppi è cosa vana" (I am a miserable being, fashioned human: believing in the blind and lame is a vain thing). The setting of her final words suggests her utter defeat. A rhetorically effective pause prefaces the rapid descending notes that set "è cosa vanna" (is a vain thing), a musical embodiment of humanity's fleeting, fragile essence. Her last utterance lends an even greater confidence to her attackers, who now join forces in a trio. Tempo, Fortuna, and Amore enjoy soloistic passages punctuated by unison singing that makes their promise to "show no pity" (pietate non ha) to "this man" (quest'huom sarà) all the more forceful. Their vocal parts become almost indistinguishable except for the bold highlighting afforded Amore on his soloistic flourish in the trio's penultimate bar, which ushers in the final statement: "I will make this man here fragile, miserable, and troubled" (Per me fragile, misero, torbido quest'huom sarà). Their trio complete, the prologue ends with a repetition of the D minor sinfonia, the "Human Frailty" motif. This repetition serves to mask the sounds of a scene shift, with its attendant exiting and entering of singers, the possible use of the flying machines, and the moving of scenery, and it allows this instrumental symbol of beleaguered humanity to have the last word before the action of the opera proper begins. By this most economical of musical means Monteverdi suggests the promise that "Human Frailty" will somehow prevail over the seemingly insurmountable obstacles in its way.

The score notes: "After the present sinfonia 'in tempo allegro' is finished, the following one begins sadly, in the bass [alla bassa], until Penelope has arrived on the scene for the beginning of her solo. This sinfonia is repeated as often as necessary to allow Penelope to get onstage [Questa sinfonia si replica tante volte insinio che Penelope arriva *in scena*]." In other words, this is an operatic vamp provided to bridge a potentially time-consuming scene shift, ensuring that the right mood will be sustained even if the machinist's magic takes longer than expected. Chafe observes, "Monteverdi's reduction of the ['Penelope'] sinfonia to a simple . . . harmony makes clear [her] destitute condition" (277). The practical and the poetic go hand in hand in Monteverdi's dramatic technique.

Scene I

The first scene introduces Penelope and her nurse, Ericlea. It also provides one of the finest examples in operatic literature of the lament, a passage where words, recitative, and arioso are "fused into a great expressive unity" (de' Paoli 481). Penelope's musical characterization is notable: she uses only recitative virtually throughout the opera until, with Ulisse safely home again, she sings an elaborate aria and then joins her husband in the duet that marks the end of the work. Her preference for recitative has led some critics to compare Penelope with another great mezzo role, that of Ottavia in *Poppea*. But although both parts require a mezzo singing actress of the highest caliber and both roles sing a huge amount of recitative, the similarity stops there. Even in the first scene of *Ulisse,* the dramatic and musical strategy with which Penelope is brought to life is completely different from what we encounter with Ottavia in the later opera. Recitative indeed forms the most-employed musical material of the first scene, but it is contrasted with significant uses of recurrent lyrical refrains and even an arioso of unforgettably melodic beauty. Unlike Ottavia, a woman whose warped values prevent her from truly "singing," Penelope has never lost her capacity for song and aria. Even her anguished recitative borders on the edge of song, a song that becomes manifest when she gives voice to her longing for her husband or fantasizes about his return.

Penelope's opening lament establishes her character and situation with great economy.

> For a miserable queen there is no end to suffering anxiety!
> The expected one doesn't arrive, and the years fly away.

[Di misera Regina non terminati mai dolenti affani!
L'aspettato non giunge, e pur fuggono gli anni.]

The reiterated E-flats—fourteen of the nineteen notes used to set
the first sentence—suggest a sense of motionlessness and emotional
stasis. Just as the note hardly changes in her opening declamation, so
too does her life seem hopelessly stalled. Both the use of musical stasis
(the reiterated note) and the sighing cadences setting words such as
"dolente" (sorrows) will delineate her recitative style throughout this
scene. Penelope's remark that "time is lame" (il tempo è zoppo) neatly
ties the emergent opera's action with the prologue. She sings "zoppo"
to a descending musical figure that recalls the character Tempo. One
critic notes that "throughout much of the opera, regardless of scene,
Penelope sings in D minor, [the] key [which] is that of Human Frailty
in the prologue, for Penelope is the victim of time and fortune . . . and
even of her love, as her final D minor in Act Three affirms" (Chafe 270).
Monteverdi and Badoaro have replaced the prologue's abstractions with
living, breathing human beings. Penelope's introductory remarks close
with another musical setting of great delicacy: "[False Hope] no longer
promises peace or healing to the old grief" (All'invecchiato male non
promettete più pace o salute). "Più" is set to a sighing figure punctuated
by a rest before the verse line is resolved by an exquisite cadence on
"pace o salute," creating a musical realization of the seemingly unat-
tainable resolution. Jane Glover suggests that the opening of the lament
implies "that this is a daily ritual into which she has been ground by the
passing of time" ("Venetian Operas" 297).

Penelope narrates the story of Helen and of Ulisse's departure to
punish her adultery, a narration portrayed by bold recitative declamation suggesting Penelope is a woman of unshakable moral conviction.
The unfairness of her situation, the chaste wife suffering "because of
the crimes of others [altrui]," reenergizes the iterative note patterns and
the sighing-figure cadence on "Per l'altrui fallo condannata innocente"
(Though innocent, I am condemned [to suffer]). After asserting that
Ulisse is "shrewd and wise: you who boast about punishing adultery,"
she again reverts to her feelings of desolation in "E intanto lasci la
tua casta consorte fra i nemici rivali in dubbio dell'honore, in forse a

morte" (At the same time you leave your chaste consort among hostile rivals—her honor and perhaps even her life in jeopardy). The iterated notes lead to yet another sighing cadence on "in forse a morte" (and perhaps even her life). As her longing for Ulisse increases in intensity, so too does the lyrical impulse of her declamation: "Ogni partenza attende desiato ritorno" (Every departure attends on a desired return). The abrupt leap from G to B-flat on "desiato" (desired) is as simple as it is striking. Desire is truly the operative element in Penelope's character, and the setting of this word lifts her musical discourse to a new level of expressiveness. It serves to launch the first of Penelope's two lyric refrains, "Tu sol del tuo tornar perdesti il giorno" (You alone have lost your day of return). These words are set to a "stupendous ascending chromatic line" (de' Paoli 481) that anticipates the "Non morir, Seneca" chorus in *Poppea*. Penelope's "Tu sol" refrain represents a melodic, lyrical utterance unlike anything Ottavia will sing in the later opera.

Ericlea now interrupts her mistress's monologue with a brief recitative identifying herself for the audience. The queen's next speech is animated by a more rapid and agitated pace, buoyed by Ericlea's moral support: "Is there then no change in my fate? Did Fortune perhaps change the volatile wheel for the stable one? And the quick sail which bears every human care through the inconstant flight for me alone does not collect a single breath." The last words, "un fiato solo," mark a climax of this new burst of indignation that in the next moment reverts to introspection: "For others the aspect of heaven of errant and fixed stars changes." This line is marked by a slower delivery and lower notes for Penelope to sing. This leads to her second lyrical refrain, "Torna, deh, torna, Ulisse!" (Return, ah, return, Ulisse!). Set to a gently undulating melodic line, the refrain forms a musical-psychological gesture that Monteverdi will reuse to punctuate the end of this second speech and the climax of the scene, a musical distillation of Penelope's character and the dramatic situation.

Penelope's agitation returns. She awaits her husband: "Deh, torna, Ulisse, Penelope t'aspetta"—again the important word "aspetta" (awaits). She will not blame her husband, since his absence cannot be due to cruelty; "Rather I charge Fate with treachery against me"

(Ma fabbro de' miei danni incolpo il fato). The brief half-rest after "danni" emphasizes the phrase "incolpo il fato," rendered striking by the musical leap Penelope makes from the first syllable to the emphatic descending line of "incolpo il fato." This arresting gesture recalls the presence of Fortuna in the prologue. Her recitative continues: "Thus in your defense, with Destiny, with heaven, I make war and create quarrels." With this bold defiance Penelope repeats her refrain, "Torna, deh, torna, Ulisse!," the same words and music heard moments before; the repetition increases their urgency. Ericlea has the next two verses: "Parting without a return cannot be the will of the stars, not to return, ah! not to return." Her words and music hint at her psychological bond with her mistress. The repeated notes of "Partir senza ritorno non può stella influir" again suggest Penelope's own musical depiction of painful stasis. Ericlea's slowly climbing vocal line on "Non è partir, non è ahi, non è partir [rest] ahi, che non è partir" seems to echo the melodic arch of Penelope's first refrain, "tu sol del tuo tornar." This musical and psychological support from Ericlea has an immediate impact on Penelope, who now launches into an unexpected aria as she imagines the prospect of her husband's return home. Even without the music, Badoaro's words are memorably beautiful.

> Torna il tranquillo al mare,
> torna il zeffiro al prato,
> l'aurora mentre al sol fa dolce invito
> è un ritorno del dì ch'è pria partito.
> Tornan le brine in terra,
> tornano al centro i sassi,
> e con lubrici passi
> torna all'oceano il rivo.

> [The tranquility returns to the sea,
> the breeze returns to the meadow,
> while the dawn sweetly invites the sun
> to a return of the day which has departed.
> The moisture returns to the earth,
> the stones return to the center,
> and with gliding steps
> the river returns to the ocean.]

These circling patterns suggest Ulisse's return is mandated by nature itself, just as the passage begins and ends with a reference to the sea. The music to which the words are set is surely among the most beautiful that Monteverdi ever composed. The aria seems to well out of the deepest springs of Penelope's soul. She begins the ravishing lyric phrase "Torna il tranquillo al mare." The composer places a rest in both the vocal line and the bass, suggesting the beginning of a new line of thought and a new form of musical expression that Penelope is beginning with hesitation. But the new ideas and the lyrical music force their way gently past these rests. As she expands the arioso she sings exquisite florid runs on "torna" ([the breeze] returns), "sol" (sun), and "dì ch'è pria" (to the previous day) that help to illustrate the meaning of the words. The "dolce invito," the "sweet inviting" of the dawn, is treated to a coaxing fluctuation of notes. This gorgeous aria melody is allowed only one more statement, "Tornan le brine," but here the ornamentation is largely stripped away, allowing the deliciously flowing notes on "e con lubrici passi" (with gliding steps) to perfectly suggest the movement of the waters. This passage is brief—and all the more powerful for its brevity. In Penelope's extreme situation, such moments of lyrical pleasure are necessarily short-lived—a "temporary lapse" signaling "a fantasy that music [is] possible" (Rosand, "Monteverdi's *Il ritorno*" 180). But this passage also affords a glimpse of an underlying beneficence in nature, an image of harmony and order that art occasionally allows us to perceive even as it documents the hindrances and inequities that beset the human condition. For all the human and divine forces arrayed against Human Frailty, this opera—like Homer's epic before it—will offer deliverance. Penelope's brief aria gives musical promise to this miraculous beneficence.

Penelope returns to recitative: "Man who lives down here, far from his origins, bears a celestial soul but a frail body." The word "celestial" (celeste) is marked by two high notes, the word "frail" (frale)—predictably enough—with low ones. Penelope is philosophizing, and the music of her recitative has become less personal, slightly more formulaic. She continues: "Soon the mortal dies and the soul returns to heaven and the body returns to dust after a brief sojourn." Again repeated high notes on "heaven" (cielo) and the low-lying ones on "returns to dust" (impolve dopo) are effective, if clichéd. We may note how far Badoaro and Monteverdi are from the dark pagan view of the afterlife found in the actual Homeric texts. Penelope's anguish comes flooding back as she repeats her first refrain, "Tu sol del tuo tornar," with its aching chromatic rise. The return of this music evokes the dramatic effect of a reopened wound. Monteverdi's use of musical styles and patterns gives this scene a musical shape that suggests the fluctuating moods of a living mind under extreme duress. The second and final statement of the "Tu sol" refrain seems to have slipped out almost unexpectedly. Penelope has just been taking comfort at the thought of the circularity of nature, which has led her to meditate on the human condition. But this philosophy is too little to hold back the floodgates of her obsession, and the music (and the psychological state it mirrors) has returned to the most biting and severe expression of her grief. The third and final statement of her "torna" refrain sets the seal on "one of the greatest scenes in dramatic literature" (Schrade 351), leaving an indelible musical and dramatic image of the longing Penelope. As with the rest of the work, the composer and the librettist have made a remarkable operatic translation of Homer's heroine. Like Mozart's Figaro or Verdi's Otello and Falstaff, Monteverdi's Penelope offers a rare example in opera of a great literary character being perfectly translated into a very different medium.

Scene 2

The next scene presents the "perfect foil and release after Penelope's sufferings" (Glover, "Venetian Operas" 299) while paradoxically revealing the dangerous moral climate that threatens the protagonists. Melanto, one of Penelope's female attendants, is enjoying an amorous tête-a-tête with Eurimaco, a servant attached to the degenerate troops of suitors who have encroached upon the Ithacan court in Ulisse's absence. Amorous banter now replaces Penelope's dignified soliloquies. The kind of lyrical melody that Penelope has kept under such tight reign now dominates the score, giving us some of Monteverdi's most sensuous love music in a scene of explosive energy. Joseph Kerman has described the effect of the entire opera as "the release of operatic energies that have been bottled up for a long time" (see Kerman, "Full Monte" 36). This sense of a renewed creative release is particularly evident in the exchange between Melanto and Eurimaco. The grave minor-key sinfonia of Human Frailty is now replaced with a jaunty major-key ritornello signaling the first great love duet in operatic history.

Although the mezzo-soprano Penelope has extolled the righteous fire that has burned Troy, her words and music suggest the chaste fires that burn within her for her husband's return. The soprano Melanto's opening aria describes a different kind of burning—an amorous fire that should be postponed only to increase one's pleasure in the conflagration. Melanto's music and character mark her as a forerunner of the soubrette type (Celletti 36). Unlike her mistress, Melanto thrives on aria, and she launches the scene with a strophic example.

> Hard are the pains
> that love suffers
> in his desire;
> but finally he cherishes
> if first he loves,
> with bitter suffering;
> if a heart is burning,
> it is a joyful fire.
> No one loses in love
> who plays out the game.
>
> Whoever is first inflamed
> by a white breast
> can expect storms;
> but riding through them
> finds love
> a serene harbor.
> If first there is weeping,
> then finally joy has its place.
> No one loses in love
> who plays out the game.

Her aria is punctuated and brought to a conclusion by the major-key sinfonia that opened the scene. Eurimaco refers directly to Melanto's "singing" in his responding aria, suggesting an element of self-consciousness in her performance before her suitor. "If a heart is burning," Melanto asserts, "it is a joyful fire." Badoaro's text indicates the gulf separating Penelope's experience from that of her servant; Monteverdi's music expands this gap. Melanto's aria, like all good strophic music, is sculpted to serve two different verses equally well. The key word, "amorosi," is granted a telling seven-note melodic flourish. "Son cari" (he cherishes) is repeated with obvious relish. The buoyant rhythm of the opening vocal bars is retarded for "gli aspri martir" (with [the lover's] bitter suffering), suggesting the sadness of these words yet containing a touch of gentle irony. In the second verse, these same notes on "porto seren" (the "serene harbor" the patient lover will attain) is equally well served by the music, suggesting now the lover's happily attained goal. The refrain that ends both verses flies in the face of the realities depicted in the prologue and the suffering that love, in its deepest manifestations, has brought Penelope: "No one loses in love who plays out the game." The flourish on "compie" (plays out) and the kittenish repetitions on "mai" (never) accentuate Melanto's frivolous and possibly immature nature.

Eurimaco responds to Melanto's strophic song with a characteristic aria of his own:

> My beautiful Melanto, delightful Melanto,
> your song is enchanting,
> your face is magic.
> My beautiful Melanto!
> Everything in you would bind and captivate anyone.
> Whoever isn't tied to you is altogether stricken.

It takes him five bars of music to say "Bella Melanto mia." The words are set and repeated to delightful melody representing amorous badinage and suggesting that Eurimaco is managing to capture Melanto's heart more with charm than with substance. Eurimaco's lovely melodic flourish on "il" in the phrase "il tuo canto" (your song) is telling. Clearly, if any word of this phrase is to be properly elaborated by vocal runs or ornament, normal musical prosody would choose "canto"—not the comparatively weak "il." Eurimaco himself will correct this "mistake" two bars later when the phrase is repeated and both "canto" and "incanto" receive the melodically appealing ornamentation they deserve. But Eurimaco repeats his "mistake" immediately with another verbally and mimetically meaningless run on "il" in the phrase "il tuo volto" (your face). Again, two bars later "volto" becomes the word treated to ornament. These are tiny details that may be easily ignored in performance but represent subtle indicators of Eurimaco's character as projected through the music. The musical elaboration of "il" makes for pretty sounds but meaningless dramatic music. As in Seneca's first scene in *Poppea,* with his fatuous elaboration of "la," Eurimaco's vocal efflorescences mark an ethically challenged character whose text and music are slightly out of harmony with each other. Eurimaco's text, his sense, and his soul are out of sync with the seductive music he is singing to win and manipulate Melanto. The music subtly convicts the character of a hypocrisy that will only emerge later within the opera. In contradiction to Monteverdi's famous formalization, Eurimaco's words are "handmaidens of his music."

The words of Melanto's response, set to a short, flexible aria, indicate that intellectually she sees through his flattering game. Her music, however, suggests that she is already succumbing to his seductive charm. In "Affected chatterer, oh, how well you know how to sing of beauty," the drawn-out elaboration of "o" over four bars—first as a rising three-note sequence, then as a long exhalation at the top of Melanto's vocal compass—suggests rising sexual excitement rather than the ironic detachment the text alone indicates. This is superb musical and dramatic craftsmanship. At moments like this Monteverdi is creating a kind of subtext for his operatic characters, suggesting the contradictions between the words a person actually says, or in this case sings, and his or her deeper inclinations and objectives. The concept of subtext is a dramaturgical technique that would not develop fully in the spoken theater for nearly three hundred years after Monteverdi.

To languishing music Melanto chides Eurimaco for "le tue dolci" (your sweet [lies]). Eurimaco answers her charge with the scene's first recitative passage, as if this less lyrical medium were a guarantee of sincerity: "It would be lies if I praised you but didn't love you, for refusing to adore an acknowledged deity is an impious lie." This does the trick, and the new lovers sing their first duet, "May the flame of the fire of our mutual love blaze up," replete with virtuoso ornamentation in which both characters indulge soloistically and in unison on "fiamma" (flame)—a word that colors the first two scenes of the opera. At the end of their duet the lovers engage in three 2-line exchanges set in recitative to continue their protestations. Melanto insists, "If you don't love me, my heart [cor mio], my soul shall turn to ice before your very eyes." In these exchanges, Melanto's repetitions of "cor mio" indicate how effective Eurimaco's seduction has been. Eurimaco's three-note setting of "cor," followed by a rather awkward rest that breaks the flow and sense of his lines "If my heart [rest] doesn't desire you constantly the earth will no longer give me room nor the heavens a roof," suggests that desire has momentarily subverted sense in his declamation. Rising passions are disrupting clear recitative prosody. Perhaps, too, Eurimaco shows cunning in making his sense harder to convey, since he will soon reveal that his sexual desire for Melanto does not prevent him from making cold-blooded recommendations about Melanto's mistress and the suitors during the height of their musical lovemaking.

They sing a second duet, this one even lovelier than the first: "You are my sweet life, you shall be my good happiness, may this beautiful knot never be dissolved." Like Shakespeare's, Monteverdi's view of humanity is a democratic one. All human beings, noble or base, good or bad, feel love, and the pleasures of love lead them to sing beautiful music. In this second duet, Eurimaco's and Melanto's voices entwine in their beautiful melody in ways that anticipate the climactic love duet of Ulisse and Penelope (as well as that of Nerone and Poppea). The relationship between Eurimaco and Melanto has its sinister and ignoble elements, but their passion for each other is real enough—at least on Melanto's side—and Monteverdi's music insists that we relate to the feelings of characters whose morality we may ultimately reject. Their unison singing of "non si disciolga mai" ([may this beautiful knot] never be dissolved) over a steady ascending bass line suggests the depths of their absorption with each other.

They return to recitative for another exchange leading to "For a fiery bosom despairs at being observed," a third duet that indicates the lovers' excited anticipation of their erotic encounter. Evidently a later copyist or music director wanted to speed the scene to its conclusion, for the Vienna manuscript, the only source for *Ulisse*'s score, omits a recitative passage from Badoaro's text that gives important expository information. The following words, contained in the libretto, are not set in the Vienna score:

> *Eurimaco:*   If beautiful Penelope
> does not yield to the wishes
> of her rival lovers,
> our secret love
> will be in danger.

The score does, however, set in recitative Eurimaco's next lines and Melanto's reply:

> Therefore you must try
> to provoke the flames in her.
>
> *Melanto:*   I'll make another try at
> that determined, obstinate soul,
> to touch again that heart
> which is a temple of chastity.

This is an evident omission from the Vienna score caused by scribal error or an ill-conceived deletion for a later revival; it is impossible to imagine Monteverdi choosing to suppress such necessary exposition by leaving it unset (see Carter, *Monteverdi's Musical Theater* 243, on deliberate and accidental cuts to the libretto). This love affair has a political significance—the lovers represent the seductive allurements of the surrounding atmosphere that threaten Penelope and Ulisse—that their next and last scene together, in the second act, underscores. Eurimaco and Melanto's love scene is capped by a repetition of their exquisite "Dolce mia vita" duet. For these lovers, unlike for Penelope, aria and lyric are the norm, recitative the exception. In Eurimaco, this tendency for song above sense has served as an indicator of his underlying character, linking him, as will be seen, with the abusive suitors.

Scenes 3 and 4

The third scene of Badoaro's libretto features a chorus of nereids and sirens who bid the elements to be still to allow the Phaeacians to place the sleeping Ulisse undisturbed on Ithaca's beach. This little scene is unset in the Vienna score and could be a deletion for a later revival or a deliberate omission on Monteverdi's part. A chorus of nereids and sirens smacks of just the sort of material Monteverdi found so uninspiring to set to dramatic music; witness the famous letter to Striggio of December 9, 1616, quoted at length in the previous chapter. The information the lines contain are not necessary to carry the plot forward. Even the allegorical abstractions of the prologue are deeply rooted in the plight of Human Frailty. Perhaps Monteverdi felt no connection to the "winds" Badoaro provided him and simply omitted them from the score. Choruses could also be prohibitively expensive in the early Venetian opera house. Perhaps also, with all the complex stagecraft about to be deployed, including another chorus of Phaeacian sailors, Monteverdi opted to minimize excessive backstage traffic. The real answer is unknowable, but this teasing gap, like others in the *Ulisse* score, tempts us to conjecture.

The score does provide a repeated bass note to cover the pantomimic action of the next scene, namely, the Phaeacians' disembarking the sleeping Ulisse on Ithaca's shore and their departure. "Here the Phaeacians' boat appears carrying the sleeping Ulisse, and, so as not to wake him, the following sinfonia [the repeated note] is played softly and always on one chord," reads the stage direction in the score. We are at a disadvantage here and must use our imaginations to realize how this transition would be realized with all the ingenuity available to the Venetian designers and machinists.

Scenes 5, 6, and 7

The implicit harmonic stasis in the droning "chord" of the so-called sinfonia will lead to a spectacular coup de théâtre, for the directions in the fifth scene call for Nettuno to arrive from the sea (perhaps from a hidden trap door) to engage in dialogue with his brother, Giove. These two gods, at least one suspended in some sort of "divine chariot" or "flying glory" so popular in Venetian stagecraft, would have created an awesomely dramatic picture as they hovered about the sleeping Ulisse and the unknowing Phaeacians. The dramatic situation, music, and implicit stage effects make the fifth and sixth scenes an example of baroque opera at its best. They offer superb opportunity for musical and scenographic display as well as rendering a truly cosmic dramatic situation with an ironic sensibility and musical grandeur to rival the tragedies of Aeschylus.

Like Tempo in the Prologue, Nettuno is cast as a grand, sepulchral bass. He may even have been sung by the same singer in early productions. Nettuno's part would certainly not suffer from audience awareness of such a doubling, because both allegorical and supernatural roles serve as a "heavy" to Ulisse and to his surrogate in the prologue, L'Humana Fragilità. Nettuno's first words are rendered with superb effect in the kind of mellifluous arioso Monteverdi reserves for supernatural figures. The declamatory delivery of his first lines, punctuated with rests that suggest a stately and pompous character, establish his power and apparent grandeur. His hatred of Ulisse, who blinded the Cyclops, Nettuno's son, compromises the sense of grandeur almost as soon as it is established: "[Humans] make war with destiny, fight with fate" ("Fa guerra col Destin, pugna col fato"). Nettuno looses much of his impressive hauteur as he indulges in *concitato*-style repetitions and rhythms, with agitated activity in the instrumental accompaniment. His next declaration, that "[humankind] dares all, challenges everything" (tutt'osa, tutto ardisce), is treated to similar excited repetition and to a rising vocal line that suggests an ironic sense of impotence in such an ostensibly mighty god. This impression is strengthened by the angry coloratura decorating "contende" in the phrase "man contends with [the will] of heaven" (l'huom col ciel contende). Nettuno regains some of his brief, earlier control as he reasons, "But if benign Giove ponders too often the transgressions of man, he holds willingly in his great right hand the idle bolts of lightning [*fulmine*]." "Fulmine" awakens Nettuno's sense of angry frustration, and he treats the word to an illustrative coloratura. In the phrase "But Nettuno doesn't suffer human guilt with his own dishonor!" (ma non soffra Nettuno col proprio dishonor l'human peccato!), Nettuno's vocal line grows in agitation, climaxing in the five-note flourish on "l'human." Although Nettuno's words ostensibly belittle mankind, his music elevates it by taking Nettuno into his upper vocal range—a delicate touch of operatic irony.

Nettuno's monologue is interrupted by a "five-part sinfonia on high" (*sinfonia alta a 5*) presumably delivered by musicians placed above the proscenium, the airborne symphony heralding the entrance of Giove and masking the sound of the machinery that will lower the king of the gods to confront his brother. (The work of Andrea and Giovanni Gabrieli and Monteverdi's own church music indicate the Venetian appetite for such antiphonal effects in instrumental placement.) The family resemblance between the divine brothers is strongly, almost humorously brought out by their music. Like Nettuno, Giove's opening lines, in arioso, are appropriately declamatory. Classical gods should sound like Giove as he salutes his brother, "Great god of the salt flood." His ringing tenor voice makes an appealing contrast to Nettuno's bass. Giove's words alone imply imperturbable control: "I am Giove by reason of my pitying mind more than by my armed hand" (Mi stabilì per Giove la mente mia pietosa più ch'armata la mano). His music implies control at first, illustrating "pietosa" with appropriately pious ornamentation. Giove's temper gets the better of him, however, as he describes his "armed hand." The rapid repetitions on "più" suggest that he is nettled by his brother's criticisms. He himself indulges in *concitato*-style rhythms when he declares, "This thunderbolt terrifies" (Questo fulmine atterra), before subsiding into reasonableness again with a sensibly illustrative flourish on "cade": "He who falls [*cade*] to earth no longer worships." His repetitions on "furioso" imply he is still feeling threatened by his brother's challenge; the music suggests contradictory emotions underlying the words.

Nettuno tells his brother of the Phaeacians' conveying Ulisse back to Ithaca against Nettuno's will: "Shame and not pity commands the pardoning of such foul deeds." Nettuno's empathetic repetitions of "shame" (vergogna) apparently win the day. Giove's anger, like his brother god's, is directed now against Ulisse and his accomplices as he aggressively repeats "castigate" (castigo): "You yourself may castigate the bold ones." Given divine permission, Nettuno describes his impending vengeance with relish, his note values lengthening as he describes how he will make the Phaeacians' moving ship an "immovable rock" (immobile scoglio). Giove closes the scene with aggressively punctuated pronouncements that allow him to regain the musical semblance of omniscience, even though all that has really transpired is that he has acquiesced to Nettuno after the latter has played upon his insecurities. Although Monteverdi's music suggests the gods' superhuman status, it has also revealed their contradictory, very human passions.

A sinfonia begins to introduce a new group of characters and to mask two more potentially noisy bits of stagecraft: Giove's ascent to the heavens and the sight of the Phaeacians' boat as it leaves Ithaca bearing its Phaeacian "chorus" of three singers: an alto, tenor, and bass. This jaunty sinfonia proves itself to be a ritornello for the Phaeacians' sea shanty.

> In questo basso mondo
> l'huomo puol
> quanto vuol.
> Tutto fa, tutto fa,
> ché 'l Ciel del nostro oprar pensier non ha.
>
> [In this world down here
> man can do whatever he wants.
> He does everything, does everything,
> For heaven has no thought
> for our doings.]

Their words and their music suggest a work song—a forerunner of so many operatic choruses to come in the next centuries. The words are ironic considering the divine argument to which we have just been privy. The contrast between divine and human perception is made more striking by having the chorus launched by a male alto, so "frail" in comparison to the "divine" bass and tenor voices that represent the gods. Both literally and figuratively, the alto inhabits the world of "human frailty." The chorus also happens to share the D minor key of L'Humana Fragilità. Their tune is set "in a deliberately narrow, restricted melodic and harmonic style, as if to caricature the idea of human frailty" (Chafe 263). All the chorus's text is sung both in unison and soloistically, ensuring that all the words and their ironic context may be savored—and that the machinist has enough time to make the spectacle of the moving boat memorable for the audience. The alto and tenor sailors are afforded solos, but the bass sings only along with the other two, ensuring that Nettuno's dark voice retains its commanding authority when he reappears to destroy the ship. Nettuno carries out his deadly magic act with recitative of pompous slowness, replete with rests that seem tailored for grand gestures from the angry god.

Alone onstage, Ulisse stirs awake. Like Penelope, he is introduced into the opera with a fine lament: "Dormo ancora o son desto?" (Do I sleep still or am I awake?). The notes setting these words hover low in Ulisse's register, taking advantage of the tenor's baritonal qualities to create a simple but perfect embodiment of a sleeper struggling to regain consciousness. The trancelike nature of the vocal writing is sustained through the hero's questions: "What place do I see? What air do I breathe? And what land do I tread on?" Glover observes that in the rests and repetitions in this passage "one can almost hear the question marks" ("Venetian Operas" 299; see also Abert, *Claudio Monteverdi* 46). There is a recapitulation of "Dormo ancora o son desto?," suggesting the circularity and confusion of the character's thoughts. Ulisse now strives to shake off drowsiness. This may be heard in the steady climb of his vocal line from the bottom to near the top of its compass in "Chi fece in me, chi fece il sempre dolce e lusinghevol sonno ministro di tormenti?" (Who causes my sweet and gratifying sleep always [to change] into an instrument of torture?). The deliciously sleepy rising and falling notes on "lusinghevol sonno" suggests the pull sleep still has on the awakening, increasingly agitated man. His awareness of betrayal compels his vocal line upward to his fanciful denunciation of sleep as "father of errors" (padre d'errori), but as he meditates on his own supposed culpability in his misfortunes, his voice sinks down again mirroring his self-disgust.

His rage returns with an accusation of the "ever-angry gods" (O Dei sempre sdegnati), a passage notable for the sudden, stabbing vocal rise on the reiterated "O." This is a musical rendering of a cry from the heart. His indignation easily melts into defeated resignation a few bars later when he begs the gods not "to take away, alas! the peace of the dead" (ma non tolgano, ahimè, la pace ai morti), his vocal line gradually fluttering to earth, as it were, on "morti." His anger at the Phaeacians erupts in his reiterated "voi" (you!) and "Feaci mancatori" (deceitful Phaeacians), with powerful jabbing notes. This circularity of his emotional journey from anger to despair returns when his vocal line drops yet again as he contemplates himself, "deserta, misero, abbando-nato." His monologue concludes with a return of his indignation when he wishes (ironically, in light of what happened just before he awoke) that his Phaeacian betrayers face treacherous winds in a "faithless ship" that may be like "a rock in the sea" (Sia delle vostre vele, falsissimi Feaci, sempre Borea inimico, e sian qual piuma al vento o scoglio in mare le vostre infide navi: leggiere agli aquiloni, all'aure gravi). This passage of invective is illustrated musically by the coloring of words such as "sempre," "vostre," "leggiere," and "aure." Ulisse's monologue introduces a passionate hero whose music perfectly reflects and projects the quick turning of his exceptional intellect. Members of seventeenth-century audiences who were familiar with *Arianna,* which Monteverdi had revived in Venice the year before *Ulisse,* may well have appreciated Monteverdi's scope—his ability to portray a hapless victim of seduc-tion in the earlier work and now the despair and anger of a warrior hero. Surely Monteverdi recalled Arianna at least subconsciously as he composed this monologue. Schrade observes: "When Ulisse blames the Phaeacians, his companions, for betraying and abandoning him, when he sings 'mi lasciate in questa riva aperta . . . misero abbandonato,' the passage is an exact duplicate of the lamenting phrase of Arianna aban-doned by Theseus" (352).

Scenes 8 and 9

Now Minerva appears before the "lost one" in the disguise of a shepherd boy. She is cast as a soprano, a forerunner of the "dramatic soprano with agility" (Celletti 37). The score directs that her gentle sinfonia is to be played as she "walks about," catching the eye of both Ulisse and the audience (the latter possibly indulging in the baroque theater's delight in cross-dressing, particularly when it compelled a woman performer to reveal more of her charms in close-fitting male attire). The sinfonia serves as a ritornello to her self-contained aria, which introduces her to Ulisse. "Dear, happy youth, which despises impious desire"—surely an ironic thought in this transvestite dramatic situation. Nevertheless her aria melody breathes fresh country air, captivating in its sense of free-dom and happiness. Her first verse closes with a repeat of her ritornello.

Her aria heightens the sense of her artificial performance as Ulisse, trapped in the "real world," can only observe her and vainly try to catch her attention with recitative. Badoaro's ironic sensibility is revealed again as the hero muses that "he can have no fraud in his breast who has no hair on his chin." Her second lyric recalls the allegorical framework of the opera with the seemingly offhand references to "limping time" (zoppo il tempo) and "flying love" (vola alato d'amor). Ulisse successfully arrests the "boy's" attention with an "aria" of his own—an arioso lasting only three and a half bars on "Vezzoso pastorello" (Charming shepherd boy). This melodic fragment is typical of the composer's melodic fecundity, which can render the simplest turn of phrase a memorable, singable tune that enchants the imagination. As soon as the dramatic need for the tune has expired, the composer drops it, never to use it again. As in so many aspects of his art, Monteverdi's melodic abundance and his iron-willed dramaturgical discipline anticipates the techniques of Wagner. Once Ulisse knows the "boy" is listening to him, he returns to recitative to inquire as to his whereabouts and ask for help, accenting his pathetic state as "a lost one" (un perduto) by repeating the phrase. Minerva's responding recitative suddenly radiates with a quiet sublimity: "This is Ithaca in the bosom of the sea, a famous port and a beach of happy fortunes. You make a joyful and grateful face at so fair a name [a sì bel nome]." "Nome" (name) is given a slow decoration lasting two and a half bars. This exquisite ornamentation allows the action to freeze for a breathless moment as the audience savors Ulisse's moment of recognition. He realizes he is home at last. The goddess continues her ruse by asking him his origin.

Ulisse's next monologue reveals his own attempts to spin a deceiving tale. He claims to be a a fugitive from Crete. The storm that he pretends brought him ashore is depicted by *concitato* rhythm and repetitions. These repetitions, and the huffing oscillations that set "The situation, shepherd, has been hostile to me" (Sin qui, pastor, hebbi nemico il caso), suggest Ulisse's fabled storytelling abilities. He paints an equally plausible image of the sea's return to calm and decorates "venti" (winds) with a flowing coloration suggestive of their recaptured quiescence. Slow, sleepy music and punctuating rests depict his exhausted sleep on the beach, then a bar of rapid music depicts the "furtive departure" (la furtiva partenza) of the "cruel Phaeacians." As Ulisse's story begins now to mesh with reality, his musical line becomes less overtly illustrative and all the more emotionally affecting. The idea of his sleeping torpor is indicated by the slow-moving declamation of his final lines—but now the music conveys a sense of real despair: "And I [*rest*] remained with my spoils on the bare beach [*rest*], unknown and alone [*rest*], and the sleep that has departed [*rest*] has left me with sadness."

At last Minerva reveals the full truth. Her vocal writing becomes more static, more "divinely" declamatory as she calls him by name and reveals her identity: "Ulisse is shrewd, but wiser still is Minerva." Ulisse's astonishment and joy is expressed in a new arioso, "Chi crederebbe mai! La Dietà vestite in human velo!" (Who would believe it! The deity veiled in human clothes!), set as a brief dancing tune. He returns to recitative to thank his protectress. His overflowing joy cannot be relegated to recitative, and he begins yet another arioso on "Hor consigliato seguo i tuoi saggi consigli" (Securely guided, I'll obey your wise counsels) to a tune expressive of great elation. This tune will prove to be a foreshadowing of the forthcoming aria, "O fortunato Ulisse."

Minerva begins to outline a plan of action. First he will be disguised so that he may observe the arrogant suitors. She assures him of Penelope's faithfulness. Each of these recitative remarks stimulates Ulisse to interject "O fortunato Ulisse," a direct anticipation of the aria to come. Minerva's reference to Penelope's "immutable constancy" (l'immutabil costanza) is superbly illustrated, with "immutably" repeated A's above a slow-moving bass progression, word painting as vivid as any of Bach's Passion music. "Now wet your brow at a nearby spring, so that you'll be unknown to others in the guise of an old man": Ulisse responds to this last recitative command with yet another bouncy arioso tune, "I will go obey, and then return" (Ad obbedirti vado, indi ritorno). Ulisse's bounty of melodies and melodic fragments suggest his overflowing emotions and excited impulses. As Ulisse exits to transform himself into the old beggar, Minerva sings an extended passage that fluctuates between recitative and arioso: "I saw vengeance when Troy burned; now it remains to me to bring Ulisse back to his homeland, to his reign; this is the anger of a goddess." Minerva is vocally establishing herself with luxurious ornamentation as a powerful divinity. Her anger will help to drive the events to follow. Her solo also serves the practical purpose of giving Ulisse enough time to disguise himself offstage. Ulisse returns "transformed" into an old man and signals his delight in disguise and playacting with another arioso, "Here I am, wise goddess!" (Eccomi, saggia Dea!), set to another tripping, happy tune. Minerva next orders the nymphs to carry his treasure to a secure hiding place. The scene closes with a brief duet for Minerva and Ulisse, "Ninfe serbate" (Guard, nymphs). Its pleasant stepping rhythm anticipates the setting of "Tod und Verzweiflung war sein Lohn" (Death and despair were his reward) in the coda of the two priests' duet in Mozart's *Die Zauberflöte.*

The next scene (act 1, scene 9) begins with a chorus of nymphs responding to the summons. This chorus is missing from the score and may well have been left out by the composer—just as the nereids and sirens were (probably) deliberately excised earlier. All that is really needed at this moment in the opera are nonsinging extras who may carry out the orders to hide Ulisse's "treasures and spoils" in a cave until he has defeated the suitors. Modern productions sometimes cover this action by repeating Minerva and Ulisse's "Ninfe serbate" duet or by having the instrumentalists repeat its tune until the action is completed.

Minerva orders Ulisse to wait for her with Eumete, the faithful shepherd (in Homer, a far-less-romantic swineherd), until she returns from Sparta with Ulisse's son, Telemaco. The sense of her impending airborne journey is aptly given by her coloratura decoration of "Sparta"—another example of the gods' tendency toward very florid ornament, the vocal equivalent of the machinist's pyrotechnics. The scene closes with a full-blown strophic aria, complete with ritornello, for Ulisse. The "O fortunato Ulisse" theme is finally allowed the breadth it deserves. This aria is made even more effective dramatically by the composer's frequent anticipation of its melody in the preceding scene. "O fortunato Ulisse" serves as a worthy climax to their scene together, displaying the full range of Ulisse's emotions. Now he happily exclaims "O, O, O," in striking contrast to his exclamations in his first despairing recitative monologue. He declares he will "leave off crying" for "sweet song," which will be "released from [my] happy heart." The section that closes each of the aria's two verses sets the line "No more shall mortals despair on earth!" (Non si disperi più mortale in terra!), a clear presentment of the justice to come that has made Homer's story so beloved over the centuries. The bracing five-bar ritornello that separates the aria's verses portrays a physical exultation.

Scene 10

This scene presents an illustration of Penelope's chaste constancy and the snares that she must contend with. Melanto attempts to break Penelope's resolve: "The bones of your husband, extinguished, incinerated, know either little or not much of your sufferings" (L'ossa del tuo marito estinto, incenerito, del tuo dolor non san poco né molto). Melanto's three repetitions of "del tuo dolor" (for your sufferings), punctuated by rests, have a cruelty born of self-interest. She cunningly praises "faith and constancy"— Penelope's core values—with a hypocritical florid ornament on "preclare" in the line "Faith and constancy are sublime [preclare] virtues" before qualifying that such faith does not extend to the dead. Melanto's growing confidence leads her into a brief concitato arioso when she sings, "A beautiful face causes war, warlike behavior displeases the dead" (Un bel viso fa guerra, il guerriero costume al morto spiace). Her "guerra" and "guerriero" induce her into the war rhythm, a bit incongruously, it seems—until we remember the Renaissance association between love and war that figures in Monteverdi's own Eighth Book of Madrigals. We are reminded of Penelope's own reflections on the Trojan War in her first monologue and the thematic significance in the opera of unbridled lust leading to destruction. Another arioso passage helps to illustrate in a flash of lightning Melanto's idea of the fleeting "best flowering of your years" (la più fiorita età) that Penelope is wasting. Glover cites this scene as revealing Monteverdi's "total commitment to situation and emotion. . . . Melanto . . . begins rather hesitatingly, her vocal line heavily punctuated with rests and repetitions. But as she gains in confidence, her music too becomes more secure, and she moves into a measured [aria]. This is just one of countless places where sophisticated dramatic awareness is translated into musical credibility" ("Venetian Operas" 296–97).

As a final bid to win over the queen, Melanto launches into a full-fledged aria, "Ama dunque, ché d'Amore" (Love then, for Love's sweet friend is Beauty. In pleasure your sorrows will fall by his arrows). The melody is as sweet and seductive as any in Monteverdi's work, a tune radiating comfort and sensuality—especially when the singer pays attention to the direction to hum part of the melody. Penelope's answering speech reveals the contradictory forces in her soul. She berates Amor as a "vain idol" and "vagabond god" whose "serene delight lasts no longer than lightning" (del suo dolce sereno è misura il baleno). The languishing quality of the setting of "dolce sereno" indicates how deeply Melanto's monologue has stirred her own longings and memories. She fights her way out of this with the thought that "a single day can change joy into grief" (un giorno solo cangia il piacer in duolo). Her musical style now shifts into an arioso that in rhythm and melody seems to gently lampoon Melanto's aria: "[Love causes] inconstancy and punishment, pain, death and suffering. The rays of an amorous heaven could change even a Jason into an Ulisse." This dancing arioso passage reveals unsuspected reserves of irony in Penelope's character. Monteverdi's music suggests Penelope's three-dimensionality; her austere stance is but one aspect of a richly sensual, deeply introspective human being. Her music is that of a woman who listens intently to the world around her and whose fierce moral stance is maintained, with enormous self-sacrifice, out of the deepest convictions.

Heartened by the ariosolike tendencies of Penelope's music, Melanto tries one more time to win the argument. A few recitative lines lead to a reprise of "Ama dunque, ché d'Amore." Penelope responds with four lines of recitative that convey all the tragic resignation of her first monologue: "One can never love again who has suffered misery. That person is stupid to return to suffering [a penar] who erred the first time." The triple iterations of "a penar" to sinking patterns of notes suggest an abyss of suffering.

Scenes 11, 12, and 13

The last three scenes of act 1 begin with a brief monologue introducing Eumete, the old retainer who remains staunchly loyal to Ulisse's memory. Jane Glover suggests that the tenor role of Eumete is "argu-ably the most straightforward and engaging character in either *Ulisse* or *Poppea*" ("Venetian Operas" 293). Eumete's character stems not only from the bardic tradition that Homer utilized but from the tradition of singing pastoral characters in *intermedi* and other proto-operatic per-formances (see also Pirrotta 257–68). But Monteverdi's music for the character lifts Eumete from cliché to three-dimensional reality, just as Shakespeare breathed life into countless stock figures.

"How, oh, how hard it is for a king to save himself from misfor-tune and evil!" Eumete sings. Monteverdi immediately establishes Eumete's character with the lovely flourish on "o," a gentle indication of the man's rustic status and of his openheartedness. This gesture will recur throughout his role as a kind of musical fingerprint. Eumete, a morally healthy human being who relishes his contact with the natural world, serves as a welcome contrast to the corruption of the court. This moral health is suggested by Badoaro's text but is made palpable by the perfect accord between the words and the tones used to set them. Eumete observes, "The more secure life than riches and fame is the poor and obscure one" (È vita più sicura della ricca ed illustre la povera ed oscura). Eumete's whole philosophy rests in these lines, and now he begins a charming aria extolling the pastoral life: "Hills, fields and woods! If there is happiness in the human condition, it is in you that the desired good finds its nesting place. Grassy meadows, in you the flower of delight is born, the fruit of liberty is gathered in you, the delight of humanity is in your leaves." He ornaments all the words a sensible person, if he or she happened to be a musician, would choose to ornament, operative words such as "campagne" (fields), "human," "sos-pirato" (longed for), "bene" (good), and "herbosi" (grassy). Eumete's lyrical tenor extols mankind in harmony with nature and simplicity. His love of his surroundings is suggested by the decoration given "voi" (your), "fiori" (flower), and "coglie" ([the flower of liberty] is gathered in you). The aria closes with Eumete's deliciously drawn-out repetitions of "delizie" (delight) in the phrase "your foliage is the delight of man" (son delizie dell'huom le vostre foglie).

Eumete's healthy normality in musical and verbal presentation is made all the more significant by his deliberate juxtaposition with Iro, the parasitic sponger attached to the suitors. The printed libretto indicates that this character's stuttering is the invention of the composer. Monteverdi freely manipulates Badoaro's text for Iro to create a verbal and musical aberration symbolizing Iro's grossly distorted nature. Iro, yet another tenor, represents all that is opposite to Eumete's verbal and musical health. He needlessly repeats words and musically ornaments weak or inoperative words. By grasping the dramatic potential of this character, Monteverdi created the first significant comic figure in opera and ensured the enormous success of the whole opera. Contemporary evidence suggests that the stuttering Iro was the hit of *Ulisse* in 1640. The following year the anonymous librettist for Monteverdi's next opera, the lost *Le nozze d'Enea con Lavinia,* was to state in his prefatory remarks to the opera's scenario that he had "made use of [a minor figure in the story] as a comic character, since I could not find in [Virgil] anyone more suitable [for such a role], and because I knew the disposition of many theatergoers, who prefer jokes like this to serious things as we see that Iro of our friend was a marvelous success" (qtd. in Rosand, *Opera* 43). One scholar sees in Iro "an unforgettable creation, almost a Falstaff 'avanti lettera,' prefiguring with his stuttering the grotesquerie of Rossinian Opera Buffa" (de' Paoli 482–83).

Iro cuts a ludicrous figure and offers much opportunity for comic by-play from a skilled singer-comedian. The aria Monteverdi gives him to launch his first scene is a veritable index of verbal and musical grotesquerie: "A cattle herdsman can [*può*] praise [*lodar*] meadows and woods." The awkward, chortling ornamentation of "può" stretches over two whole bars. Iro's stuttering inadvertently lavishes musical attention on a comparatively unimportant word in the sentence, indicating a comic inability to unite word, sense and music. A similar chortling stutter on a slightly more appropriate word, "lodar" (praise), suggests that this ornament could fall anywhere in Iro's speech. It is the musical expression of an involuntary psychological tic (see also de' Paoli 483). His stuttering intensifies in the musical setting of the lines "Sono cibo di bestie e non degli huomini" ([The grasses] are food for beasts, and not for people). Monteverdi inserted the word "pastor" into the text whenever Iro has trouble getting the word "bestie" (beasts) out. "Pastor," set to two jabbing notes, is the musical equivalent of the frustrated stamp of a foot: "Sono cibo di be- —di be- —pastor!—di be-, di be- —pastor!—di bestie e non doglie huomini." The comedy is enhanced by the donkeylike bleating that the notes and rhythm evoke, as well as the fact that Iro unintentionally resembles a "beast" when he tries to sing about them.

Rosand writes tellingly of Iro's inability to sing lyrically:

> It isn't simply that Iro does not sing. He tries but cannot. . . . In characterizing Iro as pathetically unmusical, Monteverdi sensitizes us to the nature of his own musical gifts: a mere turn of phrase, one fewer repetition, a slightly extended melodic line can make a melody where Iro could not. The composer emphasizes Iro's human deficiencies by imitating natural sounds in his utterances: he communicates in a primitive language of laughs, grunts and moans. ("Monteverdi's *Il ritorno*" 182)

Iro's music brands him as an intemperate, animalistic braggart, just as his physical appearance suggests his other incontinence. His crude boasting is illustrated with his characteristically donkeylike ornamentations of "sto" in the phrase "Colà tra regi io sto" (I live there [in the palace] with kings). His fatuousness manifests itself similarly on "qui" (here) in the phrase "You live here among the herds" (Tu fra gli armenti qui). His comic stammering resurfaces with the characteristic jabbing notes on "pastor" as he taunts Eumete that "I eat your companions, herdsman, and all your work!" (io mangio i tuoi compagni, pastor, e le tue pratiche!). Eumete drives the ludicrous Iro off the stage with a display of anger mixed with good humor: "Iro, you big eater, Iro, devourer, Iro, the talker!" Each epithet is sung slowly with mock solemnity, comically appropriate "heroic" music for the most antiheroic of figures. Eumete's impatience, however, manifests itself in the descending vocal line of "Don't disturb my peace" ("Mia pace non perturbar"). Eumete's anger erupts in the allegro arietta with which he chases the obnoxious glutton away: "Corri, corri, a mangiar!" (Run away and eat!). Iro beats a hasty retreat from Eumete and is replaced by the disguised Ulisse.

Eumete thinks he is alone again as he soliloquizes in recitative about the "generoso" Ulisse and his anxiety that a god's anger has taken the hero's life. After Eumete's remarks the score notates a slower chord pattern shifting the tonality from major to minor. In the gentlest of ways the composer suggests a momentous shift in the opera's action. Ulisse is at last making contact with someone from his old life. He sings in recitative, "If you desire the return on this day of the Ulisse you mentioned, receive this poor old man." The harmonic stasis in Ulisse's vocal line may indicate his successful enactment of his old-man disguise. But his music's gentle pace and tonal shift imparts a sense of sublimity to the scene. It is no wonder that Eumete will soon be calling the disguised Ulisse a "beggar god" (mendica Deità). Eumete's awe of the "old man" is shown by his recitative response promising him a "courteous lodging." The "beggar" exclaims in arioso, "Ulisse is alive! His homeland will see him! Penelope will have him." He returns to more somber recitative to ask Eumete to believe him (Credilo a me, pastore). Eumete responds by closing the act with an aria that welcomes the "beggar god" who has at last vanquished the shepherd's "long suffering." Eumete's despair of a moment past is gone. His aria, one of the opera's most beautiful passages, has the gentle contours of a lullaby bidding the vagabond to a secure rest. The music radiates Eumete's gentle humanity and integrity: the simple, loyal servant rejoicing in the prospect of his just master's return. The first act ends on a note of surprisingly serene expectancy.

Act 2

Minerva escorts Telemaco home from his search for his father ("Lieto cammino"). Eumete introduces the young prince to the old "beggar" who promised Ulisse's return. Left alone, Ulisse discloses his true identity to his son, and they share a tearful reunion ("O padre sospirato!") Ulisse bids Telemaco return to the palace and await instructions. Melanto reports to Eurimaco that Penelope cannot be persuaded to take a lover. In an elaborate scene, Penelope is menacingly importuned by the three royal suitors, Antinoo, Pisandro, and Anfinomo ("Ama dunque, sì, sì!"). She deflects their advances for the time being. After a ballo (the music for which is missing), Eumete arrives to announce that Telemaco has arrived back from Sparta and that Ulisse himself may soon return. The suitors plot to kill Telemaco but are dissuaded when a menacing bird, "Giove's eagle," flies overhead. Eurimaco encourages them to shower Penelope with gifts. In the surrounding forest,

Minerva instructs Ulisse in her plan to enable him to kill the suitors and regain his home. Ulisse and Eumete compare notes on the proceedings. Back at the court, Telemaco tells his mother about his visit to Sparta and Helen of Troy, who predicted the return of Ulisse. The suitors are dismissive of the new "beggar" Eumete has brought to court. Iro, sensing competition, challenges the "beggar" to a fight, which Ulisse wins handily. Penelope invites the "beggar" to remain. Next the suitors formally present their gifts to the queen. Inspired by Minerva, Penelope agrees to give her hand to whichever suitor can string and shoot Ulisse's bow. All three fail; the "beggar" asks to compete and wins. Revealing his true identity, and with his son and Eumete by his side, Ulisse proceeds to slaughter the suitors.

Scene I

The act begins spectacularly with Telemaco's first appearance, riding from Sparta with Minerva in her airborne chariot, a perfect fusion of baroque and Homeric sensibilities. The Venetian theater machinist would have delighted in designing the chariot in which the two singers were to fly. The vigorous and jaunty sinfonia that opens the scene masks the chariot's potential mechanical noise and allows the audience to take in the spectacle (and applaud) before any text is sung. Telemaco sings a brief aria to launch the scene: "Happy path, sweet voyage, the divine chariot passes as if it were a ray of light" (Lieto cammino, dolce viaggio, passa il carro divino come che fosse un raggio). The tenor Telemaco begins his role with an exquisite solo full of irresistible boyish enthusiasm. This is Ulisse as a young man, fresh from his first miraculous journey. Telemaco's ornaments on "lieto" (happy), "passa" (passes), and "raggio" (ray of light) suggest his wonder and exhilaration. These exultant flourishes are similar to the old-fashioned ornamentation usually reserved in the opera for the gods. By this means the composer indicates the kinship of the human Telemaco to his and his father's divine patroness. Telemaco next joins Minerva in a slower-paced duet that tempers the enthusiasm of his aria with a sense of awe as the "caro divino" comes to rest on the earth: "The powerful gods sail the air, plow the winds" (Gli dei possenti navigan l'aure, solcano i venti). Minerva initiates the duet, her divine authority creating the melody and ornaments she will share with her young protégé. Each of the "divine," luxuriant melismas on "l'aure" (air) is presented soloistically before being sung in unison at the duet's climax. The effect makes musical-dramatic time stand still—good dramatic strategy if the chariot is being lowered to the stage at this point—and gives a musical manifestation of the Homeric world's characteristic blurring of divine and human agency. Safely on earth, recitative is employed as Minerva offers a last warning to Telemaco not to "forget [her] counsels" lest "perils meet you" (incontrerai perigli). This last phrase is set to four rising and four descending notes punctuated by rests—the musical equivalent of an admonishing index finger. The goddess makes her exit.

Scenes 2 and 3

Eumete and Ulisse meet the newly arrived Telemaco. Eumete greets the prince with an extended solo of rejoicing, "O gran figlio d'Ulisse!" (O great son of Ulisse!). This is a splendid example of the melodic generosity and extraordinary flexibility of Monteverdi opera, a musical-dramatic form still young enough to avoid the potentially ossifying effects of traditional closed forms that would be imposed upon later baroque dramatic music. In Eumete's solo, aria melody changes and aria switches to recitative and back again with the quickness of thought. Here music is truly the handmaiden of poetry. Few composers aside from Haydn have been able to express untrammeled joy so naturally and unaffectedly. Words literally fail Eumete as he vocalizes a sequence of "o"s rising in pitch and volume in the phrase "O grand figlio d'Ulisse, o——." The effect is repeated as he reprises the aria's opening phrase with another rising sequence of "o"s added for good measure. The technique is simple, but the dramatic-mimetic conviction it carries is enormously effective. Carter observes: "Eumete's song grows from psychological excitement—hence the verbal incoherence. . . . In turn, we no longer just contemplate a given dramatic situation or emotional state; rather we are forced to share and feel it" (*Monteverdi's Musical Theater* 65).

A new, sweet melody of rising and falling contours sets Eumete's words, "And you are finally reunited with your fallen house to repair the noble ruins" (E pur sei giunto alfine di tua casa cadente a riparar l'altissime ruine). Eumete—and Monteverdi—prodigally abandon this lovely tune as the shepherd envisions the end of their years of sorrow. "Fugga, fugga il cordoglio e cessi il pianto" (Lamenting flees and sorrows end) is a new, fast-paced tune, with appropriately "flighty" ornaments on "fugga"—another delightful melody sung once and then abandoned. Eumete's next word shifts to the relative calm of recitative as he turns to his older companion on "Facciamo, o peregrino" (Let us, O wanderer). We may well expect Eumete's arioso singing to be finished, but he reverts to new melodic writing as he enjoins the disguised Ulisse to "do honor to our happiness in song" (all'allegrezze nostre honor col canto) to yet another dancelike tune. These musical shifts reflect Eumete's excited state of mind. Eumete's request for Ulisse to join him in "song" (canto) ushers in a charming duet between the older men: "Green coasts on the happy day, resplendent grasses and flowers! The breezes play with the cupids, the heavens smile on a beautiful return." The images of the beauties of the natural world, reflecting human joy, anticipate the sentiments of Penelope's act 3 aria. Along with the interaction in words and music between Eumete and Telemaco, Ulisse's own recognition of his son is an important though unscripted part of the text of any performance.

Telemaco apologizes in recitative for his own emotional reticence, "for a soul that waits [*alma ch'aspetta*] cannot be calm." Eumete, momentarily sated with melody from his duetting and aria, begins to introduce the "beggar" to Telemaco in recitative, but his excitement again overcomes him, and his music quickens in pulse and becomes more lyrical as he declares that the beggar "has assured me that Ulisse's return is not far off from this day" (egli m'accerta che d'Ulisse il ritorno fia di poco lontan da questo giorno). Ulisse is characteristically more controlled in "rational" recitative when he replies to Telemaco, promising to die if his promise is false. Eumete's emotions overflow again as he initiates yet another duet with Ulisse, one of the loveliest Monteverdi ever wrote, "Dolce speme" (Sweet hope flatters the heart, happy news charms every soul, yet fulfillment is not possible for a soul that's waiting). The emotional temperature rises as Ulisse nears the moment when he will reveal his identity to his son. Eumete's vocal line is notable for the happily sighing vocalise he gives to the end of each melodic phrase. Ulisse joins him in this tender music of happy contemplation, this "chaconne of impeccable technique" (Arnold, *Monteverdi* 113). They sing the final two verses of their duet in unison, "yet fulfillment is not possible for a soul that's waiting [*alma ch'aspetta*]," quoting the end of Telemaco's recitative from a moment before. With their words and euphonious duetting they seem to draw the still-ignorant young man into their emotional circle. All three men, though separated by age and disguise, are bound together, images of the human soul living in troubled expectation.

Telemaco sends Eumete to the palace to announce the prince's return; his repeated order of "vanne" (run) indicates that he too is excited by the "beggar's" claims. When Eumete exits, father and son are alone together for the first time. On the instant, Badoaro directs, "a ray of fire comes down from the sky, over the head of Ulisse, the earth opens, and Ulisse is swallowed up." Telemaco is left alone to deliver more than two pages of recitative—allowing the actor who has just disappeared through the trap door in the stage nearly two minutes to effect the costume and make-up change for his reappearance "in his proper form." Telemaco naturally expresses fear and amazement before beginning to worry that the vanishing figure may have been a divine sign that his father is really dead. One can hear his apprehension overtake Telemaco in the rests inserted between his words: "Ah [*rest*], dear father [*rest*], is it in this strange manner [*rest*] that heaven advises me of your death?" Rests and pitch changes vividly suggest the fluidity of changing mental states.

At this point Ulisse majestically reappears as himself, rising from below the ground. Telemaco sputters "Ma—ma—ma" (But—but—but) to ascending notes. Once his initial astonishment wears off, he turns to a short arioso, musing, "No more shall death be called bitter if in dying you learn to rejuvenate." One can feel his fear turning to wonder on the the ornamental runs given "ringiovanir" (rejuvenate). Ulisse addresses his son in his own person for the first time: "Telemaco, it's fitting that your wonder turns to joy" (Telemaco, convienti cangiar le meraviglie in allegrezze). The triple iteration of the name in the score adds a sense of momentousness to the recitative. Ulisse sets the musical pattern for the next exchange by adopting recitative with ariosos to accent a particular word or phrase. "In allegrezze" is set to a three-bar arioso in dance rhythm, recalling Eumete's melody on the same words in his aria "O gran figlio d'Ulisse." Ulisse's music is becoming more lyrical, but Telemaco is not ready to leave circumspect recitative for the emotional release of aria or duet. "Transformation is not possible for mortal man," reasons Telemaco. He declares, "The gods are tricksters" (O scherzano gli dei), treating the idea to a derisive coloratura. His father responds, "I am Ulisse! Minerva is witness, she who carried you flying though the air" (Ulisse, Ulisse sono! Testimonio è Minerva, quella che te portò per l'aria a volo). "L'aria" (air) is sung by Ulisse to a luxurious melisma similar to the "divine" ornamentation used by Minerva and her young protégé as they descended from the flying chariot. Telemaco is won over. Beyond the evidence of his eyes and Ulisse's verbal argument, his father's appropriation of "divine" music subliminally unites Telemaco with his own experience of divinity, and he now is assured of the older man's identity.

Telemaco's ascending vocalization on "O" in his phrase "O padre sospirato!" (O longed-for father!) and Ulisse's "O figlio desiato!" (O desired son!) are disarming in their frank suggestion of emotional release. The two tenors, father and son, sing a love duet almost as affecting as the later reunion of Ulisse and Penelope. Seldom if ever in the ensuing operatic heritage has the filial relationship been portrayed with such tenderness. This duet marks the true midpoint of the opera. Monteverdi's deep love for his own two sons is attested in the composer's correspondence, and the composer's own father had provided Monteverdi with invaluable moral support. The love between father and son in *Ulisse* is remarkable for its intensity. It lacks the neurotic baggage seen in the relationship between the title character and his son in Mozart's *Idomeneo,* not to mention the tortured father-son encounters in Wagner's *Ring* and Verdi's *Don Carlos.* In a similar vein, the reunion of Ulisse and Penelope at the close of the work probably represents personal associations and wish fulfillment for the widowed composer.

For the next several measures father and son trade soloistic remarks to each other, the composer insisting on a repetition of the exchange "Ti inchino! Ti stringo!" (I bow, I embrace). The implicit physical contact of child and father, separated for so many years, triggers a flowing ornamental line from Telemaco on another melismatic "o"—an indication that the joy the son is experiencing is too great for words. Father and son counterpoint each other until their unison pronouncement, "A mortal confides and hopes, all" (Mortal tutto confida e tutto spera), an extravagantly confident assertion in an opera that has given memorable embodiment to Human Frailty itself in the prologue. But the dramatic situation, with its musical expression by two ringing tenor voices, two Grecian heroes uniting in a common cause, banishes a sense of irony from the most jaundiced of listeners. The voices sing contrapuntally again until their duet ends with a final unison on "The impossible has again become true" (L'impossibile ancor spesso s'avvera). The duet's climax leads directly into an arioso by Ulisse that sends both men offstage. The melody, a sweet rising figure, is appropriately energetic to match the words "Go to your mother, go! [*Vanne alla madre!*] Go to the palace! I'll come to you again, but first I must return as an old man." These are hardly inspiring words—in fact, they are pure dramaturgical housekeeping—but Monteverdi endows their music with a melodic tenderness that suggests Ulisse's still-overflowing heart. It serves as a catharsis after the emotional expression of the past several scenes. Joseph Kerman writes: "*Vanne alla madre,* Ulisse says to the plot, as well as to Telemaco, 'go to your mother,' a (diatonic) scale up, a scale down, the same scale up again—almost shockingly simple, this, as a musical evocation of tenderness, hope, and dramatic anticipation. Monteverdi's little songs can move us as much as his affective recitative" ("Full Monte" 38). The stage is set for the first confrontation with the suitors.

Scene 4

Scene 4 affords a second and final glimpse of Melanto and Eurimaco together. Melanto tells her lover that her attempts to persuade Penelope to yield to the suitors have failed. Penelope is a "rock" (scoglio) and has a heart of "diamond" (diamante), both metaphors illustrated by suitably low notes in Melanto's register. Eurimaco abandons for the moment his long-term Machiavellian strategy and shows he is willing simply to live for the erotic moment. "Pains that are desired, troubles that are voluntary; let them enjoy the shade that hate the sun," sings Eurimaco to a short-lived dance tune. Melanto states that "Penelope triumphs in grief and in weeping" (Penelope trionfa nella doglia e nel pianto); the last three words, with their sinking cadence, smack of tongue-in-cheek. The arioso Melanto launches, with its bouncy rhythm and malicious reference to her mistress's sorrow, suggest a woman mocking emotions she can imitate but cannot understand. Eurimaco joins her in duet to close their scene: "Enjoying, laughing, sorrow is destroyed, let us love, enjoying and let others say what they will." Their purpose in the plot, as a contrast to the enduring stability of Ulisse and Penelope, has run its course. It is time for the suitors to appear and speak for themselves and not through surrogates such as Eurimaco or Iro.

Scenes 5, 6, and 7

Penelope's lonely confrontation with the suitors is an exceptional example of Monteverdi's musical drama. A large structure is built out of small musical units into a dynamic musical-dramatic edifice. Schrade writes: "This fusion of structure and expression is as characteristic of [Monteverdi's] art and aesthetic sense as it is of his dramatic and human strength. He thinks of the scene as an organism whose continuous growth must follow a preconceived form and direction" (353–54). The crowds of lawless suitors that Homer describes are economically telescoped by Badoaro into three sinister figures, Antinoo, Pisandro, and Anfinomo. (An enterprising producer is of course free to supplement their numbers with extras playing their attendants.) Antinoo, the ringleader, is a bass, Anfinomo is cast as a tenor, and Pisandro is an alto. These three men menacingly surround Penelope, their music and words alike vividly suggesting their corruption, duplicity, and latent violence. Antinoo launches the scene with a brief recitative that suggests his character in a few deft strokes: "Other queens are surrounded by servants, you by lovers. These kings pay homage to the sea of your beauty with a sea of tears." Antinoo's deeply resonant bass range has been heard before in the threatening figures of Tempo and Nettuno. Antinoo's florid ornamental run on "tu" (you) is excessive, a strained musical gesture, the musical equivalent of a disingenuous caress.

Antinoo, like his fellow suitors, is a beast who apes civilized manners. Monteverdi's setting of his words portrays a hollow, threatening figure whose expressive vocabulary aims at conventional courtliness. The result is expressive banality—witness the pat conventionality of the appropriately high notes on "bellezza" (beauty) and the clichéd droop on "pianti" (tears). The three suitors now launch the first iteration of their "Ama dunque, sì, sì" trio (Love then, yes, yes). The vocal lines rise from the bass to tenor to alto voices, the melody and words coaxing, seductive, insistent. The harsh plosive sound on "dunque" suggests the physical threat residing behind the courtly manners. Adding to the thinly disguised threat are the snakelike, hissing sibilants of the "sì, sì" traded between the three voices. Chafe notes in regard to this trio that "the repetitions of the word 'sì' foreshadow its reappearance in the final love duet, the word on which the opera ends" (Chafe 271).

The suitors' insistent melodic vigor is matched by Penelope's feisty aria response, "Non voglio amar, no, no, ch'amando penerò" (I don't want to love, no, no, for love is painful). The repeated "no"s signal her regal, dignified refusal with a descending five-note scale. Penelope's firm musical response triggers a repetition of the "Ama dunque, sì, sì" trio. The suitors press their case with the same music and words. Penelope's terse refusal has won her no respite. Penelope now tries to cajole the men with recitative: "You are so dear to me who burn with such special ardor" (Cari tanto mi siete quanto più ardenti ardete). Her ornaments on "tanto" and especially "ardenti ardete" reply in stylistic kind to the oily disingenuousness of Antinoo's first recitative. She is flattering her tormentors in their own musical language to gain time. When she sings "But don't approach me in the game of love, for the fire is more beautiful from afar than near," she is borrowing their specious courtly language and manners with the cliché of the "game of love" (amoroso gioco). Her position clarified, she reiterates her "Non voglio amar" arioso, now "a foot stamping refrain" (Carter, *Monteverdi's Musical Theater* 258). As with the trio, this repetition heightens the sense of dramatic conflict.

To break the stalemate, Pisandro, the tenor suitor, delivers an arioso plea. Like Antinoo's, Pisandro's hypocrisy is suggested by a tendency toward over-the-top ornamentation masquerading as courtliness.

But Pisandro exhibits somewhat more superficial attractiveness as he sings a lovely though stilted melody and platitudinous metaphor to woo the queen: "The leafy vine that does not embrace the tree in autumn will not bear fruit nor flower its best." His drawn-out ornamentation on "abbraccia" (embrace), extending three bars, smacks of courtly affectation but has an undeniable sensuality. The ornaments and trill on "fiorisce" (flower) would be endearing if not for the image of studied affectation he projects. Like Schubert's Erlking, Pisandro's enticements are lyrically attractive but no less threatening for that. He closes his solo with "if [the vine] no longer flowers every hand will gather it, every foot will trample it." The latent violence of this last metaphor is emphasized by Pisandro's insistent musical depictions on "ogni mano la coglie, ogni piè la calpesta." Anfinomo, the alto, now makes his bid for the queen. Like his tenor rival, he makes use of courtly love poetry replete with more horticultural metaphors: "The beautiful fragrant cedar lives, if not grafted, without fruit and covered with thorns: but when grafted, it gives birth to fruits and flowers from its thorns." The arioso starts with an individual melodic charm, but the alliteration on "f" in the repetition of "figliano frutti e fior" makes Anfinomo just slightly absurd. If the role was intended for a castrato, one might be tempted to see a level of performative irony here, a "fruitless" singer warning hollowly about fruitlessness. This possibly ironic use of the castrato can be found in *Poppea,* especially in the character of Ottone.

Antinoo weighs in with his own plea: "The ivy which grows even in spite of winter, like a beautiful, eternal emerald, if not supported, loses its beautiful green among the grassy ruins." Recitative is the natural element of Antinoo's expressive style. He is too earthbound a figure to find even the disingenuous melodiousness of Pisandro and Anfinomo. As before, Antinoo glibly overornaments "ad onta" (in spite) and "smeraldo eterno" (eternal emerald). His repeated descending runs on "rovine" (ruin) hint again at the violence below his surface manners. The suitors reunite for a third "Ama dunque, sì, sì" trio, made more threatening and insistent by all that has passed since its last appearance. Penelope's response is one of the most masterly moments in the opera. Monteverdi portrays her resolve and control while hinting at the enormous psychological toll of her position. "Non voglio amar," she sings, as if to start a third iteration of her aria. But she breaks off with three rests. "Non voglio, non voglio," she sings, the melody seeming to break apart under the emotional strain. Another brief rest indicates a change of musical-rhetorical tactics. Rather than repeat her arioso of refusal, she turns to recitative; rather than adopting the suitors' unctuous ornamental style, she sings now in her own voice. She is torn hopelessly between a "triple love," she says disingenuously, but her reflections that "tears and suffering, sadness and sorrow are cruel enemies of love" come from her heart. Frightened and emotionally battered by the suitors, she drops every strategy to deflect their advances and as a last resort pleads in an honest-sounding recitative reminiscent of passages from her opening lament. This works for the moment. The suitors, perhaps charmed by the artlessness of these pleas, launch into a new ensemble of their own to "cheer the queen," but obviously the respite can only be a temporary one.

The suitors sing "All'allegrezze"—"Now for pleasure then, to dance and song! We'll cheer the queen! A light heart falls in love at once." This trio, complete with a da capo repeat of the first section, displays all the brio of men without conscience reveling at someone else's expense, their joyful music "a grotesque contrast to the scene's tragic situation" (Osthoff 196). Glover observes: "The very relentlessness of its repetition serves to underline the ordeal Penelope is undergoing" ("Venetian Operas" 301).

In the libretto, scene 6 consists of a "Greek dance performed by eight Moors" to courtly, amorous verses that have not been set in the surviving score. The words are close to the suitors' courtship style: "Ladies in love, fair and tender, love when April smiles; joy and pleasure do not keep company with the heart when hoary age touches your tresses, etc." (translated by Derek Yeld). Either the music is lost, or, more likely, Monteverdi opted not to set it for reasons of financial and aesthetic economy. The suitors' "All'allegrezze" trio succinctly hints at the men's vulgar merrymaking. The possible gap, however, has led many productions to incorporate other music by Monteverdi into the score. In the midst of the suitors' unseemly revel, Eumete appears.

Too excited to settle on either recitative or aria, Eumete declaims to the queen and suitors that he has "very important news" (d'alte novelle, d'alte novelle). Addressing Penelope directly, Eumete sings, "O gran regina" (O great queen). Eumete's characteristic decorations of "O" here suggest his jubilant hopes, which he is unafraid to express before the suitors. He announces, "He's come back, O great queen, Telemaco your son. And perhaps the hope is not vain that I bring: Ulisse, our king, your consort, is alive. And let's hope that his longed-for arrival is not far away!" Penelope exits on somber recitative befitting her stoic attitude: "Such dubious news can either double my sorrows or change the tenor of my stars."

Scene 8

The suitors are left alone onstage. Antinoo again dominates the situation, his sepulchral voice now employing a simple, direct recitative style devoid of the prettified ornamental tendency he displayed while courting Penelope. The rests that emphasize the words "Compagni [*rest*], udiste?" (Comrades, did you hear?) suggest his authority. The rising musical line and repetitions on "a grandi e risolute imprese" (great and resolute enterprises) hint at what is to come. The last rest, in "Telemaco ritorna e forse Ulisse" (Telemaco returns [*rest*] and perhaps Ulisse), suggests a spontaneous gasp of apprehension. The notion of Ulisse's "approaching vengeance" (prossima vendetta) triggers a rapid, descending musical line covering three iterations of the verbal phrase. The danger is such that "crime must be our security." He reminds them of the depth of their offenses against the royal house. Anfinomo and Pisandro, Antinoo's obedient pupils, sing a brief duet: "Our deeds have made us enemies of Ulisse. The enemies' anger is never canceled." This duet is largely a unison declamation, with only the briefest suggestions of counterpoint. The musical-dramatic effect is of two men in terrified lockstep, fearing for their lives. Antinoo spells out their strategy in another recitative passage: "Therefore let our ardor increase." The "ardor" Antinoo now refers to is a far cry from the amorous passion he described so fulsomely to the beleaguered queen; "L'ardir s'accresca" sounds like a snarl. On "Let's take Telemaco from the living just as he arrives!" (Telemaco vicin togliam dai vivi!), Antinoo's voice descends threateningly. United by their murderous plan, the suitors sing a trio, "Sì, sì, de' grandi amori sono figli i gran sdegni; quel fere i core e quest'abbate i regni" (Yes, yes, great loves are the sons of the greatest hatreds; one wounds the heart, and the other fells kingdoms). The "sì, sì" iterations are passed between all three characters, recalling their serpentine importuning of Penelope. The drawn-out words "grandi amori," which the three share in an almost amorous unison, seem like the prelude to a love madrigal. Instead, violence erupts, with "sono figli i gran sdegni" sung to a new rapid, *concitato*-style passage. Each of them expresses rage on "e quest'abbate i regni" and lascivious longing on "quel fere i cori."

At this most dangerous moment, the stage directions require that "an eagle [fly] over the heads of the suitors." Giove's threatening sign is interpreted for the suitors in recitative by their ally, the observing Eurimaco. Eurimaco warns, "Move your steps toward crime only if you don't believe the heavens to be just" (Muova al delitto il piede chi giusto il ciel non crede). The suitors take their accomplice's hint and sing a second trio, "Crediam al minacciar del ciel irato" (I believe the threats of irate heaven, for whoever isn't afraid of heaven doubles his sin). A moment before they were united in their malevolence; now they are united in rapid music that portrays their tremulous cowardice. The effect of this trio is comic, a "grotesque" parody of *stile concitato* (Osthoff 197). The three men are reduced to palpably chattering terror.

Having failed as assassins, Antinoo rallies his troops, proposing that they woo Penelope as quickly as possible with golden gifts before her son, or anyone else, can arrive to stop them. The notions of "gold" (or) and the "arrows" (stral) of love are treated to the same unctuous overornamenting that is the salient feature of Antinoo's style of seduction. Eurimaco, relieved to have turned the men's minds from murder, sings a brief aria supporting their new strategy of gift giving, "L'oro sol, l'oro sia l'amorosa magia" (Let gold alone be the magician of love), to a dancelike tune signaling a return to the semblance of courtly values. The scene ends with a climactic trio for the suitors: "Amor è un'armonia" (Love is a harmony), the three sing in a hushed unison. "The sighs are the songs" (Sono canti i sospiri), they continue, in words and music that seem to come straight out of the *Eighth Book of Madrigals*. The rest that punctuates the word "sigh" (so-[*rest*]-spiri) is a striking mimetic effect. Their anxiety about Telemaco and Ulisse's return inspires them to play their self-appointed roles of noble lovers more vividly than ever before. But their avaricious motives can be suppressed only so long. After a discreetly placed rest they continue their self-conscious love madrigal with the mercenary observation that "they don't sing so well without the sound of gold. Whoever doesn't give presents, doesn't love."

In Homer, the suitors' plot against Telemaco occurs early in the epic and is developed more fully. Badoaro compresses this aspect of the story into this short incident, which comes relatively late in the opera's action. Consequently, the opera relegates their threat to the seriocomic bagatelle described above. The rather buffoonish cowardice portrayed here goes a long way toward denying them sympathy before their coming slaughter. Many critics and performers have followed suit and portrayed them as entirely comic throughout the opera. Historical support for this may be found in the stylistic similarities between their ensemble music and that of the *giustiniana,* popular Venetian Carnival songs traditionally performed by three sexually aroused yet impotent old men (see Rosand, "Monteverdi's *Il ritorno*" 181; Kerman, "Full Monte" 38). This is certainly a clue that the composer is placing some ironic frame around these characters, isolating them from the more sympathetic characters. But just as Shakespeare borrowed liberally from the comic tradition of the medieval vice to create his Richard III and Iago, the potent comedic elements Monteverdi has given the suitors does not warrant their being written off as entirely silly. When reduced to mere buffoonery, the suitors fail to pull their dramatic weight, and the opera suffers immeasurably. The suitors are a mixture of threatening, amorous, politic, and occasionally silly elements. To cheat them of the contradictory dimensions written into their roles (i.e., their humanity) fails to do justice either to the composer or the dramatic argument of the work.

Scenes 9 and 10

Scenes 9 and 10 are brief connecting scenes showing the preparations Ulisse, Minerva, and Eumete make for the assault on the suitors. The "Boschareccia" (woods) setting contrasts the freer natural world with the corrupted court that Ulisse must purify. This bucolic setting and the sublimely euphonious recitative Ulisse sings at the beginning of scene 9 suggests the ordered cosmos that Ulisse is attempting to reestablish: the world of divinity and humanity living in harmony. Minerva's sets forth her divine plan for Ulisse's strike to regain his home and wife. Minerva's *concitato*-style fireworks describing the moment of Ulisse's divinely sanctioned reprisal are thrilling: "E strepitoso suon fiero t'invita, saetta pur, che la tua destra ardita tutti confisccherà gli estinti al piano" (A deafening sound will invite you, then the arrows from your bold right hand shall nail them all dead to the ground). The florid coloratura on "suon" and the thrice-repeated "saetta pur" energize this description of righteous aggression. After this passage, Minerva assures him that she herself (Io [*rest*], io) will be beside Ulisse with her celestial lightening (Io starò teco e con celeste lampo). The rests that punctuate the line before and after the first "io" bridge the vocal *concitato* fury to this new idea of her divine comradeship with Ulisse in the battle to come. "They will fall victim to your vengeance" (Cadran vittime tutti alla vendetta), she assures him in a vocal passage that descends from the heights to the depths of her range. Her speech ends with the reiterated assurance that "they have not escaped punishment of heaven!" (ché i flagelli del Ciel non hanno scampo!), a passage replete with wonderfully effective "divine" fioriture (embellishments) on "hanno" and "scampo."

Eumete reports the suitors' growing fear at the mere sound of Ulisse's name. Eumete's rests portrays the fearful paralysis that has stricken the suitors: "I saw, O wanderer [*rest*], the amorous suitors [*rest*], their boldness [*rest*] failing [*rest*], their ardor [*rest*] freezing [*rest*] in their trembling eyes [*rest*], their hearts palpitating. The name of Ulisse alone transfixed these guilty souls" (Il nome sol d'Ulisse, quest'alme ree trafisse). The phrase "il nome" so excites Eumete that he repeats it to a dancing rhythm, as if he's about to begin an aria before his recitative closes. An aria does follow, a joyful two-part song for Ulisse: "I rejoice also, though I don't know why, how I laugh, though I don't know why. I am completely overjoyed, rejuvenated, by such happiness" (Godo anch'io, né so, come rido, né so perché. Tutto gioisco, ringiovanisco, ben lieto affè). The score directs Ulisse to perform his divisions on "perché" and "lieto" as if they were the laughter he is describing ("Qui rede da dovero insin a qua"), a fine example of Monteverdi's love of lifelike detail. Ironically, one other character in the opera will utilize a similar laughing effect: Iro, in his bizarre lament at the top of the third act, an echo that creates a macabre dramatic rhyme. Ulisse and Eumete leave the woods to prepare for the attack. Ulisse warns, "The thunderbolts of heaven terrify the Olympians themselves."

Scene 11

Telemaco describes to his mother his interview in Sparta with Helen. Penelope rebukes the young man for his admiration for the woman whose beauty led to war and Ulisse's disappearance. Telemaco responds that Helen, gifted at augury, has predicted the return and revenge of Ulisse. This scene contains subtle thematic relevance to both this opera and the later *Poppea*. Penelope is the center of female constancy in *Ulisse,* a symbol of Neoplatonic heavenly love, which enables the defeat of evil and the reestablishment of order. Helen of Troy is Penelope's opposite, the representative of earthly love, whose fires can literally level cities. Such dialectic arguments on the nature of love were popular with the Accademia degli Incogniti, of which Badoaro was a member. (See also Carter, *Monteverdi's Musical Theater* 246).

Monteverdi's music for Telemaco helps to project an innocent adolescent's first impressions of the greater world outside his parents' home. His love for his mother is manifested in the tapering A–B–A phrase on "regina" (queen) that closes his first sentence. In performance this simple sequence of notes suggests deep filial tenderness and respect. We are reminded of his love for his father, which had been so memorably expressed earlier in the score. His awakening sexuality is revealed in the gorgeously sensual setting of "la belleza divina" ([Helen] the divine beauty): "The beautiful Helen received me: I gazed at her stupefied" (M'accolse Helena bella: io mirando stupii). The rests that separate "io" from the surrounding text serve as a subtle musical freeze-frame suggesting the personal impact of Helen's beauty on the young man as he first sees her. The allure and danger that Helen represents, the embodiment of unlawful desire, is suggested in the setting of "I saw in those beautiful eyes the nascent sparks of burning Troy, the infant flames" (Io vidi in quel' begl'occhi, dell'incendio Trojano le nascenti scintille, le bambine faville). "Io vidi in quel' begl'occhi" is first set to gentle, mellifluous music—Telemaco is recalling his first view of Helen. Instantly the musical pulse quickens to a brief yet startling *concitato* section with emphatic verbal repetitions: "vidi, vidi quel' begl'occhi dell'incendio Trojano." The young man's passions have been aroused; he is reliving the encounter in the telling. Love for Helen is the force that can burn down cities, and even now her deleterious power can be witnessed in her innocent young admirer, who goes on to extol the worthless Paris for daring all to enjoy such a prize: "Paride," he repeats three times, each to a rising trio of notes, filled with impetuous, youthful enthusiasm. "The beautiful Greek bears in her lovely face all the excuses for the Trojans' sins" (La bella Greca porta nel suo volto beato tutte le scuse del Trojan peccato): these closing lines of the prince's speech are set in recitative of a piercing, uncanny purity. Monteverdi is suggesting not just the beauty of Helen but the ferocity of newly awakened adolescent ardor, when sensuality can rise to a point of religious exhilaration. Penelope will not stand for Telemaco's naive praise for the woman who led to so much sorrow. Helen's is "a beauty too deadly, sinful passion unworthy of remembrance," she warns her smitten son. "What a monster is that love that swims in blood" (Ché mostro è quell'amor che nuota in sangue), she says—words that could serve as a motto for Helen, the suitors, or some of the characters in *Poppea*. Penelope's attempt to disabuse her son inspires her straightforward recitative declamation, which reserves ornamental coloration for her last word, "desio"—in reference to Telemaco's "foolish desire."

Sobered by Penelope's rebuke, Telemaco declares that he has mentioned Helen because she is connected to a happy prophecy: "While in famous Sparta suddenly I was circled by the flight of an agile and happy bird. Helen, who is masterful in the science of divination and auguries, in all happiness told me that Ulisse was near." Helen's reaction and divination, "tutt'allegra mi disse ch'era vicino Ulisse," vividly break from the surrounding recitative in dancelike arioso under the emotional and dramatic pressure of the situation. Ulisse, Helen told Telemaco, will "bring death to the suitors and establish himself in his rule." Penelope's response appears in the libretto, but its music is missing from the score, almost certainly a scribal error: "May heaven grant that my life still be sustained by the frail thread of hope, and, as nature teaches the tiny seed to grow until a plant, thus, within my breast from a tiny seed the greatest joy is born" (translation by Yeld).

Scene 12

Scene 12 returns to the embattled court of Ithaca for the climactic struggle between the disguised Ulisse and the suitors. Penelope presides over this monumental scene, among the lengthiest and most ambitious in Monteverdian opera. The scene portrays two distinct conflicts leading to two different battles that mirror each other ironically; the contest of Ulisse and Iro and the contest of the bow between the suitors and Ulisse. Each struggle ends with a rousing passage in *stile concitato*. As with the first scene introducing the suitors, Monteverdi is faced with formidable organizational challenges, which he meets triumphantly. Eumete has just admitted Ulisse, disguised as a beggar, to the presence of the suitors. Antinoo's recitative, in a jabbing, threatening rhythm, denounces Eumete and the "beggar," reiterating that the shepherd "sempre . . . di perturbar la pace" (is always disturbing the peace): "You are always, always managing to disturb our peace, low-born Eumete; to make cloudy our joy, you sorrow bringer, you troublemaker. Now you've led in an infested beggar, an annoying importuner who you greedily hope will spoil our happy mood." Antinoo's insistence on "the happy mood [*mente*]," sung to a slithering six-note flourish as he and his comrades threaten and intimidate Penelope and her household, is a fine piece of musical characterization. "Civilized nobility is not cruel," Eumete insists, "nor can a great soul scorn pity which kings have from their birth." Antinoo explodes, "Arrogant plebeian! Teaching noble [*eccelse*] works is not appropriate [*non tocca*] for a vile man." His voice reaches to the heights and depths of its compass on "eccelse" and "tocca."

Iro interposes himself and inadvertently deflects the mounting tension between Eumete and Antinoo. "Leave, leave; move your feet!"
cries the suitor's gluttonous mascot; "if you are here to eat, I am here
before you" (se sei qui per mangiar son pria di te)—this last phrase
full of his characteristic stuttering. Ulisse sizes up this new "threat"
and addresses him with mock solemnity. In an initially gentle recitative establishing his old-man vocal persona, Ulisse sings, "Man of great
waist, of large perspective." He continues, "Though I am white-haired
and aged. . . ." Here Ulisse's anger breaks through the ironic mask as
he sings the phrase "my spirit is not vile yet" (non è vile però l'anima
mia), his voice rising for the triple iteration of "non è vile però." Ulisse
continues, "If high royal bounty [l'alta bontà regale] concedes so much
to me, I will trample your corpulent body beneath my foot." The words
"bontà regale" are treated to ornamentation that briefly floats at the
top of Ulisse's vocal line, registering not merely the calculated flattery
of the suitors, but something of the emotional pressures he must feel
as he sees his wife and home again for the first time in twenty years.
When called a "monstrous animal" by Ulisse, Iro is beside himself:
"I will pluck out the hairs from your beard, one by one!" In his fury,
Iro's stuttering is replaced by a ludicrous three-bar rapid arioso built
out of "barba ad uno ad uno" (from your beard one by one). In Ulisse's
response a hint of concitato rhythm tempers the words "I'll give up
my life if with force and valor I do not defeat you now, sack of straw."
Antinoo, rehearsing for his anticipated role as head of the Ithacan court,
displays his sporting side to Penelope: "Let's watch, Queen, this beautiful couple wrestling [d'una lotta], an absurd duel." "D'una lotta" is
colored with ironic ornament, the musical equivalent of a melodramatic
grimace. Antinoo, the seeming master of the situation, is unaware that
the ridiculous scrapping of Iro and the beggar is a prelude to a much
deadlier "lotta" to come.

Telemaco assures his disguised father that the field is secure for the
combat with Iro. Naturally missing the point that the grand hall will
become a real battlefield in the near future, Iro joins in: "And I also
assure you the freedom [of the field], bearded fighter." As always when
Iro's emotions are heightened, the rush of his feelings overflows in
ludicrous stuttering, here on the phrase "combattitor barbuto" (bearded

fighter), which turns into a passage of sputtering, burlesque *concitato* writing. Ulisse, as if in mockery, responds with real *concitato* style as he sings, "I accept the great challenge" (La gran disfida accetto). Iro takes his place to fight with a deliciously idiotic battle aria, "Now then, you, you! To the scuffle, to the fight!" (Su dunque! Su, su! Alla ciuffa, alla lotta!), in *concitato* rhythm. The accompanying instruments play a short battle sinfonia for the duration of the fight. The serious tone of the sinfonia, however, which serves as background music for the fight between the oafish Iro and the bedraggled beggar, has much the same ironic effect as the march rhythm and militaristic perorations that make Figaro's "Non più andrai" so memorable. Both Monteverdi and Mozart appreciated the ironic possibilities when drama and music were allowed to comment on each other.

Iro soon cries uncle—in this case, "Son vinto" (I'm defeated!), in excited repetitions over an active bass line before sinking into pseudo-tragic lament as he declares, "Ohimè," like a vanquished hero. This is not the result Antinoo wanted to see, as his stiff declamation indicates: "You, the victor, pardon him who admits defeat." His remark to Iro is more personal: "Iro, you're a good eater, but not a fighter" (Iro, puoi ben mangiar, ma non lottar). Antinoo's anger is felt in the low pitch and the snarling repetitions of "ma non lottar." Penelope, full of the true royal generosity and fellow-feeling that the suitors so conspicuously lack, formally instates the beggar at the court in dignified recitative: "Valorous beggar! Stay in court in honor and security. He is not always vile who wears poor, unsightly clothes." Penelope seems already sub-consciously drawn to the mysterious beggar, foreshadowing the later recognition scene.

Making good on their promise to shower her with gifts, the suit-ors resume their ritualistic courtship of the beleaguered queen. Both Pisandro and Anfinomo offer her gifts of crowns and "royal mantles" in exchange for her love. Each man's recitative is formal and unimagi-native, like the characters themselves. Icily formal, too, is Penelope's recitative response. It should be noted that the only surviving source for the opera accidentally confuses the alto and tenor suitors, a prob-lem that all performing versions rectify. These kinds of inconsistencies are not unknown in other Venetian opera scores. Jane Glover, in her study of Cavalli, observes: "There are four occasions [in Cavalli's operas] where a character changes clef and therefore range within the course of the opera, and several others where a character briefly slips into another clef" (*Cavalli* 73). In addition to the snafu with the two suitors, the Vienna manuscript reveals that Eumete had been partially rescored for soprano castrato, evidently in response to changed exigencies in casting.

The coming denouement is foreshadowed when Penelope refers to their present orgy of gift giving as a "noble contest and match" (nobil contesa e generosa gara): "They will not be unrewarded for these fine gifts, for when a woman is given gifts, she becomes inflamed [*accende*] with love." She indulges in an uncharacteristic coloratura complete with trill on "accende." Doubtless this causes the suitors to prick up their ears: her reserve seems to be melting at last. Her heightened use of ornamentation may be a musical symptom of Minerva's divine inspiration to propose the contest of the bow. She continues, "Now hurry, Melanto, and bring to me here the bow and quiver of the strong Ulisse; and he among you that with the heavy bow shoots the proudest arrow shall have both Ulisse's wife and his empire." The rests punctuating the phrase "havrà d'Ulisse [*half-rest*] e la moglie [*half-rest*] e l'impero" heighten the dramatic effect, building suspense. The words seem to come from her haltingly—as if from a supernatural source.

Telemaco seems to play along with the new turn of events, declaring in an ostensible aside, "Ulisse, where are you?" Penelope recoils on herself: "But what [*Ma che*] does the mouth easily promise with ah! too much discord in the heart [*discordante dal core*]?" The shocked repetitions of "ma che" are wrenching. The dissonance in her vocal line and the accompaniment that emerges on "discordante dal cor" hover throughout the rest of her speech, vividly suggesting her uncomprehending fear for what "heaven" is making her say and do: "Spirits, spirits of heaven! If I said it [*Numi, numi del cielo! S'io l' dissi*] you untied my tongue, opened the words. They are all prodigious effects of heaven and the stars." "Numi, numi del cielo" returns the music to the reassurance of the major key, a sense of stability that is immediately taken away by the aching chromatic harmonies on "S'io l' dissi."

The suitors, confident that Penelope is about to be won, burst into a trio of exuberant happiness: "Happy, gentle glory, gracious and sweet victory! Dear laments of lovers! A faithful heart, a constant breast changes trouble to serenity." The three play the role of romantic heroes to the hilt, even indulging in a minor-key passage in which they disingenuously recall the pains of love—"cari pianti degli amanti" (dear laments of lovers)—before snapping back to the major for the ensemble's conclusion. The trio gives Melanto time to retrieve the bow and arrows. The shift from Penelope's last conflicted recitation to the confident ensemble of suitors is striking. Just as striking is the return from their vigorous trio to Penelope's solo voice as she presents Ulisse's bow: "Here is the bow of Ulisse, or rather the bow of Love, which must pass to my heart." Her musical line, set low in her register with anxious, disruptive rests, helps Penelope seize center stage from the cavorting suitors. The rests, these "pauses rich with tension" (Osthoff 199), create an unforgettable moment of portentous expectation: "Ecco [*rest*] l'arco [*rest, rest*] d'Ulisse [*rest*], anzi l'arco d'Amor." Penelope's fear and hatred of the suitors is again concealed behind impeccable verbal and musical manners as she offers the bow to the alto suitor.

Each of the three suitors tries the bow and fails. The ceremony is depicted through a recurrent musical formula that asserts the ritualistic nature of the contest while building musical and dramatic tension. The progression moves downward in vocal ranges: first the alto, then the tenor, and finally the bass. A sinfonia plays each time the bow is presented to one of the suitors. This sinfonia, like the "Iro" battle sinfonia, is necessary to support the stage action. Like that earlier instrumental passage, this sinfonia takes itself quite seriously. Its tone and rhythm are urgent yet courtly, accenting the thin veneer of civilization that covers the bestial world of the suitors. It soon becomes an ironic instrumental deadpan presaging failure for the three men. The alto suitor bursts into a delightful little aria, latching on to the easy metaphor of arrows and Cupid's darts that Penelope's last speech has suggested: "Love, if you shoot me with arrows, now give force to these weapons; that in conquering I may say: if one bow has wounded me [*feri*], another bow will cure me." As in his earlier scene with Penelope, the alto suitor aims to present himself in a romantic guise to the queen and, as always, fails to fully hit his mark. His emphatic iteration of "hor dà forza, forza a quest'armi" is set to a swaggering tune. His enthusiasm for the analogy between arrows and love darts leads to a seven-note flourish on "saet-tarmi." This doesn't sound too bad, so he decorates "feri" even more elaborately in a reiterated passage that renders him slightly grotesque. He is trying too hard to strike a gallant pose; his music and prosody expose him briefly, but mercilessly, for the poseur that he is. His aria ended, the alto suitor attempts—in silence—to string the bow but fails. He resumes singing in a breathless, halting recitative: "The arm can't do it, the wrist can't do it." The use of rests here illustrates his exhausting but futile physical exertion: "Il braccio [*rest*] non vi giunge [*half-rest*], il polso [*half-rest*] non [*half-rest*] v'arriva [*rest*]" creates a strikingly realistic and slightly humorous effect that will be replicated after each of the failed attempts at the bow. The sprightly "bow" sinfo-nia sounds again—to more ironic effect—as an attendant removes the bow from the crestfallen alto and presents it to the tenor suitor.

The tenor one-ups the alto musically and dramatically. The tenor too sings an aria that verbally plays on the arrow–love dart metaphor. However, he is given music of sensuous charm and suavity when he sings, "Love, little spirit, cannot shoot arrows [*saettar*]: if he hurts mortals his arrows are merely looks [*sguardi*], not darts." The tenor's ornaments on "saettar" and his wonderful coloratura on "sguardi" shows a far greater mastery of matching word and tone than his alto rival. The tenor even breaks into a contrasting and perfectly convincing *concitato* section at "You fierce god, hurry my victory" (Tu, fiero Dio, le mie vit-torie affretta). In spite of the epic's well-known outcome, Monteverdi's music can make us believe—if only for a fleeting moment—that this suitor just might prevail. His aria ends, and he attempts in silence to string the bow. Like his alto rival, he vents his frustration in halting, breathless recitative that gives audible proof of his powerlessness before the mighty bow. Again the "bow" sinfonia sounds, unambiguously ironic because the outcome is already clear. Antinoo indulges in his charac-teristically pompous declamations. Now imagining himself without a rival and confident he can string the bow, Antinoo's final solo is more lyrical than all his previous music. He even sings an arioso, "Chi non vince in honor non vincerà" (Whoever wins not honor, does not win). When he turns to the queen he shifts back to recitative. Attempting to gain strength from Penelope's name he repeats it with a six-note ornament on the second syllable: "Penelope, I prepare myself for the supreme test by your virtue and beauty." This brief passage hints at a genuine longing on Antinoo's part. As Wagner does with the doomed giant Fasolt in *Rheingold,* Monteverdi suggests that however corrupt a man Antinoo may be, even he is capable of tender sentiment. Again silence as Antinoo's aspirations meet failure. Again the broken, gasping recitative as the bass suitor muses that "everything is true to Ulisse: even Ulisse's bow waits [*attende*] for Ulisse." "Attende," the last word of Antinoo's speech, is set near the bottom of his range, in this context a most menacing sound for Antinoo and his companions.

All three suitors have been humbled by this failure at the bow. Penelope's contempt can no longer be concealed. In recitative of noble simplicity she says just what she thinks of them: "Vain and obscure are the merits of kingly titles; the fancy royal blood, without valor, is of no avail in sustaining illustrious scepters. Who does not posses the same virtue as Ulisse is an unworthy inheritor of the treasures of Ulisse." Penelope's brave words before her disappointed and potentially violent oppressors would have struck a resonant chord in a Venetian audience. The whole story of *Ulisse* tests notions of innate versus superficial nobility in the contest between the old warrior and the indolent nobles who have been ravening his palace and land. The trial of the bow proves that Ulisse's prowess is deeper than the "fancy royal blood" of which Penelope spoke. Ulisse is entitled to his status by his own personal integrity, not merely the accidents of birth and inheritance. The Venetian aristocrats who patronized opera in the 1640s would have seen in him a reflection of themselves. The contest between Mycenaean-age warlords that Homer depicted has been made Venetian. The ultimate spiritual contest (the real "contessa gloriosa") is between the self-reliant, courageous Ulisse, a symbol of (Venetian) republican virtue, and the decadent suitors who owe their power, as so many Italian despots did outside of Venice, to inherited money and influence yet lack any personal integrity. Before the rejected suitors can respond to Penelope's scorn, the disguised Ulisse asks to try his hand at the bow—a paltry beggar following on the heels of the illustrious suitors.

> Proud youth
> doesn't always sustain valor,
> just as humble age
> is not always vile.
> Queen, in these limbs
> I keep a soul so ardent [*tengo un alma sì ardita*]
> that it invites me to the contest [*ch'alla prova m'invita*].
> The boundary I will not exceed:
> I renounce the prize and I ask only for the toil [*fatica*]

Ulisse's recitative lifts his voice to ringing high notes on "ardita" and "prova m'invita." The sense of the once-lowly hero raising to the combat is simply and beautifully evoked. Effective, too, is the stretched-out delivery of "fatica"—three long notes over a more rapid upward progression in the basso continuo—giving a picture in sound of the physical challenge to come. Penelope begins to respond in recitative—"Give the beggar the tiring task"—but her joy at humiliating the suitors, coupled perhaps with some dim awareness that her deliverer is near, leads her suddenly into a brief arioso, "A glorious contest [*contessa gloriosa*]: a contention between virile breasts and an antique frame [*fianco antico*], which will turn their flushed faces [*rossori involti*] from the fires of love to blushes of shame." She takes delight in musically painting the beggar's "antique form" (fianco antico) with drawn-out ornamentation and ornamenting "rossori," her contemptuous reference to the blushing cheeks of the amorous suitors. The accompanying instruments even play snippets of a brief ritornello, punctuating her repetitions in the last verse of the arioso. Penelope's shift from recitative to something so close to aria musically foreshadows the dramatic reversal to come.

Before handling the bow, Ulisse prays, in a brief ceremonial recitative with hints of *concitato* rhythm: "This my humble right hand arms itself on your account, O heavens! Prepare the victories, O highest gods, if the sacrifices I have made are dear to you." Another moment of musical and verbal silence, and the bow is strung. The suitors now sing their last trio, a bar of nearly motionless terror: "Wonder, stupefying, extreme prodigy!" The musical structure itself underscores the suitors' failure and Ulisse's triumph. The three suitors competed to the pattern of sinfonia, aria, or arioso; silence; and then recitative. Ulisse has moved from humble recitative to silence and now to an aria and concluding sinfonia. Here, as in all great opera, musical structure perfectly supports the dramatic action. Ulisse counters their nerveless torpor with a brief battle song, "Giove in his thunder cries vengeance! Thus the bow shoots its arrows!" Thunderclaps rumble and the instruments begin their *sinfonia da guerra* (battle symphony), signaling the beginning of Ulisse's attack and the emergence of his divine patroness Minerva on a glory above. (The libretto suggestively notes, "Apparisce Minerva in macchina.") Ulisse continues: "Minerva helps some, humiliates others; thus the bow wounds." The scene ends spectacularly to throbbing *concitato* rhythms in the accompaniment as Ulisse chants, "To the death, to the slaughter, to your ruin!" (Alle morti, alle stragi, alle ruine!), driving his enemies to their deaths amid all the musical sound and visual fury of which the baroque theater is capable.

Act 3

Grieving for his patrons the suitors, Iro utters a parody lament and resolves to kill himself ("O dolor!"). Penelope and Melanto react to the suitors' death with fear and trepidation. Both Eumete and Telemaco assure the queen that the "beggar" is really Ulisse, but she refuses to believe them. With the help of Giunone (Juno), Giove's consort, Minerva convinces the other gods that Ulisse has suffered enough ("Ulisse troppo errò"). Nettuno agrees to end his vendetta. A heavenly chorus celebrates Giove's mercy ("Giove amoroso"). Ericlea, Penelope's nurse, debates what to do, having recognized Ulisse from an old scar she saw when he was bathing ("Ericlea, che vuoi far"). Penelope refuses to believe her own eyes when Ulisse appears free of his beggar disguise. This motivates Ericlea to reveal what she saw. Still Penelope refuses to be swayed. Left alone with his wife, Ulisse reveals details of Penelope's "chaste bed," which only he has seen, and Penelope at last accepts that her suffering is over and her husband is home at last ("Illustratevi o cieli").

Scenes 1 and 2

After the impending offstage slaughter of the last act, the audience may well expect a scene of violence to follow, especially when scene 1 opens with a protracted musical cry, Iro's "O," which extends across eight bars of music. The first two bars are for solo voice, the bass clearly meant to be silent. With the bumptious ostinato pattern, the buffo nature of what is about to begin becomes clear, and the music itself reveals Iro's character after the indeterminacy of the first two bars. "I saw the suitors extinguished" (Io vidi i Proci estinti), Iro repeats three times, in ever lower sequences of notes, as if the full horror is only beginning to settle into his consciousness. Badoaro's next verse in the libretto reads, "I Proci furo uccisi" (The suitors were killed). At first Monteverdi sets these words straightforwardly. But by now Iro's passions are rising and with them his characteristic speech impediment that leads him to sing "porci" (swine) instead of "proci" (suitors)—the operatic equivalent of a Freudian slip and a fine indication of the freedom Monteverdi exhibits with his text.

Iro segues into recitative: "Ah, I have lost the delights of the stomach [*rest*] and of the gullet. Who [*rest, rest*] will help [*rest, rest*] the hungry one [*rest*]? Who [*rest*]?" Iro's mind seems to snap as he launches into a "frenetic ciaccona" (Rosand, "Iro" 152) on "Chi lo consola" (Who will console) that is striking not only for its deliberate lack of continuity with what has gone before, but for its similarity to that most famous of seventeenth-century chaconnes, Monteverdi's setting of Rinuccini's "Zefiro torna" for two tenors. The opera gains ironic ambience from the audience's recognition of "Zefiro torna," much as Mozart's audience does when the onstage band recalls music from *Figaro* during the supper scene from *Don Giovanni*. Iro's interrogative "chi"s are doubtless directed to the audience, the self-referencing musical quotation drawing the spectators even more fully into the onstage world. "Zefiro torna" is some of the most famous love music ever written, Rinuccini's "lover" transformed into a tenor duet, two voices describing their longing for the absent loved one. Now those tenor voices are briefly metamorphosed into the single Iro of immense girth, whose "lost one" is food and handouts.

"O feeble words!" (O flebile parola!), Iro exclaims, his music, appropriately enough, returning to recitative: "You'll never find one who laughs [*rida*] at the triumphant gluttony of your gullet." He sings mimetically appropriate ornaments on "rida," repeating the words with ever-longer decoration and trills until his music literally disintegrates into "real" laughter: the score directs, "He falls into a natural laugh" (Qui cade in riso naturale). How different in effect Iro's laugh is from Ulisse's when the hero gleefully learned of the suitors' fear of him in the aria "Godo anch'io, nè so, come rido"! Iro's is not the laughter of triumph or happy anticipation; it is the sign of incipient madness. Iro desperately canvasses the theater audience: "Who [*rest*] will help [*rest*] the hungry one [*rest*]? Who?" And now an expanded version of the "chi lo consola" chaconne breaks out, Iro's long-held "chi" hanging over the bass pattern for five bars. He returns to recitative as the speech darkens. "Voglio uccider me stesso" (I want to kill myself) is set to seven notes of recitative that are repeated exactly after a punctuating rest. This moment of almost matter-of-fact declamation, repeated word for word and tone for tone, is one of the scene's most unsettling details. After so many wayward musical and verbal journeys Iro "comes to rest" with a resolution to kill himself, which this most flighty of characters has the sangfroid to repeat exactly. This passage is so unnervingly serious in tone that Iro's brief descending note repetition on "non vo' mai" in the phrase "E non vo' mai ch'ella porti di me trionfo e gloria" (and not live to see [hunger] triumph and glory over me) takes on a serious cast. "For to take from the enemy is a great victory," Iro declaims in an ascending vocal line, attaining a striking climax in ringing high notes on "great victory" (gran vittoria). Iro is transforming himself into something of a comic hero—a forerunner of Molière's George Dandin or one of Beckett's outcasts, a grotesque bent on self-annihilation. Iro declaims his last words: "My courageous heart, conquer your sorrow! And before it succumbs to the enemy hunger let my body be swallowed by the tomb."

Iro is the first great comic character in opera. His monologue has been a tour de force, a parody of the operatic lament that Monteverdi himself had virtually invented with Arianna. The inspired lunacy of Iro, the *parte ridicola,* as the score reminds us at the start of this scene, is to put the murder of the suitors within a moral framework. Iro serves as a comic exaggeration of the suitors, his demented behavior reminding us of their spiritual depravity. This renders sympathy for the dead men almost impossible. Monteverdi's use of comedy, like that of his contemporary Spanish Golden Age dramatists or of Shakespeare, is one in which laughter can easily move toward tears, or, at least in this instance, toward an even more disconcerting silence.

Scene 2 in Badoaro's libretto consists of a sad procession of the suitors' souls entering hell. The score contains a note remarking that the text for this scene was not set because of its "melancholy mood." Monteverdi's editorial decision was astute, for the unset scene is pedantic and unnecessary. (It is reproduced with English translation in Rosand, "Iro" 160–62.) The composer's deletion returns the action from Iro's monologue to the protagonist's dilemma as the action moves toward the final reunion of Ulisse and Penelope.

Scene 3

Scene 3, set entirely in recitative, reveals Penelope's and Melanto's reactions to the slaughter. The two women ostensibly are speaking together, but their personal agendas are so different that we have essentially a succession of soliloquies. It is a mark of the opera's breadth of vision that the first voices heard reacting to Ulisse's slaughter of his enemies are those most sympathetic to the murdered men: Iro in the last scene, and now Melanto. Melanto, grieving secretly for her Eurimaco, who has doubtless fallen before the old man's arrows, sings short-breathed recitative phrases expressive of heightened agitation. Her rage at the suitors' attacker is indicated by her emotionally charged repetition of "Chi fu ... chi fu l'ardito?" (Who was, who was the ardent one?). She conceals from her mistress her personal investment in the suitors' fortunes with vague locutions lamenting "the pulling to earth of these temples that were erected to Cupid in those fiery breasts." The "new war" (nuova guerra) that has just been fought in her palace has left Penelope shell-shocked. Melanto sings, "Beloved widow, widowed queen, new tears are approaching. In short, completely unhappy one, every love is fatal!" With mounting anxiety over her own illicit connection with the suitors—we should remember that Melanto's counterpart in Homer and all the other servant women who were seduced by the suitors are killed by Odysseus in book 22—Melanto's vocal line climbs upward as she envisions encroaching threats: "Thus even in the shadow of the scepter, life is insecure; near the crown loathsome hands are ever bolder." Penelope replies with quiet irony, "The suitors died, and the stars they called on were indifferent attendants to their deaths." Melanto, anguished over the loss of her lover and fearful for her own safety, breaks decorum by emphatically insisting ("Penelope! Penelope!") that her mistress become "enraged" to avenge the suitors. Melanto is obviously not listening to Penelope. Penelope replies with seeming impassivity: "I cannot allow my heart to be stirred to anger or grief." It is disappointing that Melanto effectively drops out of the action from this point forward, though she figures in later group scenes around her mistress. Her affair with Eurimaco, conducted in secrecy, has apparently died in secrecy. Melanto's last major scene, all recitative and often cut from performance, is one of subtle psychological depth that reveals how far opera has come in the relatively brief period since its inception. It is difficult to recall a dialogue scene, outside of Shakespeare, of comparable, almost Chekovian elusiveness in nonoperatic drama before 1640.

Scenes 4 and 5

Eumete joins the two women in scene 4. Like Melanto, his first reference to the beggar warrior entails an excited repetition of "chi, chi" (he, he), but in Eumete the mannerism suggests his boundless love for his long-lost master. Eumete's opening recitative builds in excitation as he describes "that robust man who . . . impaled the insidious suitors." Eumete exhorts Penelope, in joyful arioso, to "take cheer again, Queen" (rallegrati, regina), before asserting, in slow declamation, that "he was, he was, he was Ulisse!" (egli, egli, egli era Ulisse!). Penelope politely refuses to be taken in. Eumete repeats his "rallegreti, regina, egli era Ulisse" arioso, as if this attractive lyrical phrase would change Penelope's mind if she only heard it often enough. In "Ulisse, Ulisse is alive, is here, is here, here, here!" the triple iterations of "here" (qui) are broken by rests and sink lower and lower in Eumete's voice as if his persuasive efforts were exhausting him, leaving him breathless. At last Penelope snaps at him: "You're stupid and blind," she sings, in terse, cutting recitative.

Telemaco joins the others in scene 5, explaining that Minerva has disguised Ulisse to help him defeat his enemies. Penelope responds, "Too often, in truth, must men on earth serve as a toy for the immortal gods. If you believe that, then you also are their toy." She effectively closes the scene with a speech of unconscious irony: "They don't have much thought, the gods up there [*lassù*] in heaven, for mortal affairs: they let the fires burn and the ice freeze: they beget the cause of pleasure and pain [*figlian le cause lor piaceri e mali*]." These last words are drawn out into a languishing vocal phrase above a gently rising bass that suggests Penelope is masochistically holding on to the painful as tightly as one would cling to the pleasurable. The situation of the mortals has reached a deadlock. The action of the next two scenes portrays the divine intervention that will allow the resolution of the action.

Scenes 6 and 7

In scene 6, Minerva lobbies Giunone in "divinely" decorated recitative to intercede with Giove for Ulisse: "We in anger and wrath have burned the Trojan kingdom.... We were offended by a Trojan, but [*ma*] we are avenged." Her fourteen-note decoration of "ma" moves, like another of Minerva's javelinlike vocal flourishes, from the top to the bottom and to the top again of her vocal line. She is stating the case for divine anger before moving to plead for merciful intercession. This shift is signaled by a couple of rests: "[*rest*] The most powerful of the Greeks [*rest*] still contends with destiny, with fate." Minerva's musical manner changes from the declamatory wrath of the earlier verses to a portrayal of a mortal's feelings. The stepping bass pattern beneath the languishingly repeated "ancor contende" (still contends) changes the tone of divine anger into one of divine compassion: "Our vengeance was the birth of [Ulisse's] wanderings [*errori*], the pleasing slaughters [of Trojans] are the offspring of his sorrows [*son figli i suoi dolori*]." Minerva's use of ornamentation and repetition forces Giunone's attention where Minerva wants it. The "divine" coloratura device is now being applied to suffering humanity rather than outraged divinity. Minerva has pleaded well, and Giunone agrees to intercede with Giove: "I will procure the peace [*pace*] and search for the repose [*riposo*] of glorious [*glorioso*] Ulisse." "Pace" and "riposo" are sweetly illustrated with two slackenings of the recitative's pulse. An elaborate coloratura on "glorioso" is as grand an effect as any Minerva has used to express divine anger. The divine musical discourse has changed before our ears; Ulisse's last obstacles are about to be removed.

Scene 7 affords potentially the greatest spectacle in the entire opera, as Giove in his "glory" joins Giunone and Minerva. Soon Nettuno will appear from the waves. The stage or backstage area must also make room for a double chorus of divine spirits of the heavens and the sea. Whether this double chorus is seen or only heard, the composer obviously desired to create an antiphonal effect between the high ("in cielo") and low ("marittimo") voices—a kind of writing that was popular in early Venetian baroque music (as in Gabrieli's canzonas for brass). After a solemn invocation to the king of the gods, Giunone bids Giove, "Incline your grace to my prayers" (Inchina le tue grazie a' prieghi miei). Giunone's recitative takes on a personal, pleading tone; her vocal phrases are slow, but the bass line moves more rapidly in a stepping motif, endowing her prayer with a sense of supernal grace. It also proves to be the launching place for a melting aria from the queen of the gods, "Ulisse has wandered too much" (Ulisse troppo errò), one of the most beautiful in the opera. The melody is built out of the six-note figure of the ritornello that punctuates Giunone's plea. Each iteration of "errò" is appropriately ornamented with a rising vocal figuration.

Giove is favorably disposed: "To me, Giunone, you have never made a prayer [*preghiera*] in vain." The tenor god's tenderness to his sister-wife is palpable in the gentle ornamentation of "preghiera." Tenderness is not an attitude Giove usually displays toward her in their numerous mythological encounters, but then again his earlier appearance revealed that Giove is already sympathetic to Ulisse. Giove confronts Nettuno with an arresting phrase, "Odimi, odimi, o Dio del mar!" (Hear me, hear me, god of the sea!). Nettuno must relinquish his anger against Ulisse, the "destined one" who has served as a mere agent or "divine champion." "Induce [*invoglie*] a gentle disposition toward him," Giove commands, his ornamentation of "invoglie" oscillating from high to low and high again—a divine command that is impossible to refuse. Giove reminds Nettuno that after Troy's fall Ulisse was "pursued by death" (errò la morte), ornamenting "errò" with a flurry of descending and ascending divisions—a musical picture of Ulisse's misadventures. Giove's next words are even more expressive: "Nettuno, pardon, O Nettuno, pardon the mortal who is crushed by his afflictions" (Nettun, pace, o Nettun, Nettun, perdona, perdona il suo duol, il suo duol al mortal ch'afflitto il rese). Giove's pleas on behalf of a mortal are simple and heartfelt. The dissonances on "duol" and "afflitto il rese" add pathos. Just in case a show of force is still needed with Nettuno, Giove closes with an aggressive coloratura: "Man isn't to blame if heaven thunders [*tuona*]."

Nettuno indicates his pacification with a gentle, slow-moving aria: "Though the waters are frigid, though the waves are icy, yet they feel the ardor of your pity." The image of Giove's "ardent pity" is treated to a wavelike ornamental pattern on the repeated phrase "di tua pietà." Nettuno is even more obsequious in the flowing setting of "Giove anco si sa, anco si sa" (Giove is already known, already known [even in the depths of the sea.]) Ulisse may now live "secure and happy." This sentiment is given its own aria in a rocking rhythm. "Giove, the loving god, makes heaven piteous through pardoning," sings the heavenly chorus of sopranos and altos. In response, the voices of the sea, made up of altos, baritones, and basses, sing, "Though it is cold, the sea is no less merciful than heaven." The text and music recall the tone of Viola's lines in Shakespeare's *Twelfth Night*: "O, if it prove, / Tempests are kind, and salt waves fresh in love" (act 4, scene 1, lines 348–49). In a unison passage, the two choirs enjoin the mortal audience, "Pray, mortal, oh, pray" (Prega, mortal, deh, prega). The two choruses deliver the moral of their observation first soloistically and then as a group, affirming that "an offended God is placated through prayer." This entire sequence, moving from Giove's imploring of Nettuno to Nettuno's renunciation of anger and the divine euphony of the celestial and maritime choirs, leads the opera into an exalted sphere. Divine reconciliation, however, with all its lavish theatrical trappings, pales before the intimate human reconciliation that brings the work to its conclusion. Utilizing a mimetic coloratura, Giove advises Minerva to placate the suitors' followers, who threaten Ithaca with war (guerra). The scene ends with a brief, cheerful aria for Minerva: "I will suppress those spirits, smother their ardor, command the peace, Giove, as it [*come*] pleases you." The aria closes memorably after an ornamental flourish on "come" that, with its fluctuation between Minerva's high and low registers, seems to bind heaven to earth in an expansive musical gesture.

The stage is set for Ulisse's true homecoming in the sublime recognition scene that will end the opera.

Scenes 8 and 9

Anticipation of this happiest of endings is built by scene 8, Ericlea's solo recitative and aria. Ericlea, the old nurse, has not been heard from since act 1, scene 1. She has recognized the disguised Ulisse, who has sworn her to secrecy. Now, with the suitors dead, she anxiously deliberates whether to tell Penelope the proof she has seen. "Will you be silent, or speak?" (Vuoi tacer o parlar?), she asks herself in repeated recitative, torn between love for her mistress and obedience to Ulisse: "To help someone who languishes, oh, how delightful!" (Medicar chi languisce, o che diletto!). The first clause is treated to verbal repetitions set to ascending chromatic lines. In a similar manner the idea of "not being able to help" (e non lo far) makes use of repetitions and stabbing dissonance. Her moral dilemma inspires charming music. On the last syllable of each of her recitative deliberations, as she recommits herself to obedient secrecy, her thoughts resolve into a refrain aria. "One must not tell all one knows," "the best thing sometimes is silence," and "silence is safer from repentance than speech"—all these prudent tags sung to the same catchy aria tune. This tune, punctuated with two different sinfonia ritornelli, contributes a sense of happy, expectant urgency to the scene. "The [aria refrain] music concretely marks her progress from her initial vow of silence, through ambivalence, to her [coming] decision to speak," Rosand observes (*Opera* 252). A figure who could easily be portrayed as a two-dimensional commedia dell'arte character is allowed to think and change through the music and its structural logic.

Penelope, Telemaco, and Eumete join Ericlea in scene 9, the two men making a last attempt to sway the queen, engaging in a duet built

entirely of rapid-fire recitative. The rapidly alternating voices quicken
the musical and dramatic pulse, heralding scene 10.

Scene 10

Scene 10 marks Ulisse's entrance for his first encounter with Penelope
without his disguise. Monteverdi's recitative rises gloriously to the
occasion. "O sweet and gentle goal of my travails, dear port of life
to which I hurry for rest [*dove corro al riposo*]": the vocal line is all
tenderness. Ulisse's emotions, which seem ready to spill over into
ecstatic, full-fledged aria at any moment, are sharply checked by the
wary Penelope. "Halt, knight, enchanter or magician!" she interrupts
in nervous, short-breathed phrases. The proto-lyrical impulse of his
first address is immediately lost in Ulisse's responses. His words and
recitative are filled with suggestions of frustration bordering on anger:
"Is this how you'll receive your husband's long-sighed-for embraces?"
Penelope's anguish matches his in her anxious repetition: "Consorte
io sono, consorte io sono, ma del perduto Ulisse" (I am a consort, I
am a consort, of the lost Ulisse). Ulisse's next words encapsulate the
humanistic trajectory of Homer's great wanderer: "In honor of your
eyes I scorn eternity. I voluntarily changed my state and destiny to
keep faith, I joined with mortality" (In honor de' tuoi rai l'eternità
sprezzai, volontario cangiando e stato e sorte. Per serbarmi fedel son
giunto a morte). Badoaro has skillfully distilled the *Odyssey*'s existential
theme into four lines of verse, set with appropriate simplicity in the
recitative. Ulisse-Odysseus's journey throughout epic and opera is an
effort to regain his mortal life and its relationships. He has eschewed
the blandishments of goddesses, with their promises of immortality, in
the hope of regaining his place by his wife and son in his own kingdom;
the vulnerable transience of the world wins out over the superhuman
promise of eternal life.

   "That valor which makes you similar to Ulisse makes you dear to
me: the slaughter of the evil lovers," Penelope sings, her strained word
choices indicating her divided impulses. "That [*questo*] is the sweet fruit
of your lie." The thrice-stated "questo" suggests a tone of growing agitation. Ulisse argues back: "I am that Ulisse" (Quell'Ulisse, quell'Ulisse

son io). Penelope's reply shows her back in complete control: "You aren't the first unworthy one who, with a lying name, attempted to find command or kingdom." Ericlea breaks her silence. "Now is the time to speak," she sings in recitative that seems about to slip into excited song: "This is, this is Ulisse, chaste and great lady" (è questo, è questo Ulisse, casta e gran donna). These two bars of arioso are left to stand like a moment of spiritual illumination as Ericlea returns to recitative. She saw the telltale scar of the wild boar as Ulisse bathed. Her tongue "at the command of Ulisse with great effort was silent." Penelope is still trapped between love and honor, a dilemma neatly highlighted by the settings of the two words: "Believing what I desire is taught to me by love [*amore*]; keeping a constant breast is the command of honor [*honore*]. My bed receives only Ulisse, only Ulisse [*sol d'Ulisse, sol d'Ulisse*]," she insists. Ulisse makes one final appeal, calling on his knowledge of her "chaste thoughts" and his "grateful memory" of their marriage bed and its embroidery, which "no other has seen."

> Of your chaste thoughts I know the customs.
> I know of the chaste bed,
> that, save for Ulisse alone,
> no other has seen.
> Every night you adorn and cover it
> with a silken cloth
> woven with your own hand,
> in which can be seen pictured
> Diana with her virginal chorus.
> That grateful memory
> has always stayed with me.

The intensity of this final revelation of Penelope's private physical and mental spaces is set to achingly expressive recitative. The gentle yet insistent iteration in the first phrase, "Io so, io so" (I know, I know), is erotically charged, as is the gradual rise in his vocal line on "e copre con un serico drappo di tua mano contesto, in cui si vede col virginal suo coro Diana effigiata." This musical ascent acts like an arc of light. The simplest physical detail of domestic existence is charged with profound spiritual significance. Ulisse repeats the word "memory" (memoria), emphasizing the final, all-important clue that reestablishes their relationship. The music from now to the end of the opera flows with a quickening pulse, one unforgettable melodic idea following the next. Penelope's recitative-bound purgatory melts into an arioso set to a gentle dancelike rhythm: "Now yes, I recognize you, now yes, I believe you, old possessor of my contested heart." The music suggests a gradual reawakening of Penelope back to the world of song and lyric aria, to life itself in the world of the opera. Penelope's tentative reentry into the world of life and song is checked, however, almost as soon as it begins, with a brief return to recitative: "Forgive my prudence [*honestà*]; I give to love alone the blame." Ulisse, home at last, begins a brief arioso of his own: "Untie your tongue, ah, untie it! For joy loosen the bonds! Let your voice utter a sigh, an *ohimè*." These words are sung to a minor-key variant of Penelope's arioso, injecting an increasing erotic intensity, especially with the languishing flourish placed on "ohimè."

Penelope's suffering is at an end, and she expresses herself in the most glorious aria in Monteverdi opera. Two strophes of lovely verse are set to a melody of infectious joy.

> Illustratevi, o cieli,
> Rinfioratevi, o prati, aure, gioite!
> Gli augelletti cantando,
> i rivi mormorando hor si rallegrino!
>
> Quell'herbe verdeggianti,
> quell'onde sussurranti hor si consolino.
>
> [Shine forth, O heavens,
> bloom again, O meadows, breezes, rejoice!
> The singing birds,
> the brooks murmuring now are, yes, happy!
>
> What verdant grasses,
> what whispering waves now are, yes, consoling.]

The strings play exuberant four-part ritornelli in vigorous response to Penelope's phrases. Penelope's latent skills as a singer are exploited to the full with heady ornamentation on "illustratevi," "rinfioratevi," "gioite," "rallegrino," and "consolino." The divisions on "The singing birds, the murmuring brooks" are as musically delightful as they are

mimetically telling. Even more suggestive are the spectacular ornaments that decorate and seem to animate the "whispering waves" (onde
sussurranti). Melody and word work together to portray the visual
world to the listener in perfectly integrated operatic art, celebrating
her return to life and love. The words and her decorative illustration
of them reinforce the theme of nature's cycles of renewal that has been
present since the opera's first scene, where Ericlea's reminder of the
patterns of nature inspired Penelope's first aria ("Torna il tranquillo
al mare"). The reappearance of this idea and the melodic fervor given
them by the composer binds the opera and imparts a satisfying closure.
Seldom has a greater sense of relief and healthy joy been expressed in
a work of Western art music.

Penelope's aria "Illustratevi o cieli" represents her full musical and
dramatic reintegration into the world. She ends the two verses with a
palpable sense of exhausted relief, expressed in a quiescent recitative:
"Indeed, what happy fate that my Phoenix rises from Trojan ashes!" One
last illustrative flourish of ornamentation on "my Phoenix" (mia Fenice)
marks the closure of her initial sense of jubilation. Destructive lust,
whether at Troy or at Ithaca, has been bested by heavenly love—the
exact inversion of the situation at the end of the next opera, *Poppea*.

The opera ends with a duet by the reunited couple, in Osthoff's
phrase "a human apotheosis" (203). Ulisse initiates it, singing a lyrical
phrase, "My longed-for sun!" (Sospirato mio sole!). Penelope responds,
"My renewed light!" (Rinnovata mia luce!). They sing a gentle minor-
key tune with solo and overlapping lines that changes the emotional
temperature from extroverted rapture to a more private, glowing tenderness. Long-pent-up emotion seems to bring them to the verge of
tears. Penelope's almost vigorous interjection, "Bramato sì" (Desired,
yes), which Ulisse will soon take up himself, is a masterstroke of musical characterization indicating the reemergence of Penelope's long-sup-
pressed sensuality. Their unison singing of "ma caro, caro" ends the first
part of their duet on a tone of ardent emotional connection. Penelope
sings a brief soloistic declamation to a drooping, suddenly mournful
chromatic line on "For you I have learned to bless my past anxieties"
(Per te gli andati affanni a benedir imparo). Ulisse takes charge, introducing a major-key tune and a text of radiant confidence: the melody

of "Don't remember the torments anymore" (Non si rammenti più de' tormenti) seems like a major-key version of the opening theme of their duet. Penelope immediately responds to Ulisse with words and music of assent: "Yes, my life, yes" (Sì, sì, sì, vita, sì, sì). Ulisse sings, "All is pleasure, all is peace!" (Tutto piacer, tutto piace), to which Penelope eagerly asserts again, "Sì, sì, sì, vita, sì, sì" (Yes, yes, yes, my life, yes). Newly invigorated by her husband's words, she sings her own lyric to Ulisse's bright new melody, "Fly from our breasts, feelings of sadness" (Fuggan dai petti dogliosi affetti), and now Ulisse sings his refrain with his own slight variant, "Sì, sì, sì, core, sì, sì" (Yes, yes, yes, my heart, yes). Ulisse and Penelope's sharing of verbal and melodic gestures is a perfect operatic expression of their unity as a loving couple. Penelope again applies her own words to Ulisse's confident tune, "All is rejoicing" (Tutto è goder), to which her husband assents: "Sì, sì, sì, core, sì, sì, sì, sì." The opera ends with a powerful affirmation of their reestablished bond in five bars of unison singing.

> Del piacer, del goder venuto è 'l di.
> Sì, sì, sì, vita
> sì, sì, sì, core
> sì, sì, sì, sì.
>
> [The day has come, of pleasure and rejoicing.
> Yes, yes, yes, my life,
> yes, yes, yes, my heart,
> yes, yes, yes, yes.]

Has any composer other than Verdi united a male and a female voice with such life-affirming confidence? Ulisse has returned; he and Penelope are united at last, for as long as art endures.

"Nothing Human Is Alien to Me"

L'incoronazione di Poppea

Having created operas out of classical myth and epic, Monteverdi turned at last to the composition of the world's first historical opera. *L'incoronazione di Poppea* represents his last and arguably greatest work. His librettist this time was Giovanni Francesco Busenello (1598–1659). Monteverdi was fortunate to encounter in Busenello the most gifted of his collaborators. Like Badoaro, Busenello was a wealthy member of the Accademia degli Incogniti, that learned society of freethinkers who were the most powerful intellectual influences over early Venetian opera. Busenello and Badoaro were friends, and an extensive poetic exchange between the two librettists has been preserved. A successful lawyer by profession, Busenello, like Badoaro, wrote for pleasure. Unlike Badoaro, however, Busenello was something of a literary genius. Busenello's work on *Poppea* places him among the greatest librettists in the history of opera, along with Lorenzo Da Ponte, Arrigo Boito, and Hugo von Hofmannsthal. Busenello's reputation rests on *Poppea* and four libretti created for Cavalli, all of which strongly influenced early Venetian operatic style. These five texts were published by Busenello in 1656 in a volume titled *Delle hore ociose*. The *Poppea* text in particular exhibits an elegant and expressive versification, a keen sense of comedy and drama, and a consummate dramatic structure that could allow the libretto to be successfully staged in the theater without any musical accompaniment. Although Busenello was far from being a doctrinaire neoclassicist, his libretto presented the composer with a beautifully sculpted drama that carefully obeyed the neoclassicist rule of time and action. From the prologue to the conclusion, Busenello's text advertises that all the events happen within a single day, and the libretto gains in dramatic impact through his discipline. Unlike *Ulisse, Poppea* contains little real action. The libretto builds its tension through the artful and varied intermingling of the characters and their psychological effect on each other (see also Leopold 213–15). Busenello's skills did not preclude Monteverdi from altering the text freely through repetition, cuts, juxtapositions, and transpositions. The libretto accompanying Nikolaus Harnoncourt's 1974 recording helpfully prints the text in the purely literary style in which Busenello left it so that one may easily appreciate Monteverdi's dramaturgical manipulations while listening to the opera.

Both *Poppea* and *Ulisse* are deeply concerned with the nature of love and desire as forces for good and evil in human life. Both works are also concerned to varying degrees with the mysterious linkage between art and power. In the last chapter we observed the self-referential undercurrents of the aging Ulisse defeating his rivals and Monteverdi himself reasserting his prowess in the operatic theater. The *Ulisse* story supports the idea of an aristocracy of merit triumphing over avaricious upstarts who threaten the commonwealth, a theme that would have appealed to the Venetian families who supported opera. *Ulisse*'s Ithaca, like Venice, can still defend itself from the blandishments of the unjust and corrupt; *Poppea*'s Rome has succumbed. It is made the subject of operatic poetry and music that is ever more alluring as it moves further from civilized restraint. Rome is ruled by Nerone, perhaps the most famous artist manqué in history until Hitler. Monteverdi had seen modern despotism while at the Mantuan court. Busenello himself had served at the Gonzaga court as the Venetian ambassador to Mantua during the period of the War of Succession. It is tempting to imagine Monteverdi and Busenello comparing notes on the Gonzaga style of rule, with its characteristic mixture of artistic cultivation and brutality. Such experiences doubtless led the older composer to bond with the younger librettist in a shared artistic vision.

Poppea is based on the true story of the Roman emperor Nero's adulterous love for a noblewoman, Poppea Sabina, and portrays events that occurred between 58 and 65 A.D. In the opera, Nerone and Poppea overcome all the human and moral obstacles that stand in their way, and the work ends with their triumphant marriage ceremony as Poppea is crowned empress. Principal sources for Busenello were the *Annals* of Tacitus, books 13—16; Seutonius's *The Twelve Caesars,* book 6; and Dio Cassius's *Roman History,* books 61—62. *Octavia,* an anonymous play attributed to Seneca in antiquity, is another major inspiration for the libretto. The sole surviving example of the *fabula praetexta,* the Latin literary term for a Roman play about Roman subjects (as opposed to Greek-based dramas), *Octavia* portrays the empress Octavia's fall from power and suggests several elements for Busenello's libretto, such as the argument between Nerone and Seneca, the characters of Arnalta and Nutrice, and Ottavia's desolate leave-taking of her friends and homeland. Most Latinists no longer believe *Octavia* to be an authentic work of Seneca; after all, he himself figures as a character in the play, though the play's action stops short of the events leading to the philosopher's death. *Octavia* is a work of "closet drama" probably composed by one of Seneca's followers, who used the medium of Latin tragic drama to create an apologia for Seneca's relationship with the corrupt emperor (see Whitman; Herington, "Octavia Praetexta"). Although he is obviously indebted to these classical sources, Busenello is extremely free with detail and chronology. For example, Seneca's death occurred in 65 A.D. and was the result of the Stoic's participation in the Pisonian conspiracy, not his objections to Nero's plans against Octavia. Octavia's banishment and Nero and Poppea's marriage had already occurred, in 62 A.D. The hapless Otho (Ottone in the opera), who had actually been married to Poppea when she began her affair with Nero, himself briefly assumed the throne before dying in a rebellion in 69 A.D. Perhaps the most significant of Busenello's changes to history and to his sources lies in his handling of the character of Ottavia. The historical Octavia is portrayed as an innocent victim by all the classical sources; Busenello paints a much darker portrait of his Ottavia, fusing some of the neurotic traits of Agrippina, Nero's murderous mother, onto the emperor's discarded consort (see Heller, *Emblems* 157).

Roman subject matter was intensely interesting for Venetian audiences, who saw themselves as the direct descendants of classical Roman civilization. The Venetians had created a republic famous for its civil government and its stability, a form of government that could be nostalgically compared to the earlier Roman Republic, rather than the decadent, autocratic Roman Empire. The papacy of the seventeenth century was a direct threat to Venetian liberty and represented a very dangerous "Rome," a Rome symbolic of the many despotisms that controlled much of Italy. The historian William J. Bouwsma observes: "Rome was thus the great adversary of [seventeenth-century] Venice, the anvil against which her political consciousness was hammered out at last" (xiii). Ellen Rosand notes, "There is some indication that [*Poppea*] could have been understood by its contemporaries as a moral lesson implying the superiority of Venice over Rome, and suggesting that such immorality was only possible in a decaying society, not a civilized nation" (*Opera* 139, see also 113). But Busenello was not an uncritical admirer of the Venetian republic. He was aware of how easily the freest of societies could experience corruption. In a letter of 1648 to his fellow librettist and friend Badoaro, Busenello wrote that Venice's only hope for spiritual renewal lay "in abandoning the new desire for luxury, the terrible struggle of ambition within offices of state, and returning to the simple ways of previous generations" (qtd. in Fenlon and Miller, *Song* 55).

Poppea is striking for its clear-eyed presentation of a world that has lost its moral compass. Virtually all its important characters are ethically compromised. Some modern commentators have taken the work to be a hymn to libertine values. After all, the Accademia degli Incogniti was notorious for its questioning of traditional sexual morality. The opera ends with the spectacular triumph of Poppea as she assumes the throne through adultery, machinations, and murder. The majority of the Venetian audience, however, could be counted on to know their Tacitus and Roman history. They could have easily filled in the gaps left by Busenello with the knowledge that shortly after the events of the opera, Nero kicked the pregnant Poppea to death during an argument and only a few years later killed himself when his army rebelled against him. One critic asserts that "Busenello's plot is . . . one of the most moral in all opera, and that this morality is sustained by the phenomenon of dramatic irony" (Savage, "Love and Infamy" 198). In contrast to *Ulisse,* the gods of *Poppea,* "even though they still intervene on occasion, . . . have lost their command over the course of the action. . . . In [the opera's] carousel of relationships, it is significant that

Amore is the only god who does not merely serve as an ornament, but intervenes at a decisive moment in the action" (Leopold 208). Far from the numinous world of gods and heroes presented in *Ulisse* and *L'Orfeo*, *Poppea* presents a darker, lonelier landscape, which its human figures animate with their destructive passions. *Poppea*'s characters are all beset by existential loneliness. Even its two principal sets of lovers lack genuine self-knowledge or deep understanding of their partners. These psychological aspects give the work its peculiar modern resonance. It is the most modern of baroque operas, the first opera that could be called realistic (see de' Paoli 495).

The opera house that premiered *Poppea* in the early months of 1643 was the Teatro Santi Giovanni e Paolo, owned by the Grimaldi family. The theater was torn down in the nineteenth century, but an architectural drawing still exists that gives historians a valuable idea about this theatrical space, with which Monteverdi would have been very familiar. Scholarly consensus now views it as the site of *Ulisse*'s 1640 premiere, and it was certainly the theater for that opera's 1641 revival. It was also the theater that had presented the lost *Le nozze d'Enea con Lavinia* (1640–41). An observer in 1663 wrote an evocative description:

> In that [theater] of SS. Giovanni e Paolo are performed the Carnival Operas with marvelous scene changes, majestic and grand appearances [of the performers], machines, and a fantastic flying machine; you see, as if commonplace, glorious heavens, deities, seas, royal palaces, woods, forests, and other handsome and entertaining visions. The music is always exquisite, presenting the best voices of the city, with the best also brought in from Rome, Germany, and other places and particularly the women with beautiful faces, rich costumes, enchanting voices, and with acting appropriate to the characters that they are playing, producing astonishment and wonder. (Francesco Sansovino, qtd. in Day 22)

The theater was intimate: five tiers of smallish boxes held about 920 people. The stage was much bigger than the auditorium, which would have made the settings appear all the more impressive to the audience (Day 26). A scenario detailing and labeling the seven stage settings of the premiere survives to which reference will be made as we explore the visual aspects of *Poppea*'s first performances. Pirrotta agues that "not having at its disposal the precision machinery devised by Giacomo Torelli for the Novissimo, where set changes took place 'turning all the parts around in one swift motion,' the scenographer must have found it expedient to alternate some fairly shallow generic sets with others that utilized the full depth of the stage and corresponded to more specific needs" (Pirrotta 268).

Textually, *Poppea* is the most problematic Monteverdi opera. It survives in two handwritten copies from revivals during the 1650s. The first score, once the property of Francesco Cavalli and apparently copied under that composer's supervision, was discovered in 1888 by Taddeo Wiel at the Biblioteca Nazionale Marciana in Venice. The second was found by G. Gasperini in 1930 at the Conservatorio di Musica San Pietro a Majella in Naples; it had been made for a revival of the opera in that city in 1651 performed by the Febiarmonici, a group of musicians who brought Venetian opera to Naples, Milan, and other Italian cities between 1644 and 1653 (Celletti 17). Like the *Ulisse* score in Vienna, both *Poppea* scores contain only the vocal lines, basso continuo, and sinfonias and ritornelli (in three parts in Venice, and four in Naples), all minus instrumental indications. Each score differs in some ways from the printed versions of the libretto. The two scores contain largely the same music, but each has significant additions and omissions unique to it. Most modern performances tend to favor the Venice score above the Neapolitan one, but several passages in the latter are too good to exclude from performance. Neither score can be directly linked to the first performances in 1643, and most productions and recordings make use of materials from both.

Modern *Poppea* scholarship, spearheaded by Alan Curtis, who produced the standard edition of the opera (1989), acknowledges that neither score perfectly represents the opera as Monteverdi saw it shortly before his death in 1643. In a famous article, Curtis detected the work of several different hands in many parts of the score ("*La Poppea Impasticciata*"). Opera production in the burgeoning Venetian commercial theater may have resembled the workshop of Rubens, who might design a painting and handle the important details himself but leave the more mundane aspects of execution to younger apprentice artists.

Monteverdi, old and in declining health, might not have been able to finish *Poppea* without help from his younger colleagues and friends. The philological investigation of *Poppea* is a necessary and fascinating enterprise, but that is not the concern of this book. *Poppea* is fundamentally Monteverdi's, even though other hands may have supplied some material for it—a ritornello here, a sinfonia there, even the occasional passage of vocal writing. I will always refer to the composer as Monteverdi, for concerns about authorship in this work, just like the pursuit of what Homer "really wrote," shift focus away from the important issue: the unprecedented depth and individuality of the work. Like the Homeric epics, Monteverdi's last opera stands as a remarkably unified work of art. In the years since Curtis's article, scholarly opinion has moved gradually back toward a more unitarian attitude in discussing the opera. Ellen Rosand argues for "the essential authenticity of the work as a whole, . . . which rests on stylistic characteristics that distinguish *Poppea* from the music of any other known composer. These include an attitude towards the text setting that marks Monteverdi's work in all genres" (Rosand, *Opera* 256, fn. 18). Indeed the opera's three acts form a beautifully organic wholeness. Eric Chafe has noted the tonal and formal unity that binds many of the seemingly divergent passages of this diverse work—one of *Poppea*'s musical hallmarks. De' Paoli eloquently describes its style of "declamation, entailing elements of recitative, of arioso, and of 'speaking song' [*parlar cantando*], felicitously mixed," in music of "spacious breadth and great simplicity" (497).

No passage in the opera has been more contested by modern scholarship than the closing coronation scene and the final duet, "Pur ti miro." The text of "Pur ti miro" does not appear in the published libretti. The words are probably by the librettist and composer Benedetto Ferrari, one of the Roman-trained artists who first brought opera to Venice, and appear in a libretto for his opera *Il pastor regio* (1641). The music from this opera does not survive. Alan Curtis has suggested that Ferrari probably composed the music for this duet in *Poppea*. Recent bibliographical discoveries, however, have demonstrated that the "Pur ti miro" duet, whoever wrote its music, was a part of *Poppea* from the beginning (see Pryer). The discovery of a manuscript libretto, the so-called Udine libretto from the time of the premiere, definitively links the final duet to *Poppea*'s first performances. Pryer also marshals convincing stylistic evidence to suggest that the duet's music could easily be the work of Monteverdi himself. Certainly the bland, derivative music, unquestionably composed by Ferrari, that flanks a performance of the *Poppea* duet on a recording led by Alan Curtis makes the reattribution to Monteverdi very plausible. In other words, whoever served as a collaborator on this opera, if there was a collaborator, knew what he was doing.

Prologue and Act I

Fortuna and Virtù argue for primacy in world affairs. Amore appears and asserts that he is the most powerful deity and that today his power will transform the world. ("Human non è"). Ottone returns to Rome and the house of his beloved Poppea ("E pur' io torno qui"), where he discovers Nerone's sleeping bodyguards. He leaves in a jealous rage. The two sleepy soldiers awaken with the dawn and begin complaining of Nerone's adulterous affair with Poppea, the empress Ottavia's grief, the influence of the corrupt Seneca, and the rebellion in the empire that Nerone refuses to address. Poppea and Nerone emerge after a night of lovemaking ("Signor, deh, non partire"). Nerone warns her that they must conceal their love until he can repudiate his wife, Ottavia. She elicits his promise to return soon. Alone, Poppea gloats that "Fortune and Love fight for me" and will help her become the next empress ("Speranza, tu mi vai"). Her nurse, Arnalta, warns her of the dangers she is in, but Poppea refuses to listen. Ottavia laments her miserable life ("Disprezzata regina"), while her nurse, Nutrice, unsuccessfully encourages her to take a lover so she can be avenged on Nerone. Seneca, Nerone's Stoic tutor, enters and offers Ottavia platitudinous advice, which she politely rejects. The young page, Valletto, rails against Seneca's supposed hypocrisy ("Madama, con tua pace"). Seneca is confronted by the goddess Pallade (Pallas Athena), who warns him that his death is near. Nerone engages Seneca in a violent argument over his right to renounce Ottavia and marry Poppea. Poppea manipulates Nerone into ordering Seneca's death. The obsessive Ottone confronts Poppea, who rejects him in favor of her ambition to become empress. Drusilla, a lady attending the empress, appears. On the rebound, Ottone proclaims his love.

The score opens with a brief sinfonia designed both to attract the audience's attention and to establish a formal tone for the ensuing dialogue through its stately rhythm. According to the 1643 scenario, a back cloth setting represents a *scena di tutto cielo* (scene depicting all the heavens; see Carter, *Monteverdi's Musical Theater* 84). Fortuna, Virtù, and Amore hover above, miraculously suspended by the theater's flying mechanisms. Fortuna, with boundless self-satisfaction, bids Virtù to "go hide herself" (deh, nasconditi, o Virtù). Fortuna begins with recitative but soon succumbs to gloating vocal ornamentation that forms an arioso. Fortuna closes her attack with an arietta on the words "whoever professes Virtue can never hope to possess riches nor glory if not protected by Fortune." Fortuna's arietta is notable for her virtuosic decoration of the words that best epitomize her values: "richezza," "gloria," and her own name, Fortuna. The melodic repetitions of "non è" in the phrase "non è dalla Fortuna" suggest a childish petulance. One would expect Fortuna to comport herself in such a shameless way. The surprisingly similar egotism and pettiness in Virtù comes as the first of the many shocks *Poppea* will offer its audience. Virtù's musical and rhetorical strategies are the same as those of her rival. Like Fortuna's, Virtù's first word is "deh" (go), followed by a rest. She then launches a virtuosic melismatic attack on "sommergiti" (sub-merge yourself), making her recitative veer close to arioso from its very outset. A brief arioso illustrates Virtù's cherished idea that she teaches "the art of navigating toward Olympus." Virtù's closing arietta is as nasty and carping as the one that closed Fortuna's presentation. After comparing herself to "God" (Dio) she spitefully notes, "That's more than anyone can say for you, Fortuna" (Che ciò non si può dir di te, Fortuna). Virtù's ornamentation on "Fortuna" directly mocks Fortuna's own luxuriating on her name. Virtù, like the humans that supposedly embody her in the opera—Ottavia, Seneca, and Drusilla—is not what she professes to be. Her propensity to jealousy and anger put her on an equal rhetorical footing with her nemesis. Virtù deconstructs herself almost as soon as she starts to sing.

Amore, like Fortuna and Virtù, is sung by a soprano but evinces greater musical and rhetorical self-control. In all likelihood the role was sung by a boy soprano. Such casting perfectly underscores the irony of his superhuman power and childlike persona: this *child* rules the world. His first lines are delivered in authoritative recitative, avoiding Fortuna's and Virtù's lyrical emotionalism. His restraint lends cumulative focus to his final arietta demanding the two others submit to his authority: "Revere me, adore me, and accept me as your sovereign." "Sovereign" (sovrano) receives two long and expressive ornamental runs that assert his dominion over the earth, Fortuna, and Virtù. The two goddesses, cowed by Amore's power, now sing a lovely duet, "Human non è, non è celeste core" (No human nor celestial heart dares to contend with Love). Amore's first "conquest" in *Poppea* is thus given a perfect musical metaphor: two soloists, whose rivalry has just been expressed in virtuosic solo singing in which they pit their musical skills against each other, are now made to sing together. Their near-interchangeable duetting reflects Amore's power to subjugate all creation. The duet frames the opening of the opera, just as Nerone and Poppea's act 3 "Pur ti miro" will mark its climax with a similar blending of voices and souls. The musical structure of both of these opening and closing duets, with their intermingling of high voices above firm treading bass lines, is also very similar: in both passages each singer's individuality is subjugated to the forces of Amore and of the basso continuo (see also Schrade 365–67). The debasing squabble between Fortuna and Virtù is ironically erased as the audience succumbs to the sensual beauty of their Love-inspired harmony. When their duet ends, Amore again commands the stage for a final recitative proclamation: "Today [*Hoggi*], in single contest, both of you, bested by me, will say that the world is changed by my merest gesture [*che'l mondo a' cenni miei si muta*]."

Scenes 1 through 4

Amore's prophesy begins to be put to the proof. The flying machines and the heavenly backdrop disappear, and the action begins to unfold in front of a setting representing the "palazzo di Poppea." In the majority of scenes in this first act, a character enters and delivers a soliloquy in supposed solitude, only to discover that he or she is not alone. This reflects the political realities of *Poppea*'s world, wherein what is normally kept private is enacted in public, and public issues are resolved for the most perversely private of reasons. The opera's pervasive eavesdropping also makes for effective stagecraft, ensuring that one scene flows directly into the next. The first such onstage audience is the sleeping guards in the shadows beneath Poppea's balcony. Throughout Ottone's solo they serve as ominous reminders of Nerone's tyrannical power.

Ottone, away on state business, has returned to Rome to serenade his lover, Poppea, beneath her balcony during the dead of night, in "the first *aubade* in the history of opera" (Celletti 33). Educated Venetians would have remembered that Otho had been sent to Lusitania by Nero in order to facilitate his affair with Poppea, who in the historical record was actually Otho's wife. Busenello portrays Ottone as Poppea's discarded lover rather than her husband. Designed for an alto castrato and usually sung nowadays by a countertenor, the role of Ottone is that of a lover whom Poppea has discarded during his absence for the brighter-toned mezzo-soprano, Nerone. It is interesting that the two largest male roles are for castrati. Busenello's historical sources assert both men's "femininity," even hinting that the two may have been lovers. Tacitus remarks that Otho was "an extravagant youth who was regarded as peculiarly close to Nero" (*Annals* 13.45). Seutonius gives more detail: "[Otho] was apparently of modest stature, with crooked feet and bandy legs, while in the care of his person he was almost feminine, plucking out his body hair and, as his hair was thinning, wearing a kind of wig fitted closely and carefully to his head, so that no one would notice it. Moreover, they say he would shave his face daily and apply wet bread to it—a practice he had taken up as soon as the first down appeared—so as to avoid ever having a beard" (*Life of Otho* 12). Otho's "bandy legs" and alleged femininity make him an ideal role for a castrato.

The scene begins with Ottone's ritornello. The tune has a sprightly, almost confident tread. Ottone's ritornello moves to a quicker pulse than his deliciously languishing aria, "E pur'io torno qui" (And so I return here). The slow, tender melody he sings is, in this sense, somewhat of an anticlimax to his livelier instrumental introduction. The slow, long-held, low notes on "torno qui, qual linea al centro, qual foco a sfera" (return like a line to the center, like fire to the sphere) give Ottone immediate musical and dramatic characterization. His serenade reveals him as a devoted, gentle, excruciatingly self-effacing lover, a bit conventional and, as will be seen, disturbingly passive. Not only does Ottone lack Nerone's power, he also lacks the emperor's perverse sexual assertiveness. Susan McClary remarks, "Each of Ottone's lines droops flaccidly to tonic" (McClary, "Constructions" 218). The opera will reveal Ottone as an obsessive personality, and "torno" (return) is a word he will characteristically come back to throughout the opera. As Abert eloquently observes, "These words enclose Ottone's entire fate" (*Claudio Monteverdi* 69). Appropriately enough, "E pur'io torno qui" is set to a returning theme. Ottone's florid melodic runs on "Ah!," which cover almost three bars, are attractive and decorous, but a shade tepid in their conventionality, as is his ornamentation on "ruscello" (stream), "luce" (light), and "appare" (appear). He underlines the serenade nature of his aria by a petite reprise on "E pur'io torno qui, torno qui qual linea al centro," accenting that this is indeed a "song" being "sung" by an operatic character and underlining the performative nature of his opening solo. The sprightly ritornello returns to close the first section of his aria.

.   In Ottone's second refrain the aria shifts to the minor key, a prefiguring of the darkening dramatic situation. This shift, occurring during lines that make specific reference to the physical surroundings on stage, may coincide with the audience's growing perception of the shadowy, sleeping guards, whose presence will shatter Ottone's happiness. "Dear beloved roof, lodging of my life, and my love, I stand here and my heart pays reverence"; Poppea's eyes, Ottone sings, will anticipate the light of the approaching day. The impression created by Ottone's aria is of a dreamy, impotent self-absorption. The "dreams" (sogni) and "sweet fantasy" (dolce fantasia) that Ottone apostrophizes of the supposedly sleeping Poppea seem more like figments of his own virtually sleep-walking musical and dramatic self-presentation. The music changes bluntly from aria to recitative on "Ma che veggio, infelice?" (But what is this I see, unhappy me?). Ottone has finally caught a glimpse of the guards, who he now realizes are not harmless "fantasmi" (phantoms) nor "notturne larve" (nocturnal shadows): their presence declares Poppea's infidelity. He makes the opera's first observation concerning inner and outer worlds: "I adore these marble columns, tearfully wooing a balcony, while Nerone sleeps in Poppea's arms." Instead of a lover serenading and happily awaking his beloved, he stands revealed a cuckold, singing music to cold stone. Poppea's home becomes a false exterior concealing betrayal, just as Ottone proves not the successful lover but an unmanly cuckold-castrato.

It has taken Ottone several verses of recitative to come to the brutal realization of where Nerone now sleeps. But rather than being stirred to some kind of action, Ottone proceeds to make a series of curiously detached observations: "[Nerone] has brought [the guards] here as protection for himself from crime. Oh, uncertain security of princes; your custodians are sound asleep." As a public figure himself, Ottone may be expected to note deficiencies in a security system. However, these comments seem strangely dissociated after the passionate expression of his aria and the bitter reversal he has just experienced in recitative. Chafe observes: "With unnerving instinct Monteverdi indicates that the hollowness of [Ottone's] generalizing words covers up a conflict; at the very point at which he observes that [Nerone's] security measures have failed, [Ottone] detaches himself from his feelings and turns away from the opportunity for vengeance it provides for him. His conflict is that of action versus inaction, and here, as in later situations, he prefers the later" (Chafe 335).

As Ottone builds toward his defeated exit, his music ironically becomes more active and veers toward arialike expression. Rather than allowing Ottone to cut a more heroic figure, the music and his words suggest his ineffectiveness via a kind of operatic self-consciousness: "Io di credula speme [rest] il seme sparsi" (I sowed the seeds of credulous hope). The rest that punctuates this line insists on our full attention to both parts of the verse. Ottone's remark is surely conventional enough metaphorically. The heightened dramatic situation, however, and the male alto voice tinge the line with irony. What "seed" could be more hopelessly "sowed" than that of a castrato? In "Ma, ma l'aria, e 'l cielo a danni miei rivolto" (But, but the air, and the heavens have overturned me to ruin), "l'aria" is a pun. Its primary meaning in this passage is obviously "air," but the increasingly arialike nature of the vocal writing creates inevitable emotional distance for the audience. It would have been hard to hear "speme" and "aria" from a castrato's mouth at a moment of heightened tension and not notice metatheatrical resonance.

Like innumerable theater pieces of the Renaissance and early baroque, *Poppea* is an artwork that is deeply concerned with both the practice and the process, philosophical and aesthetic, of making art. In Ottone's aria and recitative Amore has already exerted his influence, bringing ecstasy and now agony to a mortal walking the earthly stage below.

The soldiers' scene reveals the ruling-class protagonists from the vantage point of their social inferiors, the emperor's bumbling bodyguards. The First Soldier, a tenor, has been stirred from sleep by Ottone's mounting passion. His tepid queries of "Chi parla, chi parla?" (Who's talking?) and "Chi va lì? Chi va lì?" (Who goes there?) startle his sleeping companion awake. The Second Soldier, a baritone, awakens more quickly than his colleague. His alertness is indicated by his rapid-fire address to his friend, "Camerata, camerata!" (Comrade, comrade!), which contrast with the tenor's slower-paced "Ohimè, ancor non è dì?" (Ah me, it's still not day?).

> Second Soldier: Comrade, what are you doing?
>
> Why are you talking in your sleep?
>
> *First Soldier*: The dawn is raising its first rays.

The tenor's slow vocal line seems ready to lead him back to slumber on "I didn't sleep at all last night." The baritone goads him further, leading the tenor to curse love, Nerone, Poppea, and the army in an angry arioso before he is overcome again by halting drowsiness. The tenor is still groggy, but the baritone is on an angry roll, denouncing the sordid open secrets of the imperial marriage and the military chaos it encourages. He is a soldier—if a soldier who sleeps on duty—and his outraged professionalism leads him into an extended arioso passage: "Our empress dissolves herself in tears, and Nerone scorns her with Poppea. Armenia is rebelling, and he doesn't think about it; Pannonia is in arms, and he laughs at it. Thus, as far as I can see, the empire goes from bad to worse." Audiences in 1643 could appreciate the topicality of these words, for these same regions were again in turmoil (see Carter, *Monteverdi's Musical Theater* 272). The reference to unrest inspires a *stile concitato* passage in the vocal line and accompaniment, including a particularly realistic portrayal of Nerone's derisive laughter on the long spun-out ornaments he gives "ride" (laughter). The baritone's mimetic skills are exploited again when he gives the audience its first impression of Seneca. "[Nerone] only believes in the pedant Seneca," a line sung at the bottom of the baritone's range, prefigures and mocks the lower range in which the Stoic will sing: "That vile courtier who aggrandizes his profits by betraying his companions! That wicked architect, who builds his house on other's graves!" The two soldiers' attack on Seneca's ethics raises issues about the philosopher's integrity that are never fully addressed. Dio wrote of the historical Seneca:

> His conduct was seen to be diametrically opposed to the teachings of his philosophy. For while denouncing tyranny, he was making himself the teacher of a tyrant: while inveighing against the associates of the powerful, he did not hold aloof from the palace himself; and though he had nothing good to say of flatterers, he himself had constantly fawned [upon men]. Though finding fault with the rich, he himself acquired a fortune. (*Roman History* 61.10)

Tacitus's handling of Seneca reveals a more admirable figure (*Annals* 15.62). Busenello deliberately mixes these sometimes contradictory sources, and the opera is the richer for the resultant ambiguities. *Poppea* projects a complex world where virtually every character and action is viewed from contradictory perspectives.

The tenor caps the litany of complaints with the paranoiac order "Let not one eye trust the other, even though they always look together." This excites the two soldiers to duet: "Let's learn from the eyes not to act like fools." The two stooges who've slept while guarding the most powerful man in the world take delight in the idea of "learning": "Let's learn [*impariamo*] from the eyes." "Impariamo" is subjected to coloratura by both singers. Then the tenor observes, "But the dawn is brightening and the day comes." Their fear of the emperor and their hurried attempts to fade away inconspicuously are vividly suggested by their flustered, overlapping repetitions of "Nerone, Nerone" until, in the scene's final bar, the two men snap to attention by singing in unison, "Taciam, taciam [*rest*], Nerone è qui" (Quiet, Nerone is here). The soldiers are never heard from again. Nevertheless, their humorous by-play and bluntness of vision serve to enrich the whole opera.

The workaday, grounded vocal registers of tenor and baritone create a contrast to the soprano, alto, and mezzo characters in the surrounding scenes. They offer the audience one of the few but telling glimpses it will enjoy of the "normal" world, and their commonsense view of affairs is vital background to the action. A critic writes, "One is reminded of the guards' opening speech in Aeschylus's *Agamemnon* regarding the scandal in high places [that] is about to corrupt the whole state" (Savage, "Love and Infamy" 199).

All Busenello's historical sources are united in their portrayal of the characters of Nerone and Poppea. Nerone is uniformly condemned as an effeminate, sexually perverted sociopath who was obsessed with fantasies of his own greatness as a singer, poet, and actor. With respect to Poppea, Tacitus is the most succinct and elegant:

> Poppea had every asset except goodness. From her mother, the loveliest woman of her day, she inherited distinction and beauty. Her wealth, too, was equal to her birth. She was clever and pleasant to talk to. She seemed respectable. But her life was depraved. Her public appearances were few; she would half-veil her face at them, to stimulate curiosity (or because it suited her). To her, married or bachelor bedfellows were alike. She was indifferent to her reputation—yet insensible to men's love, and herself unloving. Advantage dictated the bestowal of her favors. (*Annals* 13.45)

The opera hardly contradicts this scathing portrait, yet the music and dramatic poetry ensure that these ostensibly monstrous personages are always compelling and profoundly human.

Monteverdi's central lovers were sung by a female soprano whose range approximated that of the modern lyric soprano (Poppea) and a mezzo-soprano castrato (Nerone). Twentieth-century revivals have used three different options for coping with the castrato question here. Nerone's part has frequently been transposed down to the tenor range. Often, in more recent productions, countertenors have been employed for the role in an attempt to have the best of both worlds, an authentic masculine presence along with something of the role's original vocal pitch. Female mezzos are certainly the most musically satisfying alternative, creating a drag performance wherein, as one critic observes, "the homoerotics of the castrati have been replaced by lesbian erotics" (Dame 151). With two female voices, the vocal lines of Nerone and Poppea can become interchangeable, as the composer envisioned: "The dissonances are very close and cause frictional moments of an almost physical nature. In the cadential notes, in unison, the lovers literally merge into each other and fuse. . . . How different from the tenor and the soprano, where the octave interval remains as an unbridgeable gap between them" (Dame 150). Both Nerone and Ottone, the principal male figures in the opera, are sung by castrati, imparting, as Osthoff observes, "the kind of sexual ambivalence often found in Caravaggio, as in the Uffizi *Bacchus*" (156). Both men are in thrall to Poppea and suffer from increasingly obvious psychosexual pathologies. Received opinion has it that seventeenth- and eighteenth-century composers virtually ignored the absurdity of castrati as lovers and heroes. Received opinion is probably correct, except when it comes to the last and most extraordinary of Monteverdi's works. Monteverdi is not ignoring the real-life sexual identity of his castrati performers; he is capitalizing on it. The use of castrati in *Poppea* reveals a psychological depth and sense of performative irony seldom encountered in operatic literature. This most artificial of baroque conventions becomes, with Monteverdi, a medium for an often uncomfortable impulse toward realism. Again the images of Caravaggio, with their uncompromising, sometimes shocking naturalistic details, spring to mind as analogies to the world of *Poppea*.

Poppea's first speech in the opera sets a musical seal on her character: "My lord, my lord, ah, don't go: let these arms circle your neck, just as your beauty circles my heart." Her first line is breathed like a sigh, hovering seductively close to melody. "Signor" is set to a two-note ascending pattern that Poppea will reuse, creating the musical suggestion of obsequiousness. Much of her music is written in repetitions of a single note, creating a hypnotic, erotic effect. Nerone, ready to resume his public persona, delivers a terse recitative response, "Poppea, let me leave," attempting to break the spell by raising the musical line. Monteverdi's rearrangements of Busenello's text—moving the first line of Nerone's speech to interrupt Poppea's fourteen-line opening clarifies the two new characters' identity, if any such clarification should be needed—reveals the composer's preference for portraying a flowing dialogue between characters. He loves the give-and-take of dialogue so much that he never hesitates to create it, even when his librettist has left him successions of block speeches. One critic notes: "The way in which Poppea ensnares Nerone and at the same time gets him to promise to marry her is a musical showpiece in the art of seduction. . . . Monteverdi [by his rearrangement of the text] gave Poppea the reins . . . with incessant questioning" (Leopold 208–9).

Poppea resumes her amorous recitative pleading with more of the dronelike effect of her first lines: "Ah, don't say you are going: even the sound of the word is bitter. Ah, I feel my soul dying [*perir*]. I feel it expiring [*spirar*]." Both "perir" and "spirar" vividly portray the conflation of death with orgasm so popular in Renaissance music and literature. Nerone attempts to gain rational control in spite of her blandishments. His next lines, set in recitative, portray a man riven by passion yet attempting to maintain the appearance of control: "The nobility of your birth does not permit that Rome should know that we are united until Ottavia— [*In fin ch'Ottavia*—]." Here is one of Monteverdi's masterstrokes. The composer makes Poppea breathlessly cut into his speech. "In fin che? In fin che?" (Until what? Until what?). Nerone is compelled to start his sentence again. "Until Ottavia no longer remains [*non riman'esclusa*]—." Again Poppea leaps at his words, cutting him off by excited questions. "Non rimane? Non rimane?" (No longer remains? No longer remains?). Nerone, now thoroughly under her sway, attempts to wipe away his earlier hesitation by completing his entire phrase. Poppea has dragged the treacherous idea out of him with her needling, reiterated questions: "Until Ottavia no longer remains due to my repudiation."

This, Nerone's first concession to Poppea, leads to the scene's first arioso. The words "Vanne ben mio" (Come, my love) are treated to attractive music in a rocking rhythm. Leopold describes the aria as "a dance-like song in which it is impossible to distinguish between joy and malice" (Leopold 209). "Vanne ben mio" is a splendid example of the opera's ironic use of beautiful music expressing horrible actions. This is followed by an aria for Nerone complete with a prefatory ritornello to announce its theme, "In un sospir, che vien" (In a sigh from the depths of my heart). Nerone is becoming aroused again, and the aria signals this by its exquisite melody and the very frequent rests in the vocal line, illustrating "the sigh which comes from the depths of my heart" and suggesting an erotic breathlessness. The tentative effect given by the frequent rests—by Nerone's vocal stopping and starting—renders the emperor a curiously vulnerable figure. This scene of erotic vulnerability is made more explicit by the setting and recitative on "O cara, cara ed un addio" (O dear one, oh, farewell), in which Nerone's vocal line moves up the staff, creating a kind of orgasmic outburst that will become a distinctive feature of his music throughout the opera. Poppea asserts herself yet again, filling the power vacuum created by her panting lover with an aria and ritornello of her own: "My lord, you always see me [Signor, sempre mi vedi], and yet you don't see me. For if it's true, that you conceal me inside your breast, then it's impossible for your eyes to look at me." The two lovers are admirably contrasted in these two arias. Nerone's minor-key "panting" aria is obviously erotic in both words and music. Poppea's words are emotionally neutral. Only her ornamental elaborations on "sempre" (always), "perché" (because), and "ver" (true) hint at flirtatiousness. She has already caught her prey and for the moment does not need to lure him. Instead, her song, abetted by a firm and steady rhythm, expresses tuneful self-confidence. Monteverdi is suggesting again that she is the power behind this relationship. Her words offer an ironic dimension to her character that also places her in a dominant position over her lover. For all his dubious attributes, no one can accuse Nerone of a keen sense of irony. Poppea is speaking in a deliberately double sense: Nerone, the foolish, murderous decadent, cannot see the real Poppea—though the opera's audience can, through the ironic layering of perception. Nerone begins an arioso, "Adorati miei rai" (My adored eyes), a slow, sultry melody that seems tailor-made for musical repetition and development. Instead, he resorts to recitative to express the words "Stay with me Poppea, my heart [rest] my dear, [rest] and the light [rest] and the light of my life." The rests suggest a return to his first aria's erotic breathlessness, and the premature abandonment of his previous arioso hints at an exhausted lover, briefly stimulated to erotic-melodic action, finding himself musically and sexually impotent. He is putty in her hands.

Poppea begins wheedling, extracting new promises and concessions from him. She repeats, "Ah, don't say that you're going; even the sound of the word is bitter; ah, I feel my soul dying, feel it dying." Faced with her renewed pleas that he stay, Nerone reverts from recitative to arioso on the platitudinous lines, "Don't be afraid, you are always with me, splendor in my eyes and deity in my heart." "Splendor" and "deità" are both subjected to predictable virtuosic ornamentation. Poppea interrupts Nerone's newest arioso. "Tornerai?" (You're returning?), she asks repeatedly, demanding an answer. Nerone attempts to assist himself with a new arioso platitude: "I can't possibly live disunited from you any more than the unity of a point may be split" (Se non si smembra la unità del punto). This curious image of the "punto" recalls Ottone's opening-aria image of the "line to the center." The verbal similarity compels us to compare Poppea's two lovers, each fond of flowery, imprecise language, each manipulated by Poppea, each sung by a castrato. Poppea has no patience for Nerone's attempt at lyrical evasion. She asks again in insistent recitative : "Tornerai?" Finally she receives an answer on her own recitative terms: "Tornerò" (I will return). "When?" "Soon." "Soon—you promise me?" "I swear it to you." "You'll keep your oath to me?" And here comes the scene's climactic promise: "And if I don't come, you come to me." Now Poppea has the emperor, and the Roman state, where she wants them. The lovers bring the scene to its close with a coda built out of languishing phrases repeated over and over, recalling the sighing figure of the Renaissance erotic "death." The lovers sing "Farewell, Nerone" and "Farewell, Poppea" back and forth as they reluctantly part in the growing morning light. In this scene we have a music in which the boundaries of recitative and aria are more than usually porous, a musical blending of eroticism "tinged with a shadow of melancholy" (de' Paoli 498).

Busenello's text for the fourth scene consists of two speeches in the published libretto—one for Poppea and one for Arnalta, her nurse. On paper the characters express two rigid attitudes in two block speeches. Monteverdi transforms this simple verbal text into a complex musical structure, creating a sense of progressing psychological conflict the words alone lack.

Poppea's speech becomes an aria, the final couplet of which will permeate the scene in the form of repeated interjections to Arnalta's warnings.

> Hope, you go on caressing my heart,
> the mind is flattered
> and you completely surround me
> with an imaginary royal mantle.
> No, no, I am not going to fear any vexation;
> Love and Fortune are fighting for me.

The trisyllabic "speranza" (hope) suggests the rhythm for the confident ritornello that begins the scene. In her aria's first two verses Poppea musically ornaments both "hope" (speranza) and "caresses" (accarezzando). Her sensuality and opportunism are encapsulated in a single strophe. Soon "flattery" (lusingando) joins "hope" and "caressing" as a characteristic word for Poppea's musical elaboration. In "The mind is flattered and you completely surround me with a royal imagined mantle," a rest separates "sia ma" from "immaginario manto." The rest and the ensuing lowering of pitch delicately emphasize Poppea's precious "imaginary [royal] mantle." The music suggests an intake of air; the lower pitch of "immaginario manto" moves the singer and her listeners from the heights of "hope" to the recesses of her ambition. The aria's final couplet is set with the rapid-fire declamation of "No, no, I'm not going to fear" (No, no, non temo) and the bold *stile concitato* outburst on "Love and Fortune are fighting for me" (Per me guerreggia Amor, e la Fortuna). The last time we heard such rhythms was during the soldiers' scene, when the Second Soldier reported that "Pannonia is taking up arms." Monteverdi has newly minted this war/sex commonplace and given it a new, ironic context.

The "speranza" ritornello is repeated for a third and final time, closing Poppea's aria. This repetition may also serve as a convenient musical tag to allow Arnalta time to enter if—as seems likely—she is not meant to be onstage for Poppea's monologue. Arnalta is written for an alto or high tenor to sing in drag, the transvestite option being the more historically authentic. Based on the nurse who attends Poppea in the pseudo-Senecan *Octavia praetexta,* Arnalta belongs to a long line of humorous old women often played by men in Continental European drama (see also Harnoncourt, *Musical Dialogue* 8). Monteverdi will give Arnalta a soul, but her roots belong in the stock characters of commedia dell'arte and Roman comedy. Arnalta's first lines are sung as recitative, in contrast to Poppea's florid aria: "Ah, child, may heaven grant that these embraces might not one day be your ruin." The rests after "Ahi figlia, figlia" (Ah, child), "abbracciamenti" (embraces), and "un giorno" (one day) suggest the nervous starting and stopping of an agitated speaker. Poppea refuses the bait and repeats the first of her aria's closing couplet lines: "No, no, non temo, no, di noia alcuna" (No, no, I'll fear no vexation). This first rephrasing of the line introduces telling variations on the textual-musical presentation. "No" is stated thrice, punctuated with a short rest. The listener has not heard this strategy before and may even be initially tricked into believing that we are about to hear entirely new material. What Busenello had written as a set speech is being broken up and manipulated by Monteverdi into one side of a dynamic, ongoing argument between two characters. Arnalta's fears suggest new ornaments to Poppea, who colors "temo" (fear) with decoration designed to put Arnalta in her place. Arnalta continues, "The empress Ottavia has discovered Nerone's love affairs, so that I am terrified and fearful that any day, any hour may be the last day, the last hour of your life." Arnalta's fears and insinuations are marked again by the use of the rests that punctuate her warnings about "the empress Ottavia," "fear" (temo), "much feared" (pavento), "every day" (ch'ogni giorno), "every hour" (ogni punto), and "your life" (tua vita). Her interlocutor having failed to find a new strategy, Poppea responds by repeating the last line of her aria, the *concitato* declamation about Love and Fortune fighting for her.

Undeterred, Arnalta delivers a third recitative warning: "Familiarity with kings is perilous, love and hate have no power over them; their self-interest is their only concern." The descending notes giving sinister color to "perigliosa" (perilous) and "puri interessi" (self-interest) make her admonitions slyer. Arnalta now opposes Poppea's lyricism with a lyricism of her own. She gets her own ritornello, a finger-wagging motif to counterbalance her mistress's music of exultant self-satisfaction. This contrasting ritornello does its work insofar as Poppea is briefly left songless. Arnalta, having captured her attention via the ritornello, goes on to a fourth recitative: "If Nerone loves you, it is just an affair. If he abandons you, you can't complain. For the least trouble, keep silent." As before, the insinuating downward swoops afforded words such as "cortesia" (affair), "dolere" (complain), and "tacere" (silent) further establish her reprimanding and possibly leering character.

Poppea, having had time to regroup, repeats her "No, no, non temo" refrain. We are again at a dramatic stalemate, though both women have proven themselves formidable musical and dramatic opponents. Arnalta's fifth recitative is an intensification of her argument: "The great breathe honor with their presence, leaving while the house is filled with wicked winds, fumes as payment for reputations." The gentle vocal rise between the words "la presenza" (presence) and "lascia" (leaving) suggests an ironic rise of voice in spoken conversation. Arnalta's ritornello is repeated to underscore her point. Emboldened, she launches a sixth recitative statement: "Perdi l'honor" (You lose honor). This passage is notable for its insinuating repetitions, accenting Arnalta's own emerging immoral core. Fruitful vices are to be preferred to ambitious ones: "Son inutili i vizi ambiziosi! Mi piaccion più i peccati fruttuosi." The intensification of the vowel reiterations creates a striking passage of musical-dramatic writing. Arnalta is a character concerned more with self-protection and appearance than with promoting a genuine morality. Her brand of recitative or song-speech seems at first that of a censorious yet sincere moralizer. But as one listens, such musical patterns begin to seem equally apt for illustrating hypocrisy and unscrupulousness. Words and music can illustrate the inner and outer content of the human being. Arnalta is beginning to enjoy herself now, just as the audience realizes her admonitions mask a character nearly as unscrupulous as the mistress she reprimands.

Arnalta's attempt to squelch Poppea's imperial ambitions compels Poppea to reiterate her "No, non temo" line. As Chafe observes, Poppea's use of the final tag lines of her aria to answer Arnalta "[create] in their insistence the effect of Poppea's refusing to listen, her blotting out everything but her hopes from her thoughts" (Chafe 318). The argument is nearing a stalemate. Arnalta decides to change her rhetorical and musical strategy: "Mira, mira, Poppea, dove il prato è più ameno, e dilettoso, stassi il serpente ascoso" (Look, look, Poppea where the meadow is very pleasant and delightful, there the serpent hides). Arnalta is at last freed from recitative, and her musical line floats an arioso of seductive allure. In her need to change Poppea's thinking she starts to think, or rather sing, like Poppea. She creates a striking musical-verbal image of the beautiful meadow that harbors the deadly serpent. The ornaments garlanding "ameno" (pleasant) recall her mistress's style of verbal highlighting. Arnalta's cautioning tale exhibits an excellent sense of suspense and surprise when the danger inherent in "the serpent" does not create agitation in the vocal and instrumental line until "la calma è profezia della tempeste" (the calm is the prophecy of the tempest). Like a sudden outburst of bad weather, the words "la tempesta" are treated to repetitions similar to Poppea's own *concitato* style, which Arnalta uses to drive home her admonition once the younger woman has had time to be lured into the magic of Arnalta's storytelling.

Arnalta fails to change her mistress. Poppea reiterates her tag lines, "Non temo" and "Per me guerreggia Amor," for a final, decisive time. Arnalta's reaction is to sing a tune that meshes perfectly with her earlier finger-wagging ritornello: "Ben sei pazza" (you are crazy if you believe that you can trust your happiness and security to a blind boy [Amore] and a bald woman [Fortuna]!"). Monteverdi reserves one more striking effect for the end of the scene: Arnalta's "anger" aria is allowed to sputter to its end in mid-repetition. "Ben sei pazza, ben sei pazza se credi . . ." (You are crazy, you are crazy if you believe . . .) suggests that the old woman has exited the stage in the middle of her song, so angry she has neglected to bring her aria to a decorous closure, as befits the end of a scene. Monteverdi has created a compelling kind of musical realism wherein an operatic character storms off the stage too overcome by anger to grant a smooth closure to her lyrical utterance. The music, words, and life of the scene are moving out of sight and earshot to continue somehow backstage, a beautifully dramaturgical trompe l'oeil.

Scenes 5 through 13

Arnalta's final broken lyric contrasts with Ottavia's stately recitative. The rest of act 1 is set "in the city of Rome." Ottavia takes Poppea's place as her scene's dominant female figure. Like her rival, Ottavia assumes an extreme emotional position and is coaxed by her female attendant to relinquish this hazardous stance. Ironically, scene 5 reverses the rhetorical position of the two female figures. Ottavia declares her agony at Nerone's behavior, yet balks at risking the anger of the gods, while her nurse (Nutrice) pleads with her to commit adultery as revenge upon her husband. Poppea-Arnalta are perfectly balanced and contrasted with Ottavia-Nutrice in Busenello's dramaturgical structure, and Monteverdi musically augments the dramatic and rhetorical contrast. The character Nutrice was inspired by the empress's attendant and confidante in the pseudo-Senecan *Octavia praetexta,* just as that ancient play had suggested the Poppea-Arnalta relationship. In *Octavia* the empress hates her husband from the outset and languishes under his unending cruelty while her nurse ineffectively consoles her to be patient and hope for the best. Busenello has altered this relationship, perhaps taking inspiration from the Penelope and Melanto scenes in *Ulisse.* Busenello's Ottavia, in this respect more like Penelope than she is like her own model of the *praetexta,* appears to love her wayward husband, longing for him to come back to her, and Nutrice, like Melanto in the earlier opera, advises her mistress to console herself with a lover. Busenello's alteration of his source deepens the emotional stakes in the opera and serves to make Ottavia's change in the second act all the more shocking.

Unlike her rival, the aria-and-arioso-addicted Poppea, Ottavia sings recitative only. Ottavia's musical style was by 1643 somewhat reactionary, closer to the recitative-heavy writing of the earliest Florentine operatic experiments than to the freer melodic style that was emerging in the 1630s and 1640s. Her exclusive reliance on recitative contrasts her character to the world around her, isolating her from her supposed moral teacher Seneca, who can himself sing arioso in moments of heightened emotion. Like Penelope in *Ulisse,* Ottavia is a great mezzo role that uses a large amount of recitative to indicate the character's emotional isolation. Nevertheless, from very early in her opera, even Penelope reveals a propensity for arioso. Ottavia does not. She is a living anachronism in the opera's musical fabric, her psychological fragility and dangerous rigidity perfectly matched by the recitative style she is given. Wendy Heller describes Ottavia's distinctive style as "a terse, angular, often colorless recitative, sometimes dissonant, other times forbiddingly consonant, but devoid of sensual chromaticism. Her preferred melodic gestures seem almost designed to negate any sense of lyricism. . . . A gasping, disjointed, and even depressed quality emerges from the short phrases" (*Emblems* 153).

The role of Ottavia was written for opera's first prima donna, the mezzo Anna Renzi. According to one contemporary source, Renzi was as "skillful in acting as she [was] excellent in music, [as] cheerful in feigning madness as she is wise in knowing how to imitate it" (qtd. in Rosand, *Opera* 96). All these attributes—acting, musicianship, and a penchant for portraying acute psychic instability—suggest Ottavia was ideally suited to Renzi's talents. Rosand observes that Renzi's roles were "tailor-made for her by composers and librettists intimately acquainted with her abilities" (*Opera* 233). Ottavia vies with Poppea as the dominant female role in the opera. Poppea's first scene reveals virtually all the essential ingredients of her character. Ottavia, however, presents a far subtler characterization and will traverse a wider arc, from her dignified first appearance to her shocking explosion of violence in act 2, which leads to her tragic final monologue in act 3. Nutrice is written for an alto or high travesty tenor and is indeed often sung by a tenor, making the character balance all the more symmetrically with Arnalta. Alan Curtis has found evidence that Nutrice and Arnalta were actually doubled by the same tenor in the 1651 Naples revival (Monteverdi, *L'incoronazione,* Curtis ed. xiii).

Ottavia's first lament breaks naturally into four rhetorical units. The first establishes who she is and her suffering, the second focuses on Nerone and his adultery, the third is taken up with her near-orgasmic fantasies of revenge, and the fourth seems to break apart verbally and musically into an impotent statement of resignation. The first two words of her monologue, "Disprezzata regina," are repeated several times, etching the new character of the "despised queen" into the audience's consciousness as well as hinting at her obsessional nature. The stage director Pierre Audi vividly described her as embodying a "river of tears" flowing through the opera (personal conversation, December 27, 2001). "Disprezzata" is sung three times, and "regina," four. Although they create a memorable musical-verbal flourish for the start of her recitative, these repetitions suggest her awareness of her social station, her pride, which, more than her broken heart, will lead her to suborn murder. Rests separate her initial self-identification as "the wronged queen, the tormented wife of the Roman monarch" from a startling succession of breathless, simple questions: "Che fò, ove son, che penso?" (What am I doing, what am I, and what am I thinking?). Her sense of wounded pride is immediately broken by these short questions, betraying disorientation and extreme psychological distress. A multidimensional character—an anguished queen with a fierce sense of entitlement, racked by painful vulnerability—is established within only a few seconds. Not until Mozart will another opera composer create such depth in a character in such a short period of stage time.

Ottavia closes the first section of her lament with odd generalizations about "the miserable sex of womankind" (o delle donne miserabil sesso), which links the role of husband with that of male children in a curiously incestuous way—not an unheard-of combination, of course, in the Roman imperial household. These child-husband creatures grow into "executioners"—they compel the female sex to "give birth to its own death" (partorir la morte). Perhaps she is thinking of Agrippina, Nero's mother, his alleged lover, and, finally, an early victim of his regime. Ottavia's vocal line includes a sighing figure, punctuated by another psychologically telling rest prefacing her attack on Nerone. As she does with "regina," Ottavia begins the next section with angered repetitions of her husband's name. Four "Nerone"s balance the four "regina"s of the earlier section. Then follows another unexpected musical and psychological insight. After denouncing Nerone as "eternally cursed at, and cursed by my griefs" (bestemmiato pur sempre, e maledetto dai cordogli miei), a rest marks a shift of tone from anger to vulnerability: "Where, ah me, where are you?" (dove ohimè, dove sei?). Busenello's bare text suggests a purely rhetorical question. Ottavia should know very well where Nerone is. Monteverdi's music suggests the words convey more than mere rhetorical force. The hesitant phrases "dove ohimè" and "dove sei" are broken by rests, suggesting the love she still feels for her husband. The composer insists that we see Ottavia not only as a neurotic and ultimately dangerous figure, but as a three-dimensional, suffering human being as well.

This passage of delicate hesitation marks the closest Ottavia can come to lyrical singing. "You happily rest and delight in the arms of Poppea": this thought becomes a reiterated outburst, resembling the *concitato* aggression Poppea had exhibited on the thought that Fortune and Love fight for her. Ottavia's lyrical singing of "felice" and "godi" betray her rage and suggest her extreme emotional and sexual frustration. Her image of Nerone in Poppea's arms recalls Ottone's remarks from the first scene, subtly linking her to the jilted lover long before we see them fatefully crossing paths. Another rest marks Ottavia's regaining of her customary stoic composure. In the third section of the lament Ottavia directly addresses Destiny and Jupiter, asking the king of the gods to rain down "lightning bolts" on her offending husband: "Destiny, if you exist, Jove, listen to me. If you have [*hai*] no lightning bolts [*fulmini*] with which to punish Nerone, I accuse you of impotence and I charge you with injustice!" The three rapid descending ornamental runs on "fulmini" portray Ottavia's spite, and the ornamented run on "hai" (you have) suggests a truly volcanic anger. "I accuse you of impotence, and I charge you with injustice": for a moment Ottavia resembles a Greek tragic protagonist defying the gods, but another telling rest in the score short-circuits Ottavia's heroics and begins her lament's anticlimactic closing section, "Ah, I've gone too far, and I reject, suppress [*sopprimo*], and bury [*seppellisco*] [my torment]." Suppression and burial are major aspects of Ottavia's mental life, and we see and hear her slump back into her passive state of "torment" (tormento) to end her first lament (on this passage see also Rosand, "Monteverdi's Mimetic Art" 125–26). Nutrice now breaks in on her mistress's soliloquy. The composer delays the last two verses of Octavia's lament, "O ciel, o ciel, deh l'ira tua s'estingua, non provi i tuoi rigori il fallo mio!" (O heavens, O heavens, turn away your wrath; don't let my fault provoke your anger!), until after Nutrice first attempts to gain her attention by repeating her name. Monteverdi's setting suggests that Ottavia may be disconcerted by her awareness of her nurse's presence and that her pleas to the heavens may be more for Nutrice's benefit than for the gods'. The composer's dovetailing increases the sense of Ottavia's estrangement from her surroundings and the difficulty of breaching the exterior and interior worlds inhabited by all the opera's characters.

Ottavia seems ready to draw out her lament further, but Nutrice at last seizes her moment and asks her to "listen, listen to the words of your faithful nurse," ushering in her own aria: "Find someone, find someone, find someone who is worthy of you, to em- — to embrace—to embrace you with pleasure" (scegli alcun, che di te degno d'abbracciarti si contenti). The verbal repetition and music create the effect of Nutrice stammering out the most embarrassing phrases to her prudish mistress. Nutrice's brief *concitato* passage reminds us of the love-and-warfare dichotomy as she elaborates the idea of erotic vengeance in "nel vendicarsi" (in revenge). The persuasive force of Nutrice's aria is helped by her accompanying instrumental ritornello. Ottavia, like Poppea before her, holds her ground in rejecting her servant's "dirty arguments" (sozzi argomenti), though the empress's responses hint at rhetorical and musical hollowness, especially when she claims that "the abused wife of an adulterous husband is mistreated, certainly, but not disgraced." The cadential phrase that ends the sentence "ma non infame" (but not disgraced) is so patently conventional as to suggest an unreflecting smugness. We can hear from Ottavia's music that she doesn't believe her own stoic platitudes. As in the preceding scene, two women are left at an impasse. Ottavia's last four lines, which conclude the scene, hint at troubling elements in her character that will eventually become a driving force in the opera's action: "If there were neither honor, nor God, I would be my own deity, and my sins I would punish with my own hand; but nevertheless I so far from sin, my heart is divided between innocence and crying." The four lines of recitative setting hint at Ottavia's inner nature. "I would be a God" is emphatically repeated—"Sarei Nume . . . sarei . . . sarei Nume stessa"—an emphasis suggesting the idea's attractiveness to the queen even as she rejects it. The hint of disingenuousness noted in "ma non infame" resurfaces in the extra emphasis given "I am so far, far from sin" (lunge, lunge dagli errori) and the stylized suggestion of a sob on "'l pianto" (crying). The empress doth protest too much.

After so many soprano and alto voices, Seneca's basso creates a pleasing contrast as he enters the scene. Seneca is the most complex and ambiguous of Monteverdi's bass roles. His deep voice lends him a sense of powerful authority. In Seneca the opera reveals its most deeply conflicted and morally ambivalent character—a fatuous theorist who dies for his theories, an accused materialist who willingly gives up all he has, a moral anchor in a world without morality. He is the second person, after Nutrice, to offer potential comfort to Ottavia. What follows, however, is a long-winded outpouring of Stoic aphorisms, as insensitive as they are unhelpful.

> Here is the disconsolate woman,
> exalted to the imperial throne
> only to suffer slavery. O glorious
> empress of the world,
> you exceed the titled ranks
> of your famous and great ancestors.
> The futility of tears
> is unworthy of imperial eyes and station.
> Thank Fortune
> who with its blows
> adds to your graces.
> The whetstone unstruck
> doesn't send out any sparks.

Monteverdi uses pompous musical gesture to point up Seneca's foibles, much as Mozart will do with Fiordiligi in *Così fan tutte*. Seneca's word painting in this scene is heavy-handed and clichéd. As an opening gesture, his voice plunges dangerously low to depict the empress's metaphorical "servaggio" (slavery). Each of the succeeding epigrammatic statements has an attractive but hackneyed musical setting. At one point, Seneca's recitative begins to grow more lyrical: "Ringrazia, ringrazia la Fortuna" (Give thanks, give thanks to Fortune), sung to an arioso whose very melodic sweetness, given the bleak situation and clichéd sentiment, seems particularly out of place. The references to "blows" (colpi) bring predictable musical depiction in reference both to Fortune's blows and to the "unstruck whetstone" (la cote non percossa). Seneca's elaborate three-measure melisma illustrating the sparks (faville) that Ottavia's whetstonelike integrity ought to set off is as musically attractive and pictorially appropriate as it is excruciatingly predictable. The phrase "Destiny's blows" (tu dal Destin colpita) conjures similar repetitions.

> But you, since you've been hit by Destiny
> should bring forth from yourself the high virtues
> of rigor and fortitude,
> greater glories than beauty.
> The charms of face, of features,
> which shine in an illustrious appearance,
> with splendid and delicate coloring
> are stolen by a few thieving days.
> But constant virtue,
> despite the stars, fate and chance,
> is never out of sight.

The "thieving days" that "steal" a beautiful physical appearance are portrayed with predictable rapid notes on "da pochi ladri dì ci son rubati." These blows of Destiny upon Ottavia reveal her "vigor" and "fortitude," all "greater glories than that of Beauty." Monteverdi's Seneca verges here into blatant parody when, in the phrase "che la Bellezza" (than that of Beauty), the article, "la," is given a ludicrous three-and-a-half-bar vocal ornamentation. What better way to depict a man out of touch with human feeling than to allow him an elaborate, inexpressive ornamentation of a meaningless word? A melisma on "Bellezza" would be predictable but at least appropriate. The long ornament on "la" suggests the character's fatuousness. Seneca's last theatrical flourish, assuring Ottavia that "constant virtue . . . knows no decay," again sinks his voice into the bass's darkest depths with a patness that makes the listener—if the "la" did not do it—question Seneca's sincerity. Ottavia, whose own integrity has already been subtly questioned by both the librettist's and the composer's choices, confirms our suspicions of Seneca with her pointed coloring of the word "artifizi" (artificialities) as she declines Seneca's proffered comfort: "You would promise me balm from poison and glory from torments. Forgive me, my Seneca, but these are empty conceits, studied artificialities, useless remedies for unhappiness." There follows an extraordinary outpouring of virtuoso musical artifice as Valletto, the empress's page, cast for either a soprano castrato or a female in drag, denounces the Stoic: "Madame, by your leave [*Madama, con tua pace*], I must vent the anger which this astute philosopher provokes in me . . . he inflames me with scorn." Valletto's hiccoughing repetitions of such words as "io" (I) and "accende" (inflamed) create the image of a young man stuttering with rage. The *concitato* style is "here carried to extremes in order to depict . . . anger [and] disdain" (Celletti 33). Valletto's verbal repetitions give his outburst comic effect. Ironically, he staunchly defends his mistress in a vocal range and musical style that inevitably remind the audience of Ottavia's husband. Valletto's comic aspect and his similarities to Nerone ensure that his emotions and reasoning, expressed with such vehemence, offer us yet another problematic, compromised individual. Valletto's outburst includes one of the most brazen, self-referential moments in opera. He tells us that the inventions of Seneca's brain, which the philosopher sees as mysterious revelations, are "but common songs" (e son canzoni*).* At this point, Valletto and his continuo accompaniment break out into a rousing four-bar quotation from Monteverdi's famous chaconne duet "Zefiro torna," which he had already utilized in Iro's comic lament parody in *Ulisse.* For a fleeting moment, Monteverdi has willfully and humorously inserted an audience-pleasing bit of self-awareness, just as Mozart was to do with the stage band playing the *Figaro* tune in the finale of *Don Giovanni.* There is gentle self-mockery here as well. For all its popularity and charm, "Zefiro torna" is a virtuoso example of mannerist word painting. Monteverdi suggests that without artistic integrity, the artist is a mere effects-monger, as the philosopher has allowed himself to become.

The last section of Valletto's speech contains more virtuoso word colorings to convey the young man's contempt for Seneca: "Madame, even his sneezes and yawns pretend to instill moral matters, and he makes everything so subtle that it would make my very boots laugh!" (Madama, s'ei sternuta o sbadiglia, presume d'insegnar cose morali, e tanto l'assottiglia, che moverebbe il riso a' miei stivali!). Sneezes and yawns could not be more realistically conveyed through music. The repeated "ei . . . ei . . . ei" leading to "sternata" is hilarious. The musical yawn in the elongated setting of "sbadiglia" harks back to the awakening soldiers of the first scene and anticipates the sleep-infused harmonics of Arnalta's lullaby in the second act. The four-note rising and falling pattern on "l'assottiglia" (to wear down or "make so subtle") vividly portrays Seneca's alleged nitpicking. Perhaps the most striking passage is reserved for the end. Seneca's style, Valletto says, is so complicated that "not even he himself, in the end, knows what he is saying" (ch'al fin neanch'egli sa ciò, che si dica). By "ciò, che si dica" Valletto is singing a capella, the continuo being silent for the better part of a measure. The sudden accompanimental silence suggests the bareness of the philosopher's sayings. Valletto is a forerunner of the soprano page-boy role, which will find its apotheosis in Oscar in Verdi's *Un ballo in maschera.*

It is typical of the poetics of this opera that neither Ottavia nor Seneca makes direct reference to Valletto's show-stopping interjection. This is a theatrical environment that tirelessly accentuates the isolation of its human figures. Even this last passionate outburst occurs in a near-vacuum as far as the text or music is concerned. Ottavia regains much dignity for her final lines before her exit, affording herself an understandably bitter verbal repetition when she describes the "diversion" (divertisca) Nerone enjoys in performing disgraceful acts. Valletto takes a final opportunity to threaten Seneca that he will ignite the Stoic's "toga, beard, and library" if he fails to help the empress. One scholar observes that Valletto's tirade "ironically foreshadows not only the ineffectuality of Ottavia's champions but also, musically, the supplanting of Seneca by Lucano, who [in the second act] replaces stoic philosophy with *'amorose canzoni'*" (Savage, "Love and Infamy" 205). Alone onstage, Seneca soliloquizes, "The royal imperial purple [*Le porpore regale*] is woven with sharp thorns, forming an undergarment for tormenting unhappy princes: the eminent crown serves only to crown their torments [*dolori*]." Although the lines are as platitudinous as before, the musical setting is simpler and less artificial. His only long vocal flourish is on the final word, "dolori" (sorrows). But now the word is an appropriate one for emphasis, and the chromaticism of its setting has an expressive context instead of the bluster Seneca lavished on "la" in the preceding scene. Seneca has had the wind knocked out of him. In this relatively chastened state he will proceed until his death in the second act.

Suddenly appearing from overhead, the goddess Pallade (Pallas Athena). sung by a soprano, captures the listener's attention with "Seneca, Seneca." Her warnings come in emotionally reserved arioso: "Seneca, I see unfavorable portents in heaven that threaten your utter ruin. If your life is to end today [*hoggi*], you will first have clear warning from Mercurio." The reference to "today" recalls Amore's promise at the close of the prologue and asserts the neoclassical unity of time over the stage action. The goddess's warning leads Seneca to a noble arioso that carries enormous conviction thanks to Monteverdi's use of word coloration and repetition: "I shall triumph, I shall triumph, I shall triumph over accident and fear" (Vincerò gli accidenti e le paure). As with the historical Seneca, Monteverdi's musical portrayal hints at the tragic compartmentalization of the private and the public or political man. On his first entrance, Monteverdi's mastery of musical gesture and artifice revealed the Stoic's pomposity and glibness. But this Seneca is also a human being capable of bravery and self-sacrifice once his social mask has been shamed away. Seneca is not a mere phony; rather, he is a flawed yet noble irrelevance in a ruthless world.

The argument scene between Seneca and Nerone was inspired by the central scene in *Octavia praetexta*. Busenello directly borrows the *praetexta*'s scheme of rigorously balanced speeches for the philosopher and the emperor. In both the Roman play and the Venetian opera, this scene figures as the definitive confrontation between rationality and passion. It would have had special impact on Venetian audiences, with its contrast between Nerone's crude argument for autocratic rule (à la Rome) and Seneca's more republican arguments. The conflict between reason and passion is musically portrayed by the simplest opposition imaginable: the extreme vocal contrast afforded by a duet between mezzo-soprano castrato and bass. In rhetorical patterning, the scene resembles classical Greek and Latin tragedy. As effective as Busenello's verbal rhetoric is, Monteverdi intensifies the drama through compositional and editorial means. Nerone's first declamation of intention concerning Ottavia is notable for the repetitions and rests written into his recitative: "I am, in short, resolved, O Seneca, O master, to remove Ottavia from her position as consort [*rest*] and to marry [*rest*], and to marry [*rest*], and to marry Poppea." The rests, along with the rising vocal pitch on each repetition, suggest a psychologically realistic detail. The defensive tyrant, eager for his old tutor's approval, seems to stutter out his momentous plans. Rosand observes that this "exaggerated text repetition signals Nerone's discomfort from the outset. . . . The emphasis must betray a guilty conscience since Seneca has not yet voiced any objection" ("Seneca" 58–59).

The musical simplicity of Seneca's reaction creates a dramatic contrast: "Sir, at the bottom of great sweetness often repentance is hidden. Feelings are a wicked councilor. They hate laws and despise reason." Seneca's recitative is striking for its lack of ornamentation and its straightforwardness. A few lines later, Nerone and his accompaniment conspire to create a vivid pictorial and musical effect when he declares that "the empire is divided, and Jove rules heaven while I hold the terrestrial scepter of the world." The word "ciel" (heaven) is sung on a sustained C above a busy descending pattern in the continuo, creating a vivid sense of Jove's sublime immovability, a force personified by the unearthly castrato voice effortlessly striding above the more "terrestrial" instrumental accompaniment. A powerful contrast comes with Nerone's next words, describing his own terrestrial omnipotence: "Ma del mondo, del mondo terren, del mondo terren lo scettro è mio, lo scettro è mio" (While I hold the the world's terrestrial scepter myself). Nero sings a concitato section melodically reminiscent of Poppea's "Per me guerreggia" from scene 4. This echo suggests the psychological similarities between Nerone and Poppea as well as the opera's deliberate blurring of the boundaries of sexual and political morality. Seneca refuses to submit to the sensual indulgence of Nerone's lyricism; however, Seneca's florid decoration of the word "furor" (the "fury" that Nerone is confusing with unmoderated will) was suggested by the ornaments Nerone bestowed on "scettro" (scepter) in his previous speech. Like the earlier scene with Poppea and Arnalta, Seneca and Nerone's musical argument features each character borrowing the other's musical style in the effort to defeat him or her. Seneca's rising anger is leading him to an increased lyricism to combat Nerone.

"Leave off this discussion," Nerone responds; "I will, I will, I will do as I wish." The petulant iterations of "will" (voglio) lead Nerone to a high G that suggests his mounting rage and the danger it brings. "Don't antagonize, don't antagonize, don't antagonize the people or the Senate," Seneca responds, his triple iteration of "non irritar" spurred on by Nerone's use of "voglio." "For the Senate and the people [*rest*] I don't care." Monteverdi's rest suggests the petulant Nerone's pause for effect before completing his provocative assertion.

Nerone moves to what he feels is his strongest justification for divorce: "Ottavia is frigid and infertile" (Ottavia è infrigidita e infeconda). The line is set using the lowest notes Nerone will sing in the entire scene. The contrasting vocal dip here is threatening in its psychological implications. The character is moving between vocal and emotional extremes with an unsettling rapidity. Another five lines of stichomythic exchange lead the two characters to a final impasse. Busenello marks this dramatic climax by Nerone and Seneca's move from stichomythic to double-line exchanges.

> *Nerone:*   Force is law in peace, and the sword in war,
>   and does not need reason.
>
> *Seneca:*   Force kindles hatred, and excites the blood,
>   reason rules humanity and gods.
>
> *Nerone:*   You are making me angry.

Gary Tomlinson writes:

> It is as if the poet were entirely oblivious to the emotional effect of his rhetorical structure up to this point. But Monteverdi was not so blind. He carefully intensified the anger of the dialogue by quickening, not slowing, the rate of alternation and by adopting the quick text repetitions of the *concitato* style:
>
> *Nero:*   *La forza, la forza, la forza, la forza è legge in pace . . .*
>
> *Seneca:*   *La forza, la forza accende gli odi . . .*
>
> *Nero:*   *. . . e spada, e spada in guerra . . .*
>
> *Seneca:*   *. . . e turba il sangue, e turba il sangue, . . .*
>
> (Tomlinson, *Monteverdi* 235)

Instead of setting Busenello's stately two-line speeches, Monteverdi brings the argument to a memorable and lyric conclusion by turning it into an animated duet. The melodic line of Nerone's "La forza è legge in pace" is strongly reminiscent of Poppea's "Non temo, non temo, no, di noia alcuna" (I fear nothing) of act 1, scene 4, a further musical association between the lovers (see Chafe 325–26). The duet brings Seneca's bass to the height of its compass when he sings "Reason rules humanity and the gods," an ironic touch musically suggesting his own mounting anger. The conflict has pushed both singers to the respective heights and depths of their vocal ranges. Nerone's sputtering rage is manifested by the repetitions and rests on "Tu, tu, tu mi sforzi allo sdegno." This begins a five-line speech in which he restates his inflexible position:

> You are making me angry; in despite of you,
> in despite of the people, and of the senate,
> and of Ottavia, and of heaven and the abyss,
> whether my wishes are just or unjust,
> today, today [*hoggi, hoggi*], Poppea shall be [*serà*] my wife.

The first line is pure *stile concitato*. The D and G that Nerone will sing on *serà* mark a climactic return to a note, suggesting an argumentative climax—and a breaking point. We have heard it before in this scene on the repetitions of "voglio." As Chafe notes, it also marks "the supreme expression of the victory of Love by force" (Chafe 328). The reiterated "hoggi" recalls again Amore's promise in the prologue. Rosand remarks that this passage's "exaggerated repetition" and other devices "[leave] hardly any time for breathing—a physiological symptom of Nerone's emotional condition" ("Seneca" 62).

In Seneca's concluding speech he returns to his usual recitative style. Nerone's infatuation "is not the failing of a king or demigod, but a plebeian crime" (non è colpa di rege o semideo, è un misfato plebeo). In illustration of the words, and in mockery of his emperor's vocal and behavioral extravagances, Seneca's voice rises to its highest pitch on "semideo," only to sink, appropriately enough, to its depths on "misfato plebeo." Nerone seems to mock Seneca with his own low notes as he dismisses him as a "filosofo insolente" (insolent philosopher). Seneca's final couplet ends the scene and paints a succinct musical image of the best aspects of his character. Rosand notes, "Never at a loss of breath—or words—the stoic philosopher concludes with the most lyrically expressive and complete phrase of the scene, a calm effusion on a Senecan precept. . . . Nerone may have the last word, but Seneca has the music" ("Seneca" 63–64). Seneca sings, "The worse side always, always, always threatens when force with reason is at odds." The repeated "always" (sempre), sung at increasingly high pitch levels, hints at the immutable values Seneca aspires to uphold. The even, rocking rhythm with which he sings "alla ragion" (with reason) nobly emphasizes the idea of reason that he extols and that stands in such sharp contrast with the rest of the opera's characters, despite Seneca's own considerable shortcomings. The scene ends as the philosopher sings an ornament on "contrasta" (in conflict), a fitting conclusion to one of the greatest argument scenes in all opera.

Scene 10 portrays Poppea's solicitation of Seneca's death. Poppea opens the scene with an arioso line that encourages Nerone's erotic reminiscences of the past night: "How sweet, my lord, how gentle were the kisses of this mouth last night?" Poppea's and Nerone's language tends to separate body parts from their owners in unhealthy ways; Poppea refers to "this mouth" (questa bocca), not "my mouth." Her final word, "baci" (kisses), is suspended on three notes, hanging in the air in a most sensual manner. In Nerone's answering recitative he fetishistically repeats certain words: "The more biting the kisses, the dearer they were." He repeats "cari" (dearer) four times, his voice rising orgasmically in pitch. Poppea now repeats phrases and employs rests, which suggest breathless erotic hesitations. "What about, what about the apples of this breast?" (Di questo, di questo seno i [rest] i [rest] i pomi?). Rosand observes: "The rests establish a rhythm of erotic impulse that serves to propel Poppea's seduction of Nerone. . . . The rests here not only contribute effectively to the mood, they actually seem designed to accommodate movement—gestures of some kind: perhaps auto-erotic in the first instance, certainly reciprocal [later]" ("Monteverdi's Mimetic Art" 131). Nerone responds, "Your breasts deserve sweeter names" (Mertan le mamme tue più dolci nomi). The words "mamme" and "dolci nomi" are repeated with increasing ornamentation. Poppea is luring Nerone from recitative into song and unreflecting passion: "What about the sweet coupling of these arms?" (Di queste braccia i dolci amplessi?). The up-and-down fluttering on "i dolci, dolci amplessi" is insistently caressing, made all the more suggestive by the rests that tease the musical line. Nerone attempts a recitative response to this last blandishment. But his recollection of their kisses, which "diffused" his "spirit" in Poppea, melts what remains of his control, and he too resorts to arioso, declaring, "No more, no more is my destiny in heaven, rather it is in the beautiful rubies of your lips."

Poppea launches into the scene's first full-fledged aria: "My lord, your words are so sweet that within my soul I repeat them to myself; and the internal repetition forces my loving heart to swoon. I hear your words, I relish them like kisses; the sensation of your sweet words is so sweet, so enlivening that, not content to flatter my hearing, they stamp the kisses on my heart." The first part of the aria is a melody of great seductive charm. The aria is also notable for the fainting effect achieved in the setting of "deliquio," vividly portraying her "swooning [heart]." In the setting of "I sensi sì soavi, e si vivaci" (The sensation [of your sweet words] is so sweet, so enlivening), Monteverdi's repetition, the breathless rest in the vocal line, and Busenello's marvelously sibilant poetry conspire to bring Poppea to new heights of musical sexuality. The "enlivening" (vivaci) power of Nerone's words suggests the aria's second section, a faster-paced refrain expressive of Poppea's impatience, which culminates in a slower, low-lying passage underlining the idea of Nerone's words "stamping [their] kisses upon my heart" (al stampar sul cor i baci). Nerone's response proclaims his intention to let her "have the title of empress" (il titolo havrai d'imperatrice). The stately setting of "d'imperatrice" impresses the notion of Poppea's imperial ascension on the minds of the audience. The words and their music are reverent, august, and, in the present context, chillingly ironic. But this is irony the audience will derive from the total musical and theatrical context. Monteverdi refuses to comment morally on his characters. *They* certainly do not find their passions and actions reprehensible. Nerone and Poppea are a pair of sociopaths ruled by selfish needs who express their passions in such a way as to make them irresistibly attractive to their auditors. Through Monteverdi's music we are made to identify emotionally with their feelings. It is only in retrospect that we evaluate these figures morally, after Monteverdi's music has brought us into touch with the darker irrational forces within us with an evenhandedness worthy of Shakespeare.

After musically crowning his lover with the stately setting of "d'imperatrice," Nerone exuberantly launches his aria: "Ma che dico, che dico, o Poppea?" (But what am I saying, O Poppea?). The music is swaying and seductive, inducing the listeners to see, or rather "hear," Poppea through Nerone's music. Nerone abases himself, if only for an instant, when he says that even being his consort is too small a recompense for Poppea (basso paragone l'esser detta consorte di Nerone). "Low recompense," "Rome," and "Italy" are set to low notes that contrast with the two much higher ones setting Poppea's "merti" and her "bel viso." Even "Nerone" is set to a descending note pattern. How can the audience resist his lyrical enthusiasm, when even the accompanimental instruments sympathetically finish his melodic refrain? The aria's second refrain reverses some of the verbal and musical patterning. Poppea's eyes "transcend nature's example," according to Nerone. At "transcendo" Nerone sings long notes at the bottom of his range, creating a thrilling illustration of his words and the depth of his feelings. This same effect is repeated and strengthened when he illustrates the "silence" (silenzio) and "wonderment" (stupore) his mistress causes those that behold her. Both words are drawn out with long low notes, giving expression to Nerone's quasi-religious awe of Poppea.

Nerone's declaration spurs Poppea to begin what seems to be a new aria: "Sublime hope [*A speranze sublimi*] lifts my heart because you have commanded it, and my modesty receives strength." Her theme is derived from the tune Nerone has just sung. The music proclaims their amorous unity, but the sense of ecstatic emotional concord lasts only two and a half bars, a telescoped version of Nerone's aria complete with its own ecstatic instrumental tag, before Poppea's murderous wheedling suspends the lyrical spell with a return to recitative: "Ma troppo s'attraversa et impedisce di sì regie promesse il fin sovrano" (But too many things cross and impede the final fulfillment of your royal promise). Poppea's "ma" instantly arrests the soaring lyricism of her aria and brings the audience and Nerone up short. Recitative is the proper element for Poppea's insinuations about the threat Seneca represents to their plans. This transition is abrupt, almost comic. (Modern listeners may think of a much later and especially effective musical and dramatic transition, also on the word "ma" [but], in Rosina's aria "Una voce poco fa" in Rossini's *Il barbiere di Siviglia*.)

Seneca, Poppea suggests, "always tries to persuade others that your scepter depends on him alone." Monteverdi dovetails the ending of Poppea's recitative with the beginning of Nerone's recitative, creating the effect of Poppea's reiterating her accusation in response to Nerone's imperious question, "Che? Che?" (What? What?). Nerone takes the bait and immediately orders the philosopher's death "this very day" (in questo giorno). Nerone ends his speech by reverting to aria for the scene's final couplet: "Poppea, be of good cheer [*Poppea, sta di buon core*], on this day you shall see what love can do." This promise is as much for the audience as for his paramour, reminding us of Amore's promised triumph in the prologue. Nerone's aria is bitingly ironic: a tyrant has just condemned an innocent man to death, and now he sings platitudes about love to an infuriatingly attractive melody. This music not only gives closure to a largely lyrical scene; its dramatic incongruity also begins to paint the progress of Nerone's growing mental and moral collapse. For Nerone, the lyric and sentiment are a perfect fit. The audience, however, may appreciate a growing discrepancy between the emperor's emotional and musical life and the circumstances surrounding him.

The libretto specifies that this sensuous yet chilling scene has been observed by Ottone. Interestingly, the discarded lover never remarks upon the plans for murder he has presumably overheard. All he can think about is his love for Poppea. After Nerone's exit, Ottone, under the watchful eyes of Arnalta, confronts Poppea for the first time. In scene 11 Busenello provides six speeches of six verses each exchanged between the former lovers. This classically balanced dialogue is a literary embodiment of hopelessly estranged people who end their argument as divided as when they began. To accent this verbal balance and the sentiments it embodies, Monteverdi creates a ritornello-and-aria melody that is repeated for each of the six speeches. The verbal balance is thus complimented by the most straightforward of musical means; however, the composer subtly varies the music to fit the words and speakers.

The exchange resembles a formal dance between the two characters, their emotions of betrayal and exasperation submerged beneath courtly manners (perhaps owing to Arnalta's presence). The ritornello's steady rhythm and melodic plangency set the mood for Ottone's pleading for the restoration of his lost love. These pleas all revolve around sensual gratification. Poppea is a "liquor" or a "meal" Ottone may look at but not consume: "Others may taste the liquor but I may only look at the container; the gates are open for Nerone, but Ottone remains outside. He sits at the mess and sates his longing while I die famished, starved for love." Ottone cuts a pathetic figure, an alto castrato begging for sex, complete with an elegant trill on "vaso" (the "container" of Poppea's body) and "rimaso" (remains) to ornament and color his watch outside the "gates" to the metaphoric "feast" of Poppea's body. The trill recurs in his second refrain at "desiri" (desire) and "aspiri" (aspire): "The longed-for harvest of my hopes, of my desires, is in other hands, and Love does not consent that I aspire to it." The instrumental ritornello darkens to the minor just before Poppea's cold-blooded response. He is to blame for his own misfortune. Destiny throws the dice, and mortals must abide by the outcome. Ottone's version of the ritornello, major keyed and pleading, returns. He complains that his "longed-for harvest" (la messe sospirata) belongs to another. We may recall the "lost seeds of hope" that this character complained of in his first scene. His erotic ornamentation on "i dolci pomi" (the sweet apples [with which Nerone may play]), borrowing Poppea's earlier description of her breasts, confirms that Ottone overheard their previous exchange, as the libretto directs.

Poppea's version of the ritornello ushers in her rejoinder, in which she cruelly suggests that Fortune gives to Ottone "her bald temples, to others her curls," recalling the allegorical figure from the opera's prologue. Poppea closes the strophic dialogue with thrilling vocal runs on "arrivar ai regni" (I'm to attain the royal station). The end of the scene is a stichomythic exchange:

Ottone: And is this the reward for my love?

Poppea: Come, that's enough, I belong to Nerone.

Monteverdi has Ottone pathetically repeat, "And is this my reward for my love?" (È questo del mio amor il guiderdone?), punctuated by the reiteration of Poppea's impatient demand, "Non più, non più" (enough, enough), before she delivers her stinging exit line, "Son di Nerone" (I am Nerone's). Ottone is left alone onstage. The printed libretto includes a brief passage between him and Arnalta missing from the Venetian score but present in the Neapolitan manuscript. Alan Curtis presumes it to be the work of "a later composer" (see Monteverdi, *L'incoronazione*, Curtis ed. 99). Whatever the music's provenance, the lines were part of Busenello's original conception, and the Neapolitan music makes an effective and bitterly ironic coda to Ottone and Poppea's scene. The tag delivers a theatrical payoff for Arnalta's eavesdropping on the previous scene, fulfilling the dramaturgical pattern of the preceding scenes, in which nonspeaking observers comment on the action. Ottone reflects on the futility of "trusting a pretty face," at which Arnalta interjects, "Unhappy boy! I'm moved to compassion by his misery; Poppea has no brain and has no pity; when I was her age I would not have made my lovers cry—with my compassion I contented all." The setting of "Poppea non ha cervello" (Poppea has no brain) sounds like vintage Monteverdi, and vintage Arnalta. The droll setting of her final line, "Per compassion gli contentavo tutti" (I contented everyone with my compassion), is bumptiously comic, reminding the listener of early Venetian opera's closeness to commedia dell'arte traditions and serving as a bit of comic relief after a succession of very serious scenes. Typically, Arnalta's comic turn, like Valletto's earlier, flamboyant display, is unremarked upon by its intended audience, reinforcing the opera's sense of the loneliness of the human condition.

Left alone, Ottone vents his wounded ego with threats to use "sword and poison" against his former mistress. The cold misogyny of Ottone's line "The weaker sex has no humanity in it, except for its shape" makes the ensuing love scene between him and Drusilla all the more unsettling. In the second act, it is Ottone who will be compelled by Ottavia to change "shape." Monteverdi finds ways of musically accenting the text's psychological realism, creating the illusion of a living character desperately trying to organize his thoughts in a moment of extreme emotional crisis. "Otton, torna in te stesso" (Ottone, return to your senses) is set to a brief melody that serves as a twice-repeated refrain, imparting a musical symbol to Ottone's reeling and obsessive thoughts. "Returning" (torna) is a characteristic mental action of Ottone, an ineffectual man condemned by his obsession with Poppea. The music of the refrain is a kind of Monteverdian idée fixe, combining musical logic and dramatic sense in the manner of the greatest musical dramatists. Chafe notes that the "Otton, torna" strain is a variant of the beginning of "E pur'io torno qui" (Chafe 293), Ottone's very first line in act 1. That earlier "torno" and this new, related melody form a verbal and musical gesture for the character of Ottone. The performative reality behind Ottone's stage figure adds an ironic element to his remarks about women being human only in shape. Performed by a castrato, Ottone represents something of the same disparity of being and essence, of inner reality and outer shape, of which he accuses "the weaker sex," a description his alto castrato voice compels the audience to consider as he embellishes the very word "figura." Ottone repeats his refrain as we see and hear him struggling to regroup after Poppea's vicious rejection. In his next recitative passage he considers the danger to his life Poppea's political ambitions present: "She's contemplating power, and if she arrives at it [*rest*], if she arrives at it, my life is lost." The pause and repetition of "e se ci arriva" creates the effect of a character thinking aloud; a word or idea comes to mind and, in a startled second indicated by the rest, leads to a larger, more disturbing idea. Ottone's new fear leads to the final repetition of his "torna" refrain. We have seen and heard him move from a wounded torpor to a state of excited paranoia. This fear is amplified in a recitative passage in which he imagines Nerone's jealousy of Ottone and Poppea's suborning "someone" to accuse him of a capital crime. As in the "e se ci arriva" passage, Ottone's quickly building fears are suggested by the rest and repetition involving "un" (someone): "She will induce someone [*rest*], someone who will accuse me." Ottone's anxiety erupts in an outburst that suggests he just might be capable of bold action after all: "I will forestall her, with sword, with sword, or with poison, I will no more nurture the serpent at my breast." The rapid notes and verbal repetitions suggest heightened agitation. The later opera seria of Handel and others would lead us into a da capo revenge aria at this point. But Monteverdi and his librettist opt for a more ambiguous and deliberately anticlimactic resolution to Ottone's soliloquy. After his violent outburst about swords and poison, a succession of rests marks a characteristic transition back to his former condition of heart-wounded stasis: "This, this is the end that I've arrived at as your lover, most perfidious, most perfidious Poppea." The whole speech and especially its musical setting mark a kind of "torna" of which Ottone is probably unaware. His obsessive nature creates a figure who is constantly spinning in place psychologically, a self-created victim of circumstance.

Drusilla is the empress's attending lady, whose proffered love Ottone has rejected in the past. Drusilla, "an early characterization of the *ingénue*" (Celletti 36), comes from Busenello's imagination, but she does have some literary and historical precedents. Canto 38 of Ludovico Ariosto's popular Renaissance epic *Orlando furioso* features a Drusilla, a woman of near-fanatical constancy to her dead husband. Busenello's Drusilla displays a comparable devotion to Ottone during the course of the opera. This parallel has led one set of critics to view Drusilla as a "heroic" figure within the opera (Fenlon and Miller, *Song* 42–43). But Busenello's Drusilla is hardly a paradigm of virtue. In the second act she cheerfully becomes an accessory to murder and reveals a ruthless self-centeredness almost as repellent as Poppea's. Seutonius's *Lives of the Caesars* (*Life of Caligula* 24) offered the librettist another, less wholesome Drusilla than Ariosto: the sister of Caligula, with whom that emperor shared an incestuous love. Surely both Drusillas, Ariosto's and Seutonius's, left their mark on the operatic character.

The first encounter between Drusilla and Ottone is a scene of extraordinary emotional ambivalence, both in the text and in the musical setting. The exchange begins in recitative. Drusilla has presumably overheard Ottone's last remark about "perfidious Poppea." "You are always with Poppea," she bitterly remarks, "either in your tongue's or thought's discourse." Ottone responds, already on the romantic rebound: "The name of the one who is an unfaithful traitor to my affections is driven from my heart, comes to the tongue, and from the tongue it is consigned to the winds." Ottone's frustrations lead Drusilla into the scene's first arioso, ironically generated by purest schadenfreude: "The court of love sometimes renders justice: you've had no pity on me, now others laugh at your sorrow, Ottone." The words "amor" (love), "fa" (renders), and "ride" (laugh) are ornamented with sadistic relish. Ottone immediately responds to the heightened emotion of her lyric outburst and makes his first protestation of love to Drusilla in an arioso of his own, a melody resembling her schadenfreude tune—surely an inauspicious beginning for a happy, meaningful relationship. A return to recitative follows in which he expresses concern for his "previous bad behavior" and his "confessed mistakes." This unpleasant recollection of his past cruelties breathlessly shifts Ottone back to arioso to make another protestation of love: "As long as I live, I'll always love you, beautiful, that soul [of mine] that was always vicious and cruel to you already repents." Beginning like the start of a new aria, the four notes on "Fin ch'io vivrò" (As long as I live) suggest Ottone's new emotional dedication. He shifts to another melodic pattern for "Already, already [my soul] repents the ancient error and now consecrates me as your servant, and friend." His repetition of "mi ti consacra homai" in descending notes indicates his desperate assurance of affection. Ottone's emotional instability is expressed by the three different arioso melodies he sings, discarding one musically promising idea for another as soon as he gives voice to it, like a desperate swimmer reaching for objects to buoy him up.

Fortunately for Ottone, Drusilla is as vulnerable as he is and responds to his musical blandishments with an arioso of her own, "Already oblivion has buried past unhappiness" (Già l'oblio sepellì), picking up Ottone's "già" from his second attempt at arioso, as well as his lyric style, in her melody. Like her new lover, she has insecurities that make her lyricism short-lived. She reverts immediately to recitative to repeatedly ask if "it is true" that he is "faithfully" united to her. "È ver, Drusilla, è ver, sì, sì" (It's true Drusilla, it's true, yes, yes), Ottone sings, in another brief surge of arioso ardor. But Drusilla's doubts are still too great for her to relinquish herself to the flow of happiness expressed in aria or duet. She continues to interrogate her would-be lover in a succession of recitative questions and answers. The music employs pure recitative for one of the opera's most emotionally revealing passages. Drusilla asks Ottone point blank, "M'ami dunque?"

(Do you love me, then?). Ottone's reply, "Ti bramo" (I burn for you), is ardent but does not directly answer Drusilla's question. When Drusilla asks again, "M'ami?," Ottone can only respond by repeating the same words, ornamenting them for greater rhetorical force: "Ti bramo, ti bramo." It is doubtful whether such realistic hesitancies and vulnerability, such multifaceted humanity in both text and music, can be found elsewhere in opera before Mozart. The moment is almost embarrassing in its emotional frankness.

Drusilla stops demanding a direct answer to the question of love: "But how could [it happen] so suddenly?" "Love is a fire," Ottone explains, "and suddenly it ascends." His rather obvious ornamentation on "foco" (fire) smacks of musical and rhetorical forcing. "Such sudden sweetness" (Si subite dolcezze), Drusilla exclaims in recitative, as if to continue in the sober style of her previous interruption. Instead she allows herself to be overcome by lyric melody in "It delights my happy heart," only to immediately arrest the song as residual doubts arise again: "But I don't understand; you love me, then?" Again Ottone evinces commitment issues by the repetition of the nonresponsive "Ti bramo": "I burn for you. Your beauty shall assure you of my love. For your sake I have impressed a new form on my heart. Believe this miracle you yourself have made." Ottone's final assertions, made in recitative, flirt with arioso on the melodious repetitions afforded "i miracoli tuoi" (this miracle of yours). Drusilla is at last convinced and expresses her contentment in an arioso of soaring happiness, "Lieta, lieta m'en vado" (I go in happiness), which comes to a beautiful melodic closure on "remain happy, Ottone" (Ottone, resta felice). She informs Ottone in recitative that she must now return to wait upon Ottavia.

Ottone's closing four lines are a soliloquy after Drusilla's exit. They represent a man who is in the first two lines desperately trying to talk himself into believing he has found a permanent substitute for his lost love. "The tempest in my heart is calm" receives an almost predictable musical illustration, the marching notes of "tempeste" resolving themselves into the long held notes on "tranquilla." Imagination and stability are not Ottone's strong suits, and he musically illustrates his second line of halfhearted self-assurance with a similarly paced setting of "To no one else shall Ottone belong but Drusilla," saving the note we heard on "tranquilla" for her name, as if to convince himself that he's at last found his emotional safe harbor. A full rest marks one of the opera's most telling transitions, the final ambivalent moment in an act, and an opera, notable for their almost unparalleled ambivalence: "And yet, despite myself, villainous Love, 'Drusilla' I have on my lips, but 'Poppea' in my heart." The use of rests, the repetitions on "et ho Poppea," and the sadly drooping musical line close the scene and act with an unforgettable image of dejection and obsessive love. Drusilla's remark, that Poppea is always in Ottone's words and thoughts, proves true after her exit. The musical irresolution of Ottone's lines leaves the action hanging in the air, a dramatic situation that has come to a moment of brief hiatus but has not resolved. If, of all Monteverdi's works, only this last scene were to survive, it would guarantee him a place with the greatest musical dramatists of all time.

Act 2

Seneca enjoys the solitude of his garden ("Solitudine amanta") just as the god Mercurio appears to announce his impending death. A Liberto (freed slave) from Nerone's guard delivers Seneca's sentence, wishing him a peaceful death ("Mori, e mori felice"). Seneca announces the imperial decree to his friends ("Amici, è giunta l'hora"). Rather than Stoic acceptance, the friends proclaim their fear of death and beg the philosopher not to die ("Non morir, Seneca"). Seneca calmly exits to commit suicide. Meanwhile the young page, Valletto, and a servant girl, Damigella, enjoy an amorous encounter, oblivious to the serious events surrounding them. Nerone celebrates Seneca's death with the poet Lucano ("Cantiam, Lucano"). Ottavia blackmails Ottone into murdering Poppea, ordering him to disguise himself for the crime by dressing as a woman. Meanwhile Drusilla exults in her newfound love ("Felice cor mio") and tries to cheer up Nutrice, who describes the sorrows of a woman growing older ("Il giorno femminil"). Ottone meets Drusilla and conveys his predicament. Drusilla happily offers to provide her own clothes to disguise Ottone for her rival's murder. In her private garden Poppea decides to take a nap, lulled to sleep by Arnalta's lullaby ("Oblivion soave"). The god Amore, from the prologue, appears and announces that he has come to rescue the unsuspecting Poppea from danger ("O sciocchi, o frali"). Ottone enters disguised in Drusilla's dress. As he readies to strike the deadly blow, Amore stops his arm, and Poppea suddenly awakes. The startled Arnalta sounds the alarm against "Drusilla," who flees the scene. Amore promises that he will make Poppea empress ("Ho difesa Poppea").

Scenes 1 through 4

The setting is Seneca's garden on his private estate. Seneca's opening monologue forms one of the opera's most effective passages of pure recitative: "Beloved solitude, refuge of the mind, sanctuaries of thoughts, delight of the intellect, which discusses and contemplates the images of heaven in their ignoble and earthly forms." Monteverdi punctuates each of these verses with rests, establishing a contemplative, serious mood. The Seneca of the country retreat is a morally healthier being than the compromised Seneca of the court, and this moral health is suggested by the dignity and appropriateness of the word setting. Gone are the pompous, expressively meaningless elaborations of articles. Instead we now hear obvious modulations, no less beautiful or appropriate for all their obviousness, on words such as "celesti" (heavens) and "terrene" (earth) that explore higher and lower notes in the bass's range. Seneca is even allowed a brief lyric flourish on "a te, a te l'anima mia lieta, lieta s'en viene" (to you [solitude], to you, my soul happily flies). The two florid runs on the repeated "lieta" (happy) anticipates similar writing for Mercurio and forms a spiritual link between the two bass roles. Seneca is soon joined by Mercurio (Mercury), the messenger of the gods, who arrives in a flying machine. The expressive exuberance of Mercurio's fioritura cries out for a complementary exuberance of baroque stagecraft. The listener is in for a pleasant shock to hear Seneca's solitary bass finally meeting his vocal match with the bass singer performing Mercurio. Their vocal kinship and singularity give musical embodiment to Seneca's "divine" virtue, which the god praises, as well as forming a pointed contrast to the opera's predominant cast of soprano, mezzo, and alto voices.

When he is told of his impending death Seneca indulges in his first substantial arioso, "O me felice!" (Oh, happy me!). This is an outburst of pent-up emotion, a little stiff and old-fashioned, like the character who sings it. It is typical of the somber poetics of *Poppea* that the promise of death is virtually the only thing which can make this character break into lyrical expression, just as his death will stimulate Nerone, Lucano, and Poppea to flights of musical effusion. Seneca realizes that "now I may confirm my writings, I authenticate my studies; the leaving of life is a blessed fate when, from divine lips, death comes." The high, resonant notes on "hor" (now) and "autentico" (confirms) and the upward soaring flourish on "sorte" (fate), as well as the even longer elaborated ornaments on "esce" (the coming [of death]), are rhapsodic, but Seneca's joy is kept in check by his natural reserve and decorum. The reiteration of "se da bocca divina" (when it comes from divine lips), a reference to the god's annunciation, will be eerily recalled two scenes later in Nerone and Lucano's macabre celebrations of Poppea's "bocca." Mercurio closes this brief scene with an aria, "Therefore joyfully prepare for the celestial voyage." His flamboyant runs on "celeste viaggio" (celestial voyage), "sublime passaggio" (sublime passage), and especially the reiterated "volo" (fly) complement his trip to heaven.

The first scene's divine pronouncement of Seneca's death is followed by its earthly annunciation, delivered by a Liberto, a freed slave, of Nerone's Pretorian guard. The Liberto begins the scene with embarrassed generalizations about about "evil" or "tyrannical commands." When he first addresses Seneca directly—"Seneca, Seneca, it is unpleasant for me to find you, though I was searching for you"—the philosopher's name is set to an unexpected dissonance suggestive of the Liberto's growing anxiety about the orders he must carry out and the gradual dropping of his impersonal mask. Seneca sets the soldier at ease with a characteristically calm recitative declamation that ends with an arioso on "I laugh [*rido*] when you bring [*porti*] me such a beautiful gift [as death]." "Rido" and "porti" are treated to pleasing, expressive ornamental flourishes. Seneca's arioso emboldens the Liberto to finally deliver his order. The soldier seems about to begin a new passage of recitative by declaring, "Nerone." Monteverdi breaks up Busenello's versification slightly to intensify the effect of Seneca's anticipation of the doom about to be announced: "Non più, non più" (No more, no more!). The interplay of the two characters suggests the phenomenon of real people nervously overlapping each other in conversation.

Liberto: Nerone sent me to you—

Seneca: No more; I understand, and will obey at once.

Another arioso adorns Seneca's verses, a grim warning that Nerone's crimes will not end with the philosopher's death: "Feeding one vice makes another vice hungry; the passage to one excess leads to a thousand; and it is ordained on high that a single abyss [i.e., crime] will open a hundred abysses." The euphonious melodic writing makes the arioso's unexpected dissonance on "abisso" (abyss) all the more effective. Monteverdi's music ensures we will remember this prediction of a man at death's door.

"Sir, you have divined correctly," the Liberto sings in two understandably relieved bars of recitative before launching into an exquisite aria, one of the opera's most memorable moments, to bid the great but flawed man an easy death: "Die, and die happy, for just as the days always are marked by the sun with light, just so your writings will give light to others' writings." The Liberto's aria gives Seneca the only nonironic tribute the opera will afford him. The Liberto has become a choric figure hinting, however obliquely, at the opera's seventeenth-century creators themselves, who, true to the Liberto's predictions, have forged a work built in no small part on the life and writings of Seneca. The "happy" (felice) death the Liberto wishes for Seneca is treated to memorable melismas, as are the self-reflexive words about the "writings of others [to come]" (scritti altrui). Seneca closes the scene with a recitative of plastic simplicity. The words "Vanne, vanne, vattene homai" (Go, go now) rise in pitch. After a brief rest his notes descend: "and if you speak to Nerone before evening, tell him I'm dead and buried." Seneca's upward and downward vocal flourish recalls Ulisse's similar "Vanne alla madre, va!" at the close of act 3, scene 3, in *Il ritorno d'Ulisse*. As in the earlier opera, the musical patterning closes a scene portraying human emotions with great simplicity. The opera's next scenes will open the floodgates of unprecedented musical and theatrical effect.

Scene 3 is one of the greatest set pieces in Monteverdi opera. It depicts Seneca's farewell to his family and disciples, described as the Famigliari, in an ensemble consisting of an alto, tenor, and bass. Seneca's newfound spiritual integration is portrayed by the music he sings to open the scene: "Friends, the hour has come to practice in deed that virtue which I've praised so much." Monteverdi gives Seneca's sonorous bass voice one of his most extraordinary passages of speech-song, a kind of endless melody in rocking rhythm. Seneca's music and words now breathe an air of unworldly resignation and calm. He closes his peroration with his most beautiful and pointed ornamentation on the word "vola," illustrating his anticipated spiritual flight to heaven. Both the composer and the librettist have ceased making the philosopher an ironic figure. He has attained a state of grace where his musical and verbal gestures cohere perfectly, where the terms "recitative" and "aria" are useless to describe a music that flows effortlessly between declamation and lyric, where ornament is an essential part of the declamation. Although the text and music have traced Seneca's liberation from the ironic contradictions that made him so problematic in the first act, he remains enframed within an operatic world of ever-deepening levels of irony. His three Famigliari, the disciples, friends, or family who should presumably be the closest people to the philosopher, on intimate terms with his personality and Stoic convictions, are now given one of the most elaborate ensemble pieces in baroque opera in order to express the unbridgeable gulf that separates the dying philosopher from all that surrounds him on earth.

The Famigliari ensemble begins with the alto, who is joined by the bass and then the tenor, all singing, "Non morir, non morir, Seneca, no!" (Don't die, don't die, Seneca, no!). This phrase rises as a jagged, harsh chromatic exclamation passing from voice to voice, creating one of the most affecting passages in Western music. Where an audience might reasonably expect a group of Seneca's intimates to begrudgingly accept their master's will, we are presented with a chorus of the most unphilosophical and un-Stoic onlookers imaginable. The three voices contrapuntally overlap for six bars, uniting to sing their phrase in a powerful unison declamation. The chromatic "Non morir, Seneca" melody rises precipitously from the depths of the collective unconscious. Even after nearly four centuries, the ensemble's short-breathed, minor-key chromatic lines, among the finest depictions in music of overwhelming, elemental terror, never fail to move an audience. Monteverdi has created a musical world that intimates yawning chaos, a world of psychological and harmonic danger that anticipates the romantics.

The numbing dread portrayed in the trio's first verse is succeeded by a contrasting passage, "Io per me morir non vo" (I would not want to die). The rhythm and texture change strikingly. The dissonant chromaticism has yielded to a more consonant, trembling seven-note pattern. The first notes are repeated rapidly, bandied between the three men contrapuntally before another strong, climactic unison statement by all three voices will end this second section just as it did the first. They are not singing for Seneca so much as for themselves. The rapid seven-note pattern embodies their animated self-interest, which leads them and the accompanying instruments into the third discrete section of the ensemble—two strophes, of four verses each, describing the very un-Stoic pleasures of this world. These verses are punctuated by a snappy, highly danceable ritornello. Seneca might as well not be onstage when his Famigliari sing:

> This life is so sweet,
> this heaven so serene,
> all bitterness, all poison,
> is in the end only a slight obstacle.
>
> If I fall into a light sleep,
> I wake up in the morning, but a tomb of fine marble
> never returns what it receives.

These lyrics and the ritornello that precedes and follows the first stanza seem to cry out for strong physical movement, perhaps dance, in this case a real tarantella to ward off death. Silke Leopold notes that these stanzas of the Famigliari ensemble "are based on the same alternating rhythm found in the dance scene at the beginning of *L'Orfeo*" (212). Indeed, the instrumental ritornello sounds almost as if it had been lifted directly from the beginning of *L'Orfeo*'s second act, the tune of Orfeo's vigorous strophic song of happiness, "Vi ricorda, o boschi ombrosi" (Shady woods, do you remember). In *Orfeo,* the happy tune emphatically expresses Orfeo's joie de vivre, making the tragic reversal of Euridice's death all the more stark and dramatic when it is announced by the Messaggiera. In *Poppea,* the Famigliari are serving a similar dramaturgical purpose: their vigorous, life-affirming music portrays the healthy sensual pleasures Seneca rejects. The tune from *Orfeo* creates dramatic irony only insofar as a clear-cut reversal of fortune is about to be announced. The tune from *Poppea* we experience to subtler and more disturbing effect. The Famigliari, ostensibly singing to Seneca in an effort to dissuade him from suicide, reveal their hopeless inability to meet their friend on his own moral and philosophical level. Their expression of Rabelaisian delight in this life and its pleasures is inappropriate advice for the old Stoic. Although Seneca makes a noble and in some measure purifying renunciation of the life that has so compromised him, we are shown his tragic isolation from even his closest friends.

Monteverdi avoids contrapuntal overlapping; each voice enunciates its text clearly in brief solos. They join together only in the final verses of the two stanzas for a homophonic statement to close the refrain. Carter notes the similarity in style between the Famigliari in this suddenly hedonistic music and the suitors' ensembles in *Ulisse.* Like the suitors' ensembles, the Famigliari's "Questa vita è dolce troppo" contains similarities to the Venetian tradition of the *giustiniana,* humorous Carnival songs featuring three old men bragging of their imaginary sexual adventures. As Carter remarks, "The Familiari need to overcome a less than illustrious precedent if we are to take them seriously" ("Re-Reading *Poppea*" 194). The Famigliari ensemble suggests a collision of two worlds: the two compositional practices Monteverdi had defined as his major approach to composition. The *prima pratica,* the more archaic counterpoint of the High Renaissance, invigorated with aching chromaticism, has formed the first part of the ensemble, and now the freer *seconda pratica* has made its deliberately incongruous appearance for the two central stanzas.

The Famigliari's stark return to the tremulous "Io per me morir non vo" marks a retreat from their forgetful exuberance and serves to usher in the reiteration of the first chromatic lines of anguish and horror, a horror only increased by its close proximity to the *seconda pratica* exuberance and life force expressed in the two central stanzas. After the climactic repetition of "Non morir, Seneca," both the Venetian and the Neapolitan scores specify a reiteration of the jaunty ritornello by the instrumental ensemble (a repetition often cut from performances and recordings). This joyful tune comes as a final reminiscence of the pleasures of life, now forming the starkest of contrasts through its placement directly following the "Non morir" music. The chromatic contrapuntal anguish is juxtaposed with the more "modern" concerted string writing, personifying the unbridgeable gap between Seneca and his followers and between an ethical life and a totalitarian state. One may justifiably wonder whether these Famigliari will have the presence of mind to preserve their master's manuscripts after all. One thinks of St. Anthony preaching to the fish and the memorable song Mahler would create nearly three centuries later, his imagination fired by a similar sense of absurd futility.

After his Famigliari have made their plea for life, Seneca calmly claims the stage again. The published libretto and the Neapolitan score present ten lines of verse omitted from the Venetian manuscript: "Suppress your sobs, send back those tears from the channels of your eyes to the founts of your souls, O my dear ones. Let these waters cleanse from your hearts the shameful stains of a thousand inconsistencies. Some other obsequies the dying Seneca requires of you than sad groans." The text is authentic Busenello and serves to make Seneca's final utterance less peremptory than it seems in the Venetian score. Perhaps Monteverdi cut the lines because the exuberance of "Questa vita è dolce troppo" had rendered the mention of "sobs" incongruous (Carter, "Re-Reading *Poppea*" 201). The Neapolitan score sets these words to pedestrian recitative. Perhaps a later composer, bothered by the abruptness of the quick "Venetian" conclusion, decided to open Monteverdi's cut and set these extra lines. Busenello clearly wanted Seneca paying a little more attention to his Famigliari, but Monteverdi himself seems to have wanted to tighten the scene as well as to increase the distance between the master and his disciples.

Seneca's last verses return us to the same mellifluous style of speech-song with which he had started the scene: "Go, all of you, to prepare my bath, where my life will run out like a flowing stream; in tepid streams I shall let flow my innocent blood, which shall with purple mark the way of my death." The rapid descending notes on "che se la vita corre come il rivo fluente" vividly portray the image of the flowing streams of blood. Seneca closes the scene and his role in the opera with a sense of hard-won dignity. To rephrase Shakespeare in *Macbeth:* nothing in his life became Seneca like the leaving it. The cuts Monteverdi made (i.e., the parts of Busenello's text he chose not to set) have a great impact on how we interpret Seneca's place in the opera. Monteverdi's cut to Seneca's closing speech removes his emotive responses to his followers, taking us directly from the followers' passionate pleas to Seneca's emotionally detached preparatory orders for his death. This cut creates a deliberate disjunction. Seneca listens but has no response to the Famigliari. They are living in different, exclusive dimensions of experience, emblematic of how *Poppea* portrays virtually all human relationships, even that of Nerone and Poppea. The complete absence of the next scene (scene 4) in Busenello's text from both scores, a depiction of Seneca's acceptance amidst a heavenly chorus of Virtues, makes the succeeding Damigella-Valletto scene all the more jarring. It is curious that Busenello, supposedly one of the Incogniti's arch-cynics, felt a scene was required that mitigated in some way the tragedy of Seneca's death and the dissonance of his followers' reaction. Monteverdi probably suppressed this apotheosis (just as he had done with the underworld scene following the suitors' deaths in *Ulisse*) and in so doing created one of the most disturbing contrasts of tone imaginable. Seneca's noble self-abnegation is followed on Monteverdi's stage not by the theater machinist's pyrotechnics, piously underscoring what has just occurred, but by the rather salacious courtship of two comparative nonentities. It would be difficult to imagine a more effective dramaturgical device to drive home one of the opera's main themes: how the amoral animal drives wreak havoc with humanity's "higher" aims when tyranny and irrationality reign supreme. The juxtaposition's effect also cuts another way: the tuneful sensuality of the servants' love scene seduces the audience, making them complicit in the ethical catastrophe. There is scarcely better evidence to be found of Monteverdi's love for contrast.

Scenes 5 and 6

Scene 5 returns us from the weighty vocal milieu of basses and tenors to an encounter between two sopranos: Valletto, the empress's page, sung by a soprano castrato or by a woman in a breeches role, and Damigella, the "girl," yet another generically named figure. Valletto has already distinguished himself as a hotheaded adolescent violently antagonistic to Seneca. Now we see him in love and lust, completely unaffected by the philosopher's tragedy. Although Valletto's words protest his innocence and confusion over the hormonal effects Damigella's beauty has on him, the sly, knowing music of his strophic aria and its complementary ritornello suggest an already accomplished young rake. His professed confusion ("I feel a certain I-don't-know-what that pinches me and delights. Do tell me what it is, girl, sweet thing") strikes the listener as a seductive but hardly innocent pose. Monteverdi's sensitivity is evident in the vividly onomatopoetic—and erotic—elaboration on "batte" (the page's reference to his rapidly beating heart) and the harmonic dip on "melenso" (the "stupefaction" he is in whenever away from Damigella). The tuneful, insinuating ritornello punctuates the end of both strophes.

Just as Valletto displays the drive and cunning of a more sexually experienced Cherubino, Damigella reveals that she is equally adept at the courtship game, responding to Valletto's aria with one of her own. Damigella's song is charged with rocking, caressing melodic patterns that give musical realization to her images of Love "playing children's games" with her "clever, dear little boy." Damigella's music is languishing, seductive, and ripe with an almost drowsy sensuality. We know at once that Valletto will not have to work much harder to bring this conquest to the bedroom. The field virtually won, Valletto can afford a moment to stop in his tracks and savor their approaching union: "Does love begin like this? Is it something so sweet? I would give, to enjoy your delights, cherries, pears, and candies" (Dunque Amor così comincia? È una cosa molto dolce? Io darei, per godere il tuo diletto, i cireggi, le pere, ed il confetto). These four verses are subjected to varied musical styles conveying the young man's fluctuating emotions. "Dunque amor così comincia?" seems to begin a new amorous aria that recalls the style of the prologue's closing duet of Fortuna and Virtù, "Human non è," extolling love as well as foreshadowing the closing duet of act 3 between Nerone and Poppea (see Monteverdi, *L'incoronazione,* Curtis ed. vii). This musical resemblance reinforces one of the opera's themes: the omnipotence of love, the force that moves the whole of creation, from emperors to valets. But Valletto's new tune is established only to be broken. The repetitions on "molto, molto dolce, molto dolce" force his lyric music into recitative. His arousal is too great to be contained by the continence of continuous melody. The exclamation "I would give, to enjoy your delights, cherries, pears, and candy," a childish expression delightfully at odds with his amatory sophistication, hints that the driving power behind this scene has shifted to Damigella. The musical setting creates a fluid analogue to Valletto's excited train of thought. The tempo slows for Valletto's last question, set in recitative, a more appropriate medium than the confident arc of melody: "But if it becomes bitter, this honey [*questo miel*], which pleases me so, will you sweeten it, tell me, my life, tell me, do?" Damigella responds with arioso: "I'll sweeten it, yes, yes" (L'addolcirei, sì, sì). The scene between the servants closes, and the world goes its Priapic way, indifferent to all that has happened onstage and all that will happen.

Scene 6 is arguably the most brilliant moment in the opera. Although the last scene portrayed the (non)reaction to Nerone's crime in the workaday Roman world, we now see the emperor's jubilation, which he shares with a new character, Lucano, the poet laureate of Nerone's court. The historical Lucano, or Lucan, as he is known to English-speaking readers, was a brilliant young poet patronized by Nero. Lucan was the author of a major epic poem, *The Civil Wars* (or *Pharsalia*), that was particularly popular during the seventeenth century. Ironically, Lucan was a nephew of Seneca. (Like his Stoic uncle, Lucan eventually fell out of favor and was forced to commit suicide after the events portrayed in the opera.) Lucan came to side against the emperor, and the poet's artistic talent awakened Nero's jealousy (see Ahl). Nero's self-image as a great artist-singer-actor-poet is well documented: his own last words before committing suicide were, "Jupiter, what an artist is lost in me!" (Dio, 63.29). His artistic endeavors and presumptions create an inescapable resonance in contemporary history with

Hitler, that most horrific of would-be artists. From earliest times, art and politics have made dangerous yet often inescapable bedfellows. Although the historical Lucan eventually opposed Nero, the operatic Lucano stands in Busenello and Monteverdi's conception as a symbol of artistic talent prostituting itself to an immoral dictatorship. In his only scene in the opera, Lucano joins Nerone in a "veritable orgy of singing" (de' Paoli 503).

Nerone's reaction to Seneca's death is portrayed in text and music as a singing competition between the emperor and his pet poet, a tenor. "Now that Seneca is dead" (Or che Seneca è morto), Nerone sings, in the descending vocal line of what seems to be the start of a recitative. Instead of recitative, though, we are exposed to the first of the scene's many audacious shocks as Nerone launches into a duet with Lucano in the form of a singing competition between two "artists": "Sing, Lucano" (Cantiamo, Lucano). Lucano picks up the hint, and his tenor voice intones a tentative "cantiam," followed by a rest, before he starts into the first ornamental statement of the word. Lucano proposes this as if it were the musical strategy for the duet to come, and Nerone leaps to outdo his "artistic rival" with his own ornamental handling of "cantiam," which lasts more than twice as long as Lucano's. Nerone is on a roll and expands the textual and melodic material of the duet as a brief solo: "[Sing] amorous songs in praise of that face which love's hand has incised on my heart." "Nel cor" (in [my] heart) breaks the quick pulse of his song and causes Nerone to slow his pace. He repeats "nel cor" three times, punctuating it with rests to create the sense that his initial celebratory impulse has almost immediately begun to turn inward and reflective. Monteverdi is suggesting the dangerous fluctuation of Nerone's moods through unexpected shifts in pulse and melody. Lucano politely waits for his master to finish his verse line, "m'ha inciso" (has incised), before reprising the "cantiamo" music, forcing his singing partner to participate in the duet he had initiated moments before. Two "cantiam"s from Lucano shift Nerone back to his earlier extroverted mood, and soon the two men, emperor and poet, are duetting in perfect synchronization: "Sing of that laughing [ridente] face in which the ideal of love has alighted." Both "cantiamo" and "ridente" are treated to florid, synchronous coloratura by both men, creating thrilling virtuosic music that seems to compel the listener to share in their joy. We, the audience, are disturbed by our psychological complicity in the beauty being created out of evil for our enjoyment.

Lucano and Nerone overlap each other as they extol the face "that inspires one to glory and influences love." As soon as they finish this sequence with their synchronous singing of "amori," Lucano again proves his willingness to lead the course of the duet his master has initiated with a repeat of "cantiam," followed by a rest. This "cantiam" suggests a return to the duet's opening, but Nerone surprises us and Lucano with a new melody in a slower tempo on "Cantiam di quel viso" (Sing of that face). Within little more than a bar Lucano rejoins his master, complimenting him perfectly in the new melody and text. In a kind of musical *largesse de majesté,* Nerone's voice drops out to allow Lucano to finish this new passage by himself, singing of the face "in which the ideal of Love has alighted" (in cui l'idea d'Amor se stessa pose). Just as Lucano finishes his phrase, Nerone gamely begins a new third tune and text, in which Lucano soon joins him. With quicker, livelier pulse the two sing of the face "that distinguishes itself from the snow with new miraculous enlivening, incarnating the passionflower." They cadence together on the luxuriant image "la granatiglia" (the passionflower). Lucano again sings a teasing soloistic "cantiam." Will Nerone create a new tune, a new image, as he did before? The emperor is noncommittal. He simply repeats, "Cantiam," and Lucano takes the lead in a gloriously exuberant recapitulation of the duet's opening melodic material, which Nerone cannot resist joining. "Let us sing about this mouth to which India and Arabia consecrate their petals and give their perfumes" is sung to music based on the duet's opening, but modified so that it slows to a standstill as they finish the verse in unison.

Lucano picks up the new idea of Poppea's mouth ("bocca") and after a pause insinuates this word soloistically as a hint and provocation for Nerone's development. As with "cantiam" before, Nerone repeats the word to himself as though hypnotized. What will happen now? A variation of the "cantiam" melody? Nerone takes the lead and begins a fourth and final section of the duet, a slow chaconne initiated by his rapt repetitions of "bocca, bocca, bocca, bocca" ([her] mouth). Monteverdi has found a musical structure to suggest Nerone's fetishistic absorption with his mistress's body, or rather one part of it (we may recall Poppea's own remarks about "the kisses of this mouth" in her last scene). The instrumental ensemble intones a ground bass beneath Nerone, who in his stupor is reduced to chanting simple words over and over. Lucano joins his master, initially repeating "bocca" but soon expanding the text of the duet. Lucano becomes the vocal ground bass of the chaconne, feeding the sense-drugged emperor a steady stream of provocative images on the theme of Poppea's mouth. Nerone is only capable of repeating "bocca, ahi!" and "ahi, destin!" (ah, destiny!) to decorate the top melodic line. In a musical and poetic sense the two men are making love to each other through the masturbatory images of the absent Poppea. The duet has reached its "Bacchanalian zenith" (Osthoff 111). No wonder contemporary directors have on occasion staged this scene to suggest a homosexual orgy. Lucano continues his ground bass of fetishistic praise of Poppea: "Mouth which gives me its lascivious, tender rubies, intoxicating my heart with their divine nectar." He "lasciviously" ornaments "lasciveggiando" and "inebria" (inebriating), drawing out and tautening the duet's musical-sexual tension to the breaking point, when Nerone gives way to a kind of musical orgasm: "Ahi! Ahi! Ahi! Destin!" Seldom has any composer created such unblushingly erotic music. The music's inherent expressive beauty, coupled with the perverse dramatic circumstances, assaults the audience's sensibilities. Our intellectual and moral selves may reject the political and ethical situation Nerone has created, but our sensu-ally receptive selves can hardly fail to be vicariously swept along on the music's tide, dissolving boundaries between right and wrong, as well as our gender or sexual identities (see also Rosand *Opera* 335, on the "libertine" aspects of the scene).

Lucano initiates a new phase of the scene with recitative. After such lyrical effulgence, this seeming return to normalcy is a relief to the overwrought senses: "You fall, my lord, you fall into the ecstasy of love's rapture, and your eyes rain down drops of tenderness, tears of sweetness." The momentarily exhausted Nerone begins to remar-shal his musical forces in a recitative of his own: "My goddess Poppea, I want to celebrate you, but my words are tiny torches beside the sun of you." Since mere words or recitative is inadequate, Nerone brings this remarkable scene to its conclusion with another self-conscious song about singing, a self-advertised solo "song" with an attractive ritornello that will mark the aria's beginning and end: "The precious rubies are your loving lips" (Son rubini preziosi). As Osthoff observes, "It is characteristic of the solo arias in *L'incoronazione* that they are inspired less by action than by the inner feelings of the characters" (111).

It should be noted that scene 7 in Busenello's 1656 published libretto was not in the opera at its 1643 premiere and almost certainly represents an afterthought on the part of the librettist that found its way into the text after Monteverdi's death. It is excluded from the 1643 scenario, the scene outline for the opera drawn up at the time of the premiere. The scene consists of a solo with Ottavia, awkwardly sandwiched between Nerone and Lucano's singing match; and Ottone's own monologue (act 2, scene 8), which precedes that character's exchange with Ottavia (act 2, scene 9). Busenello's scene 7 has all the earmarks of a librettist's later concession to a performer of the role of Ottavia, whether Anna Renzi or another early interpreter of the part. The interpolated Ottavia monologue, set to spurious music in the Naples score, serves to flesh out the empress's character, bridging the intriguing gaps in her characterization between her appearance in act 1 and her interview with Ottone. Busenello's added speech and its music make Ottavia a far more conventional operatic heroine than the one the librettist and Monteverdi created for the 1643 premiere. Busenello himself seems to have been uncomfortable with what we can now appreciate as the modernity of his original conception of Ottavia. Curious readers are referred to the excellent discussion in Carter, *Monteverdi's Musical Theater* 292–94, and the only recorded version of the opera to include the scene, the Nuova Era recording led by Alberto Zedda.

Scenes 8 and 9

After the previous scene's camaraderie between the poet and the "poet," scene 8 returns us to a more intimate sphere: a solo recitative and aria for the dejected Ottone. Ottone's words and music establish how little he has changed, despite his declared love for Drusilla. Ottone, like the emperor, is fixated on Poppea's intoxicating beauty, a fixation cunningly expressed in Ottone's music. His opening words of recitative, "I miei subiti sdegni" (Did my immediate unhappiness), contain a melodic hint of his lovely opening aria about "returning" to Poppea's house. As suggested earlier, Ottone's most dominant character trait is his eagerness to return (torno) to his hopelessly lost former happiness. His passion for Poppea has so strongly reasserted itself that he regards his earlier homicidal anger with incredulous horror: "Did my immediate unhappiness, my political situation just a little while ago induce me to thoughts of murdering Poppea?" The name of his beloved is set to a thrice-repeated note, a monotonous declamation suggesting disbelief. A brief pause then precedes a repetition of the name, which slightly lifts the musical tone and suggests rekindled longing.

Ottone's aria with ritornello expresses his self-absorbed, masochistic love for Poppea. In his first lyric, Ottone concludes that even if his former love hates him, "I will be the moon [*Clizia*] in the sun of your eyes." This passage foreshadows the gender confusion that will haunt Ottone for the rest of the opera. The moon is traditionally a female figure, the sun a male one. Ottone's words effect a gender switch, which indicates his weakening grip on his own identity. His theatrical and performative status as a castrato singer whose altered physiognomy transgresses normal gender classification makes these lines and their psychological and performative implications all the more ironic. In the second lyric, Ottone sings, "My desperate love shall be my delight [*delizia*]." "Delizia," his masochistic "delight," is treated to two florid and energizing coloraturas, the most animated passage in the entire scene. His third and final lyric allows him to indulge in a vocal flourish on "nati" in the line about his torments: "Born [*nati*] from your beautiful visage." The florid run on "nati" recalls some of the melodic contours of his first aria in act 1—particularly in those earlier passages referring to the sleeping Poppea and the "sweet fantasies" he imagined to be filling her dreams. These musical reminiscences compel Ottone to "repeat himself," musically solidifying the impression of an operatic figure locked in an obsessive, masochistic mental sate. Ottone is most himself when he sings of his doomed romantic fixation. He is a passive dreamer ironically cast in a situation demanding the kind of determined action of which he is incapable.

That hostile situation is embodied in Ottavia, who in the interim since her first appearance has become a different creature. Her suffering has destroyed all vestiges of Stoic control, and her first sung note reveals a changed woman. "Tu" (you) begins their confrontation. It is a jabbing, insistent note followed by a rest. In one instant the empress gains psychological dominance over the repressed Ottone: "You [rest], who through my ancestors were given your nobility [le grandezze]." The climbing notes on "grandezze" are imperious and threatening, a vocal mannerism new to Ottavia. This is not her only weapon, however. Monteverdi has Ottavia thrice plead, "Dammi aita" (Help me), over four measures of music. Her pleading gesture seems disingenuous after her imperious opening, but Ottone lacks the guile to sense the danger he is in. Instead he obsequiously pledges his obedience, even if it means his own "sacrifice." Ottone's unimaginative, conventional thinking is revealed in the clichéd musical setting of the word "sacrificare." Ironically, Ottavia is about to force him to make the worst of "sacrifices." Ottone's hollow musical gesture, a mere exchange of "courtesies," as he later explains, helps to lock him into an unwinnable situation. Ottavia's newfound imperiousness is given an even more fearful display: "I want your sword to write your obligation to me with the blood of Poppea; I want you to kill her." "Voglio" (I want) is sung thrice, the climbing vocal line depicting her rising excitement. A rest precedes the full pronouncement of her command: "Voglio che la tua spada scriva gli obblighi miei col sangue, col sangue di Poppea." The empathetic repetitions of D's and B's seem to stab the listener, suggesting Ottavia's new attitude borders on insanity.

Ottone is stunned, repeating, "Che uccida chi? Chi?" (Kill whom? Who?) "Poppea," Ottavia responds. Ottone still cannot believe it and repeats his question. The empress's impatience is indicated by the heightened pitch of her reiterated reply: "Poppea." At last Ottone registers the situation: "Poppea? Poppea? Che uccida Poppea?" he sings, to falling notes that vividly bespeak his despondency. Ottavia's voice rises threateningly again: "Poppea, yes, Poppea: why are you refusing what you just promised to do?" Ottone responds, "I promised that [rest]?

I promised that [rest]? Urbane [rest], humble compliment [rest], modesty of speech [rest] is customary [rest]. To what fatal penalty [rest] have you condemned me?" The musical breaks suggest a fragmented delivery, as if the character were groping for words. "What are you talking about?" Ottavia demands. Ottone replies, "I talk, I talk about the most cautious and safest means for such a great enterprise." The repeated "I talk" (Discorro, discorro) suggests another stutter and allows us to hear Ottone improvising. He breaks down again: "Am I going to die soon?" "Why these frequent soliloquies from you?" (Ma che frequenti soliloqui son questi?), Ottavia demands. "And what if Nerone learns of this?" Ottone asks. "Change your clothes," Ottavia commands; "cover yourself in women's clothes. That is an appropriate ruse for a clever assassin: and get ready to do the work." Ottavia's voice goes higher than ever by the end of this passage, suggesting a barely suppressed, harpylike fury. This passage marks one of the opera's most self-conscious moments. Ottavia has already called attention to Ottone as a stage character by referring to his "soliloquizing" asides. Ottone's position as a theatrical and operatic figure is made even more ironic when Ottavia suggests that he disguise himself as a woman ("Habito muliebre ti ricopra"). Ottavia's demand for a transvestite assassin is ludicrous on any number of levels. Divorced from the theatrical and operatic situation it is silly and improbable, at best suggesting the naiveté of the planner. Within the performative world of this opera, Ottavia's clothing suggestion serves as a deliberate comment on Ottone's "effeminate" vacillation. Combined with the fact that Ottone's role was designed for an alto castrato, the situation boarders on the hilarious. At last one of the men with the "womanly" voices will be dressed in his "appropriate" habit. Busenello's Roman sources repeatedly criticize the historical Otho's femininity. One passage in Suetonius veers close enough to the trans-vestite plot to be a possible inspiration for Busenello. In the midst of his plotting against the emperor Galba, Otho fled to the praetorian camp, "having quickly concealed himself in a lady's litter . . . getting out of the litter when the bearers flagged, and starting to run" (*Life of Otho* 7).

Neither fully male nor female, the transvestite castrato is to set out on the daring plan: the assassination of the woman for whom he impotently longs. Ottone will call himself a "monstrosity" when we

actually see him in his drag getup, and a monstrosity he is. Monteverdi
has used the performative conventions of opera to make a humorous yet
chilling commentary on the opera's action. Nerone's despotism and its
resultant crimes have led to the creation of the monstrously gendered
Ottone, a man whose romantic and political inadequacy is signified
by his castrato voice and now made doubly ludicrous by his enforced
transvestitism. The monstrosity of the castrato in a dress also contains
political and artistic resonance. Castrati had particularly flourished in
baroque Rome owing to the papal prohibition against female singers
performing in church. Roman baroque operas required castrati to don
female dress to play female roles, a musical and theatrical equivalent
of Shakespeare's boy actors playing female roles. One dominant theme
of *Poppea* is its implicit critique of "Rome" and its political and social
contrasts to the Venetian republic. The dress-wearing castrato on his
murderous mission can be seen in this light as a ridiculous and unsettling image of the decadence of Rome, a Rome seen in distinctly seventeenth-century Venetian terms. Of course, Venice had its castrati,
too, but Monteverdi is here utilizing the castrato's gender ambiguity
for dramatic and ironic point. Ottone and Nerone are such sexually
confused beings that the castrato voice represents a perfect medium for
their operatic representation. More than any other baroque or classical
opera composer, Monteverdi used the castrato voice in a paradoxically
realistic way. The audience's awareness of the sexual mutilation of the
singers portraying Ottone and Nerone actually enhances the profound
irony at the core of *Poppea*.

   After Ottone pleads for a respite to transform himself into a state of
"ferocity," a request that begs a bemused smile from the operatic specta-
tor, Ottavia's frayed patience reaches the breaking point: "If you don't
obey, I'll denounce you before Nero for having wanted to use dishonest
violence against me; and I'll see to it that you are subject to torment
and death this very day." "Se tu non m'ubbidisci" (If you don't obey) is
repeated, punctuated by a rest, at successively higher pitches, suggesting her fury. A similar process is applied to "t'accuserò" (I'll accuse
you). Her outrageous threats reach their musical and dramatic climax
in the churning dissonances between her voice and the instrumental

accompaniment on "il tormento, il tormento e la morte" (torment, torment and death). Leopold writes: "In her scheming calculation Ottavia is quite Poppea's equal. Her rapacious attack on Ottone with the command to murder Poppea, is more than *sprechgesang*: with its short fragments of sentences, repeated at higher and higher pitches, it is an outburst of hate that can hardly be portrayed more exactly in music" (Leopold 213). Ottone has nothing left but to acquiesce: "I go, Empress, to obey you." Ottone then turns to the audience for one more of his self-conscious "soliloquies," apparently unheard by Ottavia. It is almost a verbatim repeat of something he said before: "O heaven! O gods! In this extreme hour take back the day and my life!" The circularity of Ottone's thoughts is realized in Ottone's impotent repetition of a sterile verbal formula. Ottone and Ottavia exit their separate ways. The published libretto includes another unset speech by Ottavia wherein she claims Poppea's murder not only will restore her peace of mind but will cure Nerone of tyranny, "and happiness will return to the people, to the senate, to Rome, and the world" (qtd. in Carter, *Monteverdi's Musical Theater* 292). No music for this survives. If it was cut by the composer, it represents another instance of the elderly priest actually sharpening the edges of the libertine Busenello's text.

Ottavia's breakdown and descent into criminality is perhaps the greatest liberty Busenello takes with his sources. He has grafted elements of Agrippina, Nero's mother, onto the ostensibly innocent Octavia of history. Agrippina's ambition led her to suborn murder much as we see Ottavia do in this last scene. Busenello has consequently found a means for incorporating something of this notorious character into his libretto and creating an even greater challenge for the acting abilities of the great Anna Renzi. The shift in Ottavia's character is shocking, even though her words and music in the first act hinted at her possible mental instability and the hollowness of her moral bearings. This "new" Ottavia seems to have caused some of the early performers some discomfort, hence the weak and conventionalizing scene 7 mentioned earlier. These interpolations are fascinating, much like the later adaptations of Shakespeare plays in which attempts were made to "correct" works of genius.

Scenes 10 and 11

Scene 10 opens with a disconcerting outburst of joy. Drusilla sings to
Nutrice and Valletto of her newfound happiness, oblivious to the shal-
lowness of Ottone's feelings for her and the doom that is closing in on
them all. She sings about her joy in her radiant aria "Felice cor mio"
(My happy heart rejoices in my breast; after the clouds of horror I enjoy
serenity). Ironically, Drusilla's "Felice cor mio" tune is an inversion of
Poppea's "Per me guerreggia Amor" theme from act 1. The ensuing
action will suggest more unexpected parallels between Ottone's two
loves (see also Savage, "Love and Infamy" 204). The first response to
her aria from Drusilla's onstage audience is a remark by Valletto, fresh
from his dalliance with Damigella. "Nutrice," he asks, initiating a recitative exchange, "what would you pay for one day of the happy youth
that Drusilla has?" "All the gold in the world!" replies the old woman.
This exchange suggests Valletto's cruelty, which was already evident
in his outlandish baiting of Seneca. The question also ensures that the
theater audience will be able to appreciate the dramatic irony: Drusilla
only thinks she has weathered "the clouds of horror" to possess Ottone's
heart. She is so euphoric that she interposes herself between the vulnerable older woman and the teasing Valletto. "You are still young,"
Drusilla insists to Nutrice; "the sun hasn't set though the rosy morning is over." Drusilla cannot get her joy or her aria out of her system.
Her kindness to Nutrice is one of the few unselfish acts in the entire
opera, making the next scene, in which she agrees to facilitate Poppea's
murder, all the more unsettling.

Nutrice, like Arnalta, was probably conceived as a travesty part for
a tenor. The present scene contrasts a real woman's imagined happiness
(Drusilla, a female soprano) with the real unhappiness of an artificial
crone (Nutrice, a tenor) being baited by a travesty page (Valletto, a
female or a soprano castrato). The man playing Nutrice mimics female
behavior, lamenting in her aria that "the woman's day finds its evening
in the middle of the day." Nutrice claims she has arrived at the sultry,
impassable "July" of her life without benefit of love (Amore). The ironic
distancing inherent in Nutrice's appearance and music in this scene is
further suggested by the humorously descriptive use of rests in her vocal

line in the last passage of her aria: "Don't let pass green April or May: you'll sweat too much if you go voyaging in July." The mere thought of such erotic traveling past the prime of life leaves the "woman" literally breathless, "si suda troppo in Iugio [rest] a [rest] far [rest] viaggio." For all its comic potential, however, the pain of rejection Nutrice describes links her condition with the opera's gallery of tortured, lovelorn characters. Valletto leads the scene back to recitative and its conclusion. "Let's go at once to Ottavia," Valletto sings, turning to Nutrice, "my reverend grandmother!" The reference to Ottavia reminds the audience of the deadly situation of the murder plot and opens the way for Ottone's next interview with Drusilla.

Ottone encounters Drusilla, but his words and music suggest his initial unawareness of her: the frequent rests suggest his stopping for breath: "I don't [rest] I don't know where I'm going [rest]; the heart pounds [rest], the movement of my feet [rest] doesn't go together [rest]; the air that enters my breast, which [rest] I [rest] breathe [rest], finds my heart so affected, so piteous [rest] that it turns [rest] immediately into sighs." These rests are particularly suggestive on the words "quando io respiro" (which I breathe), the passage that seems to have germinated the shortness of breath implied throughout this speech. The gently oscillating notes on "il palpitar del core" (the heart pounds) describe Ottone's heartbeats. As Rosand observes of this and similar passages, "The recognition of singing as a physiological act affected by the emotions underlies the conception of musical imitation in *Poppea*. . . . Ottone's music is completely ruled by his mood, even as he projects it. The very air he breathes imitates his emotions" ("Monteverdi's Mimetic Art" 126–31).

Drusilla interrupts Ottone's soliloquy: "Where, where are you going, my lord?" Her voice seems to briefly lift his depression, and a brief duet passage ensues wherein the new lovers exchange short melodic flourishes signaling Drusilla's excited emotions and Ottone's relief on finding both a sympathetic companion and a supplier for his assassination disguise.

Ottone: Drusilla, Drusilla!

Drusilla: Where, where are you going, my lord?

Ottone: You alone, you alone, you alone I seek!

Drusilla: Here I am, here I am at your service!

This exchange subsides as quickly as Ottone gets a pledge of secrecy from Drusilla. His long held notes on "gravissimo" ensure that she appreciates the "gravity" of the secret he is about to unfold. "No longer be jealous of Poppea," he sings. Startled, Drusilla interjects a questioning "No? No?" Ottone reiterates, "Of Poppea" (di Poppea). Elated, Drusilla launches into a reprise of her aria "Felice cor mio" (My happy heart) from the previous scene. Ottone tries to drown out her aria with bitingly dissonant iterations—"Senti, senti!" (Listen, listen!)—but she sings on, with "Festeggiami in seno" ([My heart] rejoices in my breast). Ottone repeats his command, finally arresting the flow of her happy song, which is even more ironic and incongruous in the present circumstances. "I'm duty bound at this hour to a terrible command," Ottone relates, "to plunge my sword into Poppea's breast. In order to disguise myself for this enormous crime I want your clothes." Ottone's harmonically wavering recitative, mirroring the horrible command given him by the empress, finds its answer in Drusilla's firm, arioso response: "Both my clothes and blood I'd give to you." Her love is so strong, no verbal or musical hesitations have any place; indeed, she seems almost ready to burst into her happy aria again. Conspicuous by its absence is any expression of moral or ethical hesitancy over the proposed murder of her rival. Ottone responds to her striking declamation with more of his usual timid recitative—"If I can obscure myself . . . "—then seems to catch some of his new mistress's lyric optimism. He sings his next lines in an arioso: "We shall live united always in happy love." Her obvious selfless devotion and lack of moral scruple seem to rub off on Ottone, making his musical expression more colorful and dynamic. This is evident in the languishing self-pity with which he sings, "If I die, then convene with appropriate pious sorrow my funeral rites, O, O Drusilla!" and the more rapid notes that illustrate his description of his anticipated life as a "fuggitivo." "E le vesti e le vene ti darò volentieri" (My clothes and my blood I give you, voluntarily), Drusilla sings, her fast notes suggesting how eager she is to share the "fugitive" life.

Drusilla continues to show her true mettle. She orders, "Go circumspectly, proceed with caution: and know also that my fortune and my riches are yours in tribute wherever you may be. Drusilla shall prove to you to be such a noble lover, such as has not been equaled in antiquity. Let's go, for I want to strip myself and disguise you myself. But I want to know from you the exact reasons for such a horrendous deed." The stealthy preparation for the murder of a defenseless woman seems the perfect means for Drusilla to show her love for Ottone. This self-proclaimed model of female constancy has no qualms about killing—even her curiosity as to why she should help in such a "horrendous deed" can wait until after the prospective murderer is dressed in her own clothes. Monteverdi sets the seal on this troubling situation by giving Drusilla an uninterrupted reprise of "Felice cor mio." This musical reminiscence of the unclouded joy with which the previous scene began interrupts Busenello's text just before she provocatively states that she will "strip herself" to help Ottone "travesty himself" (travestirti). This is arguably the most disturbing passage in the score. The audience could appreciate the irony of Drusilla's aria at the start of the preceding scene. Now, with virtually a full disclosure of the horror of Ottone's grim commission and promising her own help in committing the crime, she buoyantly repeats the same song of joy and thanksgiving. The irony is now at the expense not of Drusilla, but of the audience. Before, the audience could pity the poor woman's emotional vulnerability and her ignorance of her situation. We presumed that had she known what Ottone's feelings were and what he was going to ask of her, she would literally have been singing a different tune. Now Drusilla knows her lover has been ordered to murder her rival and wants her to lend him her very clothing to do the deed. When Drusilla recapitulates "Felice cor mio," the audience realizes that it is they who have been the deceived character, so to speak, in the opera. Drusilla is so untroubled by the true state of affairs that she can sing her blissful aria yet again, proving that loving constancy and turpitude can easily coexist in the dark world of Monteverdi and Busenello's realpolitik. The lovers exit to prepare for the assassination of Poppea, Drusilla's promise to strip herself immediately to help him don her clothes a piquant blending of sexuality and anticipated violence.

Scenes 12 through 15

The scene is Poppea's private garden. Fenlon and Miller note that "this final sequence of three scenes in the second act constitutes both a parallel and an opposition to [Seneca's] neostoic garden of the opening three scenes" (*Song* 82). Poppea and Arnalta begin and end their scene together with two self-conscious arias. Seneca's state-sanctioned murder inspires Poppea to sensual song—"Or che Seneca è morto, Amor, ricorro a te" (Now that Seneca is dead, Love, I turn to you)—just as it did Nerone and Lucano. "Amore," "speme" (hope), and "sposa" (bride) are treated to luxurious ornamentation. The musical and verbal accenting of "Amore" prepares the way for Amore's bold intervention in the action of the opera proper.

Arnalta acknowledges Poppea's self-conscious aria: "You are always singing away [*canzoneggiando*] about this marriage." "Arnalta, I can't think, can't think of anything else," Poppea replies, the recitative reiterations of "non penso mai" an apt description of her obsession. "The most unquiet feeling is insane ambition," Arnalta cautions halfheartedly. But after this expected piety she begins to stake her claim as the new empress's servant: "But if you arrive at the scepter and the crown don't forget me, keep me close to you." The word "corone" is accented by two high notes. Instead of ridiculing Poppea's pretensions to sovereignty, Arnalta gives the idea appropriate musical respect with these august A's and unctuously begs her mistress not to forget her: "Non ti scordar" (Don't forget me) is repeated, as is "Appresso di te" (Keep me close to you). Styling herself as an experienced observer, Arnalta warns her mistress of courtly corruption and suggests Poppea will need Arnalta's proven constancy in her new surroundings. Poppea expresses one of her few unquestionably sincere utterances when she assures Arnalta, "Never doubt that for me you will always stay the same and I shall have none but you to be my confidante." This exchange recalls Drusilla, Poppea's rival, in her kind words to Nutrice, another travesty tenor, two scenes earlier.

After this rare expression of loyalty, Poppea's thoughts and music return to their most natural province, lyrics about herself. She reprises part of her scene-opening aria, "Amor, ricorro a te." This time the aria's almost drowsy self-satisfaction is evidenced by the ingenious use of rests on the repetitions of "fammi sposa." Monteverdi graphically depicts a character singing while falling asleep. Rosand observes that Poppea's "words and musical line become halting, interrupted by rests, and she then acknowledges her sleepiness in a descending line that sinks gradually to the bottom of her range" (*Opera* 339). Poppea's drowsiness has made her incapable of sustaining her aria's melody. She requests that Arnalta make a temporary bed "here in the garden" and that none be allowed into the garden "except Drusilla, or another confidante." These duties accomplished, Arnalta sings her mistress to sleep. Her words are as beautiful as their musical setting.

> May sweet oblivion lull
> your tender feelings to sleep, child.
> Rest your thieving eyes.
> Why do you open them
> for even when they are closed they steal hearts?
> Poppea, rest peacefully,
> dear and welcome lights [of your eyes]
> sleep now, sleep.

Rosand notes that the sleep and lullaby conventions of Venetian opera represent

> a dramatic device borrowed from spoken drama.... Sleep was an abnormal state of consciousness that facilitated the suspension of disbelief and thereby encouraged musical expression. It did so triply: for the singer of the provoking lullaby, for the sleeper, who could dream out loud, and for the on-stage observer, who could express himself alone.... Arnalta's soporific lullaby ... imitates sleep itself, or actually assures it, by different musical means; repetitive, circular melody within a restricted range, abnormally long held notes at cadences, and harmonic oscillations would provoke a yawn from anyone, whether on-stage or in the audience. (*Opera* 338–39)

Arnalta is repaying Poppea's loyalty to her with unforgettable words and music. Celletti describes the lullaby as "one of the finest masterstrokes in the whole history of opera."

> It is a moment of purification of a corrupt character expressing
> her feelings in the grim surroundings of the tragic death of Seneca
> and the imminent attempt on Poppea's life. The winged melody
> of Arnalta, which as it develops relies on slow vocalises . . . sets an
> example of the path [Monteverdi] followed in bringing a character
> to life by giving it to us in an alternating mood of cynicism and
> tenderness, of ordinary common sense and dreamlike effusions, in
> other words, a figure looked at from different angles, with varia-
> tion and nuance. Part of this nuance is the light patina of sensuality
> we gather as a sort of background in the poetic lullaby of Arnalta,
> now an old hag but at one time, as she confesses, a vivacious and
> hot-blooded woman. (34–35)

Arnalta is a three-dimensional character in whom smugness, greed,
loneliness, and unexpected reserves of tenderness all have a part.
With Arnalta presumably drifting off to sleep by her mistress's side,
Monteverdi and Busenello created a fascinating dramatic rhyme with
the first scene of act 1, wherein the lovelorn Ottone stumbles upon
Nerone's two sleeping guards at Poppea's window. Ottone's upcoming
entrance in Drusilla's dress before two new sleeping figures is emblematic of all the upheavals of the intervening action.

Amore, the prologue's mischievous child, descends from the proscenium, borne aloft by the magic of the theater machinist. He observes,
"Thus humanity lives in the dark, when they close their eyes, they think
they are safe from danger." Amore's recitative sets "E quando ha chiusi
gl'occhi" (When they close their eyes) to fluctuating pitches ironically
recalling the drowsy music of Arnalta's lullaby. His self-congratulatory
aria, "O sciocchi o frali," is jaunty (O stupid, weak senses of mortals,
when you fall into weary oblivion a god is vigilant over your sleep).
The descending notes ornamenting "cadete" (fall) and the rising and
the falling decoration of "sonnacchioso" (weary) mimetically decorate
while giving shape to a catchy aria melody. Amore's next two refrains
are sung to different melodic strains.

> [Mortals would] stay
> a plaything of chance,
> subject to risk and prey to peril,
> if Amore, the genius of the world, didn't look out for you.

> Sleep, Poppea,
> Earthly goddess,
> you are saved from rebel's arrows
> by Amore which moves the sun and other stars.

[handwritten margin note: M's amore]

Amore's flamboyant runs over a rock-steady rhythm in the basso continuo characterizes the setting of "Se Amor, genio del mondo, non provvede" (If Amore, the genius of the world, didn't look out) and the even more spectacular setting of "Amor, che move il sol e' l'altre stelle" (Amore, which moves the sun and other stars). This effect of rapid vocal movement over a stately basso continuo tread creates an indelible image of Amore's paradoxical flightiness and omnipotence. This last image is a direct quotation of one of the most celebrated lines in Italian literature, the close of the final canto of Dante's *Divine Comedy*. In the last canto of *Paradise*, Dante is allowed to view the face of God. Dante closes his poem with a sense of the transcendence this view of divinity has given him and its evidence of a creation bound together by divine love (Amore).

> Here my powers rest from their high fantasy,
> but already I could feel my being turned—
> instinct and intellect balanced equally
> as in a wheel whose motion nothing jars—
> by the Love that moves the Sun and other stars.

[handwritten margin note: Dante's conclusion to p272 disio]

[handwritten margin note: In Dante 'amore' is divine love]

>   (Dante, *Divine Comedy: Paradise*, canto 33,
>   lines 142–46, Ciardi transl.)

In Busenello's text, the pagan god's recourse to the tag line of Dante's masterpiece, the supreme achievement of Christian imaginative literature, is disconcerting. Just as Euripides, in his fifth-century tragedies, had secularized pagan divinity as at best a force of nature, so has Busenello suggested a similar secularization of the Christian notion of divine love: the forces that move not only the cosmos but also impel the petty lusts of Poppea, Nerone, and Ottone. The Dantean ideal of divine love is embodied by the operatic Amore, a figure similar in its sexual ambiguity to Caravaggio's famous *Triumph of Love*. Ketterer observes that the "co-opted images" from Dante "create a disjunction

[handwritten margin note: earthly lust.]

which underscores the fundamentally earthbound situation of *Poppea*" ("Neoplatonic Light" 13). But Monteverdi, through his music and the cumulative effect of the entire opera, seems to transcend Busenello's rationalism. The unrelenting irony of *Poppea* ensures that our moral sensibilities remain alert. But, miraculously, our sense of the wholeness of human experience is reenergized by our recognizing our kinship with people and situations we might have deemed hopelessly alien to our experience. We are given a potent glimpse of a cosmic wholeness, not too different from the harmonized vision Dante so eloquently stammers out at the close of his *Paradise* (see also Fenlon and Miller, *Song* 83).

Ottone enters in his rebound-girlfriend's dress and launches on a recitative monologue, unaware of the hovering Amore. Monteverdi has punctuated and even slightly rewritten the words to create a passage of probing psychological insight. Busenello's published libretto begins: "Eccomi trasformato non d'Otton in Drusilla, ma d'huom in serpe, al cui veleno e rabbia non vide il mondo, e non vedrà simile" (Here I am transformed not from Ottone to Drusilla, but from a human to a serpent, as venomous and rabid as the world has not yet seen). Monteverdi tellingly rearranges Busenello's words: "Eccomi, eccomi trasformato d'Otton in Drusilla, d'Otton in Drusilla . . . no, non d'Otton in Drusilla, no, no, non d'Otton in Drusilla, ma d'huom inserpe." The composer makes the ambiguously gendered man in a dress both more ridiculous than the poet's words suggested and also more psychologically compelling. "Eccomi" is repeated, suggesting an excitement in Ottone not implicit in the words alone. Monteverdi reworks the text to create a statement and immediate refutation. Monteverdi's Ottone asserts that he is Ottone transformed into Drusilla, and the jaunty melodic fragment with which "d'Otton in Drusilla" is set suggests he may be about to launch a lively aria rather than a long recitative passage. This "aria" is soon aborted after the repetition of "Ottone" provokes a flamboyant five-note vocal arabesque. The change of clothes seems to have momentarily liberated the tormented Ottone, but the composer, Ottone's superego, quickly quashes this "aria" with two rests and an interpolated "no." Ottone corrects himself: "No, Ottone is not transformed into Drusilla but into a serpent." Monteverdi's handling of the text is the work of probing musical and theatrical intelligence. Three centuries before Freud, the composer has manipulated Busenello's language to suggest the contradictory impulses at war in this character's psyche. Ottone, a figure characterized by his passivity and lack of "masculine" self-control, feels a brief neurotic outburst of pleasure on donning a woman's dress. This pleasure is quickly censored, and the character recalls the horrible task he is obligated to carry out. The remainder of Ottone's recitative is characterized by a proliferation of rests that break up his thoughts and direct the performer in creating the illusion of his anguished, wandering thoughts. He is a figure torn between love and hate as well as by masculine and feminine instincts. His short-breathed rhythms convey his spiritual conflict with the contrasts between the low-lying colors he gives menacing words and thoughts, such as "la vostra morte uscir dalle mie mani" (your death coming from my hands) and "funesto il fine" (fatal end). His abiding love for Poppea is evident in the caressing setting of "anima mia" (my dear one) and "e ancor io l'amo" (I still love her). (On the theme of disguise and transformation being "particularly relevant to a Venetian audience during Carnival," see Rosand, *Opera* 120–21.)

Finally, Ottone's fear of Ottavia outweighs his residual passion for Poppea, and he lifts his sword. Amore, the hovering witness, magically halts the assassin with an arioso declamation, freezing Ottone in his tracks: "Madman, rascal, enemy of my divinity, do you presume so much? I should shoot you with lightning." Amore declaims in recitative, "But you don't merit death by the hands of gods. Go unhurt from these sharp rays [*strali*]; I don't exact tribute from scoundrels." Amore channels his expressive impulse in a florid run on "strali." Ottone's castrato impotence is easily vanquished not by action, but by a coloratura flourish from a boy soprano. Poppea awakes and sees "Drusilla" helplessly frozen, "naked sword" in hand, and her cries awake the sleeping Arnalta. Arnalta closes the scene with a scene-stealing arietta: "Run! Run! Servants, maids, in pursuit of Drusilla, after her! After her! Strike her down, this monster, don't let her escape!" Arnalta's "chase" aria, a manic street call turned to song, characterizes the startled, panicked cries of the old servant scrambling to meet the emergency. Its brevity recalls Arnalta's previous scene-closing aria, "Ben se pazza" from act

1. As with the earlier aria, it is tempting here to imagine the character reprising her aria or developing it after she has left our hearing. This is true operatic suspension of disbelief and another operatic trompe d'oeil. Monteverdi has bestowed on Arnalta a peasant vitality similar to that of the Nurse in Shakespeare's *Romeo and Juliet:* a lively mixture of feeling and grotesquerie that breaks down the boundaries of commonplace mimesis. Amore can indulge in a full-fledged, though pithily brief, act-closing aria: "I have defended Poppea, I shall make her empress." The divine agency in the sordid human situation is beautifully captured in the contrast between Arnalta's rapid-fire "dalli, dalli"s and the calm, declamatory melodic assurance of the child-god's song as he proclaims his program for the opera's final act.

Act 3

Unaware of the failed assassination, Drusilla exults in her personal happiness ("O felice Drusilla, o che sper' io?"). Arnalta orders the lictor (Littore) to apprehend the attempted murderess. Nerone, learning of Poppea's close call, threatens Drusilla. Seeing herself as "a model for all lovers," Drusilla resigns herself to dying for Ottone. Ottone arrives to confess his guilt and clear Drusilla. Nerone, delighted to learn that it was Ottavia who had planned the crime, orders Ottone's banishment rather than his death, allowing Drusilla to follow her lover. Nerone announces the repudiation and exile of Ottavia. Nerone and Poppea share a scene of rapturous expectation ("Per te, ben mio"). The thunderstruck Ottavia leaves Rome for banishment and certain death ("A Dio, Roma"). Arnalta joyfully anticipates her change of status as the new empress's nurse ("Hoggi sarà Poppea"). Nerone presents Poppea to the tribunes and consuls of Rome, who proclaim her empress. A celestial entourage of Amore, Venus, and Cupids sing Poppea's praises. Nerone and Poppea celebrate their triumphal love ("Pur ti miro").

Scenes 1 through 7

The first scene returns the action to the "City of Rome," with an aria for Drusilla as she ecstatically anticipates the murder we have just seen foiled by divine intervention. The rushing five-note flourish on "o" instantly sets the tone for the aria "O happy Drusilla, O happy one, what may I not hope for?" (O felice, felice Drusilla, o felice, o che sper'io?). She is not quietly accepting the grim necessity of Ottavia's command upon Ottone, she is reveling in it, and in her role as an accomplice to murder. This opening melodic flourish is instantly contrasted with a quick tune on "Corre adesso per me l'hora fatale" (The fateful hour of my life has now arrived). The ensuing passage and the repetitions added by the composer in "Perirà, morirà, morirà, perirà, perirà, perirà, morirà, la mia rivale" (My rival is to perish, die, die, perish, perish, perish, die) is shocking in its bloodlust. Each repeated verb is set to successively higher notes punctuated by breathless rests, suggestive of Drusilla's stammering excitement. Her anticipation ends with imagining Ottone finally "being mine, mine, mine, mine, being mine" ("sarà mio, mio, mio, mio, sarà mio"). Her music here contrasts the upward vocal climb of "perirà" and "morirà" with descending notes on "mio" suggestive of emotional satiation after the violent repetitions of the imagined murder. The passage "If my clothes have served to cover him well, with your consent, O gods, I shall worship my habiliments" starts with rising notes but soon individuates itself with the upwardly flowing arabesques on "O dèi" (O gods), suggesting Drusilla's absurdly literal supplication. Ottone's use of her clothing allows her to imagine she is cutting her rival down herself. Arnalta and the Littore confront her. "There's the villain!" Arnalta declares, shocking Drusilla out of her aria and into silence.

Nerone enters, eliciting unusually demonstrative recitative from the excited Arnalta, who plays the loyal, courageous servant to the hilt. The downward vocal swoop on "Signor" suggests both excitement and officiousness. Arnalta deftly paints the situation: "Dormiva l'innocente nel suo proprio giardino" (The innocent [Poppea] was sleeping in her private garden); her verbal and musical picture recalls her striking "snake in the garden" arioso from the first act, "Mira, mira Poppea." Now the metaphor of the snake has been made real. Two fermatas punctuate the repetition of "Sopra di lei" (If your devoted servant hadn't awakened, then [rest], then [rest], the cruel blow would have fallen), maximizing the impact of the violent image on the impressionable emperor.

Nerone imperiously demands, "Why so much daring? Who incited you to this treachery?" Drusilla replies with weak, lying words and a musical line that cleaves humbly to the bottom of her range: "I'm innocent, my conscience knows it, and God knows it." "Were you led by hate or driven by an order or gold to this great crime?" The reprisal of Drusilla's recitative refrain, "I'm innocent," sends the emperor over the edge. His words, "Flagelli, funi, fochi" (Whips, flames, torture, shall drag from her the instigators, and the accomplices), verge on the self-parodic as his sadistic fantasies, set in *stile concitato,* are coupled with hopes of implicating his empress as well. This fury is so strong that Drusilla drops her pretense of innocence, only to assume another self-righteous mask, that of a martyr to love. She muses to herself, "Miserable me, before an atrocious torment shall force me to speak that which I want to hide, I would take upon myself the death sentence and the tomb. O you, whom the world calls friends, see reflected in me, what the offices of true friendship are." Her pace is slow and reflective, a contrast to Nerone's abrupt fury. Her abstraction infuriates her three antagonists.

Arnalta:	What are you twittering about, slut?
Littore:	What are you raving about, assassin?
Nerone:	What are you saying, traitor?

The furious interjections quicken the pace of Drusilla's recitative: "There is within myself a dispute . . . between love and innocence [*Amor e l'innocenza*]." Her caressing delivery of "l'innocenza" is touching in its suggestion of sincerity. The music is so convincing that some modern interpreters seem ready to forget her eager anticipation of her rival's death and her enthusiastic, indeed fetishistic dressing of Ottone to perform the deed (see especially Fenlon and Miller, who unconvincingly compare Drusilla to Penelope, *Song* 74, 82, 87). After more threats from Nerone, Drusilla finally confesses: "My lord, I was the criminal who wanted to kill the innocent Poppea." Her acquiescence is notable for her musical handling of Poppea's name. It is almost the same languishing four-note pattern Arnalta had used at the scene's start when she accused Drusilla before Nerone. Drusilla is willing, so to speak, to sing her accuser's tune.

Nerone proclaims his furious condemnation with steely control: "Conduct her [*conducete*] to the executioner at once! He should concoct [*fate*] a death for this criminal which is made worse [*inasprisca*] by long [*lunga*], terrible agony." "Conducete" and "fate" are treated to downward-swooping musical gestures characterizing the emperor's wrath. The ghastly setting of "lunga" graphically portrays lingering agonies. So, too, the oscillating notes on "inasprisca" illustrate the torturous images filling his sadistic imagination. In contrast to the violence of all around her, Drusilla is at peace with her choice of martyrdom. She hopes that her "loved one" will "just once" weep "tears of pity, if not of love [*se non d'amore*]" over her tomb. The setting of "se non d'amore" flirts with the minor key and dissonance just enough to suggest Drusilla's residual doubts about her lover's affections. In "I go as a true friend, and true lover to the cruel executioner to cover with my blood [*col mio sangue*] your sins," the composer repeats "col mio sangue" to falling notes, as if the realization of her sacrifice were only beginning to sink into her consciousness. In the nick of time Ottone enters (neither the text nor the score specifies his clothing).

Ottone and Drusilla vie with each other to take sole responsibility for the crime. Ottone's pleading wins Nerone over by implicating Ottavia as the plot's mastermind. The low-lying notes with which Ottone refers to "the death of Poppea" (la morte di Poppea) and his own anticipation of execution on "la morte" are the musical embodiment of an almost physical abjection. Drusilla cannot divert the blame to herself, even when she vies with Ottone in an arioso duet: "[The gallows] await me!" (A me s'aspetta). Ottone literally has the last word, confessing before delivering one last appeal to Nerone for his execution or banishment. Nerone now has grounds to remove his wife. He utters his verdict on the two people cringing before him. "Vivi" (Live!), Nerone proclaims, in a version of the swooping "imperial" musical gesture. Ottone's life will be spared, but he shall be banished, penniless and without title, "to the remotest desert." The composer inserts a rest as Nerone turns from Ottone to Drusilla with "And you" (E tu). Here the imperial gesture reverses itself from a downward to an ascending pattern. Nerone is intent on building Drusilla into a politically useful symbol of his clemency and as a "beloved model in our time for a woman of constancy." With Ottavia now securely in his sights, Nerone can afford to be merciful, and the sad, hapless woman before him makes for a convenient propaganda symbol. Seutonius drily remarked that the historical Nero "was fully convinced that no one was truly chaste or pure in any part of their body but that many chose to conceal their vices and hid them cleverly. And so when any confessed to him their sexual misdeeds, he forgave them all other faults" (*Life of Nero* 29). Nerone's arioso rhapsodizes on Drusilla as an "adorable paradigm of constancy" (la tua costanza un adorabil mostro). This ushers in lyrical passages expressing Drusilla and Ottone's newfound joy and relief.

Drusilla sings a memorably caressing melody on "Ch'io tragga i giorni ridenti" ([Give me permission] to spend my days happily [with Ottone]). The tune suggests beatific peace, for Drusilla is on the verge of attaining her heart's desire: Ottone all to herself. Nerone dismisses them. Ottone's relief is expressed in an energetic aria with an ecstatic staccato tune setting the words "Le virtù di costei saran richezza e gloria" (Her virtue shall be the riches and glory of my days). It's impossible to tell how much this quickening of pulse and melody is stimulated by relief at his survival and how much stems from a deepening emotional connection to Drusilla. His words do not address Drusilla herself but seem designed for his onstage auditors. In fact, he avoids addressing her directly throughout the entire scene. Drusilla responds with her own brief aria, beautifully elaborating her "ch'io tragga" tune as she envisions her future life by Ottone's side: "To live and die by you, I want nothing else" (Ch'io viva a mora teco, altro, non voglio). Drusilla will "give back all that fortune has given her [rest] that you may recognize [rest] in a woman's heart [rest] true constancy." "Una constante fede" (true constancy) is the last we hear of Drusilla and her new lover. On one level she has defied Fortune and has demonstrated her faith to her lover. Her unscrupulousness in the murder plot, however, prevents her from standing as a moral template. Nerone is left to close the scene as he condemns Ottavia in recitative notable for its pomposity: "I deliberate and resolve with solemn decree the repudiation of Ottavia, and I give the order for her perpetual banishment from Rome. Send Ottavia to the nearest coast; as soon as you can, put her on a wooden boat and commit her to the bombardment of the winds. I declare my justified anger; hurry to obey!" Nerone takes sadistic delight in ornamenting "venti," the sea winds that will carry Ottavia to her death.

Nerone now shares the stage with Poppea alone to relate their triumph. Poppea starts the scene with a bar of languishing recitative on "Signor, signor." She reasserts her seductive power over Nerone and the theater audience in supple arioso expressing her joy at surviving the assassination attempt. The scene then shifts to recitative.

Nerone:	It was not Drusilla who wanted to kill you.
Poppea:	Then who was the felon?
Nerone:	Our friend Ottone.
Poppea:	He alone?

Poppea knows her former lover only too well. Nerone tells her, "Ottavia thought of it." Now, with the last impediment to their union removed, only arioso can express their joy. Poppea's words could hardly be more cold-blooded: "Now you have a just reason for her repudiation [*ripudio*]." Monteverdi sets these words to a brief tune reminiscent of her music opening the scene. When she lights on "ripudio" she repeats the word over and over to an ascending musical line depicting ecstatic happiness, if not mounting sexual excitement. (Ironically, the tune is similar to Ulisse's melody about going to see Penelope for the first time since his arrival.) Poppea's "ripudio" arioso leads Nerone into his characteristically overcompensating declamatory style: "Today I promise you, you shall become my wife." Her hopes at the point of complete realization, Poppea sings, "Si caro dì veder non spero mai" (I couldn't hope for a more precious day), repeating "si caro dì" over and over. Nerone cannot resist "playing the emperor" again with a further proclamation.

Nerone:	In the name of Jupiter and myself, Today you shall become Rome's empress: I assure you with my royal word [*in parola regal te n'assicuro*].

With telling psychological insight, Monteverdi makes Poppea eagerly repeat Nerone's words for clarification, just as she did in their first love scene. The musical exchanges created by the composer run like this:

Poppea: In parola, in parola . . .

Nerone: In parola regal.

Poppea: In parola regal?

To make sure she understands him, Nerone reiterates the entire verse with ascending musical emphasis: "In parola regal, in parola regal te n'assicuro." His climbing vocal line lays her qualms to rest with a thrillingly assertive phrase on "n'assicuro," musically (and dramatically) settling the issue. Poppea wants to sing an aria now but is too choked with emotion: "Idolo del cor mio [*rest*], del cor [*rest*], del cor mio [*rest*], del cor [*half rest*], del cor [*rest*], cor [*rest*] mio" (Idol of my heart). Even if her "love" for Nerone is only insidious social climbing, there is no question of an ironic mask between her and her audience at this moment. The world has fallen into her hands, and she can scarcely verbalize or sing her overwhelming joy. She makes a second attempt at a musical statement: "Idol del cor mio, giunta è pur l'hora, che del mio ben godrò" (Idol of my heart, the hour has come, when I may enjoy my own). Her hesitations evaporate with her self-assured and characteristically solipsistic coloratura arabesques on "mio." Poppea is ready again for song, and Nerone immediately launches their duet. "Ne più s'interporrà noia o dimora" (No annoyance shall come between us) expresses the triumph of their love and instigates the opera's climax.

Poppea/Nerone: Ne più s'interporrà noia o dimora.
                   Cor nel petto non ho,
                   Me'l rubasti, sì, sì.
                   Dal sen me lo rapì,
                   De' tuoi begl'occhi il lucido sereno,
                   Per te, ben mio, non ho più core in seno.

                   Stringerò tra le braccia innamorate,
                   Chi mi trasfisse, ohimè!
                   Non interrote havrai l'hore beate.
                   Se son perduta in te,

In te mi cercarò,
In te mi trovarò,
E tornerò a riperdermi, ben mio,
Che sempre in te perduto esser voglio io.

[No annoyance shall come between us,
My heart is no longer in my breast—
you stole it, yes, yes,
you took it from my breast,
with the bright light of your two eyes;
because of you, my dear one, I have no heart
    in my breast.
Squeeze me in your loving arms;
you've run me through, *ohimè*!
Our happy hours shall know no interruption.
If I am lost;
Seek me in you,
I'll find myself in you,
and I shall lose myself again, my own one,
for I want to be lost in you forever.]

Whatever we may think of Nerone and Poppea, it is impossible not to vicariously share in their rapture. Their duet music proves them at this moment spiritually and sexually indissoluble. It is difficult to tell where one voice leaves off and the other begins. Nerone begins the duet with a jaunty tune on "Ne più s'interporrà noia e dimora" (No annoyance shall come between us). Poppea seamlessly joins him, only to change the tone with a slower melody of her own as she initiates the verse "Cor nel petto non ho" (My heart is no longer in my breast), sentiments and music that Nerone enthusiastically adapts and develops with her. The voices flow their separate but related lines over the continuo until Nerone emphatically declares, "Stringerò tra la braccia innamorate" (Squeeze me in your loving arms), which initiates a striking passage of homophonic declamation, the lovers are one both in word and music. "Chi mi trasfisse" (You transfix me), each sings, in three soloistic bars in a languishing descending line, before they are united homophonically again with "ohimè." A few bars later Poppea returns to her slow "Cor nel petto non ho" tune, now singing, "Se son perduta

in te, in te mi cercarò" (If I am lost, seek me in you), an idea and text
Nerone picks up. The two voices seem to move closer and closer to
the thrilling homophony they had enjoyed at "Stringerò tra le braccia."
The duet reaches its musical and dramatic climax in another moment
of exhilarating unity as both sing "in te perduto(a), in te perduto(a)"
(lost in you), before the soloistic arabesques on the words "esser voglio
io" (I want to be) that form the duet's striking coda.

The two succeeding scenes offer two different individual reactions
to the climactic action Nerone and Poppea have just celebrated. Both
the Venetian and the Neapolitan scores place Arnalta's scene directly
after the lover's duet, followed by Ottavia's famous farewell to Rome.
Most of the libretto sources, however, give these scenes in reverse
order: Ottavia first, then Arnalta. The 1643 scenario asserts this order
as well. Curtis, in his edition, follows the libretto order, and the theatrical impact of this ordering, which is followed in most performances
today, proves the libretto order to be correct. He plausibly argues that
"the renowned Anna Renzi, who sang Ottavia [in the premiere], may
have felt she was being upstaged when followed by the male comic who
played Arnalta" (Monteverdi, *L'incoronazione,* Curtis ed., 223).

Anna Renzi would probably have held her own whatever scene order
was adopted. Several contemporaries have left us their impressions
of opera's first prima donna. Benedetto Farrari wrote a sonnet in her
honor, lavishing especial praise on her performance of Ottavia's final
scene: "It is not Ottavia shedding her tears, / Excited, exposed on foam-
ing shores; / It is a monster, who, with notes high and deep / Augments
the company of the Sirens" (qtd. in and trans. by Rosand, *Opera* 385).

The empress's final solo is based on the last scene in the *Octavia
praetexta.* There Octavia, accompanied by the play's sympathetic chorus
of Roman citizens, bids a clear-eyed farewell to her homeland before
entering the waiting boat.

> But now, alas,
> My brother's bark, within whose traitorous hold
> His mother once was borne; and now for me,
> Poor wretch, his slighted sister-wife, it waits.
> No more has right a place upon the earth,
> Nor heavenly gods. Grim Fury reigns supreme.

Oh, who can fitly weep my evil plight?
What nightingale has tongue to sing my woes? . . .
The death you threaten has no terrors now
For me. Go, set your ship in readiness,
Unfurl your sails, and let your pilot seek
The barren shores of Pandateria.

(Seneca, *Octavia,* Miller trans. 885–86)

Busenello's text, however, is far more problematic. The operatic queen asserts her innocence, like the queen in the tragedy; but in the operatic context these assertions are mendacious, if not pathological. "A Dio, Roma," Ottavia's final monologue, marks a special place in an opera teeming with memorable moments. Her last solo, like her entire role, is set in pure recitative. Its opening bars are a distillation of Monteverdi's genius as a dramatic composer. The first syllable of "A Dio" is repeated three times until the entire phrase is enunciated. The effect of "A— [*rest*] A— [*rest*] A— [*rest*] A Dio, Roma" is a masterstroke. The stuttered, jagged vowel repetition suggests a previously articulate character now brought to inarticulate ruin. Ottavia is too shocked, too defeated to utter coherent speech (see also Leopold 144). Her music and text hover on the edge of chaos. She is broken psychologically and musically. Her opening bars express a kind of horror and disintegration which will not be explored again in text-based music until the *sprechstimme* of expressionist scores in the early twentieth century. The music suggests an Ottavia momentarily unable to speak, unable to sing—her immediate reaction to her condemnation. The first syllable she sings, an open "A" (fifteen times in eight bars!), is the most eloquent vocal stutter in all music. Once her immediate shock wears off, her speech becomes more intelligible: "A Dio, Roma, a Dio, patria, amici, a Dio. Innocente da voi partir conviene" (Farewell, Rome, farewell, homeland, friends, farewell. Though innocent I must leave you). Ottavia evidently believes her own protestation of innocence. Busenello and Monteverdi's portrait of mental and moral disintegration is complete. Her characteristically stark recitative style yields several evocatively picturesque or decorative details. Her grief at leaving her homeland leads her to thoughts of the all-embracing air and her sighs.

L'aria, che d'hora in hora
Riceverà i miei fiati,
Li porterà, per nome del cor mio,
A veder, a baciar le patrie mura.

[The air which hour by hour
shall receive my sighs,
shall bear them in the name of my heart
both to see and kiss the walls of the homeland.]

The thought of "the air" (l'aria) bearing her "sighs" (fiate) suggests the windlike drift of the vocal line on "Per nome del cor mio." Ottavia, not normally given to romantic depictions in her music, conjures a delicate suggestion of the wind caressing her home. The three-note cadence on "mura" (walls) is as close as she may come to melodic sweetness. Characteristically, it is the thought of caressing an object, a wall no less, and not another living being, that awakens this latent lyric impulse in her. She will repeat a similar cadential effect twelve bars later when she sings of her "beloved shore" (amati lidi). Again, not a person but a locale stirs her feelings. Ottavia is a woman perilously estranged from her world and from herself.

Ahi, sacrilego duolo,
Tu m'interdici il pianto
Quando lascio la patria,
Né stillar una lacrima poss'io,
Mentre dico ai parenti, e a Roma: a Dio.

[Ah, ah, sacrilegious woe,
you prevent me from weeping when I leave my homeland.
And I cannot shed a tear
when saying to my family and to Rome: farewell.]

She is either numb to feeling or trying to resist giving her enemies the satisfaction of seeing her tears. Chafe observes that "the palpable contradiction indicates the crux of Ottavia's nature; the split between stoicism and her true feelings drives her to empty rhetoric, producing the arresting image of a weeping without tears" (Chafe 346). Ottavia's piercing notes on "tu" (you) and "interdici" (prevents) suggest her emotions are still at the boiling point. Her repetition of the phrase "I can't shed a tear saying farewell to family and Rome" suggests a shattered woman rallying all her remaining reserves of self-control before the two rests create a poignant moment of silence to preface her final words in the opera, "a Dio." Sung to a B and two low E's, Ottavia's "a Dio" makes a satisfying closure to her monologue, recalling the stuttering A's of the scene's opening. The final words, "a Dio," sound almost conversational, like the *sprechstimme* of the opening bars, but this farewell is brief, resigned. Ottavia, the most self-deceived of all the opera's characters, leaves the stage on a note of tortured self-control and self-mastery.

Arnalta's entrance reveals the secret enclosed within her name. She has been destined all along to scale the social heights, following her mistress's fortunes (see Heller, *Emblems* 161). After Ottavia's broken stuttering, the contrast of Arnalta's triumphantly belting out the words "Hoggi sarà Poppea di Roma imperatrice" (Today shall Poppea become Rome's empress) to a melodic gesture redolent of a street vendor's ditty affords another of the opera's violent shifts of perspective and tone. No sooner does she trumpet forth her crowing, plebeian tune than she shifts to a slower, more conversational meter for "I, her nurse, shall ascend the steps of the great" (Io, che son la nutrice, ascenderò delle grandezze i gradi). The setting of "ascenderò delle grandezze i gradi" is treated to a rising sequence, a well-worn cliché that seems newly minted for this occasion. "No longer shall I be among the common and low people, who used to say to me 'hey you!'; now with sweet harmony they shall gurgle 'your ladyship!' [*gorgheggierammi il 'vostra signoria!'*]." "Gorgheggierammi" is drawn out with relish, and her new title of "'your ladyship'" is treated to an undulating note pattern suggestive of the flattery Arnalta is prepared to enjoy to the full. In "'Beautiful lady, and still youthful,' those passing in the street will say," the words "'bella donna, e fresca ancora'" are treated to arioso notable for its melodiousness, like a snippet from an antiquated popular song. It is attractive, yet clichéd, as artificial as the praise. She knows all the kind words and assertions that she is "ever young looking" will be mercenary lies spoken to win favor with her mistress. She knows she is in reality as ugly as "one of the Sibyls of ancient legend," a reality related in plain recitative in a series of notes lying at the bottom of Arnalta's range. But a lifetime of servitude and disrespect will allow Arnalta now "to drink the praise from the goblet of lies" (in coppa di bugie bevo le lodi), which is sung to an upbeat arioso with an emphatic ornamentation on "bugie" (lies).

There is bitterness behind this music's joyful bounce. This becomes clearer when she observes, "Io nacqui serva, e morirò matrona" (I was born a slave, and I'll die a lady). Her late social elevation is treated to a reminiscence of the rising-step note sequence. The cliché registers now not as an aptly chosen device but as the empty, hoary old musical trick that it is. The rising notes now grace "morirò" rather than the more apt "ascenderò." In "Mal volentier morrò; se rinascessi un dì, vorrei nascer matrona e morir serva" (I won't be willing to die; if I should be reborn one day, I want to be born a lady and die a slave), the notes describing her pauper's death appropriately move downward. Arnalta's sudden reflection on her own mortality mutes the triumphalism of her opening measures, injecting a note of bitter fatalism: "Who loses greatness dies unhappy" (Chi lascia le grandezze, piangendo a morte va). Arnalta is now singing from the heart. "Ma chi servendo sta, con più felice sorte" (Who lives a slave has a happy lot): the music becomes momentarily lively again on "con più felice sorte," but this is only a momentary lightening, "for [the slave] comes to the end of his labors loving death" (come fin degli stenti ama la morte). The brief arioso ended, Arnalta closes her solo and her role in the opera with a cold recitative declamation: "ama la morte" (loving death) are the last words she sings before the coronation of Poppea.

Scene 8

The final scene is set in "the royal palace of Rome." Modern musicology has suggested that some of the musical content of the final coronation sequence may be the work of at least one other composer. (In particular see Curtis, "*La Poppea Impasticciata,*" and Monteverdi, *L'incoronazione,* Curtis ed.) Possibly Monteverdi felt himself becoming increasingly infirm or overworked and farmed out some of the final scene to a collaborator. The authorship controversy does nothing to diminish the powerful theatrical impact of the climactic sequence. The libretto calls for the fullest use of the baroque stage. In the human sphere, Nerone, Poppea, and the chorus of consuls and tribunes enact the coronation onstage. Meanwhile, several attendant deities, Amore, a chorus of "amori," and Venus "in cielo," appear in a glory viewing the ceremony from above. Nerone launches the finale by bidding his new bride, "Ascend [*Ascendi*], O my delight, ascend to the sovereign heights, to the supreme apex [*all'apice sublime*]." Nerone lapses into arioso as he describes, with characteristic egomania, that she may "count my affections among your dearest possessions." These words, "Tra i più cari trofei, adorata Poppea, gl'affetti miei," are treated to a gorgeously sensual, rocking melodic line that anticipates a melody the chorus of consuls and tribunes will sing in Poppea's praise. The languishing "dying away" of Nerone's vocal line on "affetti miei" extends over four bars. Three succeeding bars are left for the accompanimental instruments to bring this sequence to a musical period. The effect is one of great psychological insight: the human voice and words can no longer express the depths of Nerone's contentment. The instrumental closing of his musical phrase suggests the depths of an emotion that cannot be given voice. This passage, occasionally cut from performances and even recordings, represents a delicate stroke of musical and dramatic writing of a kind only granted to the smallest handful of operatic masters. The effect will be repeated twice for both Nerone and Poppea before the entry of the chorus.

Poppea's response is given music of similar imagination and psychological depth, illustrating her entire personality: "My mind is confused by this unaccustomed splendor" (Il mio genio confuso, al non usato lume). "Il mio genio," surrounded by rests, is set to low notes in Poppea's vocal compass. The effect suggests her dreamlike awakening to the fulfillment of her ambition. This moment of torpor or suspended psychological animation is brief. "Confuso, confuso" is sung rapidly, indicating her awakening excitement. In "[My mind] has almost lost the means of thanking you [*ringraziarti*], my lord. At this high summit where you have placed me, I lack enough heart to adequately venerate you. Nature should have given us for such excessive feelings [*eccessivi affetti*] another heart in our breasts [*fabbricar nei petti*]," Poppea is fully herself again when she applies her characteristically languishing ornaments to the word "ringraziarti" (thanking you). She is as seductive as ever with her caressing runs, yet her phrasing on "eccessivi affetti" (excessive emotions) suggests something of Nerone's imperious vocal style on words such as "sublime" several bars earlier. The seductress is becoming an empress. Her florid ornaments on "fabbricar nei petti" (makes [another heart] in my breast) smack of insincerity, and the trill on "petti" is positively unctuous. Like Shakespeare, Monteverdi in his operas admits the bewildering complexity of human beings.

After protestations of love solemnized by instrumental passacaglias, Nerone summons the consuls and tribunes to pay their respects to his "dear one" (O cara), leading to a wonderful coloratura phrase. Nerone not only gives the chorus of consuls and tribunes their cue to speak, he also suggests the song they should sing. His words, "Nel solo rimirarti, il popolo e 'l Senato" (Just by looking at you, the people and the Senate begin to feel blessed), enunciate one of the bold tunes the chorus is about to sing in its act of public homage. The chorus is ushered onto the stage to a splendid sinfonia. The distinctive four-note motif suggests the background for a scene of pomp and spectacle. Its insistent rhythm may also hint that all this splendor and bustle is at core a vacuous ceremony.

The chorus's bass voices arrest attention with their declaration to Poppea, "A te, sovrana augusta" (To you, to you, august sovereign). The sense of satire is immediately apparent with the elongation of the "u" in "Augusta," which is treated to ornamentation that includes a trill. This trill on "u" delivered by hearty tenor and bass voices suggests the closest thing to a musical raspberry in music (at least until Haydn's rude comments for bassoons in his later symphonies). Its ludicrousness is only just explainable as an ornament: the consuls and tribunes don't want to lose their heads by openly insulting the new empress. Whether Nerone and Poppea pick up on their irony is up to the stage director. These choristers are clearly mocking the recipient of the empress's crown, though not the crown itself, as their glorious harmonies color their lines about "the crown [we place upon] your head" (indiademiam la chioma). "Before you, Asia and Africa bow down," the basses sing to a new, animated tune. The tenors now get their turn at the fulsome solo line with the responding phrase, "Before you, Europe and the sea which coils and divides." When the tenor and bass voices join together again on "this happy empire" (quest'imperio felici), we are reminded musically and dramatically of the enormity of Poppea's new office and, inescapably, of her unworthiness. The ornamental lingering on "felice" is humorously deadpan. The basses start a tune that had been foreshadowed earlier by Nerone at his line "Nel solo rimirarti il popolo e 'l Senato" (Just by looking at you, the people and the Senate). The basses sing "[We] now consecrate ourselves to you and give you this world imperial crown" (Hora consacra e dona questa del mondo imperial corona). This bold, rocking tune sounds magnificently impressive as the basses sing it. They are joined by the tenors just as the basses initiate a sinuous coloratura decoration on "corona" (crown). Their flowing counterpoint is arrested by their monophonic "questo, questo" (this, this), which serves as a preface to another unforgettable passage as first the basses and then the tenors take turns with "imperial corona." The ornamentation and trills added to "imperial" on the final vowel are one of the most memorable moments in operatic music. First the basses, then the tenors, then the whole chorus seem to engage in a derisive chorus of laughter even as they ostensibly grant the highest honor to Poppea. The effect may be transliterated as "imperi-a-ha-ha-ha-ha-ha-ha!" The tribunes and consuls are laughing through their teeth at the corrupt emperor and his new empress, saving their own lives by doing so on a trill. The words heap praise on Poppea; the music, raucous scorn. The effect is inescapable: the laughter ornament is heard three times, first in the basses, then tenors, then in the hilarious unison that ends the chorus (see also Savage, "Love and Infamy" 205).

A new sinfonia covers the exit of the chorus of tribunes and consuls and masks the noise of the ensuing "glory." It is easy to imagine Monteverdi's lack of enthusiasm for the chorus of cupids and the exchange between Amore and Venus. The music of the "glory" as it survives in both scores is fluent but unmemorable. Then again, whoever composed it was wise enough not to attempt to musically upstage the machinist's art. The divine intervention, however ironic, is anticlimactic, at least as the music has come down to us, and the music is marked for deletion in the Venice score.

After the hubbub of the consuls and tribunes and the divine benediction of Amore and Venus, Nerone and Poppea are allowed to present themselves one last time, not as politicians nor as self-styled demigods, but as human beings, and Monteverdi's art is always most distinctive for its focus on the human.

> Pur ti miro, pur ti godo,
> Pur ti stringo, pur ti annodo,
> Più non peno, non moro,
> O mia vita, o mia tesoro.
> Io son tua, tuo son io,
> Speme mia, dillo, dì
> L'idol mio, tu se pur
> Sì mio ben, sì mio cor,
> Mia vita, sì, sì.

> [I look at you, I delight in you,
> I embrace you, I tie you to me,
> I suffer no more, I die no more,
> O my life, O my treasure,
> I am yours, you are mine,
> My hope, say it, say
> You're my idol,
> yes, my love, my life, yes.]

The duet is in ABBA structure. The A section, "I look at you, I delight in you, I embrace you, I tie you to me, I suffer no more, I die no more, O my life, O my treasure" is set to a wonderfully languorous tune; its musical structure is similar to the "Human non è" in the prologue, the opera's first duet, in which Virtù and Fortuna celebrate Amore's power—another indication of the opera's musical coherence. Its slow, steady, rocking rhythm speaks of desire met with the ultimate fulfillment. Both Nerone and Poppea indulge in garlands of ornament on the words "Pur t'annodo" (I tie you to me) that in their counterpoint seem to bind the two singing figures together. The B section offers contrasting music of a more animated character: "I am yours, you are mine, my hope, say it, say you're my idol, you, my love, my life, yes." The two voices excitedly exchange words until they are bound together in a strong homophonic statement of "sì, mio ben, sì, mio cor, mia vita, sì." The entire section is then repeated, its urgency making the climactic return of the A section all the more effective. Paolo Fabbri calls this duet "a final summary providing an ardent epitaph to the events just staged, which overrules a generic finale in some triumphal manner to go right to the heart of the dramatic substance of the work" (*Monteverdi* 261). "Pur ti miro" is, in Bianconi's words, "a true coup de théâtre" (196).

Nerone and Poppea, singing the A refrain, bring the opera to a close. Poppea adds a piquant trill to "stringo," and the lovers' voices blend and overlap. As with their earlier duet, the listener may have trouble telling where one voice ends and the other begins. Not until *Tristan und Isolde* will operatic music attempt so bold a vision of sensual love. We may loathe the individuals who are Nerone and Poppea. The savage irony that permeates the score should leave the listener in no doubt that Monteverdi appreciates their evil. But Nerone and Poppea's emotions are real to them and to the composer, and he makes them real to us. At the height of their depravity we are reminded of our kinship with them: we all share the human capacity for destruction, violence, and corruption as well as for love, joy, and ecstasy. For all its satiric attack on absolutism, *L'incoronazione di Poppea* may represent the supreme example in Western art of Terence's maxim in *The Self-Tormentor*: "Homo sum: humani nil a me alienum puto." I am a man: nothing human is alien to me.

Epilogue: A Death in Venice

In the summer following the premiere of *Poppea,* Monteverdi felt that he needed to return to Cremona and Mantua for a visit. One of his motivations was pursuit of the ever-elusive Mantuan pension moneys. His last surviving letter, dated August 20, 1643, is addressed to the doge, asking for support in his petition to the Mantuan government. Beyond his concerns with the sums owed him, he seems also to have had a desire to see for the last time the places of his youth and early career. On his journey he received numerous testimonials to the esteem in which he was held throughout Italy. One contemporary, Matteo Caberloti, in his funeral eulogy for the composer, actually attributed the onset of his final illness to the excessive zeal of his admirers.

> While the many honorary receptions [held for him] greatly improved his spirits, they served to drastically weaken his constitution, being as he was so old and in declining health. He brought upon himself [through his travels and exertions] the final illness. Like a swan that, feeling the fatal hour near, approaches the water and there passes on to another life, singing with suaver harmony than ever, so Claudio returned in great haste to Venice, the Queen of all waters.

After a nine-day illness, Monteverdi died in Venice on November 29, 1643. He was seventy-six years old. A large funeral service was held in Saint Mark's; the music was directed by Monteverdi's successor at the basilica, Giovanni Rovetta. Monteverdi was buried at the Frari church in the chapel reserved for people from the Lombard region. Caberloti writes that "with truly royal pomp a catafalque was erected in the Chiesa de Padrini Minori de Frari, decorated all in mourning, but surrounded with so many candles that the church resembled a night sky luminous with stars" (qtd. from Fabbri, with some modifications, 265–66; Schrade 368).

Postlude

The Biblioteca Marciana lies south east from St. Mark's basilica, a stone's throw from where Monteverdi presided over musicians for the last thirty years of his life. Today visitors must force their way through the throngs of tourists vying for knickknacks and gelato, past the mask and souvenir shops along the arcade, until they face the nondescript entrance to the library. Old handwritten cards catalog much of the collection, at least that part of the collection of most interest to this visitor. The prefix "Monteverdi" yields many of the expected titles. Those of Badoaro and Busenello, hardly household names but no less essential to the baroque master than Boito and Da Ponte to Verdi and Mozart, yield a glimpse of the library's unique treasures in the field of Venetian opera. In about twenty minutes, the requested "book" arrives for perusal: a compact bundle of pocket-sized pamphlets wrapped in string and construction paper. These are the scant yet evocative remains of momentous events in the history of theater and music: the libretti published for opera houses in seventeenth-century Venice. The little booklets provided the words for the ephemeral productions that made the art of opera the aesthetic commodity it is to this very day.

The booklet for *Il ritorno d'Ulisse in Patria,* for instance, was probably in someone's hand in 1640 when he or she sat in the Teatro Santi Giovanni e Paolo, Venice's best-appointed opera house at the time, to applaud not only *Ulisse* but the aged Monteverdi's return to his operatic homeland. The booklet is in marvelously superb condition despite having weathered so many centuries. One cannot resist quietly humming the melodies to Penelope's "Torna il tranquillo al mare" and the suitors' "Ama dunque, sì, sì" while reading the old text. What secrets these yellowed papers have been privy to! Packaged along with the *Ulisse* text is the libretto of *Le nozze d'Enea con Lavinia,* by an unknown poet—Monteverdi's second contribution to the Venetian opera. The words are all that remain of this Virgilian opera, offering faint hints of lost melodies, like the piper on the Grecian urn that so captivated the imagination of Keats. It is easy to lament the loss of so many of Monteverdi's works for the theater. The gaps and discrepancies in the three surviving operas pose their own insoluble mysteries. Firmer than all brittle parchment or scholarly conjecture, however, the surviving music remains as an imperishable gift to mankind: the fruits of a long life spent in the study and fearless musical articulation of all things human.

Selected Discography
and Videography

L'Orfeo

Monteverdi, Claudio. *L'Orfeo*. Orch. Le Concert d' Astrée. Perf. Ian Bostridge, Natalie Dessay, Véronique Gens. Cond. Emmanuelle Haïm. Virgin Classics, 2004.

————. *L'Orfeo*. Orch. New London Consort. Perf. John Mark Ainsley, Catherine Bott, Simon Grant. Cond. Philip Pickett. Decca L' Oiseau-Lyre, 1992.

————. *L'Orfeo*. Orch. English Baroque Soloists. Perf. Anthony Rolfe Johnson, Julianne Baird, Anne Sofie von Otter. Cond. John Eliot Gardiner. DG Archiv, 1987.

————. *L'Orfeo*. Orch. Chiaroscuro, London Baroque. Perf. Nigel Rogers, Emma Kirkby, Guillemette Laurens. Cond. Nigel Rogers and Charles Medlam. EMI, 1984.

————. *L'Orfeo*. Orch. Ensemble Elyma. Perf. Victor Torres, Gloria Banditelli, Maria Cristina Kiehr. Cond. Gabriel Garrido, K617, 1996.

————. *L'Orfeo*. Orch. Concerto Vocale. Perf. Laurence Dale, Jennifer Larmore, Andreas Scholl. Cond. René Jacobs. Harmonia Mundi, 1995.

————. *L'Orfeo*. Orch. Concentus Musicus Wien. Perf. Lajos Kozma, Cathy Berberian, Rotraud Hansmann. Cond. Nikolaus Harnoncourt. Teldec, 1969.

————. *L'Orfeo*. Orch. Le Concert des Nations. Perf. Furio Zanasi, Montserrat Figueras, Arianna Savall. Cond. Jordi Savall. Stage Director Gilbert Deflo. BBC Opus Arte DVD, 2002.

▶ All these are fine performances. The Haïm recording on Virgin Classics is the most dramatic.

Lamento d'Arianna

Baker, Janet. *Janet Baker sings D. & A. Scarlatti, Monteverdi, H. & W. Lawes and Handel*. Testament, 2003.

Figueras, Montserrat. *Claudio Monteverdi: Arie e lamenti per voca sola.* Astrée, 1993.

von Otter, Anne Sofie. *Lamenti.* DG Archiv, 1998.

▶ All these recital discs have fine versions of this short work.

Il ballo delle ingrate and *Il combattimento de Tancredi e Clorinda*

Monteverdi, Claudio. *Ottavo libro dei madrigali, Vol. 2.* Perf. Concerto Italiano. Dir. Rinaldo Alessandrini. Opus III, 1998.

▶ This recording includes both works on a single disc.

————. *Il ballo della ingrate; Sestina.* Orch. Les Arts Florissants. Cond. William Christie. Harmonia Mundi, 1996.

————. *Il combattimento de Tancredi e Clorinda; Madrigali guerreri et amorosi.* Orch. Les Arts Florissants. Cond. William Christie. Harmonia Mundi, 1998.

▶ *Il ballo* and the *Combattimento* are available on separate Harmonia Mundi discs, each of which also includes other short works by Monteverdi.

Il ritorno de Ulisse in patria

Monteverdi, Claudio. *Il ritorno de Ulisse in patria.* Orch. Ensemble Elyma. Perf. Furio Zanasi, Gloria Banditelli, Maria Cristina Kiehr, Jean-Paul Fouchécourt. Cond. Gabriel Garrido. K617, 1998.

▶ The best uncut version available.

————. *Il ritorno de Ulisse in patria.* Orch. Concentus Musicus Wien. Perf. Sven Olof Eliasson, Norma Lerer, Nigel Rogers, Paul Esswood. Cond. Nikolaus Harnoncourt. Teldec, 1973.

▶ A reliable, unabridged performance.

————. *Il ritorno de Ulisse in patria.* Orch. Concerto Vocale. Perf. Christoph Prégardien, Bernarda Fink, Christina Högman, Lorraine Hunt. Cond. René Jacobs. Harmonia Mundi, 1992.

▶ Good singers but many cuts, interpolations, and transpositions.

————. *Il ritorno de Ulisse in patria.* Orch. Les Arts Florissants. Perf. Krešmir Špicer, Marijana Mijanovič, Cyril Auvity. Cond. William Christie. Stage Dir. Adrian Noble. Virgin Classics DVD, 2004.

▶ Christie's filmed production is excellent. The heavily cut 1973 Glyndebourne production starring Janet Baker, conducted by Raymond Leppard, and directed by Peter Hall has in the past been available from different sources on videotape. It is hoped it will be reissued on DVD.

L'incoronazione di Poppea

Monteverdi, Claudio. *L'incoronazione di Poppea.* Orch. Concentus Musicus Wien. Perf. Helen Donath, Elisabeth Söderström, Cathy Berberian, and Paul Esswood. Cond. Nikolaus Harnoncourt. Teldec, 1974.

▶ Well-sung, uncut version based on Venice score.

————. *L'incoronazione di Poppea.* Orch. Ensemble Elyma. Perf. Guillemette Laurens, Flavio Oliver, Fabian Schofrin, Gloria Banditelli. Cond. Gabriel Garrido. K617, 2000.

▶ Good performance based on Naples score.

————. *L'incoronazione di Poppea.* Orch. Bavarian State Opera. Perf. Anna Caterina Antonacci, David Daniels, Dominique Visse. Cond. Ivor Bolton. Farao Classics, 1998.

▶ Excellent live performance.

————. *L'incoronazione di Poppea.* Orch. English Baroque Soloists. Perf. Sylvia McNair, Anne Sofie von Otter, Dana Hanchard, Michael Chance. Cond. John Eliot Gardiner. John Eliot Gardiner, DG Archiv, 1996.

▶ Contains cuts and re-written accompaniment.

————. *L'incoronazione di Poppea.* Orch. Concerto Vocale. Perf. Danielle Borst, Guillemette Laurens, Jennifer Larmore, Axel Köhler. Cond. René Jacobs. Harmonia Mundi, 1990.

▶ A good performance, but there are cuts and interpolations.

Bibliography

Abbate, Caroline. *In Search of Opera*. Princeton, N.J.: Princeton University Press, 2001.

Abert, Anna Amalie. *Claudio Monteverdis Bedeutung für die Entstehung des musikalischen Dramas*. Darmstadt: Wissenschaftliche Buchgesellschaft, 1979.

————. *Claudio Monteverdi und das musikalische Drama*. Lippstadt: Kistner & Siegel, 1954.

Adams, K. Gary, and Dyke Kiel. *Claudio Monteverdi: A Guide to Research*. New York: Garland, 1989.

Aercke, Kristiaan P. *Gods of Play: Baroque Festive Performance as Rhetorical Discourse*. Albany: State University of New York Press, 1994.

Ahl, Frederick M. *Lucan: An Introduction*. Ithaca, N.Y.: Cornell University Press, 1976.

Alm, Irene Marion. "Theatrical Dance in Seventeenth-Century Venetian Opera." Diss. U of California, Los Angeles, 1993.

Anderson, Nicholas. *Baroque Music: From Monteverdi to Bach*. London: Thames and Hudson, 1994.

Aristotle. *The Complete Works of Aristotle*. Rev. Oxford translation. Ed. Jonathan Barnes. 2 vols. Princeton, N.J.: Princeton University Press, 1984. Two Volumes.

Arlt, Wulf. "Der Prolog des *Orfeo* als Lehrstück der Aufführungspraxis." *Festschrift Reinhold Hammerstein*. Ed. Ludwig Finscher. Laaber, 1986. 35–52.

Arnold, Denis. *Monteverdi: The Master-Musicians*. Rev. Tim Carter. London: Dent, 1990.

Arnold, Denis, and Nigel Fortune, eds. *The New Monteverdi Companion*. London: Faber and Faber, 1985.

Audi, Pierre. Telephone interview with author. December, 2001.

Badoaro, Giacomo. *Il ritorno d'Ulisse in patria*. Libretto with translation by David G. Evans. Booklet for *Il ritorno d'Ulisse in patria,* by Claudio Monteverdi. Orch. Concentus Musicus Wien. Perf. Sven Olof Eliasson, Norma Lerer. Cond. Nikolaus Harnoncourt. Teldec, 1971.

————. *Il ritorno d'Ulisse in patria.* Libretto with translation by Derek Yeld. Booklet for *Il ritorno d'Ulisse in patria,* by Claudio Monteverdi. Orch. Concerto Vocale. Perf. Christoph Prégardien, Bernarda Fink. Cond. René Jacobs. Harmonia Mundi, 1992.

Barbier, Patrick. *The World of the Castrati: The History of an Extraordinary Operatic Phenomenon.* Trans. Margaret Crosland. London: Souvenir, 1996.

Barlow, Jeremy. "The Revival of Monteverdi's Operas in the Twentieth Century." *The Operas of Monteverdi.* English National Opera Guide 45. London: John Calder, 1992. 193–203.

Bergeron, Katherine. "The Castrato as History." *Cambridge Opera Journal* 8, no. 2 (1996): 167–84.

Bianconi, Lorenzo. *Music in the Seventeenth Century.* Trans. David Bryant. Cambridge: Cambridge University Press, 1987.

Bianconi, Lorenzo, and Thomas Walker. "Production, Consumption and Political Function of Seventeenth-Century Opera." *Early Music History* 4 (1984): 209–96.

Bianconi, Lorenzo, and Giorgio Pestelli, eds. *Opera on Stage.* Vol. 5 of *The History of Italian Opera.* Chicago: University of Chicago Press, 2002.

Bokina, John. *Opera and Politics: From Monteverdi to Henze.* New Haven, Conn.: Yale University Press, 1997.

Bouwsma, William J. *Venice and the Defense of Republican Liberty.* Berkeley: University of California Press, 1968.

Brinton, Selwyn. *The Gonzaga: Lords of Mantua.* London: Methuen, 1927.

Brown, Kate. "Representations." In *Performing Practice in Monteverdi's Music.* Ed. Raffaello Monterosso. Cremona: Fondazione Claudio Monteverdi, 1995. 265–74.

Busenello, Giovanni Francesco. *L'incoronazione di Poppea.* Libretto with translation by Avril Bardoni. Booklet for *L'incoronazione di Poppea,* by Claudio Monteverdi. Orch. English Baroque Soloists. Perf. Sylvia McNair, Anne Sofie von Otter. Cond. John Eliot Gardiner. Archiv 1996.

————. *L'incoronazione di Poppea.* Libretto and uncredited translation. Booklet for *L'incoronazione di Poppea,* by Claudio Monteverdi. Orch. Concentus Musicus Wien. Perf. Helen Donath, Elisabeth Söderström. Cond. Nikolaus Harnoncourt. Teldec, 1974.

Cameron, Euan, ed. *Early Modern Europe: An Oxford History.* Oxford: Oxford University Press, 1999.

Carlson, Marvin. *Theories of the Theatre: A Historical and Critical Survey from the Greeks to the Present.* Ithaca, N.Y.: Cornell University Press, 1984.

Carter, Tim. "'In Love's Harmonious Consort'? Penelope and the Interpretation of *Il ritorno d' Ulisse in patria.*" *Cambridge Opera Journal* 5, no. 1 (1993): 1–16.

———. "Monteverdi Returns to his Homeland." *The Operas of Monteverdi.* English National Opera Guide 45. London: John Calder, 1992. 72–81.

———. *Monteverdi's Musical Theater.* New Haven, Conn.: Yale University Press, 2002.

———. "Re-Reading *Poppea:* Some Thoughts on Music and Meaning in Monteverdi's Last Opera." *Journal of the Royal Musical Association* 122 (1997): 173–204.

———. "Resemblance and Representation: Towards a New Aesthetic in the Music of Monteverdi." *Con che soavità: Studies in Italian Opera, Song, and Dance, 1580–1740.* Ed. Iain Fenlon and Tim Carter. Oxford: Oxford University Press, 1995. 118–34.

Celletti, Rodolfo. *A History of Bel Canto.* Trans. Frederick Fuller. Oxford: Oxford University Press, 1991.

Chafe, Eric. *Monteverdi's Tonal Language.* New York: Schirmer, 1992.

Christie, William. Interview with author, New York City, November, 2001.

Clark, George, Sir. *The Seventeenth Century.* 2nd ed. New York: Galaxy Press, 1961.

Clubb, Louise George. *Giambattista della Porta, Dramatist.* Princeton, N.J.: Princeton University Press, 1965.

———. *Italian Drama in Shakespeare's Time.* New Haven, Conn.: Yale University Press, 1989.

Cochrane, Eric, ed. *The Late Italian Renaissance, 1525–1630.* New York: Harper & Row, 1970.

Curtis, Alan. "*La Poppea impasticciata,* or, Who Wrote the Music to *L'incoronazione* (1643)?" *Journal of the American Musicological Society* 42 (1989): 23–54.

Cusick, Suzanne G. "'There Was Not One Lady Who Failed to Shed a Tear': 'Arianna's Lament' and the Construction of Modern Womanhood." *Early Music* 22 (February 1994): 21–41.

Dame, Joke. "Unveiled Voices: Sexual Difference and the Castrato." *Queering the Pitch: The New Gay and Lesbian Musicology.* Ed. Philip Brett, Elizabeth Wood, and Gary C. Thomas. New York: Routledge, 1994.

Dante Alighieri. *The Divine Comedy.* Trans. John Ciardi. New York: Norton, 1977.

Davies, Alun. "The Hellenism of Early Italian Opera." *Themes in Drama.* Vol. 3. Cambridge: Cambridge University Press, 1981. 31–45.

Day, Christine J. "The Theater of SS. Giovanni e Paolo and Monteverdi's *L'incoronazione di Poppea.*" *Current Musicology* 25 (1978): 22–38.

Dell'Antonio, Andrew. "*Il divino Claudio*: Monteverdi and Lyric Nostalgia in Fascist Italy." *Cambridge Opera Journal* 8 (1996): 271–84.

de' Paoli, Domenico. *Claudio Monteverdi*. Milan: Rusconi, 1979.

De Van, Gilles. *Verdi's Theater: Creating Drama through Music*. Trans. Gilda Roberts. Chicago: University of Chicago Press, 1998.

Dio Cassius. *Dio's Roman History*. Trans. Earnest Cary. 9 vols. London: Heinemann, 1925.

Donington, Robert. *Opera and Its Symbols: The Unity of Words, Music, and Staging*. New Haven, Conn.: Yale University Press, 1990.

Fabbri, Paolo. *Monteverdi*. Trans. Tim Carter. Cambridge: Cambridge University Press, 1994.

———. "Musical Theater in Venice." *The Operas of Monteverdi*. English National Opera Guide, no. 45. London: John Calder, 1992. 60–64.

———. "New Sources for *Poppea*." *Music and Letters* 74 (1993): 16–23.

Fabbri, Paolo, and Angelo Pompilio, eds. *Il corago, o vero Alcune osservazione per metter bene in scena le composizioni drammatiche*. Studi e testi per la storia della musica 4. Florence: Olschki, 1983.

Fenlon, Iain. "The Mantuan Stage Works." *The New Monteverdi Companion*. Ed. Denis Arnold and Nigel Fortune. London: Faber and Faber, 1985. 251–87.

———. "Monteverdi, Opera and History." *The Operas of Monteverdi*. English National Opera Guide 45. London: John Calder, 1992. 7–14.

———. *Cambridge Studies in Music*. Cambridge: Cambridge University Press, 1980.

———. "The Origins of the Seventeenth-Century Staged Ballo." *Con che soavità: Studies in Italian Opera, Song, and Dance, 1580–1740*. Ed. Iain Fenlon and Tim Carter. Oxford: Oxford University Press, 1995. 13–40.

Fenlon, Iain, and Peter Miller. "Public Vice, Private Virtue." *The Operas of Monteverdi*. English National Opera Guide 45. London: John Calder, 1992. 129–37.

———. *The Song of the Soul: Understanding* Poppea. London: Royal Musical Association, 1992.

Ferrero, Mercedes Viale. "Stage and Set." *Opera on Stage*. Ed. Lorenzo Bianconi and Giorgio Pestelli. Chicago: University of Chicago Press, 2002. 1–123.

Ficino, Marsilio. *Marsilio Ficino's Commentary on Plato's* Symposium: *The Text and a Translation*. With an introduction by Sears Reynolds Jayne. Columbia: University of Missouri Press, 1944.

Fischer, Kurt von. "Eine wenig beachtete Quelle zu Busenellos *L'incoronazione di Poppea*." *Congresso internazionale sul tema Claudio Monteverdi e il suo tempo: Relazioni e comunicazioni*. Verona: Stamperia Valdoneya, 1969. 75–80.

Freeman, David. "Telling the Story." *Claudio Monteverdi:* Orfeo. Ed. John Whenham. Cambridge: Cambridge University Press, 1986. 156–66.

Gallico, Claudio. *Autobiografia di Claudio Monteverdi.* Lucca: Akademos & Lim, 1995.

Gerson, Lloyd P., ed. *The Cambridge Companion to Plotinus.* Cambridge: Cambridge University Press, 1996.

Glixon, Jonathan. "Was Monteverdi a Traitor?" *Music and Letters* 72 (1991): 404–6.

Glover, Jane. *Cavalli.* New York: St. Martins Press, 1978.

———. "The Venetian Operas." *The New Monteverdi Companion.* Ed. Denis Arnold and Nigel Fortune. London: Faber and Faber, 1985. 288–315.

Gordon, Bonnie. *Monteverdi's Unruly Women: The Power of Song in Early Modern Italy.* Cambridge: Cambridge University Press, 2004.

———. "Talking Back: The Female Voice in *Il ballo delle ingrate.*" *Cambridge Opera Journal* 11 (1999): 1–30.

Gould, Thomas. *The Ancient Quarrel between Poetry and Philosophy.* Princeton, N.J.: Princeton University Press, 1990.

Guccini, Geraldo. "Directing Opera." *Opera on Stage.* Ed. Lorenzo Bianconi and Giorgio Pestelli. Chicago: University of Chicago Press, 2002. 125–76.

Haar, James. *Essays on Italian Poetry and Music in the Renaissance, 1350–1600.* Berkeley: University of California Press, 1986.

Hall, James. *A History of Ideas and Images in Italian Art.* London: John Murray, 1995.

Hanning, B. R. *Of Poetry and Music's Power.* Ann Arbor: University of Michigan Press, 1980.

Harnoncourt, Nikolaus. *The Musical Dialogue: Thoughts on Monteverdi, Bach, and Mozart.* Trans. Mary O'Neill. Portland, Ore.: Amadeus Press, 1989.

Heller, Wendy. *Emblems of Eloquence: Opera and Women's Voices in Seventeenth-Century Venice.* Berkeley: University of California Press, 2003.

———. "Reforming Achilles: Gender, Opera Seria, and the Rhetoric of the Enlightened Hero." *Early Music* 26 (1998): 562–81.

———. "Tacitus Incognito: Opera as History in *L'incoronazione di Poppea.*" *Journal of the American Musicological Society* 52, no. 1 (1999): 39–96.

Herington, John. "Octavia Praetexta: A Survey." *Classical Quarterly* 2 (1961): 18–30.

———. *Poetry into Drama: Early Tragedy and the Greek Poetic Tradition.* Berkeley: University of California Press, 1985.

Heriot, Angus. *The Castrati in Opera.* New York: Da Capo Press, 1975.

Highet, Gilbert. *The Classical Tradition: Greek and Roman Influences on Western Literature.* New York: Oxford University Press, 1966.

Holmes, George, ed. *The Oxford Illustrated History of Italy.* Oxford: Oxford University Press, 1997.

Holzer, Robert R. Rev. of *The Song of the Soul,* by Iain Fenlon and Peter Miller. *Cambridge Opera Journal* 5 (1993): 79–92.

Homer. *The Odyssey.* With translation by A. T. Murray. Loeb Classical Library. Cambridge, Mass.: Harvard University Press, 1980.

Horowitz, Joseph. *Conversations with Arrau.* New York: Alfred A. Knopf, 1982.

Hyginus. *The Myths of Hyginus.* Trans. and ed. Mary Grant. Lawrence: University of Kansas Publications, 1960.

Ivry, Benjamin. "Monteverdi Arrives in Milwaukee." *Opera News,* October 1988, 10–14.

Jones, Ann Rosland, and Peter Stallybrass. "Fetishizing Gender: Constructing the Hermaphrodite in Renaissance Europe." *Body Guards: The Cultural Politics of Gender Ambiguity.* Ed. Julia Epstein and Kristina Staub. New York: Routledge, 1991. 80–111.

Kelly, Thomas Forrest. *First Nights: Five Musical Premieres.* New Haven, Conn.: Yale University Press, 2000.

Kerman, Joseph. "The Full Monte: The Monteverdi Cycle at the Brooklyn Academy of Music." *New York Review of Books* 49, no. 10 (June 13, 2002): 36–38.

———. *Opera as Drama.* Rev. ed. Berkeley: University of California Press, 1988.

———. "Orpheus and the Neoclassic Vision." *Claudio Monteverdi:* Orfeo. Ed. John Whenham. Cambridge: Cambridge University Press, 1986. 126–37.

Ketterer, Robert C. "Neoplatonic Light and Dramatic Genre in Busenello's *L'incoronazione di Poppea* and Noris's *Il repudio d'Ottavia.*" *Music and Letters* 80, no. 1 (1999): 1–22.

Kivey, Peter. *Osmin's Rage: Philosophical Reflections on Opera, Drama, and Text.* Princeton, N.J.: Princeton University Press, 1988.

Konold, Wulf. *Monteverdi.* Hamburg: Rowahlt, 2000.

Kristeller, Paul Oskar. *Renaissance Thought and Its Sources.* Ed. Michael Mooney. New York: Columbia University Press, 1979.

Lauritzen, Peter. *Venice: A Thousand Years of Culture and Civilization.* London: Weidenfeld and Nicholson, 1978.

Leclerc, Hélène. *Venise baroque et l'opéra.* Paris: Armand Colin, 1987.

Lee, M. Owen. *Virgil as Orpheus: A Study of the Georgics.* Albany: State University of New York Press, 1996.

Leopold, Silke. *Monteverdi: Music in Transition.* Trans. Anne Smith. Oxford: Oxford University Press, 1991.

Leppard, Raymond. *Authenticity in Music*. Portland, Ore.: Amadeus Press, 1988.

Lindenberger, Herbert. *Opera in History: From Monteverdi to Cage*. Stanford, Calif.: Stanford University Press, 1998.

———. *Opera: The Extravagant Art*. Ithaca, N.Y.: Cornell University Press, 1984.

McClary, Susan. "Constructions of Gender in Monteverdi's Dramatic Music." *Cambridge Opera Journal* 1, no. 3 (1989): 203–23.

———. "Gender Ambiguities and Erotic Excess in Seventeenth-Century Venetian Opera." *Acting on the Past: Historical Performance across the Discipline*. Ed. Mark Franko and Ann Richards. Hanover, N.H.: Wesleyan University Press, 2000. 177–200.

Mellers, Wilfred. *The Masks of Orpheus: Seven Stages in the Story of European Music*. Manchester: Manchester University Press, 1987.

Metzger, Heinz-Klaus, and Rainer Riehn, eds. *Claudio Monteverdi: Um die Geburt der Oper*. Munich: Musik-Konzepte, 1995.

Monteverdi, Claudio. *L'incoronazione di Poppea*. Facsimile ed. of the manuscript in the Biblioteca Nazionale di San Marco, Venice. Ed. Giacomo Benvenuti. Milan: Fratelli Bocca, 1938.

———. *L'incoronazione di Poppea*. Ed. Alan Curtis. London: Novello, 1989.

———. *Tutte le opere*. Ed. G. Francesco Malipiero. 17 vols. Asolo, 1926–42.

Monteverdi Gastspiele: Opernhaus Zürich. Ed. Claus Helmut Drese. Zurich: Orel Füssli, 1979.

Morris, Jan. *The Venetian Empire: A Sea Voyage*. New York: Harcourt Brace Jovanovich, 1980.

Murata, Margaret. "Singing about Singing, or the Power of Music Sixty Years After." *In Cantu et in Sermone: For Nino Pirrotta on his 80th Birthday*. Ed. Fabrizio Della Seta and Franco Piperno. Florence: Olschki, 1989. 363–82.

Murray, Linda. *The High Renaissance and Mannerism: Italy, the North, and Spain, 1500–1600*. London: Oxford University Press, 1967.

Norman, Larry F. *The Theatrical Baroque*. Chicago: University of Chicago Press, 2001.

Norwich, John Julius. *A History of Venice*. New York: Vintage Books, 1989.

Ogg, David. *Europe in the Seventeenth Century*. 8th ed. New York: Collier Books, 1962.

O'Grady, Deirdre. *The Last Troubadours: Poetic Drama in Italian Opera, 1597–1887*. London: Routledge, 1991.

Osthoff, Wolfgang. *Das dramatische Spätwerk Claudio Monteverdis*. Tutzing: Schneider, 1960.

Ovid. *Metamorphoses*. Trans. Mary M. Innes. London: Penguin, 1982.

Palisca, Claude V. *The Florentine Camerata.* New Haven, Conn.: Yale University Press, 1989.

————. *Humanism in Italian Renaissance Musical Thought.* New Haven, Conn.: Yale University Press, 1985.

Parker, Geoffrey. *Europe in Crisis, 1598–1648.* Ithaca. N.Y.: Cornell University Press, 1979.

Parker, Roger, ed. *The Oxford Illustrated History of Opera.* Oxford: Oxford University Press, 1994.

Pascucci, Daphne. "European Stage Design in the Age of Monteverdi: Costume in Early Italian Opera and Spectacle." *Performing Practice in Monteverdi's Music.* Ed. Raffaello Monterosso. Cremona: Fondazione Claudio Monteverdi, 1995. 215–64.

Pass, Walter. "Monteverdis *Il ritorno d' Ulisse in patria.*" *Performing Practice in Monteverdi's Music,* Ed. Raffaello Monterosso. Cremona: Fondazione Claudio Monteverdi, 1995. 175–82.

Pennington, D. H. *Europe in the Seventeenth Century.* 2nd ed. London: Longman, 1989.

Pickett, Philip. "*Armonia Celeste:* Orchestral Colour and Symbolism in Monteverdi's *L'Orfeo.*" *Performing Practice in Monteverdi's Music.* Ed. Raffaello Monterosso. Cremona: Fondazione Claudio Monteverdi, 1995. 143–62.

————. "Behind the Mask." Booklet for *L'Orfeo,* by Claudio Monteverdi. Orch. New London Consort. Perf. John Mark Ainsley, Catherine Bott. Cond. Philip Pickett. Decca L'Oiseau-Lyre, 1992.

Pirrotta, Nino. *Music and Culture in Italy from the Middle Ages to the Baroque: A Collection of Essays.* Cambridge: Harvard University Press, 1984.

Pirrotta, Nino, and Elena Povoledo. *Music and Theater from Poliziano to Monteverdi.* Trans. Karen Eales. Cambridge: Cambridge University Press, 1982.

Plato. *The Collected Dialogues.* Ed. E. Hamilton and H. Cairns. Princeton, N.J.: Princeton University Press, 1961.

Plotinus. *The Enneads.* Trans. Stephan MacKenna. London: Faber and Faber, 1946.

Poe, Joe Park. "*Octavia praetexta* and Its Senecan Model." *American Journal of Philology* 110 (1989): 434–59.

Porta, Giambattista Della. *Teatro.* Vol. 1, *Le tragedie.* Naples: Istituto Universitario Orientale, 1978.

Prunières, Henri. *Monteverdi: His Life and Work.* Trans. Marie D. Mackie. New York: Dover, 1972.

Pryer, Anthony. "Authentic Performance, Authentic Experience and 'Pur ti miro' from *Poppea*." *Performing Practice in Monteverdi's Music*. Ed. Raffaello Monterosso. Cremona: Fondazione Claudio Monteverdi, 1995. 191–214.

Redlich, Hans Ferdinand. *Claudio Monteverdi: Life and Works*. Trans. Kathleen Dale. Westport, Conn.: Greenwood, 1970.

Rehm, Rush. *Greek Tragic Theater*. London: Routledge, 1992.

Ringer, Mark. *Electra and the Empty Urn: Metatheater and Role Playing in Sophocles*. Chapel Hill: University of North Carolina Press, 1998.

————. "For the Father of Opera, a Rare Family Reunion: BAM Gathers the Children of Opera's Father." *New York Times,* Arts and Leisure Section, April 7, 2002.

Rinuccini, Ottavio. *Arianna*. Libretto with translation by Patrick Boyle. Booklet for *Arianna,* by Alexander Goehr. Orch. Arianna Ensemble. Perf. Ruby Philogene, Philip Sheffield. Cond. William Lacey. NMC,1998.

Roche, Jerome. *The Madrigal*. 2nd ed. Oxford: Oxford University Press, 1990.

Rogers, Nigel. "Some Thoughts on Monteverdi's *Orfeo* and a Suggested Alternative Ending." *Performing Practice in Monteverdi's Music*. Ed. Raffaello Monterosso. Cremona: Fondazione Claudio Monteverdi, 1995. 183–90.

Rosand, David. *Myths of Venice: The Figuration of a State*. Chapel Hill: University of North Carolina Press, 2001.

Rosand, Ellen. "The Bow of Ulysses." *Journal of Musicology* 12 (1994): 376–95.

————. "The Descending Tetrachord: An Emblem of Lament." *Musical Quarterly* 65 (1979): 346–95.

————. "Iro and the Interpretation of *Il ritorno d'Ulisse in patria*." *Journal of Musicology* 7 (1989): 141–64.

————. "Monteverdi's *Il ritorno d'Ulisse in patria* and the Power of 'Music.'" *Cambridge Opera Journal* 7, no. 3 (1995): 179–84.

————. "Monteverdi's Mimetic Art: *L'incoronazione di Poppea*." *Cambridge Opera Journal* 1, no. 2 (1989): 113–37.

————. *Opera in Seventeenth-Century Venice: The Creation of a Genre*. Berkeley: University of California Press, 1991.

————. "The Opera Scenario, 1638–1655: A Preliminary Survey." *In Cantu et in Sermone: For Nino Pirrotta on his 80th Birthday*. Ed. Fabrizio Della Seta and Franco Piperno. Florence: Olschki, 1989. 335–46.

————. "Operatic Ambiguities and the Power of Music." *Cambridge Opera Journal* 4, no. 1 (1992): 75–80.

————. "Seneca and the Interpretation of *L'incoronazione di Poppea*." *Journal of the American Musicological Society* 38 (1985): 34–71.

Rosenthal, Albi. "Aspects of the Monteverdi Revival in the 20th Century." *Performing Practice in Monteverdi's Music.* Ed. Raffaello Monterosso. Cremona: Fondazione Claudio Monteverdi, 1995. 119–24.

Rosselli, John. "From Princely Service to the Open Market: Singers of Italian Opera and Their Patrons, 1600–1850." *Cambridge Opera Journal* 1, no. 1 (1989): 1–32.

————. *Singers of Italian Opera: The History of a Profession.* Cambridge: Cambridge University Press, 1992.

————. "Song into Theater: The Beginnings of Opera." *The Cambridge Companion to Singing.* Ed. John Potter. Cambridge: Cambridge University Press, 2000. 83–95.

Saslow, James M. *The Medici Wedding of 1589: Florentine Festival as Theatrum Mundi.* New Haven, Conn.: Yale University Press, 1996.

Savage, Edward B. "Love and Infamy: The Paradox of Monteverdi's *L'incoronazione di Poppea.*" *Comparative Drama* 4 (1970): 197–207.

Savage, Jack. "The Spanish Contribution to the Birth of Opera." *The Operas of Monteverdi.* English National Opera Guide 45. London: John Calder, 1992. 65–71.

Savage, Roger, and Matteo Sansone. "*Il corago* and the Staging of Early Opera." *Early Music* 17 (1989): 495–511.

Schrade, Leo. *Monteverdi: Creator of Modern Music.* New York: Norton, 1950.

Segal, Charles. *Orpheus: The Myth of the Poet.* Baltimore, Md.: John Hopkins University Press, 1989.

————. *Singers, Heroes, and Gods in the Odyssey.* Ithaca, N.Y.: Cornell University Press, 1994.

Sempe, Skip. "Old Passions, New Players: Monteverdi and the Need for a New Kind of Authenticity." *Musical Times* 134 (1993): 371–75.

Seneca. *Four Tragedies and Octavia.* Trans. E. F. Watling. Harmondsworth: Penguin, 1987.

————. *Octavia.* Trans. Frank Justus Miller in *The Complete Roman Drama.* Ed. George E. Duckworth. Vol. 2. New York: Random House, 1967.

Seutonius. *Lives of the Caesars.* Trans. with an introduction and notes by Catherine Edwards. Oxford: Oxford University Press, 2000.

Sevieri, Maria Paola. *Le nozze d'Enea con Lavinia.* Recco: Ferrari, 1997.

Shearman, John. *Mannerism.* London: Penguin Books, 1987.

Shepherd, Michael, ed. *Friend to Mankind: Marsilio Ficino, 1433–1499.* Bury St. Edmunds, Shepheard-Walwayn, 1999.

Sherman, Bernard D. "Singing Like a Native: Alan Curtis, Rinaldo Alessandrini, and Anthony Rooley on Monteverdi." *Inside Early Music: Conversations with Performers.* Ed. Bernard D. Sherman. Oxford: Oxford University Press, 1997. 133–56.

Smith, Patrick J. *The Tenth Muse: A Historical Study of the Opera Libretto.* New York: Schirmer, 1975.

Solomon, J. "The Neoplatonic Apotheosis in Monteverdi's *L'Orfeo.*" *Studi musicali* 24 (1995): 27–47.

Somerset-Ward, Richard. *Angels and Monsters: Male and Female Sopranos in the Story of Opera.* New Haven, Conn.: Yale University Press, 2004.

Sørenson, Villy. *Seneca: The Humanist at the Court of Nero.* Trans. W. Glyn Jones. Chicago: University of Chicago Press, 1984.

Sternfeld, F. W. "Aspects of Aria." *Con che soavità: Studies in Italian Opera, Song, and Dance, 1580–1740.* Ed. Iain Fenlon and Tim Carter. Oxford: Oxford University Press, 1995. 111–17.

————. *The Birth of Opera.* Oxford: Oxford University Press, 1993.

Stevens, Denis. *Monteverdi in Venice.* Madison, Wis.: Farleigh Dickinson University Press, 2001.

————. *Monteverdi: Sacred, Secular, and Occasional Music.* London: Fairleigh Dickinson University Press, 1978.

Stevens, Denis, ed. and trans. *The Letters of Claudio Monteverdi.* Cambridge: Cambridge University Press, 1980.

Stevens, Denis, and Nigel Fortune, eds. *The New Monteverdi Companion.* New York: Norton, 1968.

Stravinsky, Igor. *Themes and Conclusions.* London: Faber and Faber, 1972.

Striggio, Alessandro. *L'Orfeo.* Libretto with translation by Avril Bardoni. Booklet for *L'Orfeo,* by Claudio Monteverdi. Orch. New London Consort. Perf. John Mark Ainsley, Catherine Bott. Cond. Philip Pickett. Decca L'Oiseau-Lyre, 1992.

————. *L'Orfeo.* Libretto with uncredited translation. Booklet for *L'Orfeo,* by Claudio Monteverdi. Orch. Concentus Musicus Wien. Perf. Lajos Kozma, Cathy Berberian. Cond. Nikolaus Harnoncourt. Teldec, 1969.

Strinati, Claudio, and Rossella Vodret. *Caravaggio and His Italian Followers: From the Collections of the Galleria Nazionale d'Arte Antica di Roma.* Venice: Marsilio, 1998.

Sullivan, J. P. *Literature and Politics in the Age of Nero.* Ithaca, N.Y.: Cornell University Press, 1985.

Tacitus. *The Annals of Imperial Rome.* Trans. Michael Grant. Harmondsworth: Penguin, 1981.

Taylor, A. E. *Platonism and Its Influence.* New York: Cooper Square, 1963.

Tomlinson, Gary. *Metaphysical Song: An Essay on Opera.* Princeton, N.J.: Princeton University Press, 1997.

————. *Monteverdi and the End of the Renaissance.* Berkeley: University of California Press, 1987.

————. *Music and Renaissance Magic: Towards a Historiography of Others.* Chicago: University of Chicago Press, 1993.

van der Kooij, Fred, and Rainer Riehn. "*Orfeo* oder die Ohnmacht der Musik." *Claudio Monteverdi: Um die Geburt der Opera.* Ed. Heinz-Klaus Metzger and Rainer Riehn. Musik-Konzepte 88. Munich: Bosch-Druck, 1997. 94–104.

Vince, Ronald W. *Renaissance Theatre: A Historiographical Handbook.* Westport, Conn.: Greenwood, 1984.

Virgil. *Ecologues, Georgics, Aeneid 1–6.* Trans. H. Rushton Fairclough. Cambridge: Loeb Classical Library, 1994.

Wallis, R. T. *Neoplatonism.* 2nd ed. Indianapolis: Hackett, 1995.

Walton, J. Michael. *Greek Theatre Practice.* London: Methuen, 1991.

Whenham, John. "The Later Madrigals and Madrigal Books." *The New Monteverdi Companion.* Ed. Denis Arnold and Nigel Fortune. London: Faber and Faber, 1985. 216–47.

————. "A Masterpiece for a Court." *The Operas of Monteverdi.* English National Opera Guide 45. London: John Calder, 1992. 20–28.

Whenham, John, ed. *Claudio Monteverdi: Orfeo.* Cambridge: Cambridge University Press, 1986.

Whitman, Lucile Yow. *The* Octavia: *Introduction, Text, and Commentary.* Berne: Haupt, 1978.

Index

All works cited below are by Claudio Monteverdi, unless otherwise indicated.

Track Descriptions and Listing

L'Orfeo, René Jacobs/Concerto Vocale
From harmonia mundi HMC 901553.54

1. Toccata (1:49)

   This jaunty fanfare, which opens *L'Orfeo*, was probably the ceremonial entrance music for Monteverdi's patron, the Duke of Mantua. The late Renaissance wind and percussion instruments create a bracing sonority that immediately captures the listener's attention. The toccata serves as introduction not only to *L'Orfeo*, but to the entire operatic tradition. (See discussion chapter 3, pp. 45–46).

2. La Musica Prologue, Efrat Ben-Nun, soprano (6:33)

   After the toccata, the allegorical figure of Music herself introduces the audience both to the story of the semi-divine singer Orpheus (Orfeo) and to the new style of performance in which it will be presented: a drama in music. The prologue's instrumental refrain or ritornello will reappear at pivotal moments in the later action. Monteverdi is here prefiguring something of Wagner's leitmotif technique nearly three and a half centuries in the future. (See discussion chapter 3, pp. 46–49).

3. "Possente spirto," Laurence Dale, tenor (5:06)

4. Ritornello (harp): "Orfeo son io," Laurence Dale, tenor (4:39)

   Here, in one of the first great set pieces of operatic music, Orfeo pleads with the forces of the underworld to return his beloved wife to him. According to classical mythology, Orfeo was the greatest singer who ever lived, capable of moving not only humans and animals, but inanimate nature as well through his powers of performance. Monteverdi utilizes every device of vocal and instrumental technique to convey the most powerful of human emotions. His elaboration of the words through stunning vocal ornamentation is both musically thrilling and powerfully dramatic. (See discussion chapter 3, pp. 66–70).

Il ballo delle ingrate, William Christie/Les Arts Florissants
From harmonia mundi HMT 7901108

5. Ballo (4:49)

    This is one of Monteverdi's best-known purely instrumental passages. It comes from a *ballo,* a late-Renaissance courtly musical and theatrical entertainment. This *ballo,* written for a royal wedding, warns courtly ladies to gratify their lovers or run the risk of being condemned to hell as one of the *ingrate,* or ungrateful ladies. The instruments offer hauntingly somber music for the ghostly *ingrate* dancers. (See discussion chapter 4, pp. 105–106).

Il ritorno d'Ulisse in patria, René Jacobs/Concerto Vocale
From harmonia mundi HMC 901427.29

6. Penelope's opening scene: "Di misera regina," Bernarda Fink (Penelope), Jocelyne Taillon (Ericlea), mezzo-sopranos (10:50)

    Opera's first great heroine, Queen Penelope, laments her husband Ulisse's long absence. Penelope's attendant, Ericlea, comforts her. Penelope pleads with the gods for his safe return with a searing repeated motif, "Torna, deh, torna, Ulisse!" Penelope sings a brief, delicate aria describing the returning patterns in nature ("Torna il tranquillo al mare"), hoping that fate will allow Ulisse a similar return. (See discussion chapter 6, pp. 148–153).

7. Iro's lament: "O dolor!" Guy de Mey, tenor (6:02)

    Iro, the stuttering glutton, is opera's first vividly drawn comic character. His solo parodies the idea of operatic lament. Instead of grieving over lost love, as Penelope does in the passage above, Iro grieves over the loss of the free food he had been receiving before Ulisse's return. While the music accents Iro's comic ludicrousness, it also suggests, rather disturbingly, that the character is going insane. Monteverdi, like his near contemporary Shakespeare, is notable for the psychological complexity of his characters. (See discussion chapter 6, pp. 199–201).

8. Aria and duet: "Illustratevi, o Cieli," Bernarda Fink, mezzo-soprano; Christoph Prégardien, tenor (4:10)

    Reunited with her husband at last, Penelope sings one of early opera's most glorious arias, then engages in a touching duet with Ulisse, which ends the opera. Throughout this opera, Monteverdi creates music that is fully equal to the nobility and humanity of Homer's great epic. (See discussion chapter 6, pp. 209–211).

L'Incoronazione di Poppea, René Jacobs/Concerto Vocale
From harmonia mundi HMC 901330.32

9. Seneca and his disciples: "Amici, è giunta l'ora," Michael Schopper, bass; Dominique Visse, counter-tenor; Gerd Türk, tenor; Andreas Lebeda, baritone (5:51)

    The philosopher Seneca has been ordered by the tyrannical Roman emperor Nero (Nerone) to commit suicide because of Seneca's opposition to Nerone's adulterous affair with Poppea. Seneca calmly relates this distressing news to his friends and disciples in flowing recitative, while their struggle to dissuade him from death utilizes vocal ensemble, solo singing, and the help of the instrumental accompaniment. As with Mozart, Verdi, and Wagner, Monteverdi proves himself a master musical dramatist, creating music that thrillingly vivifies every moment on stage while revealing profound insight into the characters' complex, often contradictory personalities. (See discussion chapter 7, pp. 264–268).

10. Nerone, Lucano scene: "Or che Seneca è morto," Guillemette Laurens, mezzo-soprano; Guy de Mey, tenor (7:34)

    Nerone and the court poet, Lucano, partake in a decadent "singing competition" celebrating Seneca's death and the beauty of Poppea. This scene is a musical and dramatic tour de force, revealing the opera's uniquely disturbing irony. Monteverdi and his librettist have used ancient Roman history to create a striking commentary on the Italy of their own time—a world of dangerous autocrats, political corruption, and an often deliberate blurring of state-sponsored art and reality. (See discussion chapter 7, pp. 271–273).

11. Poppea and Arnalta's "lullaby" scene, Danielle Borst, soprano; Christoph Homberger, tenor (6:58)

    Poppea, also happy that Seneca is out of the way, decides to nap in her garden. Arnalta, her nurse, a role designed for a comic tenor in drag, sings Poppea to sleep with one of the loveliest lullabies ever written. As in the Iro passage from *Ulisse,* a character who has been used primarily as a comic foil here reveals an unsuspected depth of human feeling. (See discussion chapter 7, pp. 285–286).

12. Ottavia: "Addio, Roma," Jennifer Larmore, mezzo-soprano (4:21)

    The shattered empress Ottavia faces exile and certain death. Her brief monologue, complete with stammering, shell-shocked repetitions created by the composer, makes hers one of the most coveted mezzo roles in early opera. Her musical characterization throughout the opera is notable for its psychologically compelling suggestion of emotional turmoil and dangerous instability. (See discussion chapter 7, pp. 299–301).

13. Nerone, Poppea duet: "Pur ti miro," Guillemette Laurens, mezzo-soprano; Danielle Borst, soprano (4:18)

    Nerone and Poppea celebrate their marriage and her coronation in music, which suggests their sexual and psychological union. Since Nerone was designed for a mezzo-soprano castrato singer (here sung by a female mezzo), his vocal music can become perfectly blended with that of his new bride. One of opera's most celebrated love duets, its authorship has been questioned by some scholars in recent years. There is no question, however, about the music's beauty and unforgettable dramatic power. (See discussion chapter 7, pp. 306–307).